Matthias Eckermann

Venture Capitalists' Exit Strategies under Information Asymmetry

GABLER EDITION WISSENSCHAFT

Matthias Eckermann

Venture Capitalists' Exit Strategies under Information Asymmetry

Evidence from the US Venture Capital Market

Deutscher Universitäts-Verlag

Bibliografische Information Der Deutschen Bibliothek
Die Deutsche Bibliothek verzeichnet diese Publikation in der Deutschen Nationalbibliografie; detaillierte bibliografische Daten sind im Internet über <http://dnb.ddb.de> abrufbar.

Dissertation Technische Universität Dresden, 2005

1. Auflage Januar 2006

Lektorat: Brigitte Siegel / Nicole Schweitzer

Der Deutsche Universitäts-Verlag ist ein Unternehmen von Springer Science+Business Media.
www.duv.de

Umschlaggestaltung: Regine Zimmer, Dipl.-Designerin, Frankfurt/Main
Druck und Buchbinder: Rosch-Buch, Scheßlitz
Gedruckt auf säurefreiem und chlorfrei gebleichtem Papier
Printed in Germany

ISBN 3-8350-0126-4

Preface

This book has been submitted as dissertation at the Faculty of Business Management and Economics at Dresden University of Technology, Germany on January 19, 2005. Throughout the completion of this thesis, I received much encouragement and advice from mentors, colleagues and friends. I would like to take this opportunity to thank all of them.

First of all, I would like to express my gratitude to my supervisor Prof. Dr. Michael Schefczyk for providing a fruitful research atmosphere at the SAP Chair for Entrepreneurship and Innovation at Dresden University of Technology. His comments and support helped me develop and complete this thesis. Moreover, I thank Prof. Schefczyk for supporting my ambitions to conduct research in the United States.

Second, I am especially grateful to Prof. Andrew L. Zacharakis, Ph.D. for hosting me as visiting scholar at Babson College and for supervising my project during this time. This thesis benefited tremendously from his knowledge and from his outstanding support. His encouragement and support also helped me survive less productive times.

A great debt is to Prof. Dr. Herman Locarek-Junge who accepted the burden of being my second examiner at Dresden University of Technology.

The final paper benefited tremendously from conversations with several experienced researchers and practitioners in the United States. I want to thank Elaine I. Allen, Lowell Busenitz, Bill Bygrave, Les Charm, David Hsu, Ernest Parizeau, Elizabeth Riley and Shaker Zahra for their support. Moreover, I enjoyed fruitful discussions with my office colleagues Robert Dietrich, Jochen Neubecker, Frank Pankotsch and Jörg Wylegalla at Dresden University of Technology as well as Santeri Korri and Christian Vintergaard at Babson College. Their curiosity raised many questions which greatly improved this thesis. I owe special gratitude to Julio Perez for his outstanding technical support.

Financial support from the German Academic Exchange Service (DAAD) is gratefully acknowledged.

Last but not least, I would like to thank my mother for her extensive support during my time as a doctoral student and before. It is a pleasure for me to dedicate this dissertation to her.

Matthias Eckermann

Table of Contents

Table of Figures

Table of Tables

Abbreviations

CAPM	Capital Asset Pricing Model
CEO	Chief Executive Officer
CFO	Chief Financial Officer
CR	Concentration Ration
CVC	Corporate Venture Capital
DCF	Discounted Cash Flow
EVCA	European Venture Capital Association
GDP	Gross Domestic Product
GEM	Global Entrepreneurship Monitor
IPO	Initial Public Offering
IRR	Internal Rate of Return
LBO	Leveraged Buy-Out
M&A	Mergers and Acquisitions
MBO	Management Buy-Out
MBI	Management Buy-In
NASDAQ	National Association of Securities Dealers Automated Quotation
NVCA	National Venture Capital Association
P/E	Price/Earnings
PE	Private Equity
PMC	Projected Marginal Costs
PMR	Projected Marginal Return
PMVA	Projected Marginal Value Added
R&D	Research and Development
SD	Standard Deviation
SDC	Securities Data Company
SEC	Securities and Exchange Commission
SEM	Structural Equation Models
VC	Venture Capital
VCF	Venture Capital Firm
VIF	Variance Inflation Factor

1. Introduction

The term 'Venture Capital' (VC) denotes resources that specialized investors provide to start-ups in order to help them commercialize their mainly high-technology ideas.[1] The early stage character of these projects makes VC investments exceedingly vulnerable to information asymmetries ex-ante and ex-post to the investment decision.[2]

Research has long identified different states of information asymmetry that exist between entrepreneurs and venture capital firms (VCFs) – especially during the initial investment decision process. In fact, VC investments progress through several new investment cycles. Information asymmetries between incumbent and outside investors occur at every investment round although their extent declines.[3] Eventually, the incumbent VCF's[4] exit is subject to information asymmetries too – between incumbent inside and outside follow-on investors.[5]

Even though follow-on investors perform due diligence, they experience information spreads in that they cannot access every relevant piece of information. Either, prospective investors suffer from lower levels of specific knowledge or their access to information is limited by the entrepreneur and the VCF withholding less favorable details.[6] Hence, the new investors' due diligence only reflects their constrained perception of the venture's value.[7] In fear of information disadvantages at exit, prospective investors discount their valuation to be compensated for their adverse selection risk and for their due diligence costs. Moreover, if prospective investors do not recognize existing potentials, they cannot incorporate these potentials into their assessment and assume lower valuations. Information asymmetry leads to lower exit valuations and distresses the VCF's proceeds from the investment.[8]

This thesis investigates information disadvantages of follow-on investors and looks into VCFs' strategies to overcome the costs of asymmetric information between inside and outside investors at exit. This dissertation's underlying hypothesis states that the more pronounced information asymmetries are, the higher acquirers discount

---

[1] Black/Gilson (1998), p. 245; Cumming/MacIntosh (2001), p. 445f.; Lam (1991), p. 137

[2] Coase (1984), p. 231; Constantinides/Grundy (1989), p. 445f.

[3] Admati/Pfleiderer (1994), p. 371f.; Busenitz/Fiet (1996); Cornelli/Yosha (2003), p. 1; Gompers (1995), p. 1461

[4] This analysis always refers to VCFs as the incumbent risk capital investors; new VCFs that buy out incumbent VCFs are termed as follow-on investors.

[5] Cumming/MacIntosh (2001), p. 449; Lam (1991), p. 144

[6] Cumming/Fleming (2003), p. 4ff.

[7] Cornell/Shapiro (1988), p. 14; Cumming/MacIntosh (2001), p. 449

[8] Lin/Smith (1998), p. 242

their offers.[9] In managing informational asymmetries at exit, the VCF can increase its profitability.

1.1 Venture Capital Investments and Divestments

The VC investing process lasts several years and involves a multitude of different activities. VCFs start with gleaning and selecting high potential investment opportunities which they provide with funding.[10] In order to prevent the venture's management from engaging in self-beneficial behavior, VCFs monitor their venture investments closely and stage capital infusions according to the accomplishment of interim goals.[11] Besides supervising the venture's progress, the VCF's managers provide managerial support; they offer management assistance and access to their networks of potential customers, suppliers or financial service providers.[12] The VCFs' active involvement in their ventures distinguishes them from other types of rather passive equity investors. VCFs also stand out in that they initially stipulate measures enabling them to terminate changes in the private firm's ownership structure and shape divestment strategies in their favor.[13]

Researchers proclaim a direct correlation between entrepreneurial activity and economic growth. Entrepreneurship represents a major determinant of economic prosperity. According to the GEM 2000 Executive Report, about half of the difference in levels of economic growth across nations can be explained by the presence or lack of entrepreneurial activity.[14] The importance of VC financing for economic growth derives from the fact that VC funding spurs entrepreneurial activities. The financial and non-financial resources VCFs provide enable start-ups to circumvent typical growth constrains such as of the inaccessibility of traditional sources of finance or of established industry networks.[15] Particularly for high-technology start-ups, VC finance plays a significant role in that it fosters the commercialization of innovations.[16] VCFs have substantially promoted the emergence of new sectors such as the semiconductor-industry and the biotech-industry.[17] Research concludes that the existence of a thriving VC-industry represents a major factor for entrepreneurial and economic

---

[9] Cornell/Shapiro (1988), p. 14

[10] Dotzler (2001), p. 6

[11] Amit/Brander/Zott (1998), p. 445; Barry (1994), p. 8ff.; Barry/Muscarella/Peavy/Vetsuypens (1990), p. 450; Gupta/Sapienza (1992), p. 349f.; Ruhnka/Young (1991), p. 119f.; Schmidt (2003), p. 1139

[12] Davila/Foster (2003), p. 691; MacMillan/Kulow/Khoylian (1989), p. 311

[13] See discussion in sections 3.1.1 and 3.1.2

[14] Reynolds/Hay/Bygrave/Camp/Autio (2000), p. 4 and p. 13ff.

[15] See discussion in sections 2.2 and 2.3.1

[16] Empirical studies provide evidence that VC plays a considerably higher role in the financing of innovative start-ups than loans; see Jordan/Lowe/Taylor (1998), p. 23; Kortum/Lerner (2000), p. 674ff.; Cassar (2004), p. 262f.

[17] Bhide (2000), p. 141; Cowie (1999), p. 13; Timmons/Bygrave (1986), p. 163

growth. A study commissioned by the National Venture Capital Association (NVCA) reports that VC-backed firms accounted for almost $1.1 trillion of the U.S. GDP and created 12.5 million jobs in the year 2000.[18] Further empirical research has proven that the availability of VC significantly enhances the nationwide creation of wealth and employment in countries with an active VC market.[19] Figure 1 illustrates a slight tendency between VC markets and GDP per capita across selected countries.

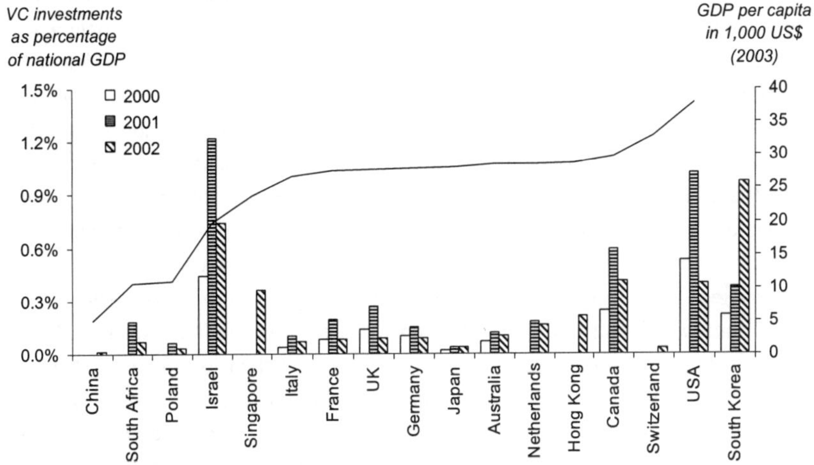

Figure 1: VC investments as percentage of national GDP[20]

VC funding does not represent a long-term financing option. The VCF's business principle is to nurture ventures until they reach sufficient sizes and credibility to access follow-on finance.[21] The VCF's commitment is rewarded only upon withdrawal.[22] Given the non-existence of revenues in early stages, VC investments cannot distribute annual dividends.[23] VC research has already recognized the exit's importance. Scholars demonstrate that a VCF's success is not only driven by its ability to identify and to manage venture investments but also by its capabilities in exiting portfolio

---

[18] http://www.nvca.org/nvca06_25_02.html; accessed on September 12th, 2004

[19] Gompers/Lerner (1999a), p. 5ff.; Jeng/Wells (2000), p. 242; Gompers/Lerner (2001a), p. 146ff., summarize recent research on the impact of VC on economic growth

[20] GEM Monitor (2003)

[21] Aghion/Bolton/Tirole (2000), p. 2; Gupta/Sapienza (1992), p. 349

[22] Albach/Hunsdiek/Kokalj (1986), p. 166; Black/Gilson (1998), p. 256; Brück (1998), p. 18; Zemke (1995), p. 70

[23] Bartlett (1999), p. 84; Brück (1998), p. 75f.; Cumming/Fleming (2003), p. 2

companies efficiently.[24] Petty, Bygrave and Shulman (1992) point out, that VCFs create or lose substantial values at exit.[25] Given the importance of exits, the question of how to improve the exit behavior must be of interest for every VCF.[26] This thesis focuses on the exit stage in the VC financing process by taking the point of view of the VCF. It researches the question of how VCFs shape their exit strategies under information asymmetry.

The focus of this dissertation requires that the term "exit" captures information disadvantages of new investors upon exit. Hence, exit has to incorporate the initial investment of the follow-on investor regardless of whether he acquires only a small fraction or the whole venture. This definition embodies the occurrence of original information asymmetries between inside and outside investors. All subsequent capital infusions of the same follow-on investor are less affected by information asymmetries because the investor's involvement enables him to learn about the venture.[27] Moreover, the VCF's influence on further exit decisions declines once an exit in this sense is initiated. VCFs lose their preference rights by converting their mezzanine instruments into common equity. Their remaining equity stakes are treated like other ordinary stakes. In addition, the VCF relinquishes board seats or board seats may be added thereby diluting the VCF's influence. In essence, the VCF releases its tight control over the venture's management and loses its clout to terminate alternative exit strategies. The initial withdrawal represents the only chance for the VCF to actively manage information asymmetries through the proper exit strategy.[28] An exit transaction in this sense occurs in an initial public offering (IPO) or in a merger or acquisition (M&A) when the VCF exchanges its stakes in the venture against the acquirer's publicly listed stock or cash.

1.2 Information Asymmetry as Overall Problem

This section introduces the underlying research stream. After contrasting the two central research strands in finance, this section sets out the overall problem originating from information asymmetry between incumbent inside and prospective outside investors. This dissertation is consequently embedded in the context of the theory of economics of institutions.

---

[24] E.g., Berglöf (1994), p. 247; Cumming/MacIntosh (2003), p. 512; Lin (1996), p. 56; Lin/Smith (1998), p. 243f.

[25] Petty/Shulman/Bygrave (1992), p. 48, yet, they fail to quantify these potentials; see also Shepherd/Zacharakis (2001a), p. 59

[26] Shepherd/Zacharakis (2001a), p. 59

[27] Cumming/MacIntosh (2003), p. 512f.

[28] Cumming/MacIntosh (2003), p. 515; Lin/Smith (1998), p. 242

1.2.1 The Neoclassic Economics' Research Stream

The neoclassic economics' normative research question focuses on the impact of a company's financial decision making – particularly with respect to the equity ratio and the dividend payout policy – on its valuation.[29] To reduce complexity and isolate structures of interest, neoclassic economics neglect aspects of asymmetrically distributed information. Research models within the neoclassic stream simplify matters in that they presume "perfect markets" in which:[30]

- every participant possesses the same quantity and quality of information
- information is costless so that it is available to everyone without limitations
- homogeneous expectations prevail so that everybody draws the same conclusions from this information
- transactions are costless
- markets are equally easy to access for both, firms and individuals if they want to buy, sell or issue securities

Modigliani and Miller's (1958) article on the firm's financing strategy represents a popular analysis within this research stream which exemplifies the typical approach in neoclassic economics.[31] Modigliani and Miller presuppose information to be uniformly distributed between the firm and outside investors as well as buy/sell transactions to be costless. Modigliani and Miller argue that since information is publicly available and costless, market participants immediately recognize when a firm's financing structure becomes marginally sub-optimal.[32] In terms of Modigliani and Miller, investors then take over the firm and optimize its capital structure. Thereafter, they harvest the marginal difference between the ex-ante and ex-post valuation by selling the firm. Given this adjusting mechanism, Modigliani and Miller conclude that the firm's valuation is not driven by its financial decisions. According to Modigliani and Miller, the firm's valuation is rather determined by the availability of alternative investment opportunities to the firm.[33]

In accordance with Modigliani and Miller (1958), neoclassic economics regard the methods of financing as a procedure for sharing the company's uncertain future profits. The firm's financial structure, however, does not determine the likelihood of occurrence of these proceeds and consequently does not influence a company's

---

[29] Schefczyk (2004), p. 129

[30] Carpenter/Petersen (2002), p. 54; Fama (1978), p. 273f.; Ross/Westerfield/Jaffe/Jordan (1996), p. 386ff. and p. 416ff.; Schefczyk (2004), p. 129f.

[31] Modigliani/Miller (1958), S. 261ff.; see also Fama (1978), p. 272ff.; Schmidt (1985), p. 423; Titman (2002), p. 101f.; Schefczyk (2004), p. 129ff., provides an overview on financial theories and their central research questions

[32] Fama (1978), p. 272f.; Perridon/Steiner (1997), p. 305; Ross (1977), p. 23

[33] Fama (1978), S. 272f.

valuation.[34] The neoclassic economics' presuppositions narrow the research focus down to analyzing the allocation of a company's uncertain future proceeds.[35]

When allowing for the reality of imperfect markets, the neoclassic economics' propositions that financing decisions only determine the allocation of future returns to shareholders but exert no influence on a firm's valuation are not valid. In fact, information dissimilarities occur in every financing transaction.[36] Consequent research evolves on investigating financing structures that incorporate aspects of non-perfect financial markets and yet optimize the firm's valuation. The questions arising in the context of information inefficiency[37] are addressed in several approaches in the theory of economics of institutions in which this analysis is embedded.[38]

1.2.2 Theory of Economics of Institutions and Information Asymmetry

The reality of bilateral financing relationships is neither characterized by evenly distributed information nor by homogeneous expectations. The theory of economics of institutions presumes that information is always distributed asymmetrically in advance to every financing transaction imposing an adverse selection problem on the investor.[39]

The state of information symmetry characterizes a setting of evenly distributed information; every party accesses the same sources of information and draws similar conclusions. If information is unequally distributed, one party suffers from an informational disadvantage. An asymmetric distribution of information can arise accidentally or is imposed by one party. Information disadvantages occur unintentionally, if one party cannot access information which is available to others due to its limitations in expertise and resources.[40] Information dissimilarities can also be effectuated by market participants who refuse to reveal relevant information in order to secure benefits from this state or from lowering another party's disadvantages.[41] The types of intended information asymmetries include hidden characteristics, information and intentions. Figure 2 provides an overview on the different types of information asymmetries.

---

[34] Hartmann-Wendels (1987), p. 17

[35] Fama (1978), p. 272ff.; Schmidt (1985), p. 423

[36] Constantinides/Grundy (1989), p. 445f.

[37] Information inefficiency prevails if information between parties is distributed asymmetrically and this market imperfection imposes costs on one or more parties.

[38] Hax (1991), p. 63ff.; Pape/Beyer (2001), p. 629f.; see also Schefczyk (2004), p. 129, who discusses further approaches

[39] Constantinides/Grundy (1989), p. 445f.; Eisenhardt (1989a), p. 58; Leland/Pyle (1977), p. 382f.

[40] Myers/Majluf (1984), p. 189

[41] Schefczyk (2004), p. 150

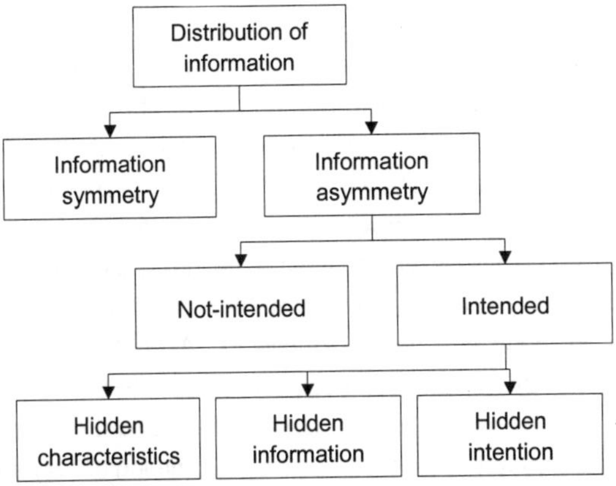

Figure 2: Types of information asymmetries[42]

To obtain information advantages in advance to closing financing contracts, a party can hide its negative characteristics against other parties. If it reveals its characteristics entirely, the contractual partner is likely to modify the transaction's parameters to its distress. For the first party, hiding potentially negative characteristics thus proves less costly as opposed to revealing all characteristics. A party can also neglect to share particular information about the investment opportunity which may negatively influence an upcoming transaction. Hidden information inhibits the negatively affected party from enforcing its claims during the negotiations in advance to the transaction and simultaneously allows the other party to extract personal benefits from the deal. For the same reason, a party may hide its true intentions to other parties before and after contracts are entered. If the other contracting parties recognize its deteriorating ambitions, contracts may not be concluded or modified to impede this behavior. The new contracts in turn distress the first party's individual utility.[43]

Hidden characteristics, information and intentions prevent outside investors from precisely evaluating an investment opportunity resulting in the so-called "adverse selection" problem.[44] Akerlof (1970) defines adverse selection as the problem of ex-ante asymmetrical information concerning the intrinsic quality of the project which restrains the committing parties' evaluation of the project.[45] Because no efficient markets that bring investment opportunities and capital providers together exist, an investor will not be compensated for information disadvantages against the investees

---

[42] Based on Amit/Brander/Zott (1998), p. 441ff.; Carpenter/Petersen (2002), p. 42; Deeds/Decarolis/Coombs (1997), p. 32; Picot/Dietl/Franck (1999), p. 91; Spremann (1990), p. 566

[43] Amit/Brander/Zott (1998), p. 441f.; Bell (2001), p. 90f.

[44] Amit/Brander/Zott (1998), p. 441f.; Schefczyk (2004), p. 150f.

[45] Akerlof (1970), p. 489f.; Hsu (2000), p. 9;

by more favorable investment conditions. In fact, the investor has to expect the investee to hide information regarding the likelihood of failure of the business in order to increase chances of being financed.[46] In the absence of reliable information on individual investment opportunities, investors are forced to base their investment decisions on average attributes of all available investment opportunities.[47] High quality investments will consequently receive the same conditions as low quality opportunities. Thereupon, high quality projects leave the market as they perceive the allocation of capital as unfavorable. The central effect of this adverse selection problem is that it generally results in inefficient market allocations. Akerlof shows that the extreme consequence of the adverse selection problem manifests in vanishing markets because the only equilibrium price of the market is zero and therefore no transactions will occur at all.[48] In line with Akerlof's reasoning, Cumming (2004) argues that equity investors only attract firms with low return potentials as the financing conditions based on the average quality assumption are unfavorable for high-potential firms.[49] Thus, equity investors always face substantial adverse selection risks through hidden characteristics, information and intentions.

The theory of economics of institutions researches the occurrence of adverse selection in financing transactions and the costs adverse selection imposes on investors. The theory presumes that every transaction is executed in an institutional framework of norms and rules. The framework warrants security and regularity for all exchanges of goods and capital. It also stipulates dispositions to punish violators which, for instance, conceal pertinent information. This institutional system enables a relatively frictionless economy while impeding the occurrence of Akerlof's extreme conclusion of vanishing markets.[50] The costs of creating, modifying and maintaining the institutional framework are typically defrayed by governments, municipal authorities or other institutions.[51] Individual participants carry only the variable costs of single transactions. According to their occurrence in a financing process, these costs can be subdivided into:[52]

- Costs for initiating a financing contract, such as costs for searching and processing information regarding the quality of the investment opportunity to reduce the adverse selection risk

[46] Hsu (2000), p. 9
[47] Schefczyk (2004), p. 150f.
[48] According to Akerlof's example of the market for used cars, Akerlof (1970), p. 489f.
[49] Cumming (2004), p. 1
[50] Oviatt (1988), p. 64; Richter/Furubotn (1996), p. 7
[51] Richter/Furubon (1996), p. 49
[52] Richter/Furubon (1996), p. 50f. and p. 318ff.

- Costs for concluding the financing contract, for instance, costs for negotiations, for decision making or for consulting external experts
- Costs for monitoring and controlling the investment throughout the transaction

The theory of economics of institutions seeks to explain why the reality of markets differs from ideal equilibriums of neoclassic models by examining these transaction related costs.[53] The theory of economics of institution's central research question asks how transactions and intermediation can be performed efficiently.[54]

1.2.3 Imperfect Markets as Origin for Venture Capital Transactions

Scholars ground several entrepreneurial research streams on settings of information asymmetry. Economists of the Austrian research stream, for instance, reason that entrepreneurial initiatives evolve from asymmetric information about market resources. An individual's information advantage offers unique entrepreneurial opportunities that have not been exploited by others yet.[55] Following this argumentation, entrepreneurial activities generally emerge from information asymmetry between entrepreneurs and their environment. Thus, neoclassic models cannot capture the characteristics that set entrepreneurial settings such as emerging markets apart from established environments.

Similarly, neoclassic models are not suited to explain the occurrence of VC because their premise collides with the crucial premise of entrepreneurship finance. Given the neoclassic economics' simplified research settings, no outside investor suffers from information disadvantages about the venture. Everybody accesses similar information and predicts the same progress.[56] A venture can immediately tap every source of funding once the entrepreneur decides that the business is worth pursuing. In the neoclassic setting, financial intermediaries – such as VCFs – that are specialized in gathering and processing information about venture investments do no exist.

The emergence of VC finance for early stage ventures originates from market imperfections.[57] In general, information asymmetry hampers prospective investors' due diligence. Investors in young private companies encounter the following types of information asymmetry ex-ante and during the financing relationship:

---

[53] Richter/Furubon (1996), p. 340f.

[54] Merton (1995), p. 23

[55] Soh (2003), p. 729, see Kirzner (1997) for a detailed discussion of the Austrian approach; see also Minniti (2004), p. 637f.

[56] Hayek (1945), p. 519, argues that in this case, financial problems remain purely logical problems; see also Heitzer (2000), p. 123f.; Pape/Beyer (2001), p. 629f.; Prester (2002), p. 158f.

[57] Merton (1987), p. 484; Misirli (1988), p. 40f.

- *Hidden characteristics:* The entrepreneur's skill set plays an important role for the businesses prosperity. The lack of skills is commonly regarded as a disadvantage handicapping the venture's progress. In order to obtain funding, entrepreneurs with a lack of skills may be prone to conceal their shortcomings during the investor's due diligence.[58]
- *Hidden intentions:* Entrepreneurship research acknowledges the entrepreneur's ambition to extract individual benefits to the distress of the venture investor's financial commitment.[59] To obtain funding, entrepreneurs may hide their true ambitions prior and during the investment period.
- *Hidden information:* Entrepreneurs may want to hide failures such as design flaws or negative customer feedbacks in advance and during the funding period in order to attract capital respectively to maintain the funding relationship.
- *Hidden actions:* Hidden information and intentions allow the entrepreneur to hide actions during the financing period. The entrepreneur may, for instance, decide on a strategy that does not maximize the businesses valuation but adds to his expertise in certain technologies enabling him to start new businesses. Since his opportunistic behavior is not recognized by outsiders, it does not entail negative consequences for the entrepreneur.[60]

In essence, entrepreneurs may be privy to information that negatively affects financing contracts and transaction parameters.[61] Sapienza and Gupta (1994) conclude that the lack of external control imposes serious problems for governing venture investments on outside financiers.[62] Because outside investors suffer from information disadvantages and opportunistic strategies of entrepreneurs, they abstain from investing in new ventures.[63] In contrast, VCFs have developed a multitude of experiences in previous investments. They have established unique capabilities to cope with the problems of information asymmetry in start-up finance. Thus, VCFs can extract favorable risk-return profiles from venture investments.[64] VC research concludes that information asymmetries mainly account for the existence of VC as an early stage financing instrument. VC intermediates exist because asymmetric infor-

---

[58] E.g., Fried/Hisrich (1994) p. 30f.; Sapieza/Gupta (1994), p. 1618ff.

[59] E.g., Admati/Pfleiderer (1994); Berglöf (1994); Hellmann (1998); Kaplan/Strömberg (2003); Sahlman (1988)

[60] Kaplan/Strömberg (2004), p. 2177ff.

[61] The entrepreneur's behavior as well as its implications for the VC finance process are deepened in section 2.3.2 c)

[62] Sapienza/Gupta (1994), p. 1618; Eisenhardt (1989a), p. 64

[63] Bourgeois/Eisenhardt (1988), p. 816, argue that this state is even more severe for ventures that apply high or revolutionary technologies

[64] Amit/Brander/Zott (1998), p. 441; Barry (1994), p. 4; Davila/Foster/Gupta (2003), p. 691; Gompers (1995), p. 1487; Gompers/Lerner (2000), p. 127; Hsu (2000), p. 9

mation and inherent uncertainties prevent common equity investors from direct engagements.[65] Rather, common equity investors seek intermediation by specialized VCFs.[66]

1.2.4 Information Asymmetry upon Exit

Throughout the VC investment, the VCF closely monitors the entrepreneur's progress. In doing so, the VCF learns about the venture and participates in newly emerging information. Hence, the VCF's information disadvantages against the entrepreneur decline continuously during the VC process. By the time the VCF desires to exit, its information disadvantages against the entrepreneur have virtually vanished.[67]

VCFs are confronted with asymmetric information upon exit again when they sell their stake in the venture to outside follow-on investors.[68] Akin to the VCF's adverse selection problem at the initial investment decision,[69] the prospective investor encounters an investment risk and suffers from uncertainty about the venture's quality. Following psychological risk theory, prospective investors perceive risk when they are aware of the array of the investment's possible future outcomes and know the probabilities of occurrence attached to each outcome. Yet, they do not know which scenario eventually materializes. Prospective investors are uncertain about an investment, if they cannot even foresee the array of the investment's future outcomes.[70] Both, risk and uncertainty originate from the follow-on investors' lack of information.[71] Nevertheless, the follow-on investor's uncertainty does not entirely result from his information disadvantage against inside parties. Provided a perfect market, all investors suffer from the same uncertainties and risks about an investment. Both, the insider's and the outsider's valuation incorporate equal uncertainties and risks and deliver similar results. In the sense of neoclassic economics, this dissertation presumes that the uncertainties and risks inside and outside investors share do not affect the financing transaction; the perfect market consideration implies that once an entrepreneur perceives an investment as favorable, any outside investor will too. Imperfect markets, however, afford the inside investor with an information advantage and increase outsiders' uncertainties and risks. This analysis presumes that the follow-on investor's investment decision depends on the extent of this information

[65] Murray (1994), p. 60

[66] The intermediation role of VCFs will be explicitly examined in section 2.3.1 b).

[67] Admati/Pfleiderer (1994), p. 371; Amit/Glosten/Muller (1990), p. 103ff.; Davila/Foster/Gupta (2003), p. 692; Neus/Walz (2001), p. 1; Prasad/Bruton/Vozikas (2000), p. 168f.

[68] Lam (1991), p. 144

[69] Akerlof (1970), p. 489f.; Amit/Brander/Zott (1998), p. 441ff.; Eisenhardt (1989a), p. 61

[70] Galbraith (1973), p. 5

[71] Tichy (1981), p. 204ff.

spread. The present dissertation does consequently not research general investment risks and uncertainties but rather those risks and uncertainties that information dissimilarities impose on follow-on investors. Incumbent parties have to overcome this information spread to facilitate a transaction. At the VCF's exit, follow-on investors suffer from the following non-intended and effectuated information gaps:[72]

- *Accidental information asymmetries about the venture*; the follow-on investor suffers from a lower level of specific knowledge in comparison to incumbents (entrepreneur and VCF) preventing him from assessing the project's prospects and values. Kohers and Kohers (2001) exemplify that outsiders experience particular difficulties in evaluating high-tech firms since they do not possess intimate knowledge about new technologies.[73]
- *Information asymmetries effectuated by entrepreneurs* who engage in self-beneficial behavior and withhold less favorable details such as characteristics, intentions or information.[74] E.g., entrepreneurs may conceal management failures and design flaws to secure their position in the company and further funding.[75]
- *Effectuated information asymmetries by the VCF* that conceals its real incentives to withdraw or negative information that would lower the follow-on investor's valuation.

Information asymmetry at exit imposes an adverse selection problem on the outside follow-on investor.[76] Follow-on investors perform due diligence to resolve their information disadvantages.[77] In doing so, they accrue costs for searching and processing information.[78] These information costs correlate with the extent of information disadvantages the prospective investor seeks to alleviate; if he must mitigate greater information spreads, the due diligence becomes more expensive. This consideration induces new investors to find an equilibrium in which they acquire some information but accept a certain extent of uncertainty. To be compensated for their information costs and the remaining uncertainty, prospective investors discount their valuation.[79] From the VCF's perspective, the prospective investors' information disadvantages

---

[72] Based on Carpenter/Petersen (2002), p. 54f.; Cumming/Fleming (2003), p. 4ff.; Cumming/MacIntosh (2001), p. 449; Deeds/Decarolis/Coombs (1997), p. 32; Janney/Folta (2003), p. 364; Sah/Stiglitz (1986), p. 716f.

[73] Kohers/Kohers (2001), p. 36; also see Campbell (1979), p. 915

[74] Cable/Shane (1997), p. 149

[75] Janney/Folta (2003), p. 362; Keasey/Short (1997), p. 76

[76] Keasey/Short (1997), p. 76; also see Akerlof (1970), p. 489f.

[77] Harvey/Lusch (1995), p. 7; Hayek (1945), p. 522ff.; Salop/Salop (1976), p. 619

[78] Sah/Stiglitz (1986), p. 716f.

[79] Barnea/Haugen/Senbet (1981), p. 8; Cornell/Shapiro (1988), p. 14; Cumming/MacIntosh (2001), p. 449

are either costly to mitigate or to accept at exit. VCFs consequently face the problem of finding a solution that maximizes the overall outcome.[80] Therefore, VCFs must understand the interplay between discounts and information spreads as well as the impact of information inefficiency on their behavior upon exit.

Figure 3 illustrates all possible information asymmetries between the central parties in the VC context. Given the purpose of this study, the present analysis contemplates a simplified model. Upon exit, VCFs have eliminated their information disadvantages against the entrepreneur through their assistance and monitoring activities. Additionally, this study presumes that the co-investor's goals resemble those of the lead investor in that both desire to maximize the transaction's financial outcome. In essence, this study focuses on the information gaps between inside parties embodying the entrepreneur and the VCF and the outside party – the follow-on investor.

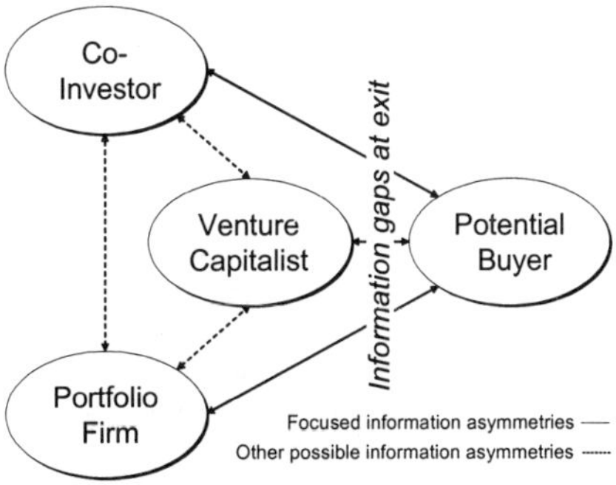

Figure 3: Interrelations and possible information asymmetries in VC finance[81]

[80] Lin/Smith (1998), p. 242

[81] The presence of co-investors refers to VCFs' syndication of VC investments; see section 2.3.1 c)

1.3 Literature Overview and this Study's Focus

Schefczyk (2004) suggests a scheme to classify the VC literature. He sets out the different perspectives taken by the researcher and the focus on investment stages. Regarding the perspective, Schefczyk distinguishes three layers in VC finance: the fund investors', the VCFs' and the portfolio companies' points of view.[82] Schefczyk also discerns funding events, such as early stage funding through VCFs or later stage capital infusions by private equity investors. To categorize this study, Schefczyk's classification is extended. This dissertation adds a third dimension that looks into the investment process of a single transaction beginning with the due diligence and ending with the investor's withdrawal. This study researches the withdrawal from venture investments by taking the point of view of a single VCF. The analysis exclusively regards the exit process as source of returns and considers previous states as given. Figure 4 illustrates the focus of this thesis compared to all possible emphases in VC research.

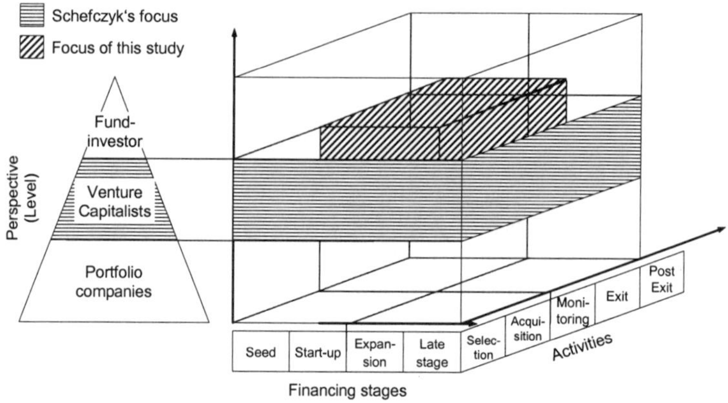

Figure 4: Perspectives in VC research[83]

Even though exits play a vital role for every VCF, attention has only been paid to a few aspects of VCFs' exits.[84] The majority of exit related studies focuses on one specific exit route. Most often, this has been the IPO[85] emphasizing the VCF's certifi-

[82] Barry (1994), p. 4ff. provides examples for research on the relationship between VCFs and entrepreneurs; further examples are Bygrave (1987); Elitzur/Gavious (2003); Lerner (1994b); moreover, Sorensen/Stuart (2001) look into network structures and syndication in VC transactions

[83] According to Schefczyk (2004), p. 179

[84] Section 4.1 sheds further light on the literature on exits

[85] E.g., Barry/Muscarella/Peavy/Vetsuypens (1990); Bergström/Högfeldt/Westin (1995); Brav/Gompers (1997); Megginson/Weiss (1991); Shepherd/Zacharakis (2001a)

cation role and the impact of the VCF's presence on the issue's underpricing.[86] Both themes are related to information inefficiency that restrains the prospective investors' due diligence. However, these studies do typically not involve the investment's characteristics but only the VCF's general ability to mitigate information concerns of outside investors. Some studies examine trade sales or alternative exit vehicles with different emphases.[87] Relander, Syrjänen and Miettinen (1994), for instance, find that the entrepreneur's attitude towards an acquisition by industrial investors influences the exit's performance.[88] Only Lam (1991) addresses the question of how VCFs can add value by selecting one particular exit vehicle. Yet, he fails to provide empirical evidence. Recently, Schwienbacher (2002) and Fleming (2003) have compared exit vehicles highlighting the VCF's selection of high-quality candidates for IPOs while the remaining ventures only accomplish private transactions.[89] Scholars also contrast the advantages of private and public finance in different settings. But these analyses merely reflect a corporate finance perspective instead of considering a VC context. Also, this work hardly involves information asymmetry concerns.[90]

Other scholars put the emphasis on particular exit strategy options, such as the VCF's timing decision[91] or partial exits[92]. Both directions are driven by the need to mitigate follow-on investors' information disadvantages. The first research stream argues that VCFs delay exits until the venture has accomplished visibility or capital markets become less sensitive for investment risks.[93] In exiting partly, VCFs seek to the overcome potential investor's quality doubts in that they signal their confidence in the transaction's success. This consideration is also related to the method of payment; while cash payment is associated with a complete exit, compensation through shares in the acquirer-company ties the VCF's proceeds to the transaction's outcome. [94]

Contractual conditions for successful exits have also been studied. This research stream either contemplates the allocation of control rights depending on the venture's performance[95] or lock-up provisions underwriters device in IPOs. While contractual

---

[86] Allen/Faulhaber (1989); Booth/Chua (1996); Espenlaub/Tonks (1998); Grinblatt/Hwang (1989); Welch (1989),

[87] E.g., Relander/Syrjänen/Miettinen (1994) and Petty/Shulman/Bygrave (1994) analyze trade sales; Murray (1994) secondary purchases by financial investors

[88] Relander/Syrjänen/Miettinen (1994), p. 139f.

[89] Schwienbacher (2002), p. 7f.; Fleming (2003), p. 9

[90] E.g., Subrahmanyam/Titman (1999); Zingales (1995)

[91] Brück (1998); Neus/Walz (2001); Schwienbacher (2001); Tykvová (2003)

[92] Cumming/MacIntosh (2003)

[93] E.g., Chemmanur/Fulghieri (1999); Maksimovic/Pichler (2001)

[94] Cumming/MacIntosh (2003), p. 513ff.

[95] E.g., Berglöf (1994); Cornelli/Yosha (2003); Cumming (2002); Gompers/Lerner (1996); Hellmann (2000)

provisions are required to preclude opportunistic behavior, lock-up provisions prevent insiders from exploiting their informational advantages against new share holders by selling stakes shortly after going public.[96]

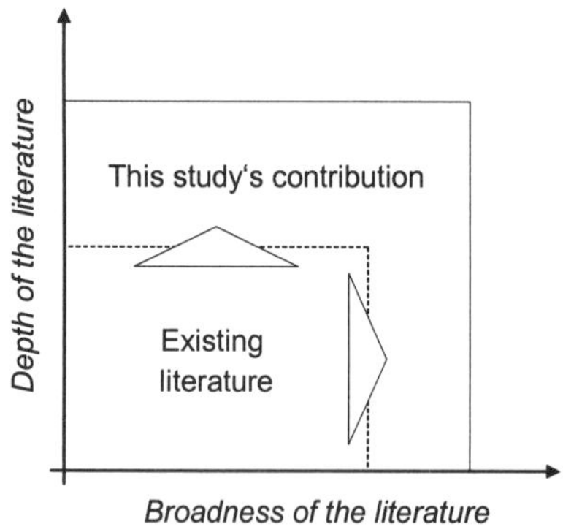

Figure 5: This study's focus contrasted to the existing literature

The existing literature suffers from two shortcomings. First, even though single exit strategy aspects have been examined in the context of information asymmetry, hardly any study incorporates more than one theme in a comparative analysis. Since most exit-related aspects have only been scrutinized separately, the literature neglects their interrelatedness. Second, the VCF's interactions with outside parties to facilitate exits have not been explored yet. Research has already indicated that VCFs can make a difference in exits.[97] Only it has never been asked how. As illustrated in figure 5, this thesis deepens the VCF's interplay with outsiders upon exit and examines the VCF's holistic approach to exiting ventures including interdependencies of exit strategy options.

1.4 Purpose of this Dissertation

The present dissertation researches whether and how information asymmetries between VCFs and prospective investors affect VCFs' exit strategies. This study presumes that information asymmetries prompt the acquirer to discount his valuation at exit. VCFs can improve their profitability by incorporating the prospective investors' informational concerns in their exit behavior.[98] The study seeks to identify the most

---

[96] Aggarwal/Krigman/Womack (2002), p. 106; Bradley/Jordan/Yi/Roten (2001), p. 465; Field/Hanka (2001), p. 471ff.; Gompers/Lerner (2000), p. 209

[97] E.g., Barry/Muscarella/Peavy/Vetsuypens (1990); Gompers (1996); Megginson/Weiss (1991)

[98] Cornell/Shapiro (1988), p. 14

appropriate strategies for a multitude of scenarios on the basis of empirical findings on recent transactions.

Timmons and Bygrave (1986) note that the VC industry is often perceived as an agglomeration of homogenous firms.[99] Fried and Hisrich (1988) as well as Gompers and Lerner (1999) contradict this notion. They show that VCFs are in fact heterogeneous organizations because of their individual genesis.[100] In support of this notion, Cumming (2002) as well as Elango, Fried, Hisrich and Polonchek (1995) conclude that substantial differences across VCFs stem from varying objectives, strategies or resources which are distributed unevenly in the VC industry.[101] These differences translate into different approaches of VCFs in nurturing young companies.[102] This study picks up the idea of differences among VCFs; the analysis contrasts exit strategies across the VC industry in order to identify common and divergent behavior patterns upon exit. Following Sah and Stiglitz's (1986) reasoning about decision making in heterogeneous versus homogenous settings, this dissertation presumes that when common patterns prevail in a heterogeneous environment, they have generally proven successful.[103] Commonly applied exit patterns thus constitute successful exit strategies. If behavior patterns vary across transactions, no general success strategy has emerged in the last decades of VC finance. For those findings, this dissertation concludes that no impact on the exit's success exists.

In respect to its methodical approach, this study gains consolidated findings by inducing general theories from empirical observations.[104] Researchers often criticize this approach because, in the sense of Popper's (1994) critical rationalism, empirical data sets only reflect singular observations rather than the whole population. Popper argues that general theories cannot be induced from sample observations. In fact, data samples only allow researchers to refuse a theory if an observation collides with this theory.[105] However, the findings of this empirical analysis on the one hand contribute to common knowledge in excluding falsified assumptions. On the other hand, the levels of significance indicate the likelihood of occurrence of predicted events. Thus, the outcome guides further research.[106]

---

[99] Timmons/Bygrave (1986), p. 163

[100] Fried/Hisrich (1988), p. 22; Gompers/Lerner (1999a), p. 4

[101] Cumming (2002), p. 2; Elango/Fried/Hisrich/Polonchek (1995), p. 158

[102] Barney (1991), p. 103; MacMillan/Kulow/Khoylian (1989), p. 35ff.

[103] Sah/Stiglitz (1986), p. 716ff.

[104] Induction denotes a process in which few perceptions are generalized to form a theory. In this context a theory is referred to as an interim assumption which has not been disproved yet; see Blum (1994), p. 17f.

[105] Popper (1994), p. 42

[106] Schefczyk (2004), p. 10f.

The study pursues two partial goals which can be characterized as an explorative and a confirmative one:

I. Building an analytical model to derive hypotheses represents the explorative goal. To warrant high-quality results, the research model has to embody major sources of information asymmetry between the inside and outside investors. In addition, it must address the VCF's options in shaping exit strategies. To identify these aspects, the existing literature has to be screened and suggestions gathered of how VCFs shape exit strategies. As the available literature may not entirely capture the VCFs' practical considerations, further inspirations are drawn from interviews with practitioners. Research hypotheses are then derived from the combined insights.

II. Empirically validating the hypotheses and connecting the VCF's options in reacting to information asymmetries and researching interdependencies constitute the confirmative goal. Therefore, two data samples have to be collected which form the basis of the empirical analysis.

The findings will be summarized and, thereafter, further research questions are deduced. Nonetheless, in the sense that management research addresses applied problems and strives at providing applicable solutions, this study complements practical solutions for VCFs.[107]

1.5 Structure of this Study

The remainder is structured as follows. Chapter two presents a detailed analysis of the VC-financing concept. It pays particular attention to the development process of start-up companies as regards their need for capital and their constraints in accessing external sources of funding. Based on the critical discussion of possible funding options, the concept of VC finance will be introduced. Chapter two then discusses the VC process and embeds the exit in the VC concept.

Chapter three examines the VCF's exit. It discusses specific provisions VCFs arrange when they enter an investment. This chapter then dwells on exit means and analyzes the exit process by taking the perspective of a single VCF. Finally, chapter three describes the present situation for VCFs' exit transactions and highlights problems emanating from the recent development of capital markets and the VC industry markets.

Chapter four provides an overview on the relevant literature. Then, chapter four reverts to the findings of chapters two, chapter three and the literature analysis and builds a model of how information asymmetries affect the VCF's exit behavior. The model describes the impact of information dissimilarities on the VCF's exit strategy in

---

[107] Steinmann (1978), p. 92; Ulrich (1981), p. 19

the form of research hypotheses. Moreover, chapter four reports the explorative pilot studies that are undertaken to improve the model's quality.

Chapter five introduces this dissertation's research methodology. Initially, the variables are defined. Thereupon, chapter five describes the data collection and characterizes both, the original data sample and the survey data sample. Finally, chapter five provides brief insights on the statistical devices that will be employed to validate the research model.

In chapter six, the research model will be tested based on either the survey or the original data sample. Initially, the research hypotheses are validated by using bi-variate and multi-variate test methods. Second, this chapter employs a hierarchical cluster analysis in order to detect unforeseen patterns of how VCFs facilitate their exits. The cluster analysis' results are tested for their contribution to the original research model.

Chapter seven wraps up the results. It summarizes the findings from a scientific perspective and then outlines this thesis' insights for practical use. It also reviews the analysis' limitations and shortcomings. Chapter seven then derives the need for subsequent research and inspires new research questions. Figure 6 illustrates the structure of this dissertation and highlights how every chapter's findings flow into the analysis in subsequent chapters.

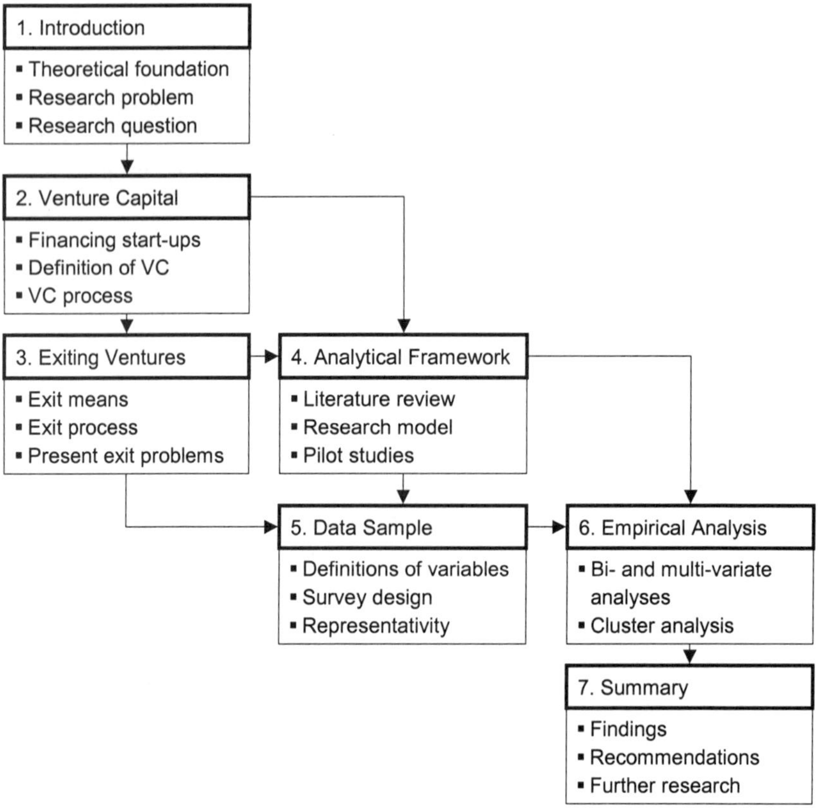

Figure 6: This study's structure

2 Venture Capital Investing

This section introduces the rationale of VC financing and builds the theoretical basis for the following considerations. First, the necessity of VC funding for start-ups will be outlined by contrasting an emerging company's need for capital with its limited access to traditional funding. Then, this chapter addresses the questions of how VC fills the financing gap of start-ups and what motives the different participants pursue with their engagement in VC. The VCF's expectations towards venture investments are discussed in particular. This chapter concludes in distinguishing different types of VC investors.

2.1 Development Stages and Financing Requirements of Start-ups

As a matter of fact, financial requirements of start-up companies mutate throughout their evolution. This chapter discusses the different development stages through which a company passes from the origin to its maturity. For every stage, this section sets out the firm's demand for funding. Based on the evolution process and the altering financial requirements, this chapter outlines VC as a funding option for entrepreneurial ventures.

2.1.1 Product-Life-Cycles and Start-ups' Development

Even though scholars sometimes regard the evolution of young companies as an individual process, a fundamental construct underlies every start-up's development. Since most start-ups are founded upon only one product, their progress is closely linked to the life-cycle of the product itself.[108] Not until the start-up commences to offer further products or services does this linkage decouple.[109] Modeling a product's life-cycle originates from the assumption that the development of the product, as indicated by its market share and the cash flow or profit it generates, follows a general trajectory of different consecutive stages. Product life-cycle models respectively firm life-cycle models aim at describing this process.

New products and hence young companies are frequently subject to risk and uncertainty since inside and outside investors cannot foresee the project's potential outcomes and their probabilities.[110] Life-cycle models project the typical development of start-ups to describe how risks and uncertainties about the product's acceptance,

---

[108] Engelmann/Juncker/Natusch/Tebroke (2000), p. 25; Schiereck (1973), p. 55; see Schumpeter (1939), Vernin (1966) or Hirsch (1967) for a general discussion on product life-cycle models

[109] Schween (1996), p. 96; an overview on development models of companies is provided in Mellewigt/Witt (2002), p. 84f.; a further discussion can be found in Ruhnka/Young (1987), p. 169

[110] Ruhnka/Young (1991), p. 118

its market share and its returns to the firm decrease over time.[111] Product-life-cycle models usually separate the periods of product development, market introduction, growth, maturity, saturation and degeneration.[112] Entrepreneurship research picks up this scheme and discerns three major stages through which a venture passes: the early stage mainly comprising the product development, the expansion stage including both the market introduction and the growth period and the late stage in which the company faces maturity, saturation and finally degeneration in cases where no new products are launched.[113]

Several limitations underlie life-cycle models of both product and start-ups. In general, these models tend to simplify the genesis of products or companies in order to generalize their propositions. Life-cycle schemes do not account for a venture's unique characteristics. Neither is every stage precisely separated from others, nor can the transition from one stage into the next one be determined exactly. In fact, this process is a fluent metamorphosis in which parameters change constantly. Assigning a start-up or product to one stage is mostly inaccurate if the stage's definition is drawn narrowly. In addition, product life-cycle models presume that one stage succeeds the previous one. However, a company or product may already fail during an early level or it enters a later stage without progressing through intermediate stages given favorable respectively unfavorable conditions. Nevertheless, life-cycle models are useful to sketch the typical evolution of a company in that they provide a referential framework with criteria visualizing achievements and ahead lying tasks for every development level.[114] Figure 7 provides an overview on the contents of these stages and the major risks associated with every level.

---

[111] Brophy (1992), p. 393

[112] Gerpott (1999), p. 216ff.; Heyde/Laudel/Pleschak/Sabisch (1991), p. 5ff.; Pleschak/Sabisch (1996), p. 17f. and p. 65; Räbel (1986), p. 85f.; Schiereck (1973), p. 53ff.

[113] Fischer (1987), p. 13; Nevermann/Falk (1986), p. 72; Wrede (1987), p. 22; Zemke (1995), p. 29

[114] For critics on product-life-cycle models see Betsch/Groh/Lohmann (1998), p. 230; Engelmann/Juncker/Natusch/Tebroke (2000), p. 30; Seppä/Laamanen (2001), p. 216

<table>
<tr><td colspan="2" rowspan="2">Firm's development level</td><td colspan="2">Early stage</td><td rowspan="2">Expansion stage</td><td colspan="2">Late stage</td></tr>
<tr><td>Seed</td><td>Start-up</td><td>Bridge</td><td>MBO/MBI</td></tr>
<tr><td colspan="2">Activities</td><td>▪ Product designing
▪ Market research
▪ Prototyping</td><td>▪ Founding the company
▪ Preparing for production
▪ Gathering marketing-activities</td><td>▪ Entering production
▪ Introducing the product to market
▪ Financing further growth</td><td>▪ Preparing
- an IPO or
- a sale to a strategic investor</td><td>▪ Takeover through an internal or external management team</td></tr>
<tr><td colspan="2">Profits and losses</td><td colspan="5">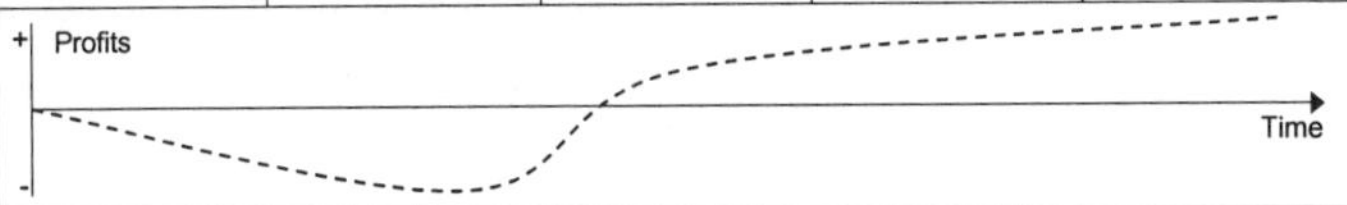
</td></tr>
<tr><td rowspan="6">Major risks</td><td rowspan="2">Market risks</td><td colspan="5">▪ Market potential does not suffice; market development is unfavorable
▪ Economic trends are unfavorable; industry sector suffers
▪ Competition increases</td></tr>
<tr><td colspan="2"></td><td colspan="3">▪ Lack of market acceptance</td></tr>
<tr><td rowspan="2">Business risks</td><td colspan="5">▪ Product cannot be produced at competitve costs; production lacks flexibility
▪ Lack of management skills and resources</td></tr>
<tr><td colspan="2">▪ R&D fails to meet objectives in respect to outcomes, time or budget</td><td colspan="3">▪ Products do not attain sufficient revenues or market shares
▪ Organization, coordination and structures are inefficient</td></tr>
<tr><td rowspan="2">Financial risks</td><td colspan="5">▪ Insolvency, venture is running out of money and cannot finance the next steps</td></tr>
<tr><td colspan="2">▪ Venture does not accomplish next funding round</td><td colspan="3">▪ IPO windows close; venture cannot attract follow-on funding and replace VC finance</td></tr>
</table>

Figure 7: Development levels of start-ups[115]

2.1.2 Early Stage

The term "early stage" refers to the period in which the business is set up. Scholars subdivide this level into the "seed"- and "start-up"-stage.[116] Throughout the seed stage, the entrepreneur develops an innovative idea around which he builds his firm.[117] He may generate an entirely new technology, imitate existing technologies or replace an obsolete technology. Irrespective of the idea's innovativeness, setting up a new business is connected with elementary uncertainties and risks for the entrepreneur as well as for outsiders. Initially, the entrepreneur has no evidence for the market's acceptance of his conception. When entering an emerging market, the entrepreneur additionally encounters uncertainties about the technical feasibility of his conception and the eventually dominant product design.[118] Many early stage firms entering the same industry do not succeed in producing the dominant design and

---

[115] Based on Achleitner (1999), p. 569ff.; Bauer (1995), p. 1660; Benjamin/Margulis (2000), p. 179ff.; Klemm (1988), p. 41; Schefczyk (2004), p. 38ff.; Schmidkte (1985), p. 50; Ruhnka/Young (1991), p. 122

[116] Eisele/Habermann/Oesterle (2002), p. 3; Engelmann/Juncker/Natusch/Tebroke (2000), p. 26f.; Schefczyk (2004), p. 40f.

[117] Allen/Faulhaber (1989), p. 306

[118] Baum/Silbermann (2004), p. 415; Huyghebaert/Van de Gucht (2004), p. 670

vanish.[119] Uncertainties also remain about appropriate marketing strategies.[120] Baum and Silberman (2004) add that the inexperience of the entrepreneur adds to the risk of mismanagement in early stage ventures.[121] The overall risk for every investor – including the entrepreneur – during the seed stage concerning the product's feasibility, the market's acceptance and appropriate strategies represents the highest throughout the evolution of the business.[122] Accounting for this risk and related uncertainties, the entrepreneur explores the basic feasibility of his conception in order to select the most promising idea.[123]

The business requires funding to progress through the successive research and development (R&D) stages towards tests of its commercial viability. The venture's capital requirements even grow with the complexity or novelty of the idea; new high technology products usually require more R&D expenditures than low technology or just modified products.[124] Yet, the entrepreneur's expenses for R&D, preliminary models or market studies are entirely uncovered by revenues at this stage.

The start-up period follows the seed stage and is prefaced by the company's legal foundation. While activities in the seed stage center on fundamental R&D activities, the entrepreneur sets out to commercialize his idea during the start-up stage. He assembles prototypes and conducts tests in selected market segments. The pretests afford the entrepreneur with experiences about the technical feasibility and about customers' preferences so that he can initiate improvements. The adaptation of the insights from the preliminary tests reduces the risks and uncertainties about the product's market acceptance and technical feasibility. Eventually, the young company prepares to enter production and stepwise implements a marketing concept. At this point, the entrepreneur typically begins to experience an overload of tasks. Particularly entrepreneurs with backgrounds other than in business suffer from their shortage of specific management knowledge on commercializing ideas. Entrepreneurs in the start-up stage thus hire additional staff to complement missing expertise.[125] In doing so, the entrepreneur alleviates risks regarding the management's quality.

The additional expenditures for the production implementation, staff hiring, market tests and initial marketing measures are still not covered by earnings given that

[119] Busenitz/Fiet (1996); Eisenhardt/Schoonhoven (1990), p. 506
[120] Allen/Gale (1998), p. 70
[121] Baum/Silberman (2004), p. 415
[122] Bygrave (1988), p. 137
[123] Norton/Tenenbaum (1993a), p. 432
[124] Schmeisser/Krimphove (2001), p. 7
[125] Picot/Schneider/Laub (1989), p. 366 and p. 381f.

the product has not been introduced to the entire market yet. That is why the need for capital even tends to increase within this stage as compared to the seed stage.

2.1.3 Expansion Stage

At the beginning of the expansion stage, the venture takes on production and introduces its readily developed product(s) or service(s) to the market. Companies at this stage concentrate on increasing their coverage of domestic markets rather than on R&D activities. To meet the upcoming demand, expansion stage ventures have to enlarge their production and distribution systems. Most important, the business proves its financial and technical viability once the product succeeds in the market. Both, cash flow and profits attain positive values so that a growing part of expenditures is covered by revenues. Eventually, the start-up can self-finance its expenditures.[126] The product's performance reduces risks and uncertainties about the R&D outcome and the overall business concept. The company moreover establishes a track record allowing outsiders to assess the product's quality and its market. In addition, organizational structures and reporting systems evolve enabling the firm to provide historical data for outsiders' due diligence. In fact, start-ups matured to this stage hardly differ from established companies of the same industry featuring a similar size. The entrepreneurial risk components of market acceptance and management skills merely vanish.[127] The commercial take-off lowers the dependency on external funding in that the firm begins to accumulate internal funding.

Firms at a later expansion stage may enter foreign markets. In order to meet the requirements of remote markets, the firm has to assimilate the original products to local demands and develop appropriate sales structures. In domestic markets, firms at this level diversify their product ranges in order to increase market shares and to meet the upcoming competition. Every strategy causes uncertainty about the market's acceptance. Yet, the firm gains expertise that lowers uncertainties in comparison to earlier stages. These activities are necessary investments in the future requiring considerable amounts of capital which may exceed the start-ups internally generated resources.

2.1.4 Late Stage

The late stage is characterized by declining margins, toughened competition, new substitute products and the market's saturation.[128] In terms of product life-cycles, one-product companies within the later stage have passed the peak of total sales and face the degeneration of their products. At this stage, their activities center

---

[126] Engelmann/Juncker/Natusch/Tebroke (2000), p. 27f., Schefczyk (2004), p. 41

[127] Huyghebaert/Van de Gucht (2004), p. 677; Matz (2002), p. 13f.

[128] Fiet (1995), p. 553; Merkle (1984), p. 1061; Nevermann/Falk (1986), p. 75

on strengthening market positions and improving structures and efficiency in repetitive processes. Eventually, firms in the later stage are forced to take measures to renew their actual product range in order to stretch the product's life-time. Alternatively, the firm can launch a new generation of products. The company's life-cycle then combines the firm's current product life-cycle with the new product's life-cycle. Thus, the firm alleviates its dependency on the original product or service. The company's risk profile changes too; the firm now aggregates different product- and market-risks in a portfolio that compensates failures in one business with success in other endeavours. Nevertheless, both strategies require funds. If the firm cannot finance these projects through internally generated funds, it will seek outside sources again.

With introducing new products and technologies, the company's management faces new challenges. In comparison to earlier stages when the start-up's management commercializes familiar inventions or concepts, new products and technologies require different knowledge and expertise. Besides new products, later stage management encounters competition and is confronted with changing customer preferences. The new challenges, the incumbent management faces during the late stage, differ considerably from the main tasks in previous stages. The entrepreneurial management team's skills do eventually not suffice anymore to guide the venture's expansion in new markets and technologies. If the incumbent management's decisions are driven by false presumptions the firm's resources are not allocated optimally. Companies in later stages consequently hire external management teams to complement their expertise.[129] The launch of new products and hiring of external management impose new risks as the product's viability and the management qualities are unknown ex-ante. Both measures also prove costly and may not be covered by the revenues anymore.

In essence, a start-up's prosperity is indicated by its pending need for capital. Start-ups that fail to raise sufficient funds cannot proceed to higher development levels.[130] The next section addresses the funding of start-ups from their genesis to their initial floatation.

2.2 Start-Up Finance

The venture's financing constitutes one of the major limitations for its growth.[131] Financing defines corporate actions to raise money to fund operations.[132] Financing activities involve the configuration of two dimensions. On the one hand, the entrepre-

---

[129] Picot/Schneider/Laub (1989), p. 366 and p. 381f.; Wupperfeld (1994), p. 115

[130] Cornell/Shapiro (1988), p. 6

[131] Cassar (2004), p. 261

[132] Perridon/Steiner (1997), p. 341 and p. 344

neur has to specify the financial instruments. On the other hand, he has to decide on which sources of capital to tap.[133] Drawing this distinction is important because both, inside and outside investors can simultaneously participate in a company through debt and equity instruments but require different prerequisites and varying reward schemes. The following sections discuss which alternatives are accessible for start-up companies during their maturity process.[134]

2.2.1 Financial Instruments

In every financing transaction, the basic choice of instruments is between debt and equity. Both options differ in their risk- and return-profiles.[135] Debt on the one hand is repayable on a guaranteed repayment schedule and provides the lender with a prior claim on the company's assets. Providing a company with a loan is less risky than investing equity in the same firm if certain conditions exist (e.g., collateral and steady cash flows). Hence, lenders claim less compensation in comparison to fully liable equity investors. Debt by comparison with equity tends to be passive, except that prior to entering contracts the lender will impose certain conditions on the borrower. To guarantee the steadiness of future cash flows and prevent the management from opportunistic decisions, debt investors demand appropriate governance structures such as a board of directors with independent members or an accounting system that constantly monitors the company's financials.[136] In the absence of voting rights for loans, debt investors cannot influence the company's management after contracts are signed. Pure debt usually occurs in the form of an ordinary bank loan.

Ordinary equity on the other hand has no specific maturity, bears no contractual rate of return and affords the holder certain rights and privileges making him an active participant in the management and supervision of the company. The holders of ordinary equity represent the final owners of the business. Equity investors hold the lowest claim against the firm's assets. Thus, pure equity represents the riskiest part in the financial structure of the company's balance sheet. As reward, equity investors obtain the total excess of assets over liabilities. The risk and the potential return of ordinary equity are greater than those of ordinary debt. Ordinary equity typically occurs in the form of common shares of a company. In fact, common equity is rarely used in VC finance because the VCF's claim over the liquidation value would equal the entrepreneur's claim. In this case, the remaining assets are distributed among the VCF and the entrepreneur according to the relative equity ownership. However, if the

---

[133] According to Graf/Gruber (2001), p. 504

[134] Picot/Laub/Schneider (1989), p. 28ff., consider the development of a start-up as a result of a combining process of financial resources

[135] Schierenbeck (1973), p. 29

[136] Norton/Tenenbaum (1993b), p. 34; Perridon/Steiner (1997), p. 374f.

entrepreneur does not carry the costs of failure alone anymore, he becomes prone to acting opportunistically. Thus, VCFs seek to secure a senior claim on the firm's assets exceeding the entrepreneur's claim.[137]

As financial instruments have become more sophisticated, many variations combining elements of straight debt and equity have emerged – the so called "mezzanine"-instruments. Mezzanine capital features more than just one form of capital gains (e.g., interest payments and dividends after a conversion) and offers reduced liability to investors.[138] The fundamental advantage of mezzanine instruments in the VC context is that they allow VCFs to participate in the company's growth while at the same time protecting their investments in case of liquidation.[139] The most usual forms of mezzanine financing sorted by descending equity features and increasing debt characteristics are:

- The preference share is a contract that offers holders preferred participation over common equity holders upon liquidation. Preference shares holders obtain a dividend, provided that the profits suffice. If not, it is common to arrange that any unpaid dividends will be distributed at some time in the future when profits become available. Unlike common equity, investors cannot exercise control over the company.[140]
- Convertible preferred shares resemble preferred shares. In addition, they grant the holder upside participation in the form of common equity issued upon conversion. Similarly to preference shares, convertible preferred stock provides downside protection in the form of a liquidation preference. Conversion is triggered by performance so that the holder maintains his superior claim on the firm's assets in case of failure. Convertible preferred shares also allow for tax advantages over equity and preferred equity. The additional right of conversion translates into a higher valuation of convertible preferred shares in comparison to common or preferred shares for tax purposes. If convertible preferred shares are converted into common shares, this value spread is not subject to taxation.[141]

---

[137] Jain (1999), p. 225

[138] Heitzer (2000), p. 26; Leitinger/Strohbach/Schöfer/Hummel (2000), p. 75f.

[139] Golland (2000), p. 35ff.; Heitzer (2000), p. 26; Sherling (1999), p. 173

[140] In fact, the preferred participation can be further distinguished: in a "cumulative if earned preference", the preferred shares are satisfied prior to the common shares for the duration of one year. In contrast, "cumulative preferences" recompense the preferred shares for all past losses accrued. As for VC finance, VCFs usually chose non-cumulative dividend rights as it is perceived impossible for the start-up to achieve gains in its first years. A more detailed discussion is provided by Benton/Gunderson/Robinson (1997), p. 8–9; Bartlett (1999), p. 84ff.

[141] Bagley/Dauchy (1997), p. 202; Benton/Gunderson/Robinson (1997), p. 6–7

- Debt with warrants represents a form of loan supplemented with a warrant. The warrant allows the holder to purchase shares of common stock at a fixed price within a specified period while still collecting interests on the loan to the company.[142]
- Convertible debentures allow the creditor to convert his outstanding debt into common stock at a predetermined price. Convertible debentures differ from debt with warrants in that the creditor does not receive loan payments after converting his debt into stock anymore. In turn, the borrower must not repay the entire loan if the lender chooses not to exercise his warrants.[143]
- *Subordinated convertible debt* is similar to convertible debentures except that the creditor has a lower claim on the assets in the case of liquidation.[144]

Today, a company's financing decisions involve more than one instrument. Firms minimize their financing costs in that they offer investors tailor-made contracts to tap the cheapest capital sources. Nevertheless, the convertible preferred stock has emerged as the most prominent financial contract in the VC industry in the U.S. because it combines debt and equity characteristics to the advantage of the VCF. Norton and Tenenbaum (1992) report that VCFs favor the use of preferred shares regardless of the deal's specifics. Megginson and Mull (1991) find that 41.9 % of the VC-backed companies have convertible preferred stock in their capital structure as compared to 12.6 % of non-VC-backed firms.[145]

2.2.2 Sources of Finance

Not only has a company to decide which financial instruments it employs, it has also to choose the source of capital. Generally, two categories exist: internal and external sources of capital. The central distinction is drawn on the different perspectives of internal and external investors. Inside investors hold private information about the company to which external investors are not exposed. External investors thus suffer from information disadvantages preventing them from entirely understanding the firm's risks and potentials.[146] Figure 8 illustrates the different sources of capital and their categorization.

---

[142] Norton/Tenenbaum (1993b), p. 35; Sherling (1999), p. 167f.

[143] Leitinger/Strohbach/Schöfer/Hummel (2000), S. 77f.; Sherling (1999), p. 167f.

[144] Leitinger/Strohbach/Schöfer/Hummel (2000), S. 77f.; Sherling (1999), p. 167f.

[145] Barry (1994), p. 9f.; Bratton (2002), p. 892; Cumming (2002), p.6; Megginson/Mull (1991); Norton/Tenenbaum (1992), p. 27f.; Schmidt (2003), p. 1139

[146] See section 1.2 for a detailed discussion; Gompers/Lerner (2000), p. 128

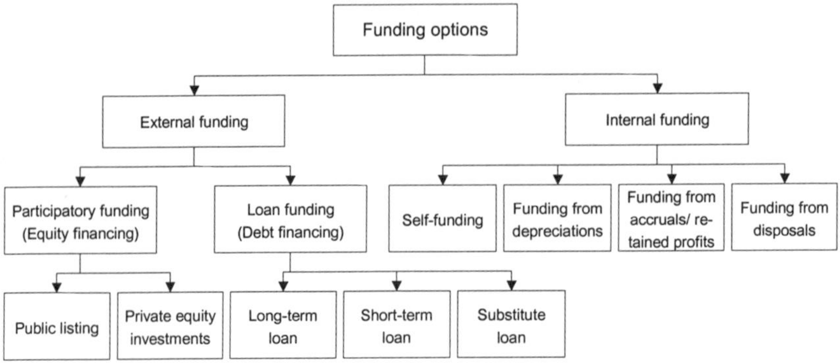

Figure 8: Internal and external financing options[147]

Internal sources of capital comprise all funds the company has already accumulated through retained profits, from depreciation and accruals, from proceeds of divestments or from funds provided by inside investors. For young start-ups, the entrepreneur usually serves as internal capital provider.[148] Both sources are limited; internal funding can only provide those resources the firm has generated previously or which are covered by the founder's wealth. Unless the entrepreneur endows the firm with sufficient capital, internal sources of young companies are scare since the venture generates little to no revenues in its early stages.[149]

Outside funding requires the firm to approach external investors through issuing shares to the public, offering equity-related stakes to institutional, strategic or other investors or incurring debt. As regards the limitations of outside funding, external equity and external debt have to be distinguished because debt- and equity-investors differ in their objectives and requirements.

External equity investors seek returns above the market rates by accepting elevated investment risks attributed to equity investments in single companies.[150] The act of exploiting external equity sources equals an exchange transaction of present funds for future claims on the venture's uncertain cash flows.[151] This transaction bears the difficulty of appraising the venture's future development for the external investors. External equity investors perform due diligence to anticipate the venture's future earning potential and assess the investment risk. The availability of external equity to the venture is contingent on the outside investor's appraisal of the venture's

---

[147] Perridon/Steiner (1997), p. 342

[148] Büschgen (1985), p. 221; see figure 8

[149] Baier (1996), p. 104

[150] See also Capital Asset Pricing Model (CAPM) , section 2.3.3 c)

[151] Graf/Gruber (2001), p. 504; Schneider (1992), p. 614

risk-return-profile.[152] Overcoming the prospective equity investors' uncertainties about the venture's quality represents a key challenge for start-up firms. Janney and Folta (2003) hold that managing outside investors' information gaps distinguishes successful and unsuccessful start-ups; the latter are more likely to run out of money before they generate revenues.[153] Besides, the entrepreneur's willingness to shift control rights to the investor limits the accessibility of external equity. Because the entrepreneur does not carry the costs of failure alone after receiving outside equity funding, he may prioritize opportunistic strategies to increase his private wealth.[154] This behavior, however, distresses the equity investor's investment. In order to prevent the management from opportunistic behavior, equity investors demand control rights constraining the investment to the entrepreneur's willingness to share corporate control.

Since debt investors lend money in exchange for fixed cash flows in the future, they do not participate in the firm's success in excess of these interest payments.[155] Instead of assessing uncertain future potentials, external debt investors desire to protect their investment from failure. Sufficient assets to collateralize the loan as well as steady and predictable cash flows to fulfil interest payments constitute compelling prerequisites for incurring debt. Even if the venture can provide sufficient collateral and cash flow, the accessibility of external debt remains difficult for young start-ups because banks hardly grant small loans. Banks prefer to grant large credits in contrast to small loans in order to achieve a higher dispersion of their fixed costs for a preliminary due diligence.[156] As a consequence, external debt finance is bounded to the firm's assets, cash flows and typically to the loan's volume too.

2.2.3 Structuring the Start-up's Finance Throughout Its Development

A venture progresses through several rounds of financing. At every stage, the entrepreneur has to anticipate how much capital the start-up requires. Accordingly, he has to specify which sources and which instruments – aggregated to the financial structure – to apply.[157]

Several theories suggest rationales for adopting a specific financial structure. Cassar (2004) distinguishes two principle frameworks that emanate from different types of financing costs: the static-trade-off and the pecking-order theory. The static trade-off setting considers the impact of increased debt funding; the costs of princi-

---

[152] Gompers/Lerner (2000), p. 128

[153] Janney/Folta (2003), p. 363f.; Leitinger/Strohbach/Schöfer/Hummel (2000), p. 83

[154] Jain (1999), p. 225

[155] Stiglitz (1985), p. 146

[156] Gerke (1993), p. 620f.; Schefczyk (2004), p. 68

[157] VC will be introduced in the following section

pal-agency problems and bankruptcy are contrasted against the tax shield from interest payments.[158] In the absence of revenues in the venture's early stages, the contemplation of tax advantages does not contribute to this analysis. The pecking-order theory ascribes the choice between debt and equity to the costs of informing outside investors. Information costs dependent on the extent of risk and uncertainty, investors associate with the investment. The pecking order predicts the following sequence: internal equity and debt provided or secured by the founder, short-term debt, long-term debt and finally external equity.[159] This analysis follows the pecking order but shows how the VC concept breaks up this traditional order by offering external equity capital to early stage ventures.

At its genesis, two factors limit the venture's access to external sources of capital. First, start-ups are typically not endowed with sufficient assets to collateralize debt investments.[160] In their early stages, ventures consume capital for creating knowledge. This knowledge is tied to individuals and bears not transferable value in case the business fails. Thus, it cannot serve as collateral.[161] External debt financing at early stages is consequently limited to the company's and the entrepreneur's personal assets serving as collateral.[162] Second, start-ups in contrast to established companies cannot exhibit track records or historical data (e.g., financial statements, references for the management, etc.) to facilitate an outside investor's due diligence.[163] In the absence of detailed knowledge about the project, external equity investors fail to assess the company's true value. They find only unfavorable risk-return profiles stemming from apparently high market and technological risks. These risks prevent external equity investors from investments in early stage ventures.[164] The pecking-order proclaims that the entrepreneur's personal funds remain the only option since the entrepreneur is best aware of the venture's value at this stage.[165] In addition, the entrepreneur may receive supplements in the form of equity investments or loans from close external investors such as his family and friends. Besides, the entrepreneur can also apply for a loan on his personal assets.[166]

Provided that the concept proves viable, the venture's capital requirements exceed the entrepreneur's own and his immediate entourage's resources rapidly. Still,

---

[158] Cassar (2004), p. 263f.

[159] Howorth (2001), p. 79, provides an overview on studies confirming this pecking order; see also Berger/Udell (1998), p. 624; Cassar (2004), p. 264; Myers/Majluf (1984), p. 219ff.

[160] Carpenter/Petersen (2002), p. 54f.; Murray (1994), p. 60; Ruppen (2001), p. 27

[161] Cornell/Shapiro (1988), p. 14; Murray (1996), p. 42

[162] Murray (1994), p. 60

[163] Eisenhardt/Schoonhoven (1990), p. 504

[164] Schefczyk (2004), p. 68

[165] Myers (2001), p. 81; Cassar (2004), p. 264

[166] Bruno/Tyebjee (1985), p. 65; Allen/Udell (1998), p. 625

the start-up is not able to access debt financing exceeding the loans on the entrepreneur's personal assets since the firm neither owns sufficient assets nor has it a steady cash flow to collateralize and repay the debt investment. The initial assets of start-ups rather include intangible assets, such as tacit knowledge gained through R&D. In essence, the accessibility of debt financing remains limited until the venture exhibits a steady cash flow over several consecutive periods and invests in tangible assets. Even later on, debt remains constrained until larger loans are required. Traditional equity financing in the form of passive investments is limited too because external investors' suffer from ex-ante uncertainties and fear unfavorable risk-return profiles. Institutional or strategic equity investors do not possess the capabilities to evaluate and supervise early stage investments.[167] Unless the firm has proven its viability, external equity funding is essentially not accessible. At this stage, only venture capital becomes an option – as will be discussed in chapter 2.3.1 a).[168] Given the high investment risks, VC investments occur in the form mezzanine instruments. These mezzanine instruments protect the VCF's investment from the entrepreneur's opportunistic behavior, limit the VCF's loss in case of a failure and allow it to participate in the venture's success.[169]

After accomplishing break-even, internal financing through retained profits becomes available to finance expansion. First revenues and a looming product acceptance during the expansion stage produce new information about the viability of the business. These accomplishments reduce ex-ante uncertainty of outside investors. The venture can then tap external equity financing of strategic investors seeking a window in new technologies or markets.[170] Equity investors at this stage will demand preference rights to secure their investment in case of both failure and the entrepreneur's opportunistic behavior.[171]

As the company enters the expansion stage, its need for capital commensurately grows. At the same time, the company's looming business allows it to lever the cash flow and investments in assets by incurring external debt funding. Upon expansion, the outside investors' ex-ante uncertainty and information gaps decrease given that the product's market acceptance and technical viability become apparent. At this stage, the company has built a track record of successful interactions with customers, suppliers or strategic partners.[172] Moreover, the firm's market activities generate

---

[167] Merkle (1984), p. 1061f.

[168] Venture finance includes not only VC but also Corporate Venture Capital, funding by business angles, etc., see section 2.3.4

[169] Barry (1994), p. 9f.; Bratton (2002), p. 892; Cumming (2002), p.6; Norton/Tenenbaum (1992), p. 27f.; Schmidt (2003), p. 1139

[170] Breuer (1997), p. 325

[171] Bratton (2002), p. 892; Cumming (2002), p.6; Schmidt (2003), p. 1139

[172] Eisenhardt/Schoonhoven (1990), p. 504

public information that allows outsiders a more detailed assessment of the company. The more the company matures, the easier it becomes for external equity investors to value it and the less investment risk remains. Eventually, the investment risk attains a level commonly perceived for every other firm of similar size in the same sector. At this point, the venture can access public capital markets with a variety of debt or equity instruments. Once the company's issues are publicly traded, it has virtually access to every financing instrument. Firms at this stage can improve their capital structures and balance the costs of capital with the risk-return requirements of investors.[173] IPOs of equity and debt instruments also help fund further growth in new markets through new products or acquisitions. Beyond this, the extended equity position after an IPO of equity allows the firm to incur debt by levering the new funds.

Throughout later stages, companies oftentimes alter their ownership structure, for instance, to revise preference rights or majority stakes.[174] The restructuring of major share holder positions requires the company to access bridge financing. "Bridge financing" denotes interim funding provided by outside investors to help companies to cover expenditures for a certain period of time. Bridge financing hence enables the venture to replace equity positions of incumbent investors. However, bridge financing is only a short-term solution until new permanent funds become available.[175]

In some cases, the ownership structure is revised substantially and corporate control is transferred. If an external management team discovers a strategy of reallocating the firm's resources more efficiently – so that future free cash flows produce values in excess of the company's current valuation – a buyout transaction occurs. Such a transaction provides returns for present and new investors; the incumbent owners obtain a higher valuation than they can generate and the new management team receives the spread between the transaction's valuation and the valuation after restructuring.[176] Even though MBO investors infuse equity, they lever their contribution through borrowing against the target's future cash flows. In essence, the MBO transaction involves substantial debt investments.[177] Accordingly, this type of transaction is also referred to as leveraged buyout (LBO).

Figure 9 illustrates the successive financing phases of a venture from its genesis until it is floated on a stock market or sold to private investors. Conditional on the venture's state, figure 9 highlights the type of financing contracts and the most likely source of finance as projected by the pecking order.[178] Moreover, figure 9 reflects the

---

[173] Zemke (1995), p. 35

[174] Black/Gilson (1998), p. 261; Schmidt (2003), p. 1140

[175] Harris (2002), p. 59

[176] Ambrose/Winters (1992), p. 89; Arzac (2001), p. 16

[177] Arzac (2001), p. 16

[178] Howorth (2001), p. 79; see also Myers/Majluf (1984), p. 219ff.

impact of VC finance on the company's capital stock. Initially, VC financing adds to the firm's equity position. The strengthened equity position in turn enables the firm to lever the VCF's infusion and increase debt funding. In excess of that, researchers show that the VCF's presence improves the firm's access to bank loans in that the VCF certifies for steady cash flows.[179] In essence, VC financing boosts the venture's financing structure helping overcome financial constraints throughout the venture's development.

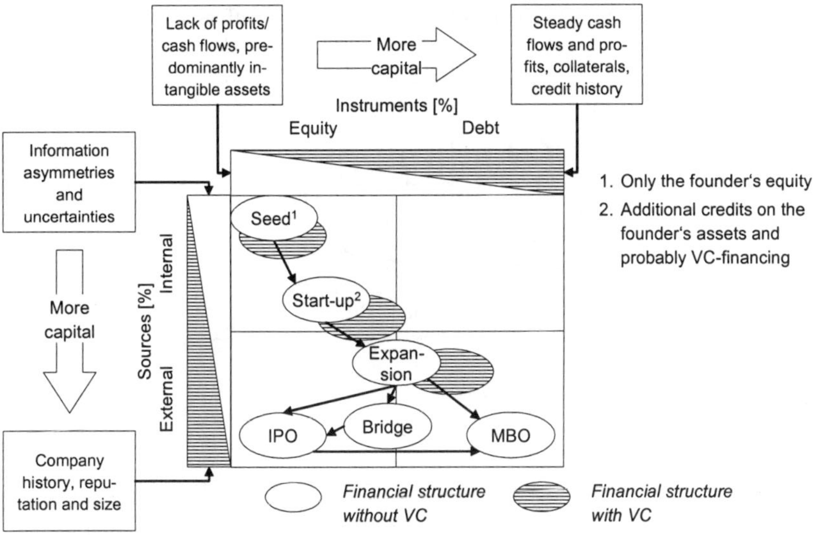

Figure 9: Mutation of the financial structure and the impact of VC

2.3 The Venture Capitalist's Business Model

This chapter deepens the understanding of the VCF's business model and looks beyond the brief introduction given in chapter one. Initially, this section delves into every participant's role in VC finance. The exchange of goods/services and capital among the VCF and its environment throughout an investment and the processes and measures VCFs employ to facilitate these transactions are examined.[180] The analysis of the VCF's business model provides the basis for the analysis of VCFs' exits.

---

[179] Busenitz/Fiet (1996); Lam (1991), p. 141

[180] See Stähler (2001), p. 38ff., for typical contents of an analysis of business models

2.3.1 Motives to Engage in VC Finance

This section examines which resources, services and funds VCFs exchange with other participants in the financing process including the start-up, the fund-investors and the follow-on investor (private investor respectively the public market in case the venture goes public).[181] It sheds light on the incentives of the involved parties to engage in VC finance. These incentives are essential for the existence of VC finance. This section elaborates that VCFs cannot survive in the absence of start-ups to finance, fund investors to obtain capital from or follow-on investors to buy out the VCF.

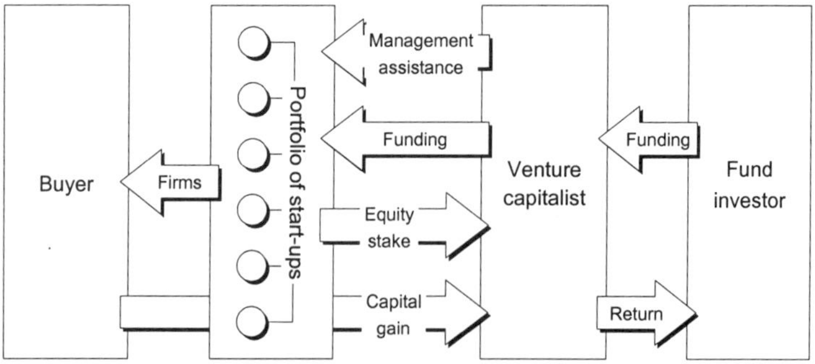

Figure 10: Exchange transactions in VC finance[182]

a) Start-ups and the venture capitalist

Start-ups represent the recipients of the VCF's services. Although entrepreneurs may have auspicious ideas, they usually lack the necessary capital to fund the entire process of commercializing their invention.[183] For two reasons, VC constitutes a financing option that is particularly well suited to meet the requirements of young start-ups or even of a seed-idea distinguishing VC from other forms of equity investments.

In the absence of external capital, the entrepreneur cannot invest in R&D activities and infrastructure to commercialize his idea. Only VC addresses this financing gap in that VCFs provide equity capital infusions to start-ups despite the risks.[184] VCFs accept the risk of investing in early stage firms while the combination of intangible assets, oftentimes inexperienced founders, negative earnings, unproven concepts and the absence of a track record deters debt providers and institutional or

---

[181] See figure 10

[182] Based on Schmidtke (1985), p. 111

[183] Gompers/Lerner (2000), p. 127

[184] Gillner (1984), p. 12; Kulicke/Müller (1994), p. 18; according to Zider (1998), p. 132, more than 80 % of the VCF's financial contribution will be invested in infrastructure required for further growth

strategic equity investors.[185] From the entrepreneur's perspective, VC financing bears the advantage of outside equity finance. Unlike debt, VC finance does not require the investment's protection through the businesses or the founder's personal assets. Moreover, the entrepreneur does not commit to repay the VCF's investment – not even in case of a failure.[186] VC requires no fixed interest payments which burden the start-up's cash flow at early stages. Both, the VCF and the entrepreneur essentially face the same investment risk of commercializing innovative products in not yet emerged markets and experience similar motivations to work against the odds of launching the new business.[187]

Contingent on the timing of the initial investment, scholars distinguish between seed and start-up finance.[188] Seed finance supports the development of an idea; the entrepreneur requires funds to improve his concept and to prepare a business plan. Seed finance typically ranges about a few hundred thousand dollars. Start-up finance addresses the equity gap arising in the start-up period and covers expenses related to marketing and the mass-production of the venture's products. Start-up finance can amount up to several million dollars.[189]

Second, VCFs offer assistance to entrepreneurs in the form of management know-how and experiences.[190] The VCF's support helps commercially inexperienced entrepreneurs to overcome managerial obstacles.[191] Moreover, the entrepreneur benefits from accessing the VCF's exclusive network of industry contacts with potential suppliers, customers and service providers such as consultants or accountants.[192] Sapienza (1992) observes that entrepreneurs particularly appreciate the VCF's strategic advice – more than accessing networks.[193] Through sharing knowledge and granting access to critical resources, VCFs shorten the time the venture requires to enter the market. VC thus boosts the start-up's prosperity.[194] Several

---

185 Barry (1994), p. 3; Birmingham/Busenitz/Arthurs (2003), p. 2; Boocock/Woods (1998), p. 36; Eisenhardt (1990), p. 504

186 Schween (1996), p. 15

187 Heitzer (2000), p. 25

188 Lam (1991), p. 137

189 Siegert (1991), p. 34

190 Davila/Foster/Gupta (1997), p. 691; Sweeting/Wong (1997), p. 127

191 Amit/Brander/Zott (1998), p. 442; Barry/Muscarella/Peavy/Vetsuypens (1990), p. 448; Bascha (2001), p. 5; Sweeting/Wong (1997), p. 127; Timmons/Bygrave (1986), p. 161

192 Davila/Foster/Gupta (2003), p. 691; MacMillan/Kulow/Khoylian (1989), p. 31f.; however, when offering wrong or bad strategic input, VCFs can also hinder the venture's growth, see Steier/Greenwood (1995), p. 348ff.

193 Sapienza (1992), p. 12

194 Spekman/Forbes/Isabella/MacAvoy (1998), p. 758f.

studies confirm that VC-finance enhance start-ups' growth and value creation over those of non-VC-backed ventures.[195]

In exchange for its financial and non-financial contributions to the start-up, the VCF obtains equity and mezzanine stakes.[196] In most VC markets, convertible preferred shares constitute prominent instruments since they advantage VCFs in two respects. Convertible preferred shares grant the VCF geometrical participation in the prospering company. Geometrical returns are generated through the conversion rights inherent in the convertible preferred share.[197] Simultaneously, convertible preferred shares reduce the downside potential in case of a failure. Common stock is employed rarely since the VCF would invest without having a superior claim over the entrepreneur with respect to assets and cash at liquidation.[198]

Besides, VCFs seek participation in the corporate governance so that the entrepreneur has to accept a loss of control to the VCF. VCFs are almost always represented in the venture's board and usually occupy several directors' positions. A stronger board representation of VCFs increases the entrepreneur's receptivity to financial, operational and strategic advice. VCFs also use their board presence to supervise the management and initiate strategic changes if necessary.[199] Most important, the VCF's managerial control reduces the likelihood that the entrepreneur will engage in self beneficial behavior. Thus, VCFs ensure that the entrepreneur pursues only strategies that optimize all share holders' profits equally.

b) Fund investors and the venture capitalist

The VC fund investors, such as banks, pension funds, endowments, insurance companies or wealthy individuals, represent another group of participants in the VC system. They wish to allocate capital to risky investments with high return potentials. But VC fund investors do not possess the time and expertise to oversee single transactions.[200] VCFs collect their funds and manage the investment process on the behalf of the VC fund investors.[201] VC funds are commonly structured as limited partnerships in which the fund investors subscribe to the fund as partners with limited liability while the VCF serving as general partner is not confined in its liability. Con-

---

[195] As shown in a study by Coopers & Lybrand for the EVCA, EVCA (1996); a major research track compares VC-backed and not VC-backed start-ups reflecting the VCF's contribution to the venture's performance. The central findings show that firms that receive VC funding outperform others; see Mull (1994); Megginson/Weiss (1991), p. 883; Schilit (1991), p. 37f.; Cornelli/Yosha (2003), p. 1ff.

[196] See section 2.2.1

[197] Bartlett (1999), p. 85f.; See section 2.2.1 for a detailed discussion

[198] Norton/Tenenbaum (1992), p. 23

[199] Barry/Muscarella/Peavy/Vetsuypens (1990), p. 460ff.

[200] Gompers/Lerner (2000), p. 127

[201] Barry (1994), p. 4; Bowden (1994), p. 308

tracts limit the partnership's life-time – usually to ten years.[202] During the first two to five years, the fund investors commit to advance up to a certain amount of money.[203] It takes a fund typically three years to entirely invest its capital in start-ups.[204] The VC fund's contractual goal is to maximize the fund's terminal value.[205] After the fund ceases to exist, its resources are distributed among the limited partners and the VCF. The VCF's compensation stems from annual management fees which typically amount to 2 % of the fund's face value and from carrying interests in the fund of up to 20 % of the appreciated value.[206] The fund investors receive the remaining of the appreciated value.

The fund concept embodies two general advantages for investors. First, finance research posits that by building a well diversified portfolio, investors can reduce their investment risk without giving up returns. Every rational and risk adverse investor desires a well diversified portfolio.[207] In general, a diversified portfolio is easier to create the more capital the investor has at his disposal. VC funds embark on this rationale and collect money from a multitude of capital providers. Because the VC fund combines the resources of several investors, it can compose a larger portfolio of start-up investments than individual investors can.[208] Consequently, the fund can diversify its investment risk more effectively. The past performance of VC funds in the United States confirms this argumentation; Barry (1994) finds that VC funds are hardly subject to unsystematic risks because they spread their investments across sectors and development stages and thus diversify their portfolio risk.[209]

Second, engaging VCFs as intermediates lowers the fund investors' transaction costs. VCFs repeatedly invest in start-ups. In doing so, they accumulate unique expertise in all stages of the VC process which lowers transaction costs in subsequent deals.[210] Barry (1994) argues that VCFs capitalize on their experience particularly throughout the detection and selection of investment opportunities.[211] Given their expertise, VCFs are able to select investment opportunities more effectively and effi-

---

[202] Gompers/Lerner (1996), p. 465

[203] Lin/Smith (1998), p. 244

[204] Blake (1999), p. 81f.

[205] Hax (1964), p. 436

[206] Bygrave (1994), p. 17; in fact, the VCF's compensation varies across funds, see Chiampou/Kallett (1989), p. 3; Gompers/Lerner (1999), p. 6, note that compensation agreements range from 1.5 % to 3 % as regards the management fee

[207] Perridon/Steiner (1997), p. 118f.

[208] See Benston/Smith (1976), p. 216, for mutual funds in general

[209] Barry (1994), p. 7

[210] Amit/Brander/Zott (1988), p. 441; Schmidt (2003), p. 1139; see Williamson (1990), p. 69, for transaction costs

[211] Barry (1994), p. 4

ciently than unspecialized investors.[212] During the investment period, VCFs contribute their knowledge to the venture's decision making process and positively impact the venture's risk-return profile. Their experience also allows VCFs to track the venture's progress and monitor the entrepreneur's behavior better than unspecialized investors.[213] Moreover, the VCF grows a multitude of industry contacts that diminish frictions in acquiring, managing and ultimately selling ventures.[214]

Research holds that VC finance exists because of VCFs' superiority in managing risk and exploiting transaction cost advantages. Amit, Brander and Zott (1998) argue that VC finance has emerged because VCFs' specialized skills to select and monitor the entrepreneurs' activities allows them to manage early stage investments more effectively than the VC fund investors.[215] VCFs consequently accomplish more favorable risk-return profiles for their venture investments and return higher profits to their fund investors. Their continuous involvement in VC finance enables VCF to act as informed agents in markets with imperfect information and to lower costs that stem from information inefficiency.[216] Employing the VCF as intermediate allows fund investors to participate in the VCF's transaction costs advantages.[217]

c) Co-investors and the venture capitalist

VCFs frequently involve other VCFs in their investments. This strategy is commonly referred to as the syndication of investments.[218] Syndication serves both, the incumbent and the new VCFs in several ways. First, as outlined above, larger portfolios are exposed to less unsystematic risk given that they can diversify better. Syndication allows VCFs to aggregate their portfolios and increase diversification. In doing so, VCFs reduce their exposure to unsystematic investment risks.[219]

Second, syndication allows the participating VCFs to share their expertise in selecting and monitoring venture investments. VC-syndicates can improve their decision making at the initial and every subsequent investment stage. Sah and Stigliz (1986) find that organizations, in which investment decisions are made only, if several independent and qualified observers agree, are superior to those in which

---

[212] Boocock/Woods (1998), p. 37

[213] Barry (1994), p. 4; Birmingham/Busenitz/Arthurs (2003), p. 2; Gupta/Sapienza (1992), p. 349; Jain (1999), p. 223

[214] Sahlman (1990), p. 500

[215] Amit/Brander/Zott (1998), p. 441ff.; Gompers/Lerner (2000), p. 130

[216] Chan (1983), p. 1543

[217] Benston/Smith (1976), p. 215ff., note that employing intermediates is appropriate if the intermediate can lower costs of information asymmetries and risks; see also Leland/Pyle (1977), p. 382; Chan (1983), p. 1560; Misirli (1988), p. 111f.

[218] Florida/Smith (1990), p. 353

[219] Bygrave (1987), p. 139

projects are funded after a single affirmative decision.[220] VCFs circulate investment proposals to syndicated investors to try to convince other VCFs to commit capital. In pooling their experiences and knowledge, syndicates reduce information dissimilarities between investors and investees. Thus, syndicated investments are attributed with lower investment risks in relation to non-syndicated investments.[221] Syndication additionally enhances VCFs' monitoring and management assistance after the investment is entered. The entrepreneur is supervised by several instances and gains access to the VCFs' combined resources and experiences.

d) Follow-on investors and the venture capitalist

Follow-on investors succeed the VCF in providing growth capital to the venture. Regardless of their type or affiliation, follow-on investors benefit from VC in that VCFs grow new generations of investment opportunities. The VCF's professional assistance and monitoring over several years helps VC-backed start-ups to manage much of the risk. By the time of the exit, VCFs offer follow-on investors investment opportunities in emerging markets that have already proven their financial viability and feature reduced entrepreneurial risks. Had the venture failed, the VCF would have abandoned it and disposed it to the management team or specialized financial investors earlier.[222] Similar to manufacturing, VCFs create value by combining several input factors, such as entrepreneurial ideas, expertise and capital. Through selling their products, VCFs reap their returns.[223]

VC research discerns two general types of follow-on investors. Public investors on the one hand represent scattered investors in capital markets that buy a company's equity issue. Research suggests that VC-backed IPOs feature lower investment risks in comparison to non-VC-backed companies because of the VCF's active involvement and careful selection of IPO candidates.[224] In subscribing to the issue and acquiring the venture's stock, public investors reward the VCF for its services.

Private investors on the other hand constitute industrial investors seeking to acquire entire firms. In general, private investors wish to stretch their portfolio of businesses and technologies without incurring the costs and risks of developing the innovation internally. Rather, industrial investors buy proven concepts from VCFs.[225] Acquisitions of VC-backed firms prove particularly useful if:

---

[220] Sah/Stiglitz (1986), p. 716ff.

[221] Bygrave/Timmons (1992), p. 440ff.

[222] Barry/Muscarella/Peavy/Vetsuypens (1990), p. 448

[223] Brück (1998), p. 15; Dieckhaus (1993), p. 171

[224] E.g., Barry/Muscarella/Peavy/Vetsuypens (1990), p. 448; Busenitz/Fiet (1996); Megginson/Weiss (1991), p. 879f.; Neus/Walz (2001), p. 17; see section 3.1.1 a)

[225] Frick/Torres (2002), p. 114

- the acquirer desires to inject new life into its business through launching new products and accessing new markets.[226] Cable and Shane (1997), for instance, note that new business opportunities are oftentimes recognized solely by entrepreneurs.[227] Through buying new ventures, matured corporations can access innovative business concepts and emerging markets.
- the investor wishes to access new technologies, unique skills or intellectual property exclusively held by innovative ventures.[228] Merrifield (1988) underlines the importance of acquiring new technologies for incumbent businesses in order to maintain their competitive advantages.[229] In the case of new technologies, innovative start-ups develop vital pieces of knowledge to which industry incumbents have no access. In fact, the complexity of modern technologies and rapidity of technological change limit the ability of incumbent companies to rely solely on their internal knowledge.[230] Investments in entrepreneurial businesses grant private investors access to innovative technologies and simultaneously to skilled employees.[231]
- an incumbent firm wishes to eliminate competitive threads emanating from new ventures and thus initiates a takeover.[232]

Further incentives resemble common motivations for M&A activities. M&A motives depend on the acquirer's position in the value chain relative to the venture's business. Acquirers take over ventures that provide input factors, if they wish to move downstream in the supply chain to ensure long-term supply and to reduce costs. Alternatively, private investors seek to move upstream to gain access to new markets by buying a start-up that purchases their products. Yet, common motivations, such as developing synergies in production or procurement, do usually not prove viable in the VC context. On the one hand, ventures that are sold to private investors lack sufficient sizes; the bigger the venture gets, the more likely are VCFs to float it instead of selling it privately.[233] On the other hand, the uniqueness of the venture's technologies does not enable the acquirer to achieve synergy effects through merging the target's operations into his own business.[234]

---

[226] Achleitner (1999), p. 140; Gaughan (1999), p. 133; Picot (1998), p. 11

[227] Cable/Shane (1997), p. 144

[228] Alvarez/Barney (2001), p. 139f.; Cumming/MacIntosh (2003), p. 514

[229] Merrifield (1988), p. 172

[230] Lane/Salk/Lyles (2001), p. 1141ff.

[231] Blonigen/Taylor (2000), p. 50ff. ; Ranft/Lord (2000), p. 296

[232] Cumming/MacIntosh (2003), p. 517; Schröder (1992), p. 252; Temple (1999), p. 101f.

[233] Mikkelson/Partch/Shah (1997), p. 284; Wang/Sim (2001), p. 343 and p. 353; Wright/Robbie/ Romanet/Thompson/Joachimsson/Bruining/Herst (1994), p. 96

[234] Achleitner (1999), p. 139; Gaughan (1999), p. 133ff.; Picot (2000), p. 5f.

2.3.2 The VC-Financing Process

Different views about the VC process prevail among the three central parties – the entrepreneur, the VC fund investors and the VCF. The perspectives of the entrepreneur and the fund investors vary particularly with respect to fundamental activities. From the entrepreneur's perspective, VC financing constitutes a unique event; entrepreneurs almost always set up only one VC-backed business in their life-time.[235] In the context of VC, entrepreneurs primarily look into the accessibility of resources that help grow the business. VC financing is the result of a temporary financing decision that fills the gap between the venture's actual capital endowment and its requirements. Limited partners regard their VC related activities in the context of their commitments to VC funds as an ongoing process. They permanently have to find optimal allocations for their capital. Thus, the fund investors' VC related activities center on selecting, continuously monitoring and re-allocating their resources either to VC funds or to alternative investment opportunities. The VCF acts as intermediate between both parties. The VCF's view consequently captures both perspectives. VCFs perceive the VC process as a cycle with the repeating activities of allocating the limited partners' funds to VC investments. Besides, VCFs deal with the sequence of activities that concentrate on the execution of one particular investment. Most scholars hence describe the VC process from the point of view of the VC to encapsulate the entrepreneur's and the fund investor's perceptions.

To simplify matters, the following discussion only pays attention to the process of a single start-up investment as illustrated in figure 11. Researchers agree on the distinction of the following activities that are sequentially carried out by VCFs from the initial capital gathering to the eventual returning of the proceeds to the limited partners.

---

[235] Westhead/Wright (1998), p. 174f; Wright/Robbie/Ennew (1997), p. 228f.

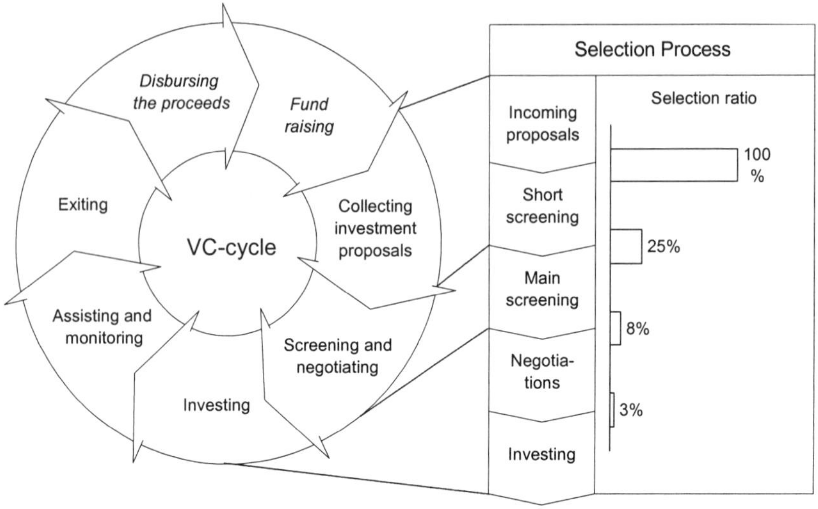

Figure 11: The VC financing cycle[236]

a) Fund raising

In order to raise capital for VC investments, VCFs initiate a VC fund. Raising funds takes several months. Throughout this time, the VCF's management team promotes its fund concept and investment focus. The VCF also advertises its track record of previous investments. The track record demonstrates the VCF's specialized skills in nurturing ventures in the targeted investment focus. The track record distinguishes the VCFs from other VCFs that compete for fund investors.[237] Once the fund's objective is achieved, the fund is closed to further investments. Thereafter, the VCF governs the capital for the fund's specified life time.

Researchers denote those activities in which the VCF attracts and returns the fund's capital to its limited partners as the VCF's passive business. The passive business does not involve the execution of venture investments itself. The VCF's financing activities constitute the VCF's active business.[238] The VCF's active business is a process that typically progresses through these steps: attracting business proposals, evaluating and selecting them, negotiating and entering investments, monitoring the portfolio firms and finally cashing-out.[239]

---

[236] According to Albach/Hunsdiek/Kokalj (1986), p. 168ff.; Fried/Hisrich (1994), p. 30ff.; Schefczyk (2004), p. 40ff.

[237] Matz (2000), p. 37

[238] Roesner (1968), p. 74; Schröder (1992), p. 71f.

[239] Bell (1999), p. 54ff.; Schröder (1992), p. 39f.

b) Collecting investment proposals

Already during the fund raising process, the VCF begins to glean investment proposals. In order to increase the number of proposals and thus the probability of participating in high potential investment opportunities, VCFs engage in several promotion activities.[240] First, VCFs meet entrepreneurs and gather investment proposals on company presentations, marketing events or on entrepreneurial franchise fairs.[241] Well established VCFs also receive inquiries from entrepreneurs on a regular basis due to their publicly known track record of successful VC-investments – even without relation to their marketing activities. Second, investment proposals stem from the VCF's network of financial service providers. Unlike an entrepreneur approaching the VCF, referred investment proposals bear the advantage of third-party certification through the VCF's network. The prospects of a follow-on assignment of these service providers warrants the VCF certitude that they will only endorse outstanding business proposals. Otherwise, the relationship suffers distressing the service provider's long-term profits. Third-party certification essentially helps the VCF to overcome initial information asymmetries. Most frequently, such trustworthy contacts embody lawyers or investment bankers. Fried and Hisrich's (1994) provide empirical evidence that most successful VC investments stem from references of third-parties rather than from entrepreneurs submitting proposals.[242]

c) Screening and negotiating

Financiers always face the problem of picking the best investments.[243] Evaluating and selecting investment opportunities hence constitutes a central step in every investment process regardless of the investment class or the investor. However, two reasons account for an even higher importance of a deliberate due diligence for VC investments as compared to investments in publicly traded securities of well established companies. First, investors' efforts to perform due diligence on a publicly traded security carry little reward because the market's pricing reflects all available information.[244] VC investment opportunities, however, are not exposed to public scrutiny and VCFs cannot take a free ride on the market's supervision. Thus, the valuation of start-ups remains relatively uncertain. Second, modern financial theory posits that investors in public securities are virtually not exposed to company-specific risks; investors in public companies can eliminate the unsystematic risk by diversifying their portfolio of stocks. The portfolio's market risk rather than the individual investment's

---

[240] Matz (2002), p. 37f.; Schmeisser/Krimphove (2001), p. 235f.

[241] Betsch/Groh/Lohmann (1998), p. 227f.; Bascha (2001), p. 19; Dotzler (2001), p. 6f.

[242] Fried/Hisrich (1994), p. 31

[243] Keasey/Short (1997), p. 76

[244] Lasfer/Melnik/Thomas (2003), p. 1959f.

risks determines the investor's return in the long run. Diversification is, however, limited for VCFs since they are not able to spread their investments to a similar extent. VC investments rather require concentrated capital infusions limiting the diversification of firm-specific risks. In essence, discriminating investment proposals is crucial for VCFs because no objective market valuation exists such as for publicly traded securities and the VCF is exposed to higher firm-specific risks.[245]

VCFs initially screen incoming investment proposals – usually in the form of a business plan – and exclude those inquiries that apparently do not correspond with the very basic requirements. A common rule of thumb holds that the transaction must eventually yield five times the VCF's investment.[246] At this stage, VCFs rely on their experience to assess whether the proposed business can accomplish sufficient market shares and margins to satisfy the return requirement. Up to 90% of the incoming proposals are usually rejected after the initial screening because the VCF identifies shortcomings regarding the viability or return potential.[247]

In the second evaluation round, the VCF devotes more time to an intensive assessment of the remaining proposals. Throughout this due diligence, the VCF establishes a sound understanding of the businesses competitive advantage and viability. Yet, VCFs cannot access every information that is relevant for a complete evaluation of each proposal; either the entrepreneur is privy about information or the VCF would have to incur substantial costs to close the information gap.[248] The VCF's due diligence rather focuses on a few but crucial selection criteria. VCFs examine two key factors that are widely recognized as prerequisites for successful venture investments.[249] On the one hand, the business concept must promise a significant market potential in the near future. In this context, VCFs anticipate the holding period the business requires for gaining a sufficient size and credibility to be sold in public or to private investors.[250] The growth potential or size of the relevant markets reference the future earning potentials and indicate whether the business will exhibit a sufficient size to attract public investors in an IPO.[251] Further emphasis is put on the businesses uniqueness and proprietary rights. Uniqueness and proprietary protection serve as barriers for new market entrants and preserve the VCF's investment.

---

[245] Bhide (2000), p. 142

[246] Fried/Hisrich (1994), p. 30

[247] Fried/Hisrich (1994), p. 32; Pfirrmann/Wupperfeld/Lerner (1997), p. 55

[248] See sections 1.2.3 and 1.2.4 for a detailed discussion of information asymmetries

[249] This contemplation mainly follows the notion of Fried/Hisrich (1994); see also Timmons/Muzyka/Stevenson/Bygrave (1987), p. 111ff., who identify five factors as key indicators of a successful venture: product-market characteristics, competitive dynamics, business economics, business performance and management team; see also Amit/Gloster/Muller (1990), p. 102f.; Brettel (2002), p. 306

[250] Shepherd/Zacharakis (2001a), p. 59

[251] Elango/Fried/Hisrich/Polonchek (1995), p. 159; Hinkel (2001), p. 36; Yosha (1995), p. 3ff.

On the other hand, the VCF's evaluation strongly focuses on the entrepreneur's abilities. Research provides vast evidence that a venture's success largely depends on the quality of the management team.[252] The risk of weak management immediately lowers the investment's prospects of yielding appropriate internal rates of return (IRRs) on the VCF's capital infusion. In order to reduce the risk of poor management, VCFs assess the entrepreneur's background, track records from previous projects and achievements in prior jobs. In addition, VCFs draw on the entrepreneur's meticulousness in preparing the business plan and presenting the proposal.[253]

Because successfully exiting ventures is of direct importance for VCFs, VCFs anticipate future exit scenarios before entering the investment. For instance, they investigate which strategic buyer may become interested in the venture or whether the venture will attract public investors. Cumming (2002) points out that if the VCF cannot foresee how to sell the venture, it almost always refuses to fund the proposal.[254] However, the VCF takes into account that the markets' interests in certain technologies or products as well as the public investors' preferences undergo changes with the evolution of new businesses. E.g., in recent years, investors have developed substantial interests for computer hardware, internet or biotechnology ventures. Thus, ventures stemming from such a promising stream of innovations are likely to be funded in spite of the fact that exit vehicles are not foreseeable upon the initial investment decision.[255]

Besides examining the businesses prospects and its exit chances, the VCF values the business in its current state and projects future valuations. Valuation plays an important role for the VCF's return calculations. VC investments do usually not disburse interim payments to compensate investors given their little capital endowment and lack of profits throughout the commercialization process. Only the valuation at exit accounts for the VCF's return.[256] Yet, the absence of a track record and uncertainties about the venture's future development hamper the use of conventional valuation methods. Corporate finance methods either benchmark valuations of established companies on the basis of price/earnings ratios (p/e ratio) or calculate a company's discounted cash flow (DCF).[257] For computing the p/e ratio, a company must possess a stock price which is put in relation to the firm's earnings. In fact, until the portfolio company has not accomplished an IPO, it cannot yield a trading price. A

---

[252] Fried/Hisrich (1994), p. 28; Riquelme/Watson (2002), p. 396; Schwienbacher (2002), p. 2; Wang/Sim (2001), p. 339

[253] Fried/Hisrich (1994), p. 30f.; Sapienza/Gupta (1994), p. 1618ff.

[254] Cumming (2002), p. 2; Matz (2002), p. 39; Schröder (1992), p. 251; Temple (1999), p. 101; Weitenauer (2000), p. 287; Wupperfeld (1994), p. 101

[255] Gompers/Lerner (2000), p. 206

[256] Wupperfeld (1994), p. 101

[257] Seppä/Laamanen (2001), p. 216

DCF valuation computes the risk adjusted values of future cash flows and derives the company's net present value. However, predictions about the venture's future cash flows remain highly uncertain given that the venture's development cannot be foreseen. VCFs rather revert to alternative valuation methods such as multiples on the basis of revenues or cash flows.[258] VCFs benchmark these multiples against similar companies and draw conclusions about the relative position of the firm.[259] Based on these considerations, the VCF establishes an understanding of the venture's risk-return profile and decides on whether to reject or to fund the venture.

A positive outcome provided, both parties – the entrepreneur and the VCF – enter negotiations on the deal's specific terms. The amount of capital the VCF provides, its board representation and control rights over the exit are determined in the so called "term sheet".[260] Moreover, VCFs stipulate precautions for cases in which the business fails to accomplish predefined milestones or for situations in which the start-up outperforms the plan. If the venture underperforms, the entrepreneur is forced to render equity stakes to the VCF. These provisions provide incentives to the entrepreneur and prevent him from acting opportunistically.[261] Depending on the business and the industry sector, the extent of these measures varies. For instance, high technology investments with a higher risk for failure generally entail more milestones than low technology companies.[262]

d) VC financing period

After closing the investment contract and committing the first round of capital, the VC financing period commences. Throughout this period, VCFs encounter typical problems of bilateral financing relationships. These problems emanate from differences in the individual goals of the VCF and the entrepreneur. Scholars discriminate two typical behavior patterns in VC relationships that originate from differing interests: principal-agent problems and moral hazard.

According to Jensen and Meckling (1976), a principal-agent relationship occurs if two parties with differing objectives, information and influence are involved in a project and one party (the principal) employs the other party (agent) to carry out a task.[263] The principal-agent framework is a rather general framework in social sciences. Principal-agent relationships are prevalent in every financing relationship in-

---

[258] Cornell/Shapiro (1988), p. 14; Kaplan/Ruback (1996), p. 48f.; see Keeley/Punjabi (1996), p. 114f., for further discussions; see Langer/Thiele (2001), p. 254, for valuation of immaterial assets such as tacit knowledge

[259] Koeplin/Sarin/Shapiro (2000), p. 94

[260] Bartlett (1999), p. 80

[261] Matz (2002), p. 39; see Mirrlees (1997) for a general analysis of this "Carrots and Stick" system

[262] Gompers/Lerner (2000), p. 164

[263] Cable/Shane (1997), p. 145; Jensen/Meckling (1976), p. 308

cluding VC finance.[264] The principal-agent framework is frequently applied to issues of compensation,[265] acquisition strategies,[266] board relationships,[267] financing structures,[268] vertical integration[269] or VC finance.[270] Given that the agent pursues private interests and that the principal cannot monitor the agent's behavior, the delegation of tasks imposes the costs of the agent's opportunistic behavior on the principal.[271] Principal-agent costs are found to negatively correlate with the tangibility of the venture's assets. The more intangible or firm-specific the venture's assets are, the less value they bear in case of liquidation and the more difficult it becomes for principals to retrieve their investment if the agent engages in self beneficial behavior.[272] The principal-agency theory suggests that appropriate control- and incentive-systems lower these costs and align the agent's behavior with the interests of the principal.[273]

According to Eisenhardt (1989a), moral hazard roots back to the agent's lack of efforts in pursuing contractually fixed goals.[274] Moral hazard arises in situations in which the agent does not carry the full consequences of his actions.[275] This situation can be ascribed to two reasons. First, the principal would accrue too much cost by completely supervising the investee's actions. Hence, he does not entirely monitor the agent's actions but rather audits the project's status periodically. Hence, the principal cannot entirely isolate the agent's contributions or omissions to the project's outcome.[276] Second, the contract cannot anticipate every future scenario. Bounded rationality prevents the principal from understanding all possible influences on the contract's outcome by the time the contract is set up. In essence, the principal can neither design contracts that completely stipulate the agent's actions nor can he observe the compliance of these contracts. Thus, the principal cannot contractually assign the full consequences of the agent's actions to the agent. Moral hazard describes the agent's exploitation of the contract's incompleteness; the agent can hide negative information or engage in self-beneficial behavior without being liable for his omissions in fulfilling the contract.

---

[264] Brander/Amit/Zott (1998), p. 443

[265] E.g., Eisenhardt (1985)

[266] E.g., Amihud/Lev (1981)

[267] E.g., Fama/Jensen (1983); Kosnik (1987)

[268] E.g., Argawal/Mandelker (1987); Grossman/Hart (1988); Jensen/Meckling (1976)

[269] E.g., Anderson (1985), see also Eisenhardt (1989a), p. 58f.

[270] E.g., Cable/Shane (1997); Gompers (1995); Sapienza (1992); Sapienza/Gupta (1994)

[271] Eisenhardt (1989a), p. 61; Higashide/Birley (2002), p. 60

[272] Gompers (1995), p. 1462

[273] Bell (2001), p. 90

[274] Eisenhardt (1989a), p. 61

[275] Kotovitz (1987), p. 549

[276] Gompers (1995), p. 1462

As for VC finance, the VCF adopts the role of the principal and the entrepreneur the agent's role. Both moral hazard and principal agent problems result from the VCF's information disadvantages against the entrepreneur prior and after the initial investment decision.[277] Both patterns affect VC-finance in particular as VCFs are frequently engaged in a relatively uncertain environment regarding markets, technologies, management teams, etc. which entail high information spreads.[278]

Research has identified two general mechanisms by which principals can cope with principal-agent and moral hazard problems. First, the principal can monitor the agent's behavior by employing reporting systems, budgeting or board representation.[279] Second, the principal can arrange for outcome-based reward schemes. In essence, principals have to create incentives for the agent to align the agent's interests with the principal's so that both parties pursue similar goals.[280]

VCFs apply both mechanisms. By providing management assistance and monitoring to the venture, VCFs aim at lowering the costs from principal-agent and moral hazard problems.[281] Gorman and Sahlman (1989) dwell on the VCF's involvement in the venture and examine monitoring patterns. They find that VCFs spend nearly half of their time supervising their investments. On average, a VCF commits a total of 110 hours per year to assisting and monitoring one venture investment.[282] Schröder (1992) and Barry (1994) further investigate the contents of the VCF's non-financial contributions. According to them, the VCF typically supervises and assists on financial and managerial problems.[283] Nevertheless, VCFs acknowledge the entrepreneur's abilities to build the business. VCFs thus avoid taking away the entrepreneur's autonomy by getting involved on a daily basis.[284]

Following the budgeting recommendation, VCFs also apply staging mechanisms. Staging means that the VCF does not infuse the entire investment at once but divides it into several tranches depending on the venture's actual needs. Investment stages usually address particular development steps such as the completion of a prototype, successful market tests, readiness for production or the achievement of certain sales volumes. For every stage, the entrepreneur obtains just enough funding to

---

[277] Kaplan/Strömberg (2004), p. 2177f.

[278] Amit/Brander/Zott (1998), p. 444

[279] Ripperger (1998), p. 50

[280] Eisenhardt (1989a), p. 61; Gompers (1995), p. 1461; Kreps (1990), p. 592f.; Norton/Tenenbaum (1993b), p. 34; see Mirrlees (1997), p. 1311, for a fundamental discussion

[281] Matz (2002), p. 39; Ruhnka/Feldman/Dean (1992), p. 137ff.

[282] Gorman/Sahlman (1989), p. 235f.

[283] Barry (1994), p. 5; MacMillan/Kulow/Khoylian (1989), p. 35ff.; Sahlman (1990), p. 505; Schröder (1992), p. 232ff.; Elango/Fried/Hisrich/Polonchek (1995), p. 165, find that VCFs devote on average 20 hours per month to monitoring every portfolio company.

[284] Admati/Pfleiderer (1994), p. 395

promote the business to the next step without having the freedom to engage in self-beneficial behavior.[285] If the entrepreneur fails in reaching the next step, the VCF imposes two sanctions. On the one hand, the VCF can condition further capital infusions on the assignment of more stakes to it.[286] On the other hand, it can abandon the company.[287] Staged financing essentially reduces the entrepreneur's incentives and freedom to act opportunistically.[288]

In addition to that, VCFs monitor entrepreneurs by holding board seats and disproportionally high voting rights in relation to their actual ownership position.[289] Thus, the VCF participates in the entrepreneur's decision making and can prevent opportunistic behavior. Baker and Gompers (2001) assert that the board composition of VC-backed IPOs differs significantly from those of non-VC-backed IPOs. The boards of VC-backed firms feature a lower percentage of inside and instrumental directors and have higher ratios of VC managers and affiliates.[290]

Furthermore, VCFs arrange for performance related contracts that punish entrepreneurs in case they cannot comply with the predefined plan. These so-called ratchets transfer equity shares to the VCF if the entrepreneur fails to accomplish interim goals.[291] Thus, the VCF aligns the entrepreneur's interests with its own.

e) Exiting investments

While prior efforts aim at building the venture's intrinsic value, the exit concludes the VC investment process. At exit, the VCF harvests the outcome of its financial and non-financial contributions to the venture. The need to exit reflects the limited life-time of VC funds after which the funds' resources have to be disbursed; the VCF's investment horizon is terminated not to exceed the fund's life-time.[292] VC fund investors arrange precautions that oblige the VCF to return the fund's resources either in cash or liquid securities.[293] The VCF utilizes exit vehicles to convert its illiquid stakes in the venture into cash or more liquid stakes.[294] Chapter three deepens the discussion of exits.

---

[285] Sahlman (1990), p. 473 and p. 503

[286] Sahlman (1990), p. 506f.

[287] Gifford (1997), p. 459; Gompers (1995), p. 1461; Sahlman (1990), p. 507

[288] Admati/Pfleiderer (1994), p. 371f.; Bergemann/Hege (1998), p. 704; Busenitz/Fiet (1996); Cornelli/Yosha (2003), p. 1

[289] Kirilenko (2001), p. 565; Sorensen/Stuart (2001), p. 1553

[290] Baker/Gompers (2001), p. 11ff.

[291] Brück (1998), p. 125; Murray (1996), p. 47; Pogue (1991), p. 60; Wright/Robbie/Romanet/Thompson/Joachimsson/Bruining/Herst (1994), p. 107

[292] Barry (1994), p. 4; Gompers (1996), p. 469; Sahlman (1990), p. 492

[293] Sahlman (1990), p. 492

[294] Albach/Hunsdiek/Kokalj (1986), p. 166; Zemke (1995), p. 70

f) Distributing the proceeds

After exiting an investment or at the latest by the time the VC fund is terminated, the VCF returns the resources to the limited partners. By disbursing the limited partners' stakes, the VCF closes one loop of the VC cycle.

2.3.3 The Venture Capitalist's Return Requirements

In general, a financing transaction occurs only if the prospective returns comply with the new investor's return requirements.[295] The investor's requirements towards the investment's return vary across investment classes, investment duration and risks. The fact that investors (VC fund investors, VCFs and entrepreneurs) attribute VC investments with accelerated risks, higher uncertainties and greater illiquidity in comparison to other investment classes translates into greater return expectations.[296] This section sheds light on return expectations in VC finance and the VCF's requirements in particular.

Researchers distinguish three layers of performance perception in VC finance of which the VCF's perspective constitutes just one point of view. First, limited partners require an appropriate compensation for committing their capital to the VC fund.[297] They base their future allocation of capital on their experiences with the current fund's profitability. The VCF's view constitutes the second level. Since VCFs depend on the limited partners' supply of capital, the fund investors' objective shape the VCF's return requirements. Usually, the VCF's fundamental goal is maximizing the VC fund's value.[298] However, some capital suppliers pursue alternative goals. Corporate venture capitalists (CVCs) primarily desire to access new technological knowledge and emerging markets whereas governmental initiatives put the emphasis on job-creation and economic development.[299] For simplicity, this analysis focuses on profit-minded VC investors and excludes other objectives than purely financial ones. The third level addresses the performance expectations of the venture and the entrepreneur himself. The preliminary condition to be selected for VC finance is that the start-up complies with the VCF's requirements. Consequently, the start-up has to align the vast majority of its goals to those of the VCF throughout the VC duration in order to obtain funding. The principal-agent theory, however, acknowledges that the

---

[295] Birmingham/Busenitz/Arthurs (2003), p. 3; Chmielewicz (1970), p. 241
[296] See section 2.3.2 c)
[297] Sahlman (1990), p. 491f.
[298] Hax (1964), p. 436
[299] See section 2.3.5

entrepreneur may also pursue goals different from those of the VCF which affect his perception of success.[300]

Researchers evaluate success in VC finance on the basis of four dimensions: capital market indicators, financial statement indicators, profit indicators and subjective success indicators.[301] Figure 12 contrasts the return dimensions to the three groups. Given the focus of this thesis, the following discussion delves explicitly into the VCF's return expectations towards venture investments.

	Capital market indicators	Financial statement indicators	Profit indicators	Subjective success indicators
Investors	▪ Performance of the fund's shares if quoted ▪ Low volatility	▪ Cash flow to the fund ▪ Fund's costs	▪ Net return to the investors (IRR_3) ▪ Exit-values ▪ Multiples	
Venture Capitalist	▪ Underpricing ▪ Long-term performance ▪ Liquidity/trading volume	▪ Cash flow to the VCF/VC-fund ▪ Avoidance of insolvency	▪ Return on harvested investment (IRR_1) ▪ Returns on current stales (IRR_2) ▪ Multiples	▪ Reputation building ▪ Track records
Portfolio Company	▪ Market capitalization ▪ Low underpricing	▪ Return on investments ▪ Cash flows ▪ Liquidity	▪ Market share ▪ Growth	▪ Brand name ▪ Firm's reputation ▪ Experience gains

(Investors ↔ Venture Capitalist: Returns / Funds; Venture Capitalist ↔ Portfolio Company: Returns / Cash, Assist.)

Figure 12: Success indicators in VC finance

a) Capital market indicators

Capital market indicators apply solely to publicly listed ventures. Capital market indicators comprise measures that are observable on the public markets such as the company's pricing or the share's volatility. These indicators mirror the market's fundamental opinion about the venture. To establish a vivid trade in which the venture's stock becomes liquid, the public market must look on the venture positively. Unless public markets do not develop for a listed venture, the firm's stock is not tradable. The illiquid nature of VC investments represents a major concern of VCFs because VCFs' investment strategies aim at achieving most of the returns through capital gains in IPOs. Upon exit, the market's positive opinion translates into liquidity allowing the VCF to divest in the after market. If illiquid, the VCF cannot dispose its stakes at proper valuations.[302]

When a company is floated, the issue's underpricing represents a further concern of VCFs. Underpricing depicts the value spread between an issue's initial offering price and the closing price on the first day of trading. Underpricing stems from

[300] These problems are addressed in the principal-agent theory; this study discusses principal-agent theory problems in the VC context in section 2.3.2 d)

[301] E.g., Jakoby (2000), p. 52ff.; see also Schefczyk (2004), p. 195ff., for a differing contemplation

[302] Ivanova/Tzvetkova (2001), p. 177

different valuations of inside and outside investors with the latter suffering from informational disadvantages. Accordingly, the extent of underpricing correlates with the degree of information asymmetry between inside and outside investors.[303] Table 1 illustrates this argumentation reporting findings on different levels of underpricing across industries and VC-backed issues versus non VC-back issues. Barry (1989), Franzke (2001) and Habib and Ljungqvist (2001) observe that VCFs care more about underpricing the more shares they include in the IPO. Underpricing then causes a direct wealth loss for the VCF and prevents stock sales in the IPO.[304]

Average first-day underpricing	Aggarwal et al. (2002)	Bradley/ Jordan (2002)	Franzke (2001)	Habib/ Ljungqvist (2001)	Meggin-son/Weiss (1991)	Ritter (1987)
VC-backed issues		23.3 %	26.5 %*		7.6 %	
Non-VC-backed issues		14.3 %	32 %*		13.5 %	
Internet IPOs	66.2 %	37 %**				
Non-internet IPOs	35.2 %					
Overall	50.4 %	18.4 %			10.6 %	15 %
Historical	15 %			13 %		

* Median ** Biotechnology, semiconductors and software

Table 1: Underpricing as reported in previous studies[305]

b) Financial statement indicators

From the point of view of the VCF, financial statement indicators do not directly translate into returns. Yet, they help convey information about the venture to prospective investors. Financial statements contain information about the venture's asset structure, its profitability etc.. They report the accumulation of values in terms of tangible assets, contracts, etc. which in case of liquidation allow investors to retrieve their investments. Besides, financial statements possess high credibility because they are certified by auditors. Potential investors usually assess investment opportu-

---

303 Bradley/Jordan (2002), p. 613; Certo/Daily/Dalton (2001), p. 34

304 Barry (1989), p. 1100f. Franzke (2001), p. 13; Habib/Ljungqvist (2001), p. 434

305 Aggarwal/Krigman/Womack (2002), p. 115; Bradley/Jordan (2002), p. 601; Franzke (2001), p. 16; Habib/Ljungqvist (2001), p. 433; Megginson/Weiss (1991), p. 893; Ritter (1987), p. 275; the distribution of average first-day underpricings varies considerably across studies because the data samples underlying each study stem from different periods and some studies explicitly focus on abnormal underpricing during hot issue markets

nities on the basis of the firm's public statements.[306] Statements that indicate a viable business resolve prospective investors' uncertainty at exit and enhance the VCF's withdrawal. If the contents of the venture's financial statement do not satisfy outside investors, the venture cannot tap public markets and may be rejected by industrial investors.

c) Profit oriented indicators

Profit oriented indicators represent the most prominent success measures in VC finance – on the level of the VCF and individual investments – since they directly reflect the VCF's ability to maximize the VC fund's capital.[307] Even though Bygrave (1992) notes that hardly any standards for measuring the profitability of VC-investments have emerged, two proxies have become widely accepted: the return multiples and the IRR.[308] The IRR is already recommended by the European Venture Capital Association (EVCA).[309]

The absolute profitability of a VC-investment can easily be computed; if a VC investment attains a valuation at exit that exceeds the total capital inflow, the project yields a capital gain. The return multiple extends this contemplation in that it relates compounded efforts to the terminal outcome. An investment's return multiple is defined as the ratio of cash outflow to investors in terms of dividends or valuation at exit to the total cash inflow, such as the initial investment and subsequent capital injections.[310] A common rule of thumb holds that a venture must return five times the VC investment in order to compensate the VCF for exposing its capital to the investment risk.[311] Das, Jagannathan and Sarin (2003) argue that return multiples are an appropriate measure to assess an investment's profitability. But return multiples suffer from shortcomings because they incorporate neither the investment's duration nor the risk.[312]

$$C_0 = \sum_{t=0}^{n} CF_t (1+r)^{-t} + E_n (1+r)^{-n} - I_n \quad \textit{(Basic formula to compute the IRR)}$$

---

[306] Fassin/Lewis (1994), p. 49f.

[307] In fact, studies utilizing principal-agent frameworks oftentimes exclude other success indicators than financial ones, e.g. Hellmann (1998); Kirilenko (2001)

[308] Barry (1994), p. 6; Bygrave (1992), p. 442; Bygrave/Fast/Khoylian/Vincent/Yue (1989), p. 94ff.

[309] EVCA (2003), p. 75ff.

[310] Return multiples occur under several other names too but basically incorporate the same parameters and allow for the same conclusion. Aliases are Cash-in/Cash-out Ration, Ration of Distribution to Paid-in Capital, or Residual Value to Paid-in Capital, when accounting for the fact that VC-backed companies hardly disburse dividends, to name only few; see Bader (1996), p. 142; Das/Jagannathan/Sarin (2003), p. 2ff.; Fleming (2003), p. 13f.; Perlitz/Peske/Schüffel (1999), p. 1

[311] Fried/Hisrich (1994), p. 30

[312] Das/Jagannathan/Sarin (2003), p. 2ff.

The internal rate of return represents a measure that additionally captures the investment duration. The IRR includes the initial investment I_0, the terminal exit valuation E_n, the annual sums of disbursed dividends and further investments CF_t. The IRR r is computed by iterating the annualized rates of return an investment accomplishes in n years until the net present value C_0 attains zero. However, a VC investment's IRR can only be calculated after the investment is exited and all parameters are known. Likewise, IRRs for VC funds are only computable after the VCF has withdrawn the fund's stakes from all investments. Fried and Hisrich (1994) report that a successful VC investment returns an IRR of 40 % compounded annually over a holding period of five years. Such an IRR equals a return multiple of 5.4. The same yield over ten years, however, requires 28.9 times the original investment.[313] Yet, the required IRR decreases from early stage to late stage investments since the investment risk abates.[314] Table 2 exemplifies expected IRRs across different investment stages as reported in the literature.

Even though the IRR is the most widely spread measure, its practical application is subject to several limitations as pointed out by Bygrave (1992).[315] First of all, the measurement of IRRs varies substantially across the VC industry because VCFs record their data individually for different periods of time. Some VCFs process information immediately after terminating an exit transaction. Other VCFs calculate their IRRs only on a monthly or even yearly basis. In the latter case, measures are computed as if the transaction had taken place on the last day of the reporting period. Given these differences, IRRs are not comparable across the VC industry. Second, inferring IRRs from exited investments requires intimate information about the VC-partnership's agreement to incorporate the allocation of proceeds between the limited and the general fund-partners. The question arises when and how the fund's gains are disbursed. In general, researchers assume the following procedure. The limited partners retrieve their investment first. The remaining gains are generally splitted so that the general partners receive 20 % and the limited partners 80 %.[316] Yet, this method represents just a rule of thumb and varies across VCFs. Third, VCFs publish interim statements to promote further fund raising activities. These IRRs are, however, subjective estimates. Since the new fund's promotion overlaps with actual venture investments, ventures are not exited by the time of the interim statement.[317] The valuation of investments that are not exited yet is proposed by a valuation committee

---

313 The ratio of 5.4 times the original investment reflects an annual growth of 140 % over five years (140 %^{5}); the same applies to the ratio for a 10 year-holding period (140 %^{10})

314 Seppä/Laamanen (2001), p. 216

315 Bygrave (1992), p. 443f.; EVCA (2003), p. 75ff.

316 Barry (1994), p. 4

317 Schefczyk (2004), p. 196ff.

and thus subjective. Finally, even though the IRR takes the investment duration into account, it does not ex-ante include risk aspects.

Financial research has developed several approaches that integrate risk considerations into profit measuring. The most prominent model is the Capital Asset Pricing Model (CAPM).[318] In general terms, the CAPM provides a procedure to evaluate an investment by relating its risk to its expected return. The model originates from the idea that investors demand additional returns if they are asked to accept higher investment risks.[319] An investment's risk is indicated by the volatility of its returns; the more the returns vary the higher the investment risk. The investment risk can be subdivided into a systematic component and an unsystematic component. The systematic risk results from market or economy-wide influences and affects the returns of every single company within the same industry sector. The unsystematic risk, in contrast, is an individual feature – attributed to a single firm. In general, investors can minimize their exposure to unsystematic risk by spreading their investments over companies and sectors. As a consequence, misfortune in one asset is most likely compensated by the fortune of another asset. An optimal-constructed portfolio of assets can even reduce the unsystematic risk to zero exposing the investor only to the systematic risk. According to the premises of the CAPM, financial markets do not reward exposure to unsystematic risks; they only reimburse systematic risks.[320]

VC investments are subject to substantial systematic and unsystematic risks. VC investments typically operate with new technologies in emerging markets subjecting the VCF to substantial systematic risks. For instance, biotechnology or computer and software firms show extraordinarily high variances in their returns in comparison to firms in more conventional industries such as retail or manufacturing.[321] Moreover, VCFs focus on early stage investments; early stage investments feature greater unsystematic risks than later stage investments because the venture's commercial take-off is hardly predictable by the time the VCF enters the investment.[322] VCFs' typical portfolio performances reflect the higher risks that VCFs incur by funding start-ups. Bergeman and Hege (1998) point out that three out of ten VC investments record entire losses. Another three firms accomplish only break even. Two are likely to yield modest profits whereas only the remaining two account for sufficient profits to cover the losses from other investments and providing reasonable returns.[323] Ruhnka

---

[318] See Schefczyk (2004), p. 197ff., for further risk models

[319] Peridon/Steiner (1997), p. 504

[320] Sharpe (1964), p. 425

[321] Amit/Brander/Zott (1998), p. 441

[322] E.g. Black/Gilson (1998), p. 245; Gaida (2002), p. 147; Leitinger/Strohbach/Schöfer/Hummel (2000), p. 89; Levin (2001), p. 1–5; Pfirrmann/Wupperfeld/Lerner (1997), p. 9; Wright/Robbie/Romanet/Thompson/Joachimsson/Bruining/Herst (1994), p. 84;

[323] Bergemann/Hege (1998), p. 704

and Young (1991) observe a similar distribution and conclude that only 30 % of the VCF's investments are eventually successful. Another 30 % yield marginal profits while the remaining investments fail.[324]

VCFs pursue two strategies to reduce their exposure to unsystematic risks. VCFs seek diversification and specialization. Following the predication of the CAPM, VCFs can diversify their investments across different industries and companies in order to minimize their risk exposure. Especially those VCFs with an emphasis on seed investments may seek to spread investments so that they reduce their unsystematic risk. Yet, VCFs depend on the availability of suitable investment proposals to accomplish diversification and on exact information to assess each investment's unsystematic risk. Specialization represents another approach to control portfolio risks.[325] The assumption of complete diversification is not necessarily appropriate, when an investor can achieve cost advantages or alleviate risks by employing his accumulated expertise and specialized skills in related industries or product areas.[326] In fact, VCFs pursue both strategies; they specialize in a particular industry but spread their investments over numerous ventures to minimize the unsystematic risk component.

Moreover, VCFs integrate risk considerations in their selection process in that they assign risk adjusted thresholds of required IRRs to every investment proposal.[327] Over the past, research has devoted much attention to illustrate expected rate of returns of VC funds and individual VC investments. Martin and Petty (1983) compare publicly traded VC funds with mutual funds. They show that VCFs have to exhibit higher returns than their counterparts in order to compensate their fund investors for the higher average investment risk.[328] Chiampou and Kallet (1989) analyze 55 private VC funds by breaking them into two groups. Chiampou and Kallet find that the investment returns of the 35 older funds over the period 1978 to 1987 average 24.4 % per annum against a standard deviation of returns of 51.2 %. The younger funds perform much more poorly yielding only a 5.4 % annual return. Overall, Chiampou and Kallet report that based on the dispersion of average returns for the matured sub-sample, VC fund investors risk more than investors in S&P 500 stocks. In addition, Chiampou and Kallet report that younger funds are even riskier than older VC funds.[329]

---

[324] Bhide (2000), p. 143; Gompers/Lerner (2000), p. 6; Ruhnka/Young (1991), p. 119

[325] Bygrave (1987), p. 151

[326] Norton/Tenenbaum (1993a), p. 435

[327] Barry (1994), p. 4; Temple (1999), p. 45ff.

[328] Martin/Petty (1983), p. 409f.

[329] Chiampou/Kallet (1989), p. 1ff.

Concerning individual VC investments, Cochrane surveys the distribution of returns. He observes in his sample of roughly 8,000 VC-backed companies from 1987 to 2000 that approximately 15 % yield a return multiple greater than 1,000 %. For 15 % of the VCF's investments, he reports losses. 35 % of the ventures cannot return their investment.[330] Huntsman and Hoben (1980) examine 110 venture investments by three VCFs. They assert that a VCF's return depends on outliers. The average annual return over the sample period from 1960 to 1975 is 18.9 %. However, after eliminating the top 10 % of investments, the average return drops to -0.28 %.[331] Huntsman and Hoben observe a high variability of VC investments' returns and conclude that a VCF's success dependent highly on few outstanding investments.[332] Bygrave and Stein (1989) find that the overall annualized rates of return decrease with every successive round of VC a portfolio company receives. Bygrave and Stein attribute this finding to the reduced uncertainties and risks in later round investments.[333] A subsequent enquiry in VC related studies yields the following average IRR expectations for individual VC investments in different stages; the results are reported in table 2.

	Wetzel (1981)	Golder (1984)	Barron (1984)	Ruhnka/ Young (1986)	Glad-stone (1988)	Bovaird (1990)	Bowden (1994)	Bygrave (1997)	Temple (1999)
Seed	50 %			73 %			50 - 70 %	80 %	
Start-up	50 %	> 50 %		54.8 %	> 50 %			60 %	50 %
First stage	37.5 %	40 - 50 %		42.2 %	40 - 60 %			50 %	
Second stage	30 %	30 - 40 %		35 %	30 - 40 %			40 %	30 - 35 %
Third stage		25 - 30 %		35 %	20 - 30 %		25 - 40 %	30 %	20 %
Exit stage	22.5 %			35 %				25 %	
Average			20 - 29 %			> 40 %			

Table 2: Expected IRRs of VC investments across different stages[334]

d) Subjective expectations

Subjective expectations comprise qualitative measurements which are not directly measurable. In the context of VC finance, the VCF's reputation gains represent a prominent subjective return from successful investments. Reputation is important to VCFs for several reasons. First, reputation allows certification which reduces the heterogeneity of valuations of VCFs and prospective outside investors in subsequent exit transactions. A good reputation with public markets or corporate investors en-

---

[330] Cochrane (2001), p. 10

[331] Huntsman/Hoben (1980), p. 48, table 4

[332] Huntsman/Hoben (1980), p. 49

[333] Bygrave/Stein (1989), p. 295

[334] Barron (1984), p. 11ff.; Bovaird (1990), p. 70; Bygrave (1997), p. 197; Gladstone (1988), p. 114; Golder (1984), p. 52; Ruhnka/Young (1991), p. 189; Temple (1999), p. 47

ables VCFs to convey credible signals about a venture's quality at exit. Thus, reputation literally reduces costs related to informational asymmetries. For IPO exits for instance, the VCF's reputation alleviates underpricing.[335]

Second, highly reputable VCFs find it easier to raise capital for follow-on funds as their outstanding ability in nurturing start-ups is mirrored in their reputation with fund investors or investment advisors.[336] An excellent reputation also helps VCFs to increase the likelihood of being considered for co-investments from other VC-providers which would not involve either new funds or small unsuccessful organizations. Finally, the number of investment proposals from start-ups seeking VC finance positively correlates with the VCF's reputation so that prestigious VCFs receive more proposals to select from.[337]

2.3.4 Types of Venture Capital Firms

As noted earlier, VCFs are heterogeneous organizations differing in their objectives, strategies and resources.[338] The few common features that VCFs share in general are their focus on nurturing early stage and high-technology companies with capital and management assistance.[339] VCFs typically prefer private investments in emerging high-technology sectors that promise an enormous growth but entail comparatively high risks and uncertainty.[340] Sectors in which VC investments frequently occur are semiconductors, computer software and hardware, communication and biotechnology.[341]

However, ongoing distinctions between categories of VCFs are drawn on the basis of their ownership structure and particularly their objectives.[342] The VCF's primary goal derives from the objectives of the parent company or fund investors. Two different types of VCFs occur typically: independent VCFs and captive VCFs.[343] VCFs are denoted as being independent if they are owned and run by teams of private individuals. Independent VCFs raise capital from various outside sources – normally institutional sources – on a competitive base. VC fund investors evaluate the VCF's performance in advance to their commitment and select only the best performing

---

[335] E.g., Barry/Muscarella/Peavy/Vetsuypens (1990), p. 448 and p. 469f.; Megginson/Weiss (1991), p. 881

[336] Gompers (1996), p. 136

[337] Bygrave (1988), p. 143ff.; Lerner (1994a), p. 17

[338] Cumming (2002), p. 2; Elango/Fried/Hisrich/Polonchek (1995), p. 158; Timmons/Bygrave (1986), p. 163

[339] E.g., Lessat/Hemer/Eckerle (1999), p. 94; Prester (2002), p. 9; Temple (1999), p. 1ff.; Weimerskirch (1999), p. 9ff

[340] Black/Gilson (1998), p. 245; Lam (1991), p. 137

[341] Ambrose/Winters (1992), p. 90

[342] Brettel (2002), p. 306; Schefczyk (2004), p. 19

[343] Robinson/van Osnabrugge (2001), p. 32; Schefczyk (2004), p. 34ff.

VCFs. It is essential for independent VCF to achieve superior investment returns and to demonstrate their competence to VC fund investors in order to secure their continuity.

Captive VCFs are subsidiaries of financial institutions, such as banks or insurance companies, managing investments on behalf of the parent group. Corporate venturing represents a popular type of captive VC investors. Corporate venture capitalists (CVCs) are primarily funded by an industrial corporation. These corporations use VC financing to gain insights in emerging technologies or companies. In exchange for providing funding and support, CVCs entities gain access to new business opportunities helping the parent company to fulfil its strategic objectives. While the strategies of VCFs funded by financial institutions hardly differ from independent VCFs, the CVCs' investment strategies derive from the parent company's industry focus. CVCs have to keep in touch and potentially influence technological development rather than maximizing direct investment returns.

Special types of VCFs are those affiliated to governments, local authorities or other state enterprises. They have the mission of promoting particular policies, such as innovation, regional development, employment, etc. These VCFs contribute to the implementation of municipal policies by supporting specific initiatives and the creation in the sector or region of interest.

2.4 Conclusive Remarks

In developing new technologies and commercializing innovative business models, start-ups create uncertainty and unique risk profiles. They consequently lack access to other sources of external funding than VC. VCFs represent organizations which provide equity finance to start-ups to fund their early growth and facilitate their access to alternative sources of capital.

Upon the initial investment decision, the VCF suffers from information disadvantages against the entrepreneur. Entrepreneurs may keep negative information to themselves in order to attract VC. Besides, hardly any public sources for information about emerging markets and technologies exist from which VCF could learn about a venture. Evaluating early stage ventures in emerging technologies thus proves particularly difficult for the VCF.

Throughout the VC investment, the VCF is vulnerable to the entrepreneur's opportunistic behavior which the VCF cannot completely control due to information disadvantages. However, VCFs have developed a unique expertise to work against these odds. They employ a variety of monitoring systems and contractual measures to eliminate opportunistic behavior. Their ability to minimize information gaps prior and during the VC investment distinguishes them from other investors. It forms the basis of their competitive advantage and allows them to realize attractive portfolio returns. In essence, VC intermediates exist because the asymmetric information and inherent uncertainties of young innovative ventures prevent common equity investors from direct engagements.

Eventually, the VCF has to reap the return from its commitment to the venture. Given that the capital endowment of start-ups is usually very thin allowing for no annual disbursements, VCFs are only rewarded upon divestment. At exit, the VCF virtually benefits from the venture's improved access to alternative financing options in that it sells its stakes to follow-on investors. The exit consequently constitutes an elementary step for the VCF's success and continuity. The following chapter deepens the rather general discussion of exits.

3 Exiting Ventures

After chapter two has outlined the emergence of VC and the principal process patterns that underlie VC investments, this chapter concentrates on the exit as the final step in VC investments. Initially, this chapter analyzes common instruments such as contractual agreements, exit vehicles and the general exit process patterns from the VCF's perspective. Thereupon, this chapter examines the present challenges VCFs face at exit. The insights from this analyses guide the development of the research model in the subsequent chapter.

3.1 The Venture Capitalists' Exit Means

This section examines how VCFs facilitate exits within the VC relationship. First, this chapter discusses the means VCFs have at disposition to enforce exit transactions in their favor. The literature distinguishes two basic types of means: exit vehicles facilitating the conversion of the VCF's stakes in the venture into cash and stocks and contracts serving as enforcement of the VCF's exit ambitions at any time.

3.1.1 Exit Vehicles

VC fund investors stipulate that the VCF has to return their investments either in cash or liquid securities.[344] VCFs employ a variety of exit vehicles to convert their illiquid stakes in venture investments into cash or liquid securities. The fundamental distinction between exit vehicles is drawn in the type of the follow-on investor. Corporate Finance theory distinguishes public and private investors.[345] Public investors comprise all investors that buy new issues on public markets while private investors represent individuals or organizations that acquire the whole firm. In the VC context, the group of private investors is subdivided into the most internal investor – the entrepreneur – and financial or industrial investors. Further distinctions such as the time to prepare the exit derive from the various requirements of the targeted investor.[346]

Findings on the occurrence of these exit vehicles vary across studies given that the underlying data samples are composed differently. Cochrane (2001) and Gompers and Lerner (1998) for instance look into early stage investments in the U.S. while Wright, Robbie, Romanet, Thompson, Joachimsson, Bruining and Herst (1994) collect data on later stage investments in the UK.[347] Besides, the distribution of exit ve-

---

[344] Pape/Beyer (2001), p. 636; Sahlman (1990), p. 492

[345] Achleitner (1999), S. 137; Jansen (1999), p. 31

[346] Bascha (2001), p. 36

[347] Cochrane (2001), p. 8; Gompers/Lerner (1998), p. 2167; Wright/Robbie/Romanet/Thompson/Joachimsson/Bruining/Herst (1994), p. 94f.

hicles also changes over time as environmental factors such as the public markets' conditions allow for a higher IPO ratio in some periods as compared to other periods.[348]

For the VC market in the U.S., Das, Jagannathan and Sarin (2003) report, that the probability for a venture to be exited via an IPO amounts to roughly 20 % to 25 %. They show that the likelihood for an acquisition ranges between 10 % and 20 %.[349] Gompers and Lerner (1998) note that 31 % of the ventures in their sample accomplish an IPO. In contrast, 29 % are sold privately.[350] Cochrane (2001) observes that roughly 22 % of VCFs' investments result in an IPO in contrast to slightly more than 20 % in M&A transactions.[351] Amit, Brander and Zott (1998) report from their data sample that an average of 16 % of VCFs' investments accomplish an IPO. 10 % of the VCF's investments are acquired by industrial investors, 13 % by financial investors and 37 % of the ventures are redeemed by their management. Write-offs account for 17 %.[352] Wright, Robbie, Romanet, Thompson, Joachimsson, Bruining and Herst (1994) find that only a quarter of all transactions in their data sample are exited at all. The most common form of disposing MBO investments in the UK is the trade sale followed by buy-backs whereas IPOs account for not more than 5 %.[353]

Given these findings, it is difficult to compute an overall ratio for a specific exit vehicle on the basis of previous research. Recent studies only agree that not more than roughly one third of those VC investments that are exited by these means accomplish an IPO; M&A transactions occur slightly less often.

a) Initial public offering

In an IPO, the VCF floats its stakes in the venture to public markets. In general terms, an IPO represents the process in which a stock in a closely held company is sold to the general public for the first time.[354] Gompers and Lerner (1998), however, note that the actual withdrawal begins not until one year after the initial quotation. Lock-up arrangements limit the VCF's sales in the IPO to only few percentages.[355] IPOs are consequently based on the expectation that a liquid market will develop

[348] Cumming (2002), p. 4; Lerner (1994a), p. 313f.
[349] Das/Jagannathan/Sarin (2003), p. 2 and p. 8
[350] Gompers/Lerner (1998), p. 2167
[351] Cochrane (2001), p. 8
[352] Amit/Brander/Zott (1998), p. 460, figure 5
[353] Wright/Robbie/Romanet/Thompson/Joachimsson/Bruining/Herst (1994), p. 94f.
[354] Brigham (1985), p. 584; Cumming/MacIntosh (2003), p. 513; Fassin/Lewis (1994), p. 39
[355] Gompers/Lerner (1998), p. 2167

after the venture's initial quotation. Only a continuously liquid market allows the VCF to sell its stakes after the lock-up period has expired.[356]

Not every venture can go public. The IPO exit requires the candidate to fulfil several prerequisites. These requirements are imposed either by institutions, such as the future market places, the SEC, the investment patterns of public investors and the VCF itself.[357] Contingent on the targeted market segment, IPO candidates must prove a critical size and reasonable revenues.[358] Pre-matured IPOs are only accomplishable in a few sectors such as in biotechnology.[359] Moreover, the IPO candidate must exhibit enough growth potential and state a credible strategy to accomplish prosperity. Schwienbacher (2002) points out that IPOs require a sufficient size and profitability in order to catch public investors' attention. The public market's attention in turn warrants that a liquid market develops for the new issue.[360] IPO candidates must also possess a proper organizational structure featuring a board of directors and an appropriate internal reporting system to comply with SEC rules for publicly listed companies.[361] Researchers furthermore find that VCFs carefully select their IPO candidates even if the external conditions are in favor of an initial public listing and the SEC would permit the quotation. Schwienbacher (2002) and Fleming (2003) argue that VCFs are concerned about their reputation with public markets. A good reputation eases the VCF's access to public markets with future IPO exits. In order to protect their reputation, VCFs only choose high quality investments for a floatation and opt for M&A transactions to divest low quality firms.[362] Due to these requirements, those companies that eventually go public have undergone an intensive screening and selection process.

Cochrane (2001) notes that the perception that the IPO is the most profitable exit vehicle is heavily biased by the VCF's selection of IPO candidates. For instance, Bygrave and Timmons (1992) find that IPO exits generate profits almost five times greater than the second most profitable exit mechanism, the trade sale.[363] This no-

---

[356] Ivanova/Tzvetkova (2001), p. 177

[357] E.g., Deeds/Decarolis/Coombs (1997), p. 32; Ravasi/Maschisio (2003), p. 382; Maksimovic/Pichler (2001), p. 460ff., find that public finance is more likely for companies that have proven their viability

[358] Mikkelson/Partch/Shah (1997), p. 284

[359] Lerner (1994a), p. 294

[360] Schwienbacher (2002), p. 7; Temple (1999), p. 103f.

[361] Engelmann/Juncker/Natusch/Tebroke (2000), p. 153ff.; Weitenauer (2000), 395ff.; Witt/Schmidt (2002), p. 753

[362] Fleming (2003), p. 9; Schwienbacher (2002), p. 7f.

[363] E.g., Bygrave/Timmons (1992), p. 27f.; Sacirbey (2000), p. 3; Lam (1991), p. 148; Busenitz/Fiet (1996), p. 2

tion, however, ignores that only the VCF's best ventures become public companies.[364]

Researchers offer several rationales why an IPO is more profitable than a private transaction. Zingales (1995) demonstrates that the incumbent's greater bargaining power against public investors in relation to private investors results in higher valuations for IPOs. Zingales reasons that public markets feature numerous investors as opposed to only few acquirers in private markets. Public markets are thus entirely competitive while private investors do not rival for investment opportunities. Zingales elaborates that a few private investors – unlike scattered public investors – can pressure incumbents on pricing concessions given that the incumbent has only a few alternatives.[365] Zingales concludes that incumbents can secure higher valuations in floating their firm because of their greater bargaining power against public markets.[366] Fleming's (2003) findings empirically sustain Zingales' conclusion. Fleming observes that the returns drawn from IPOs significantly exceed those from other exit vehicles. He reports a mean IRR of 76.1 % for IPO whereas trade sales only yielded a mean IRR of 27.3 % and secondary purchases 18.2 %. Fleming can also validate this assumption when employing multiples to assess the profitability of exits instead of IRRs.[367]

Lam (1991) delves into VC settings studying how VCFs maximize their proceeds by facilitating IPOs. Lam argues that the absence of public information about a venture increases estimation risks for both public and private investors. To be compensated for the higher risk, investors add discounts to transactions in information inefficient settings. However, Lam outlines that firms that go public supply investors with new information and resolve information spreads. VCFs capitalize on the improved information efficiency in that they postpone their actual cash out after information asymmetries are alleviated through the IPO. Conversely, the VCF sells its stakes all at once in the private transaction. Thus, the VCF does not participate in the private investor's new insights after the deal is closed. Lam concludes that the higher information efficiency surrounding public ventures generally advantages the IPO over the trade sale in that it lessens discounts.[368]

Subrahmanyam and Titman (1999) demonstrate that public finance is cheaper than private funding in information efficient settings and vice versa. In their framework, a firm accrues initial information costs when it tries to convince outside investors. Information costs are driven by the number of interested investors and their ex-

---

[364] Cochrane (2001), p. 1

[365] Zingales (1995), p. 425f.

[366] Zingales (1995), p. 426

[367] Fleming (2003), p. 18

[368] Lam (1991), p. 148

pertise with similar projects. First, Subrahmanyam and Titman argue that when two parties acquire the same information, the information they actually receive is likely to differ. Subrahmanyam and Titman give two reasons for why public markets can nonetheless exploit this imperfection better than private investors. On the one hand, Subrahmanyam and Titman set out that public investors outnumber private investors and thus receive a greater variety of information. On the other hand, public markets exchange their knowledge so that every single public investor capitalizes on the venture's emission of different information. Conversely, private investors do not confer about their information.[369] Second, Subrahmanyam and Titman consider that investors may discover valuable information serendipitously.[370] Serendipitously acquired information mostly concerns observations from the firm's environment such as customer preferences etc.. Akin to their initial argumentation, Subrahmanyam and Titman posit that public investors are more likely to recognize serendipitous information given that they outnumber private investors.[371] Subrahmanyam and Titman elaborate that public financing is less expensive when information is easy to acquire for new investors and serendipitous information plays a considerable role. Subrahmanyam and Titman conclude that firms go public when they have already gained visibility for instance by launching new products while firms that require funding for internal projects, such as reorganizations, prefer private funding.[372] Likewise, Cumming and MacIntosh (2001) maintain that information disadvantages of follow-on investors vary. As proposed by Subrahmanyam and Titman, Cumming and MacIntosh stress that different types of follow-on investors resolve different types of information asymmetries. Private investors are more capable of evaluating new technologies and markets given their related experiences. Public investors, however, are superior in gathering and processing information about established markets and products. Cumming and MacIntosh argue that VCFs target those investors that suffer from the least information disadvantages. For innovative ventures, VCFs choose private investors and the IPO for non-innovative settings. In doing so, VCFs minimize discounts and maximize the exit value.[373]

Wang and Sim (2001) observe that a firm's industry affiliation influences the occurrence of IPOs. They find that VC-backed high-technology ventures are more likely to go public than low technology ventures. Wang and Sim argue that public follow-on investors suffer from virtually no capital limitations as opposed to private investors. Wang and Sim set forth that only public investors can raise sufficient capital to satisfy

---

[369] Subrahmanyam/Titman (1999), p. 1047

[370] Subrahmanyam/Titman (1999), p. 1047

[371] Subrahmanyam/Titman (1999), p. 1075

[372] Subrahmanyam/Titman (1999), p. 1075

[373] Cumming/MacIntosh (2001), p. 451f.

the immense capital requirements of high-technology ventures while private investors are confined in their resources.[374] Their sample data reflects that high-technology firms are more frequently brought public (55.4 %) than low-technology firms (37.1 %).[375] Conversely, low-technology firms accomplish more secondary purchases or buy-backs given that low-technology ventures call for less follow-on funding.[376] Wright, Robbie, Romanet, Thompson, Joachimsson, Bruining and Herst (1994) come to a similar conclusion. In their sample of MBO transactions in UK, they find that only a quarter of all VC investments completed in the period from 1985 to 1991 were exited at all. The most common form for exiting MBO investments is trade sales. IPOs occurred in not more than 5 % of the exit transactions.[377] Most interestingly, Wright et al. observe significant differences in companies' average sizes across exit vehicles. Exits of larger MBO transactions are more likely to lead to IPOs than smaller investments. In their sample, only 16.2 % of exits with an investment volume below £ 10 million are floated, compared to 35.3 % of those transactions above this value. Wright et al. conclude that trade sales are constrained to certain investment volumes while public investors are virtually unlimited in their financial resources.[378]

Nevertheless, trade sales sometimes turn out to receive higher valuations if specialized investors include synergy effects or technological advantages in their offer.[379] Moreover, IPOs impose considerable costs on the issuing firm. The costs directly associated with initial quotations span legal, auditing and underwriting fees. Zingales (1995) points out that investment bankers charge on average 14 % of the funds raised for their services.[380] Costs that are incurred indirectly comprise the time and efforts the venture's management and the VCF devote to promoting the offering. In addition, indirect costs accrue through the dilution associated with sales of underpriced shares. In fact, the offering is regularly priced below the market's price to create incentives for public investors to invest.[381] In essence, the IPO may turn out to be the more expensive exit transaction, if the advantages do not trade off the higher costs.

As regards the relation between the entrepreneur and the VCF in advance of the exit, IPOs generally create fewer conflicts than a trade sale. The IPO enables the entrepreneur to regain corporate control. Black and Gilson (1998) assert that the po-

---

[374] Wang/Sim (2001), p. 343 and p. 353

[375] Wang/Sim (2001), p. 347f.

[376] Wang/Sim (2001), p. 352

[377] Wright/Robbie/Romanet/Thompson/Joachimsson/Bruining/Herst (1994), p. 94f.

[378] Wright/Robbie/Romanet/Thompson/Joachimsson/Bruining/Herst (1994), p. 96

[379] Cumming/MacIntosh (2001), p. 556; Wright/Robbie/Romanet/Thompson/Joachimsson/Bruining/Herst (1994), p. 94fff.

[380] Zingales (1995), p. 425

[381] Bartlett (1999), p. 135, see section 2.3.3 a)

tential to exit through an IPO allows the entrepreneur and the VCF to enter a self-enforcing implicit contract over the venture's control. In approaching an IPO, the VCF agrees to return control to a successful entrepreneur assuming that the entrepreneur retains a sufficient block of shares. The prospects for an IPO-exit essentially provide entrepreneurs with incentives to perform well.[382]

At the same time, IPOs feature a particular problem for the VCF. The IPO mutates the venture's ownership structure from few block holders into a number of scattered investors. Ang, Cole and Lin (2000) as well as Pagano and Röell (1998) examine the implications of the dilution of the VCF's ownership on the quality of corporate governance. In general, Ang, Cole and Lin as well as Pagano and Röell find that small, scattered stake holders perform corporate control less intensively than large block holders. Large investors tie their success to fewer but greater investments. They desire to control the investment's fortune by intensively monitoring the management's actions. Conversely, scattered share holders seek risk reduction primarily through diversification. Scattered investors hence spread their monitoring efforts over a multitude of investments which reduces their supervision of individual firms.[383] An IPO dilutes the VCF's influence and thus shifts control from the VCF to the entrepreneur. Moreover, the public firm is no longer depending on staged capital infusions by the VCF since it can access public markets now. By floating the venture, VCFs essentially step back from controlling measures such as budgeting or staging for instance.[384] Yet, the VCF cannot cash out at that point.[385] The IPO hence subjects the VCF to principal agent risks and calls for a sound relationship and trust between the VCFs and the entrepreneurs.

b) Trade sale

In a trade sale, the portfolio company is sold to one industrial investor.[386] Particularly those firms that do not match the requirements for an IPO with respect to size or profitability are subject to trade sales.[387] Not only do trade sales represent a viable exit vehicle for firms that cannot go public, the trade sale's return exceeds the IPO's return in some situations. In line with Cumming and MacIntosh (2001), Wright, Robbie, Romanet, Thompson, Joachimsson, Bruining and Herst (1990) outline that the private investor's background enhances his understanding of the company's business and enables him to recognize higher values in the firm's technologies. Private

---

[382] Black/Gilson (1998), p. 260f.; D'Souza (2000), p. 1ff.; Lorenz (1989), p. 129; Temple (1999), p. 103

[383] Ang/Cole/Lin (2000), p. 84; Chemmanur/Fulghieri (1999), p. 273 ; Pagano/Röell (1998), p. 188

[384] Black/Gilson (1998), p. 261

[385] Cumming/MacIntosh (2003), p. 515; Lin/Smith (1998), p. 242

[386] See section 3.3.3 for a detailed analysis of motives to select either means

[387] Temple (1999), p. 109; Gompers/Lerner (2000), p. 6

investors also benefit from synergies or access to new technologies elevating their profit from the transaction over the venture's stand-alone valuation while public markets consider solely the latter. Public investors may thus come to lower valuations than private investors.[388] Schwienbacher (2001) relates higher valuations in trade sales to the venture's product-market characteristics. Schwienbacher sets out that if a new business threatens an incumbent firm's market position, the latter is prone to buy the venture in order to eliminate rivalry. In this sense, Schwienbacher outlines that if industrial incumbents' market positions are negatively affected by the venture's products VCFs can bargain higher valuation levels. If the threat proves powerful enough, an industrial incumbent's offer will ultimately exceed the IPO's return.[389] Schwienbacher extends this contemplation arguing that the venture's degree of innovation moderates its competitive threat to industrial incumbents.[390] He stresses that the more innovative the venture is the less it jeopardizes incumbent firms' market positions. Schwienbacher concludes that since industrial investors perceive less pressure to eliminate the high technology venture's competition, innovative businesses are less likely to be acquired.[391] Finally, Lerner (1994a) outlines that in times of low equity valuations, companies avoid public markets. They prefer private financing because it is less affected from public investors' scepticism and renders a more objective valuation.[392] The occurrence of trade sales is consequently subject to the capital markets' conditions too.

The trade sale as exit vehicle entails a considerable disadvantage from the entrepreneur's point of view. In the trade sale, the entrepreneur cedes corporate control to the industrial investor and will lose his non-financial benefits from managing the venture. Although agreements can be implemented to ensure that the entrepreneur will stay in the firm after the sale, this transition may cause conflicts between the entrepreneur and the incumbent VCF.[393] Despite this conflict, VCFs regard trade sales as attractive since this transaction form ends the VCFs engagement in the portfolio firm promptly. Trade sales also provide immediate payments in cash or marketable securities to the VCF.

c) Secondary purchase

A transaction similar to the trade sale is the secondary purchase. While the VCF disposes the venture to industrial investors in a trade sale, the secondary purchase

---

[388] Cumming/MacIntosh (2001), p. 556; Wright/Robbie/Romanet/Thompson/Joachimsson/Bruining/Herst (1994), p. 94ff.

[389] Schwienbacher (2001)

[390] Schwienbacher (2001), p. 2

[391] Schwienbacher (2001), p. 3

[392] Lerner (1994a), p. 300f.

[393] Bascha (2001), p. 41

marks the disposal to merely financially motivated investors.[394] Secondary purchases occur in cases in which a portfolio company still needs assistance to prosper. If the VC fund approaches termination, the VCF recycles investments in medium or low performing companies which attract neither public nor private investors in that it sells the venture to other VCFs. Secondary purchases also allow new VCFs to replace incumbent VCFs and help turn around struggling ventures.[395] In essence, secondary purchases represent a viable solution if the incumbent VCFs desire to exit while the venture cannot access public markets yet or achieve a trade sale.[396] This transaction form implies a low potential for conflicts since the entrepreneur maintains his position and the VCF receives immediate cash.

d) Buy back

The buy back through the portfolio company's management or founders represents an alternative exit route. This mechanism is only considered to serve as back-up exit route. It is primarily applied to stalling ventures that cannot achieve exits in one of the above discussed ways.[397] In fact, the chances for a buy back are limited. A buy back requires the entrepreneur to dispose over additional capital to buy out the VCF. Thus, the VCF cannot expect to receive a high price if it decides on a buy back.[398]

e) Liquidation

When a business ceases its operations, it becomes subject to liquidation. If VCFs cannot accomplish an exit via one of the four routes examined above, the liquidation represents the terminal occasion for investors to retrieve some values from the venture. Implicitly, liquidation serves as an exit where not the whole company but its assets are sold to provide liquidity to incumbent investors. However, before any resources are distributed to equity investors, the debt providers are satisfied. What remains is disbursed according to the equity structure.[399] Even though liquidation preference warrants the VCF to be served before the remaining equity investors gain access to the venture's resources, it can usually not secure the entire investment. In the worst case, a liquidation event may not return any capital.[400] Liquidating a ven-

---

[394] Temple (1999), p. 110; Bascha (2001), p. 41
[395] Brück (1998), p. 41
[396] Temple (1999), p. 110
[397] Bartlett (1999), p. 88
[398] Brück (1998), p. 40
[399] Brück (1998), 39f.
[400] Schefczyk (2004), p. 49; Schwienbacher (2001), p. 7

ture makes sense at least from a financial perspective when an investment is likely to fail but the absorbed funds still exceed the claims of debt providers.[401]

3.1.2 Contractual Exit Means

The VCF's exit represents an inevitable step in the VC cycle given that VC financing is ex-ante temporarily limited. The divergent interests of the entrepreneur and the VCF about the future distribution of power and responsibility eventually clash at exit. This conflict can cause a principal-agent problem in that the entrepreneur works towards hampering the VCF's exit.[402]

The VCF's involvement in commercializing the entrepreneur's business conditions that the entrepreneur shifts substantial control power to the VCF. For the duration of VC funding, the entrepreneur has to accept the VCF's monitoring and active participation in the firm's decision making. Inherent in the VCF's investment is the right to block decisions. At exit, the VCF sells the rights attached to the investment either to private or public investors. As set out in section 3.1.1, each type of follow-on investor implies a different distribution of future corporate control. Black and Gilson (1998) point out that the prospects for the entrepreneur of losing corporate control to industrial investors may create conflicts between the entrepreneur and the VCFs. While VCFs seek to maximize profits at exit, the entrepreneur's benefits from setting up a venture include more than the sale's proceeds. Westhead and Wright (1998) fathom that entrepreneurs start businesses to earn monetary and non-financial benefits such as reputation and prestige.[403] By surrendering control to a private investor, the entrepreneur loses his non-financial benefits.[404] If the entrepreneur is not compensated for giving up his non-financial benefits in a private transaction, he is likely to oppose this exit vehicle. In an IPO, however, the entrepreneur can regain corporate control and keep his non-financial benefits. Black and Gilson (1998) conclude that IPO exits consequently generate fewer conflicts between the VCF and the entrepreneur.[405]

Besides the choice of exit vehicles, timing issues may stimulate conflicts between the VCF and the entrepreneur. First, VCFs desire to center their exits on peaking stock markets to maximize the valuation.[406] Second, VCFs are concerned about their reputation with fund investors, industrial investors and public markets. Exiting

---

[401] Brück (1998), 40; Wang/Sim (2001), p. 340.

[402] According to Bästlein (1997), p. 34, conflicts arise due to divergent perceptions of values, disagreement on the distribution of power etc.; see also Schwienbacher (2002), p. 3

[403] Westead/Wright (1998), p. 189; see also Brück (1998), p. 87f.; Pagano/Röell (1998), p. 192

[404] Westhead (1998), p. 189

[405] Black/Gilson (1998), p. 260f.; Temple (1999), p. 103

[406] Lerner (1994a), p. 294

represents a way for VCFs to build their reputation for successfully growing ventures.[407] Gompers (1996) reports that particularly young VCFs rush their ventures into early exits in order quickly establish track records. As Gompers (1996) notes, unseasoned VCFs even accept that the venture's immaturity at exit harms the venture's progress.[408] Early exits additionally allow VCFs to re-assign their human resources to new investments – especially when the current portfolio has matured to an extent where private or public markets become accessible.[409] However, the entrepreneur may feel that his venture cannot survive alone by the time the VCF desires to exit. Rather, the entrepreneur wishes to continue the VC process in order to receive further funding and support. The divergent timing strategies result in conflicts as well.

To minimize the impact of these conflicts on their exit ability, VCFs condition their commitment on the incorporation of contractual exit means. VCFs precisely stipulate rights warranting them to determine the type of follow-on investor and the timing. Even though the spectrum of rights occurring in VC finance is wide and their application varies across investment stages, industries and VCFs, some rights occur in almost every VC contract granting the VCF the flexibility either to accomplish an IPO or to close a private sale at any time.

Prior to going public, every company has to file a registration with the SEC. The SEC must approve the filing before the candidate can float its shares. Moreover, the company has to register the incumbent investors' stock with the SEC that is to be included in the IPO.[410] A major concern of VCFs is their influence on the registration of their equity stakes. Prior to closing an investment contract, VCFs typically claim registration rights allowing them to time the IPO and include their shares in the quotation. In exchange, the entrepreneur oftentimes receives veto rights to block an IPO in the first three years after the VCF's initial investment.[411]

If the entrepreneur holds the majority of common equity stakes and thus voting rights,[412] VCFs can ex-ante not terminate a private transaction. For this scenario, VCFs arrange precautions to protect their minority stakes. Such rights are termed "tag along rights". If the entrepreneur initiates a sale of his stakes, tag along rights

---

[407] Gompers (1996), p. 136

[408] Black/Gilson (1998), p. 256; Gompers (1996), p. 133f.; Prester (2002), p. 135;

[409] Aghion/Bolton/Tirole (2000), p. 2; Barry/Muscarella/Peavy/Vetsuypens (1990), p. 449; Kanniainen/Keuschnigg (2000), p. 2; Lorenz (1989), p. 37; Sidler (1997), p. 193

[410] Brück (1998), p. 139; Certo/Daily/Dalton (2001), p. 35; Sahlman (1990), p. 504

[411] Aghion/Bolton/Triole (2000), p. 27

[412] As discussed in section 2.2.1, VCFs preferably hold convertible preferred shares up to the exit

force the entrepreneur to include the VCF's minority stakes in any transaction. Then, VCFs must not remain in the business without the initiator.[413]

In those settings in which the VCF holds a majority equity stake, for instance after redeeming its convertible preferred shares, the VCF secures "drag along rights". Drag along rights eliminate the claims of minority owners in an acquisition. Drag along rights enable the VCF to force minority share holders to join in the transaction. This means is designated to protect majority share holders as industrial buyers only look to gain absolute control over an acquisition target. Without this option, M&A transactions do typically not materialize. In some cases, tag along and drag along rights count in turn for the entrepreneur too.[414]

3.2 The Exit Process

After the previous section has introduced exit means, this section sets out the exit process by taking the perspective of VCFs. It discusses basic steps which underlie every exit decision. Furthermore, this section demonstrates how VCFs consider and utilize typical means such as staging and exit related provisions throughout the exit process.

3.2.1 Differences and Common Characteristics of Exit Processes

Relander, Syrjänen and Miettinen (1994) argue that exiting ventures is a diffuse process because it is affected by numerous factors such as industry trends, public markets, involved VCFs etc.[415] In addition to that, every investment, industry or exit vehicle calls for different preparations. Depending on the chosen exit route, the withdrawal may be a singular event or span a number of activities lasting several months. SEC rules, for instance, hinder VCFs to sell large stakes to outside investors after the IPO or after the lock-up period has expired.[416] Sometimes VCFs do not even seek to dispose their stakes in a venture all at once but exit partially. In doing so, VCFs demonstrate their confidence in the venture's long term performance to follow-on investors.[417] However, the need for exiting ventures is always determined by the limited life-time of the fund.

Two arguments explain why VCFs must carefully plan their exits. First, Montgomery, Thomas and Kamath (1984) provide evidence on the general benefits of well

---

[413] Tag along rights are also referred to as co-sale rights; Brück (1998), p. 63ff.

[414] Brück (1998), p. 63ff.

[415] Relander, Syrjänen and Miettinen (1994), p. 150

[416] If an IPO does not include a lock-up agreement, the founding shareholders may sell immediately on the first trading day, provided they meet the provisions of SEC Rule 144.This rule permits shareholders to sell stock they have owned for a specific time period while restricting the number of shares that come to market over a three-month period.

[417] E.g., Cumming/MacIntosh (2003)

prepared divestures. They show that definite divestment strategies eventually fetch higher proceeds than reactionary divestures on short term opportunities. They reason that a deliberate evaluation of divestment options and a thorough matching between the divestment object's resources and environmental opportunities are more likely to increase the transaction's returns than unreflective or reactive responses to sudden events.[418] Second, the VCF swaps its convertible shares into common equity at the exit. At this point, the VCF loses the preference rights and dilutes its influence on the venture's management. Since the venture will not re-assign similar preference rights to the VCF, exiting is an irreversible process. Given that the VCF ultimately releases control over the management when embarking on the divestment, the VCF loses its clout to initiate changes in the exit strategy ex-post. The VCF's exit hence needs to be anticipated and prepared carefully.[419] Because of the vital part exits play in the VC process, VCFs must plan their exit related activities. VCFs advance through the following steps towards their withdrawal.

3.2.2 Supporting the Initial Investment Decision

VCFs embark on gathering exit relevant information even before they commit the first round of funding. As section 2.3.2 c) sets outs, VCFs look for exit opportunities in every investment proposal they receive. In the absence of exit prospects, the VCF rejects the request. In addition, VCFs anticipate the venture's development, growth and future cash flows. According to Ruhnka, Feldman and Dean (1992), a venture's growth represents an important predictor for possible exit strategies; if the venture promises only little growth, prospects for a successful IPO decrease. Yet, insufficient growth forecasts do not destroy the venture's prospects for less profitable exits via a trade sale or a buyout.[420] For these scenarios, VCFs identify strategic acquirers with a possible interest in acquiring the company's technology, knowledge, products or market shares. Based on these considerations, the VCF sets out an exit plan detailing possible exit dates and exit routes.[421]

If the VCF decides to invest, it enters negotiations with the entrepreneur. At this stage, the VCF arranges for contractual provisions. VCFs stipulate registration rights for a possible IPO exit and tag along respectively drag along rights for private trans-

---

[418] Montgomery/Thomas/Kamath (1984), p. 831; see also Brück (1998), p. 16; Duhaime/Patton (1980), p. 46

[419] See section 1.1

[420] Ruhnka/Feldman/Dean (1992), p. 138 and p. 147f.

[421] Misirli (1988), S. 34

actions.[422] The VCF also delegates its managers to the venture's board to represent the VCF's interests and eventually its exit-ambitions.[423]

3.2.3 Monitoring Internal and External Conditions During the VC Period

Throughout the VC process, VCFs observe the venture's environment and monitor the investment's progress. A widely used technique by VCFs to learn more about their ventures during the VC process is the staged infusion of capital.[424] At any stage, the VCF audits the investment on the basis of new information that has surfaced since the last investment stage. The venture does not receive further financing until it satisfies the VCF's desire for new information.[425] Based on this information, the VCF revises the original exit plan and identifies new exit opportunities. Changes become necessary if the venture fails to accomplish interim goals or if the investment exceeds the predefined expectations. Moreover, VCFs look out for possible industry investors that want to enter the venture's industries and track IPO activities of similar ventures. Relander, Syrjänen and Miettinen (1994) picture this process in the following matrix.[426] If a scenario materializes in which an exit becomes feasible, the VCF has to balance the present transaction's proceeds against possible future returns and decide on whether embarking on the divestment or not.

---

[422] See section 3.1.1

[423] Barry/Muscarella/Peavy/Vetsuypens (1990), p. 460ff.; Kirilenko (2001), p. 565; Sorensen/Stuart (2001), p. 1553

[424] See section 2.3.2 d)

[425] Admati/Pfleiderer (1994), p. 371f.; Bergemann/Hege (1998), p. 704; Busenitz/Fiet (1996); Cornelli/Yosha (2003), p. 1

[426] Relander/Syrjänen/Miettinen (1994), p. 151

Most expected exit route	Investing	Adding value	Exiting
IPO class	- Analyse exit choices - Agree on the deal structure for successful floatation - Determine alternative exit routes and agree on the conditions with other shareholders - Identify potential trade sale buyers if IPO fails	- Plan the time for quotation - Prepare for exiting through alternative exit routes just in case - Keep the contract network posted on the venture's performance to increase the possibility for a good trade sale offer if necessary	- Determine the best stock market to exit into - Plan the quotation - Consider unexpected trade sale offers
Trade sale class	- Analyse exit choices - Design an appropriate deal structure for exiting - Identify buyers - Network with potential buyers - Map the technology and corporate strategies of the buyers	- Present the portfolio of ventures to buyers - Monitor the strategic moves of potential buyers - Identify the best possible intermediaries to be used - Estimate the best time to exit the venture with respect to the resources	- Note the final deadline for exiting and act - Active selling through networks - Use intermediates - Ad hoc trade sales - Note that each trade sale offer requires time to be examined
Question mark class	- Avoid investing in ventures with obscured or poor exit possibilities - Divest lemons early - Cluster ventures for trade sale	- Exit the living dead now - Active selling through networks - Consider MBO, MBI or management earn-outs - Consider other types of financial restructuring	- MBO, MBI, earn-out or other types of financial restructuring - Starting your exit-planning here might be risky

Time →

Figure 13: Selection scheme for suitable exit vehicles[427]

Changes in the venture's environment may also induce VCFs to review their exit plans. Most frequently, researchers name looming hot issue markets as example for improving external conditions for the VCF's exit. Black and Gilson (1998) examine the general interplay between VC activities and stock markets in a cross-country study. Black and Gilson find that well developed capital markets are crucial for the existence of an active VC industry. Capital markets allow VCFs to tap virtually unlimited public funding and benefit from hot issue markets.[428] Ibbotson and Jaffe (1975) first document hot issue markets and discover cyclical patterns in the IPO market in which IPOs yield higher than average initial returns.[429] Ritter (1984) confirms this finding using a later time period. He concludes that hot issue markets continue to exist and occur periodically.[430] Similar patterns are more recently observed by Ljungqvist and Wilhelm (2003).[431] Neus and Walz (2001) and Ofek and Richardson (2003) ascribe the emergence of hot issue markets to elevated investor optimism. Public investors essentially accept higher uncertainties and risks during hot issue

---

427 Relander/Syrjänen/Miettinen (1994), p. 152

428 Black/Gilson (1998), p. 256ff.

429 Ibbotson/Jaffe (1975), p. 1027

430 Gompers/Lerner (2000), p. 206; Ritter (1984), p. 238f.

431 Ljungqvist/Wilhelm (2003), p. 723

markets and thus boost an issue's short-term performance.[432] IPO research also observes that a few initial floatations in an emerging industry trigger many subsequent listings and lead to IPO waves. In every IPO, the issuer releases new information that allows public markets to assess markets, technologies and business models.[433] Thus, IPOs essentially increase information efficiency and improve financing conditions for following listings.[434] A dynamic arises in which firms seek to capitalize on the increased information efficiency from previous IPOs of similar industries by tapping public finance.[435] In the VC context, Lerner (1994a) and Wang and Sim (2001) set forth that VCFs seek to capitalize on investor optimism and IPO waves in that they float their ventures in times of peaking stock markets to maximize the exit's valuation. When public markets suffer from low valuation levels, VCFs either provide another funding round or target private investors instead.[436] Shepherd and Zacharakis (2001a) and Giot and Schwienbacher (2003) exemplify that the recent hot issue markets have resulted in shortened holding periods for ventures. VCFs exploited hot issue markets in that they exited relatively earlier than in cold issue markets.[437] These findings show that the public market's optimism and dynamic moderate the restrains of information asymmetry and uncertainty on the VCF's exits. In times of hot issue markets, public investors become less sensitive for information spreads allowing VCFs to float ventures more easily whereas VCFs encounter more informational concerns and scepticism in public markets in cold issue periods. In essence, hot issue markets may provide strong incentives for VCFs to alter their exit plans towards immediate floatation to capitalize on high equity valuation levels.

3.2.4 Deciding on the Exit

The VCF's first decision pertains the exit's timing.[438] Stoughton, Wong and Zechner (2001) acknowledge that ventures progress through several financing stages. Up to a certain stage, ventures are backed by private investors – in the context of this thesis by VCFs. After a while, the venture gains access to other private investors and to public markets.[439] From this stage on, the VCF can reap the profits from its engagement in that it sells the venture to follow-on investors. Cumming and MacIntosh (2001) hold that the VCF's exit timing thereafter depends on the relation of

---

[432] Lowry (2003), p. 5; Ofek/Richardson (2003), p. 113f.; Neus/Walz (2001), p. 17

[433] Ljungqvist/Wilhelm (2003), p. 723

[434] Lam (1991), p. 148

[435] Chemmanur/Fulghieri (1999), p. 271

[436] Lerner (1994a), p. 300, reports a mean equity index of 4.05 for IPOs and only 3.05 for private funding; Wang/Sim (2001), p. 342

[437] Giot/Schwienbacher (2003), p. 7; Shepherd/Zacharakis (2001a), p. 66

[438] Section 4.1 analyzes the literature on VCFs' timing decisions

[439] Stoughton/Wong/Zechner (2001), p. 377f.

the marginal value, the VCF can add through a further commitment, to the marginal costs of its efforts. VCFs exit optimally when their marginal costs begin to exceed the marginal value added.[440] However, Gompers (1996) finds that unseasoned VCFs' timing decisions are driven by yet another consideration. Unseasoned VCFs experience ambitions to quicken their reputation building process and consequently schedule exits before the managerial optimum.[441] In addition, VCFs' exit decisions may be triggered by unexpected circumstances as set out above. An industrial investor approaching the VCF may induce changes in the exit strategy and cause an early trade sale.[442] The decision of when to dispose a portfolio company also depends on the capital market's condition. Peaking stock markets, for instance, drive the VCF's decision to bring a venture public.[443]

Second, the VCF has to match the venture's condition with the requirements of either public or private follow-on investors to determine the exit vehicle. Most VCFs initially seek to float their companies given that the IPO is commonly regarded as the most profitable exit route.[444] If the venture does not fulfil the requirements for an IPO, the VCF faces three choices. First, the VCF can sell the venture to industrial investors in a trade sale. Second, if no exit is foreseeable but the venture prospers, the VCF can commit to further funding and assistance. Thus, the VCF enables the venture to tap public or private equity markets in later periods. Third, the VCF can abandon the investment and try to retrieve its investment in a liquidation event or a less favorable exit vehicle such as the secondary purchase or the buy back. Relander, Syrjänen and Miettinen (1994) reason that the VCF only reverts to this option if the venture fails in completing important interim goals such as concluding R&D activities or unsuccessfully entering the market. At any later stage, the VCF reconsiders the scheme pictured in figure 14.

Finally, VCFs have to determine their involvement in the exit transaction to optimize the outcome.[445] Habib and Ljungqvist (2001) set out that VCFs can reduce the underpricing of IPO exits by promoting the issue. Habib and Ljungqvist exemplify that the VCF attends roadshows or negotiations with follow-on investors to disperse their concerns. Habib and Ljungqvist find that VCFs also enlist prestigious investment bankers as means to promote their exits.[446] The investment banker promotes the

---

[440] Cumming/MacIntosh (2001), p. 448

[441] Gompers (1996), p. 133ff.; Gompers/Lerner (1999a), p. 30; Milgrom/Roberts (1982), p. 283; Zemke (1995), p. 145f.

[442] Schröder (1992), p. 252; Temple (1999), p. 101f.

[443] Giot/Schwienbacher (2003), p. 7; Lerner (1994a), p. 300; Shepherd/Zacharakis (2001a), p. 66

[444] See section 3.1.1 a)

[445] Stoughton/Wong/Zechner (2001), p. 377f.

[446] Habib/Ljungqvist (2001), p. 434f.

new issue on roadshows and to institutional investors or looks out for private investors if the venture moves towards a trade sale.[447]

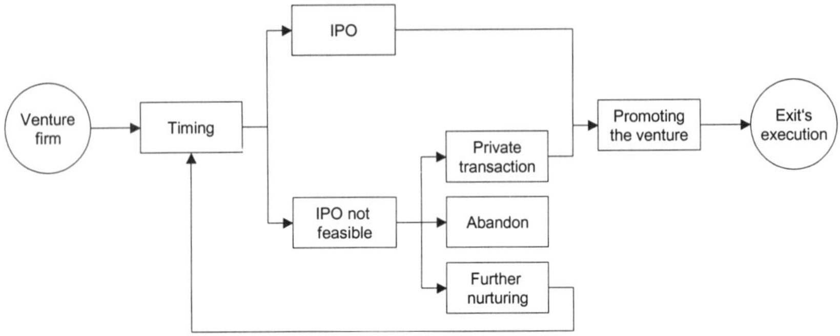

Figure 14: Decision-based framework of the exit process

3.2.5 Executing the Transaction

Once the decision to exit is made, the VCF executes the transaction. However, the execution of private and public transactions varies substantially. Private transactions entail the investor's due diligence and negotiations about the deal structure. Over a brief period of time, corporate control is then transferred to the new investor.

The IPO, however, involves different activities and lasts several months. Usually, the IPO process commences with the VCF hiring an investment bank to serve as underwriter. The investment banker performs the due diligence and determines the IPO-price's filing range. However, this price is subject to negotiations and changes according to the demand for the stock. The actual IPO begins with the offering firm filing the S-1 registration statement with the SEC. The initial floatation becomes effective within 20 days after the SEC's approval. In the U.S., VC-backed companies usually target the National Association of Securities Dealers Automated Quotation (NASDAQ) for their initial listing. NASDAQ was especially set up to meet the requirements of young, growing companies.[448]

However, the IPO itself does not serve as exit vehicle; usually, the incumbents are required to stick to their stakes even after the IPO for a lock-up period.[449] Lock-up provisions represent typical contracts between insiders of the floating company and the investment bankers. The underwriter obliges incumbent investors not to dispose their shares for a specific period after the initial listing.[450] It is commonly held that

---

[447] Booth/Chua (1996), p. 293; Certo/Daily/Dalton (2001), p. 35
[448] Fassin/Lewis (1994), p. 39
[449] Gompers/Lerner (2000), p. 209
[450] Bradley/Jordan/Yi/Roten (2001), p. 466f.

immediate insider sales signal that the issue is overvalued and destroy chances for a liquid after-market.[451] Lock-up provisions hinder insiders from exploiting their information advantages over the public market by cashing out through the initial floatation. By preventing early sales, lock-up agreements tie the insiders' proceeds to the share's performance in the long term. Insider selling prior to the expiration is allowed only if the lead underwriter accedes to the divestment. Aggarwal, Krigman and Womack (2002) report that incumbents sell on average only 25.9 % of their stake in the IPO.[452] The lock-up arrangement forbids the original investors to sell further shares for a period of 180 days after the IPO. Until the lock-up agreement expires, trading is usually limited to the portion of shares that is initially issued. Besides, the VCF's IPO exit is subject to SEC rule 144. SEC rule 144 imposes limitations on insider sales at any time allowing the VCF to divest only over a long time frame.[453]

Accordingly, Gompers and Lerner (1998) observe that the incumbents' divestments start twenty months after the initial floatation. Gompers and Lerner spot a skewed distribution with the median of shares being distributed after more than one year. In the first three month after the IPO, only one percent of the distributions occur due to the limitations of the lock-up provision.[454] Because the actual withdrawal begins not until one year after the initial listing, IPO exits require the development of liquid markets afterwards to warrant successful exits.[455] However, Aggarwal, Krigman and Womack (2002) report that in 16 % of the IPOs insiders sell shares before the lock-up period expires in spite of the lock-up agreement.[456] Brav and Gompers (2003) observe a similar distribution and emphasize that in roughly 15 % of their sample IPOs insider sales occurred in advance of the lock-up expiration.[457]

3.3 Recent Exit Trends

This section examines recent trends and the circumstances in which VCFs accomplish exits today. The discussion elaborates changes triggered by the plunging

---

[451] Aggarwal/Krigman/Womack (2002), p. 106; Bradley/Jordan/Yi/Roten (2001), p. 466; Field/Hanka (2001), p. 471ff.; Gompers/Lerner (1998), p. 2167; Gompers/Lerner (2000), p. 209

[452] Aggaral/Krigman/Womack (2002), p. 117

[453] Field/Hanka (2001), p. 471; see also Field/Hanka (2001), p. 471, Fn. 1, for a deeper discussion of SEC rule 144; see www.law.uc.edu/CCL/index.html for SEC rules. Rule 144 generally applies to corporate insiders such as officers, directors or anyone else holding more than 10 % of the outstanding securities. They may sell their shares to the public only if the following conditions are met: 1) the securities have been held for at least one year; 2) current financial information must be made available to the buyer, e.g., in form of 10K and 10Q reports; 3) the seller must file Form 144 with the SEC no later than the first day of the sale; 4) if the securities were owned for between one and two years, the volume of securities sold is limited to the greater of 1 % of all outstanding shares. But there are exceptions for private sales to qualified investors, such as industrial or financial investors.

[454] Gompers/Lerner (1998), p. 2167

[455] Ivanova/Tzvetkova (2001), p. 177

[456] Aggarwal/Krigman/Womach (2002), p. 120

[457] Brav/Gompers (2003), p. 16, table 5

stock markets, by the development of the VC industry and concludes with actual challenges VCFs face upon exit.

3.3.1 Declined Stock Markets and the Overhang of Portfolio Companies

Black and Gilson (1998) find that functioning IPO markets are crucial determinants for a vibrant VC industry.[458] Likewise, Lerner (1994a) and others find a strong correlation between the average share price performance in national equity capital markets and the number of VC-backed companies that go public across all countries with established VC-markets.[459] In the era between 1999 and 2000 when stock markets peaked,[460] successful IPOs appeared virtually independent from the level of development of the issuing company.[461] The skyrocketing market boosted investors' optimism about new issues easing VCFs' exits.[462] During this period, many VC-backed start-ups were brought public at tremendously high valuations.

Since then, the markets have dropped sharply and investor optimism has abated. It turned out that new issues were systematically overpriced during the hot issue markets. The declining equity valuation levels in 2000 resulted from investors' disappointment about these overstated issues.[463] In 2003, the number of IPOs was only 15 % of the number of the hot year 1999. In the same period, VC-backed IPOs slumped even more to 13 % compared to the level of 1999. Today, the declined stock markets allow for fewer VC-backed IPOs at far lower valuations.[464] With the IPO option becoming less likely, VCFs are forced to consider other exit vehicles, such as trade sales, secondary purchases and even buy-backs. Alternatively, VCFs can postpone their exits and wait for new hot issue markets if the fund's remaining life time permits the delay.

---

[458] See section 3.3.2 a)

[459] Lerner (1994a), p. 300f.; Neus/Walz (2001), p. 17; Shepherd/Zacharakis (2001a), p. 66; Giot/ Schwienbacher (2003), p. 7; Wang/Sim (2001), p. 342

[460] See figure 15

[461] Sacirbey (2000), p.3

[462] Ofek/Richardson (2003), p. 113f.; Reynolds/Hay/Bygrave/Camp/Autio (2000), p. 48

[463] Chang (2004), p. 721f.; Lowry (2003), p. 5

[464] Lowry (2003), p. 5

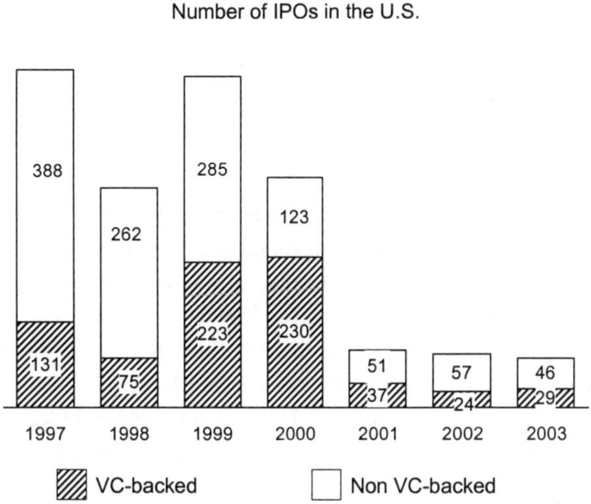

Figure 15: IPO-trends in the U.S. VC-market[465]

The conditions of public markets in turn influence financial decisions of young companies. As Lerner (1994a) demonstrates for the biotechnology sector, young start-ups are more likely to seek VC-financing during hot issue market periods while they tend to finance their projects through alliances with larger companies in times of poor market performances.[466] Considering an investment horizon of 5 years, those VC-investments entered in the era 1999 to 2000 have now matured. Yet, the number of VC-backed IPOs and the number of portfolio companies sold privately have declined constantly since 1999.[467] The number of new investments made since the hot issue period has by far exceeded the number of withdrawals until now – even when accounting for the high failure rates in VC finance. Currently, VCFs have a significant overhang of VC investments and face pressure to exit them given that their funds approach termination. The NVCA, for instance, reports that VCFs have entered far beyond 9,000 venture investments in the years 1999 and 2000. Even when considering the lowest probability for an IPO of 10 % to 20 % as reported by Amit Brander and Zott (1998), between 900 and 1,800 IPO exits are to be expected in the subsequent years.[468] However, figure 15 reports only 90 actual floatations of VC-backed

---

[465] See www.nvca.com

[466] Lerner (2003), p. 442; see also Leleux/Manigart (1994), p. 69; Reynolds/Hay/Bygrave/Camp/Autio (2000), p. 48; Reynolds/Hay/Bygrave/Camp/Autio (2001), p. 24

[467] See figure 15; NVCA (2003); Das/Jagannathan/Sarin (2003), p. 8

[468] See section 3.1.1; Amit/Brander/Zott (1998), p. 460, figure 5

firms revealing an enormous overhang of not exited ventures in VCFs' current portfolios. A similar calculation applies to the number of M&A exits since 2000.[469]

3.3.2 Increased Competition in the VC-Industry

Cochrane (2001) notes that the VC industry has become highly competitive – particularly since essentially no barriers exist that prevent individuals or organizations from entering the VC market.[470] The hot issue markets in the past two decades in which IPO exits were awarded with astronomical profits have spurred the emergence of new VCFs. From 1980 to 1989, the number of existing VCFs competing for investors and investment opportunities has tripled.[471] From 1997 to 2000, the number of operating VCFs has doubled from 393 to 792. Both, the number of VCFs and the amount of VC funds have peaked in the year 2000 as illustrated in figure 16. After the "dotcom" bust and the slump in the IPO markets, the number of VCFs has abated again. This decline stems – among other factors – from the shakeout of those firms which were not able to accomplish successful exits and in consequence did not attract enough capital to recycle their funds.[472] However, figure 16 shows that the number of existing VCFs still exceeds the level of 1998 and that the shakeout continues. Nowadays, VCFs are forced to demonstrate their ability of successfully nurturing ventures to attract investors if they want to recycle their funds and if they wish to participate in future hot issue markets.

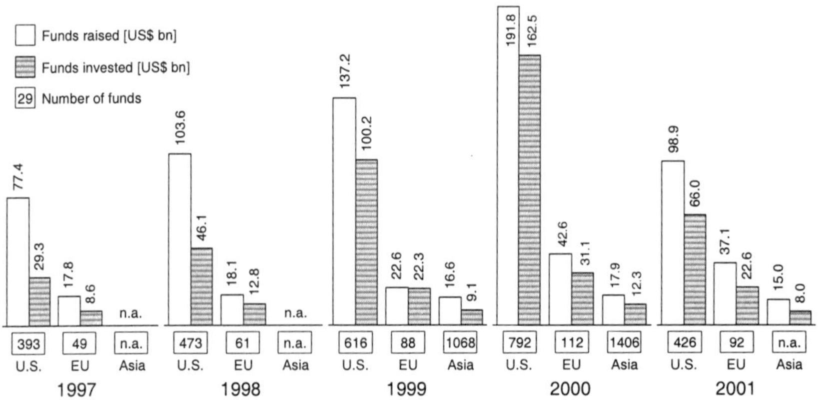

Figure 16: Growth trends in the U.S. VC-market[473]

---

[469] See www.nvca.com

[470] Cochrane (2001), p. 2

[471] Gupta/Sapienza (1992), p. 347

[472] Inderst/Müller (2004), p. 320f.

[473] SDC Platinum, 06/10/2003

In addition, the market shares of alternative fund providers such as individual investors ("Business Angles"), corporate subsidiaries offering VC or strategic alliances have grown considerably as reported by Burns (2003) and Elitzur and Gavious (2003).[474] Today, VCFs face an increasing rivalry from business angles and CVC entities – mainly for new investment opportunities but also when searching for follow-on investors.

3.3.3 Current Challenges for Venture Capitalists' Exits

The VC-industry has already recognized the gap between the actual exit opportunities and VCFs' demand. From their representative study across the European VC markets, Wall and Smith (1997) report that 70 % of the participating VCFs admit to have problems when exiting their investments. Wall and Smith identify three odds that hamper VCFs' exits. Even though Wall and Smith's study reports the situation in the year 1997, the findings match the current problems in the U.S. VC industry. Wall and Smith highlight three exit-problems that VCFs face in the context of the recently plunging stock markets.[475]

- *Lack of institutional buyers*: Due to currently suffering stock markets, an IPO exit cannot attract institutional buyers.
- *Lack of strategic or financial buyers* (for alternative exit-routes): First, most companies can currently not raise external equity to pay for an acquisition given that the present stock markets do not allow for new issues at favorable prices.[476] Second, even if incumbent industrialists intend to acquire a venture without raising external funds, they would value the target according to valuations actually attained at stock markets – in fact not favorable terms for the VCF.
- *Uncooperative management of the venture*: Valuations currently accomplishable in an IPO or acquisition are not favorable for both the management and the founders of the start-up. But in contrast to the VCFs, the management's investment horizon is not limited. In order to achieve higher valuations in future hot issue markets, entrepreneurs and managers may seek to delay the exit.

Wall and Smith summarize that VCFs profit from hot markets, such as in the period from 1999 to 2000, yielding numerous exit-options until the markets slumped in late 2000 and 2001. Today, illiquidity has grown to a major concern for VCFs as op-

---

[474] Burns (2003), p. 30; Elitzur/Gavious (2003), p. 710f.

[475] Wall/Smith (1997), p. 6f., the study is based on interviews with 30 European VCFs; see Burns (2003), p. 29, for the VC-industry in UK

[476] Burns (2003), p. 31

portunities for successful exits of VC-investments have become less abundant. Nowhere is that more apparent than for VC-backed IPOs.

3.4 Conclusive Remarks

Exiting is an important step in the VC cycle. Thus, VCFs devote much attention to elaborate proper exit strategies from their initial investment on. In addition, VCFs stipulate a variety of measures that allow them to divest at almost every time regardless of the entrepreneur's agreement and carefully approach the exit transaction.

Researchers address a variety of factors that impact the VCF's exit decisions. The discussion in this chapter has shed light on factors affecting the exit vehicle and the exit timing. Throughout the VC process, VCFs observe and revise their initial exit strategy until they have identified a favorable setting to accomplish a profitable exit. Only then do VCFs launch the exit and promote the venture to prospective investors.

However, the discussion neglects the constraints of VCFs' exits. Given the focus of this study, information asymmetry represents the central obstacle impeding exits or at least imposing costs on the VCF by the time of the withdrawal. Either way, information asymmetry impacts the VCF's proceeds from the exit. The subsequent chapter dwells on the literature and develops a model that describes VCFs' exit behavior under information asymmetry.

4 Building an Analytical Framework

On the basis of the literature and advancements of theoretical models, this chapter develops the research model that underlies the empirical analysis. The research model relates information asymmetries between inside and prospective outside investors about the business and eventual departures of entrepreneurial team members as well as VCFs' abilities to resolve uncertainties of prospective investors to the VCF's exit strategy. Initially, this chapter sets out the relevant literature and the theoretical constructs underlying the research model. Then, this chapter derives 20 hypotheses on how VCFs react to information inefficiency at exit. This chapter concludes with adjusting the hypotheses to the findings from four qualitative pilot-studies in which the research model is pre-tested.

4.1 Exit Strategies in the Literature

The purpose of this section is to identify previous research on VCFs' exits that inspires the subsequent research model. This section sets out how this thesis finds relevant research. The findings are reported in an aggregated form.

Initially, the literature focus needs to be sketched. Given the purpose of this study, an article, working paper, book chapter etc. becomes relevant if it addresses the occurrence of financing transactions in general. Relevance is furthermore determined by two criteria: the article's focus on particular categories of investees and types of investors. Research that addresses financing transactions of matured firms is less likely to contribute to the present analysis in comparison to papers looking into financing events of entrepreneurial ventures. Relevant articles hence emphasize financing transactions either in general or in an entrepreneurial context. Work that takes the perspective of a debt investor does not address the particular problems attributed to equity investments in early stage ventures. Given that VCFs look to replace their equity stakes, relevant articles must address equity financing events. The closer an article's emphasis comes to the focus of the present dissertation, the more pertaining it is. If findings relate VCFs' exit decisions to information dissimilarities, they will be considered in the research model. If findings shed light on other dependencies, they will be used for controlling the research model for other influences than information asymmetry.

The literature analysis pursues two strategies to identify possibly all relevant work concerning VCFs' exits: screening relevant journals and discovering related findings in a bibliometric analysis. In order to identify these articles, the literature analysis searches the major journals for articles that obviously center on VCFs' exits.

Therefore, the recent issues (from 1988 to 2004) of the following peer review journals are systematically screened:[477]

- Entrepreneurship Theory & Practice[478]
- Financial Management[479]
- The Academy of Management Journal[480]
- The Journal of Business Venturing[481]
- The Journal of Finance[482]
- The Journal of Financial Economics [483]
- Venture Capital[484]

Working papers are found by browsing public sources such as the Social Science Research Network[485] and the internet. The inquiries use terms such as "exit", "divestment", "IPO", "trade sale" and "venture capital".[486]

This procedure may, however, suffer from too narrow a focus; the preceding analyses may have improved the awareness of important research. Yet, this awareness only concerns the entrepreneurial finance field. In order to spread the literature search in relevant fields other than those explicitly involving VC or entrepreneurial finance without dropping the focus on VCFs' exits, a bibliometric analysis is applied. Generally, scholars employ bibliometric analyses to quantify and describe patterns of publications in a particular research stream. Bibliometric analyses help identify core research strands and determining the mutual impact of individual articles in the field.[487] Whenever an author cites another author, a bibliometric relationship is established. Bibliometric research traces relationships between articles by screening the references.[488] In the context of this study, a bibliometric analysis is pursued to root back ideas from recent articles on VCFs' exits to their original concepts. Being aware of the original concepts improves the literature analysis in two ways. First, it provides a sound understanding of the emergence of relevant research streams. Second, the

---

[477] See Schefczyk (2004), p. 177f., for a similar approach

[478] E.g., Murray (1996); Shepherd/Zacharakis (2001a)

[479] E.g., Cumming/MacIntosh (2001); Johnson/Miller (1988)

[480] Yielded no results

[481] E.g., Chang (2004); Janney/Folta (2003)

[482] E.g., Barry (1989); Brav/Gompers (1997); Megginson/Weiss (1991)

[483] E.g., Barry/Muscarella/Peavy/Vetsuypens (1990); Black/Gilson (1998); Gompers (1996); Lerner (1994a)

[484] E.g., Wang/Sim (2001)

[485] www.ssrn.com

[486] E.g., Franzke (2001); Giot/Schwienbacher (2003); Neus/Walz (2001); Schwienbacher (2001); Schwienbacher (2002)

[487] Osareh (1996a), p. 150ff.

[488] Osareh (1996a), p. 154f.; Osareh (1996b), p. 217ff.; Potter (1988)

insights gained throughout the bibliometric analysis inspire a selective broadening of the literature focus on other research bodies than the VC strand. Based on the enhanced understanding of core research streams, the literature analysis screens the references of the newly discovered articles and gleans further articles. The broader focus consequently contributes new concepts to the analysis of VCFs' exits.

Before embarking on the bibliometric analysis, the procedure's beginning and end have to be determined. As for this study, the most recent articles or working papers that clearly address VCFs' exits constitute the point of origination:

- Cumming and MacIntosh (2001) and Neus and Walz (2001) outline that they examine the timing of VCFs' exits.
- Wang and Sim (2001) as well as Schwienbacher (2002) concentrate on the VCF's choice of exit vehicles.
- Cumming and MacIntosh (2003) shed light on the extent of VCFs' exit transactions in the U.S. and in Canada.

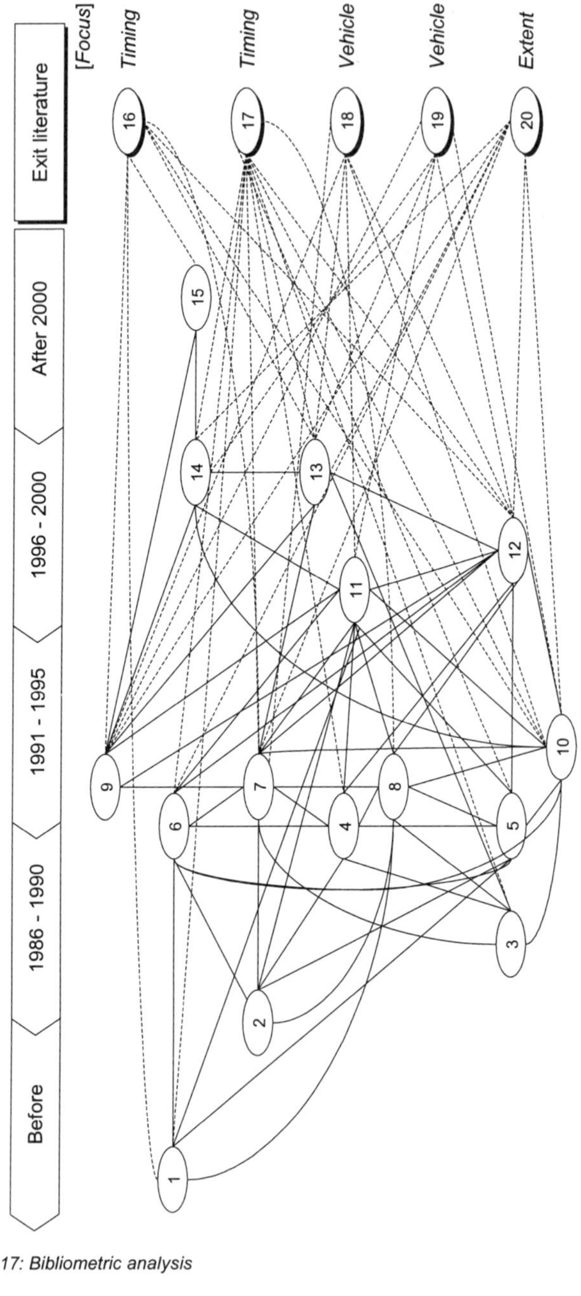

1: Leland/Pyle (1977), 2: Ritter (1984), 3: Booth/Smith (1986), 4: Allen/Faulhaber (1989), 5: Grinblatt/Hwang (1989), 6: Welch (1989), 7: Barry et al. (1990), 8: Carter/Manaster (1990), 9: Sahlman (1990), 10: Megginson/Weiss (1991), 11: Lerner (1994a), 12: Gompers (1996), 13: Black/Gilson (1998), 14: Hellmann (1998), 15: Kaplan/Strömberg (2003), 16: Cumming/MacIntosh (2001), 17: Neus/Walz (2001), 18: Wang/Sim (2001), 19: Schwienbacher (2002), 20: Cumming/MacIntosh (2003)

Figure 17: Bibliometric analysis

The analysis stops when VCFs' exits are related to apparently basic research concepts on corporate finance. Figure 17 illustrates how the significant articles are interrelated. Considering that every research paper quotes several other scholastic papers, bibliometric research exponentially gains complexity and therefore has to be focused. Due to this complexity, figure 17 only illustrates publications and their bibliometric relationships that were cited more than ten times in the screened literature. In doing so, figure 17 separates the most influential articles in the field. Moreover, figure 17 isolates three terminal articles. These articles constitute origins of research streams with substantial impact on the VC field. The illustration relates them to the recent publications on VCFs' exit transactions even if they are not cited anymore. These articles are:

- Leland and Pyle (1977) represent the utmost end of the analysis. They derive the general need for financial intermediation – and hence for VC finance – from imperfect markets. In their sense, financial intermediates such as investment banks or VCFs act as information broker between inside and outside investors. The intermediate's service helps resolve information dissimilarities between insiders and outsiders and reduces transaction costs.[489] As for the present analysis, Leland and Pyle inspire the focus on the presence of financial intermediates in exit transactions.
- Ritter (1984) relates the occurrence of public finance instead of private funding to the hot issue market phenomenon.[490] In doing so, he spurs a research stream on how equity valuation levels affect a company's financing decisions. Control hypotheses on the timing of exits and on the decision between public and private finance evolve from his findings.
- Booth and Smith (1986) initiate a wide research body on certification mechanisms in financing transactions that help VCFs to cope with information asymmetry.[491] This idea founds the basis of a research body centering on the role of certification upon exit through the VCF or third-parties which the research model picks up.

Figure 17 exemplifies that Allen and Faulhaber's (1989) article as well as Grinblatt and Wang's (1989) work on underpricing are discovered throughout the bibliometric analysis. Both articles are not directly related to VC but provide insights in the consequences of the VCF's actions during the exit. In fact, the research model reverts frequently to these articles. The bibliometric analysis also contributes articles

---

[489] Leland/Pyle (1977), p. 382f.

[490] Ritter (1984), p. 215f.

[491] Booth/Smith (1986), p. 261ff.

of Subrahmanyam and Titman (1999) and Chemmanur and Fulghieri (1999) that focus on information costs arising when firms want to tap public or private funding.

The following table summarizes the findings of the existing literature pertaining VCFs' exits. Table 3 follows the decision model introduced in section 3.2.4. The findings are discussed in depth in the relevant sections on the research model and on the control variables which account for alternative explanations. The discussion of exit vehicles is embedded in section 3.1.1 which examines exit routes in general.

Exit Strategy Options	Category	Article	Findings
Timing	External influences	Black/Gilson (1998)	- Well developed capital markets are crucial for the existence of a vivid VC industry - Vivid public capital markets allow VCFs to tap public finance for exits and to benefit from hot issue periods[492]
		Lowry (2003); Ofek/Richardson (2003); Neus/Walz (2001)	- Public investors accept higher uncertainties and risks during hot issue markets boosting IPOs' short-term performances[493]
		Lam (1991); Ljungqvist/Wilhelm (2003)	- Follow-on IPOs in emerging markets benefit from higher information efficiency established through prior IPOs[494]

[492] Black/Gilson (1998), p. 256ff.

[493] Lowry (2003), p. 5; Ofek/Richardson (2003), p. 113f.; Neus/Walz (2001), p. 17

[494] Lam (1991), p. 148; Ljungqvist/Wilhelm (2003), p. 723

		Lerner (1994a); Wang/Sim (2001)	- VCFs capitalize on hot issue markets by timing their exits accordingly - In the absence of hot issue markets, VCFs delay exits or target private investors instead[495]
		Shepherd/Zacharakis (2001a); Schwienbacher (2003)	- The occurrence of hot issue markets shortens holding periods of VC investments[496]
		Shepherd/Zacharakis (2001a)	- Regional conditions affect the speed to IPO of VC-backed firms[497]
	Industry affiliation	Chemmanur/Fulghieri (1999); Cumming/MacIntosh (2001); Shepherd/Zacharakis (2001a)	- High technology ventures require longer holding periods than low-technology ventures since follow-on investors must resolve greater information spreads[498]
		Giot/Schwienbacher (2003)	- Internet firms accomplish IPOs faster than firms in other sectors - Their IPOs are accelerated through higher investments and closer monitoring[499]

495 Lerner (1994a), p. 300; Wang/Sim (2001), p. 342

496 Giot/Schwienbacher (2003), p. 7; Shepherd/Zacharakis (2001a), p. 66

497 Shepherd/Zacharakis (2001a), p. 66

498 Chemmanur/Fulghieri (1999), p. 271; Cumming/MacIntosh (2001), p. 446; Shepherd/Zacharakis (2001a), p. 66

499 Giot/Schwienbacher (2003), p. 3 and p. 13f.; for signaling theory see Certo (2003), p. 434; Keasey/Short (1997), p. 75f.; Marshall (1998), p. 1081

	Information costs	Chemmanur/Fulghieri (1999)	- Incumbents contrast information costs of IPOs and private finance when deciding on external funding - If no information about the firm is public, private finance becomes cheaper[500] - Firms go public if they exhibit track records and have circulated information in public[501]
	Venture's progress	Bygrave/Stein (1989)	- Successful VCFs nurture ventures until they establish credibility with follow-on investors - Returns from IPOs correlate positively with holding periods[502]
		Giot/Schwienbacher (2003)	- VC durations decline if VCFs commit to a more intensive monitoring[503]
		Wright et al. (1994)	- The number of exits peaks after a holding period of 3 to 5 years - Afterwards it declines because only "living dead" ventures remain[504]

500 Chemmanur/Fulghieri (1999), p. 250f.

501 Chemmanur/Fulghieri (1999), p. 252 and p. 269

502 Bygrave/Stein (1989), p. 295

503 Giot/Schwienbacher (2003), p. 12

504 Wright/Robbie/Romanet/Thompson/Joachimsson/Bruining/Herst (1994), p. 97

		Cumming/MacIntosh (2001); Neus/Walz (2001)	- VCFs terminate investments when the projected marginal value added as a result of their efforts becomes less than the projected marginal costs of these efforts - Thereafter, the VCF's commitment becomes inefficient[505]
	VCF's characteristics	Gompers (1996)	- VCFs without track records rush their investments into IPOs to quicken their reputation building process[506]
		Neus/Walz (2001)	- Reputation allows older VCFs to exit earlier given that it certifies for the transaction[507]

[505] Cumming/MacIntosh (2001), p. 447f.; Neus/Walz (2001), p. 17

[506] Gompers (1996), p. 135f.

[507] Neus/Walz (2001), p. 17

		Lerner (1994a)	- Seasoned VCFs are more effective in centering their exits on hot issue market periods than their unseasoned counterparts - Seasoned VCFs execute IPOs more effectively and efficiently - Seasoned VCFs raise less investor-scepticism if they delay exits because of their greater credibility[508]
Exit vehicle	Advantages of IPO exits	Zingales (1995)	- The incumbent's greater bargaining power against public investors in relation to private investors results in higher valuations for IPO exits[509]
		Cumming/MacIntosh (2003); Lam (1991)	- Firms that go public supply investors with new information - VCFs capitalize on the improved information efficiency in that they cash out after the actual IPO[510]

[508] Lerner (1994a), p. 312

[509] Zingales (1995), p. 425f.

[510] Cumming/MacIntosh (2003), p. 512f.; Lam (1991), p. 148

		Subrahmanyam/Titman (1999)	- Firms go public if they have gained visibility while firms that require funding for internal projects, such as reorganizations, prefer private funding[511]
		Cumming/MacIntosh (2001)	- Follow-on investors resolve information asymmetries differently - IPOs impose less information costs in non-innovative settings[512]
		Wang/Sim (2001); Wright et al. (1994)	- VCFs float high-technology ventures because public finance is not limited and can satisfy the immense capital requirements of high-technology ventures - Private investors are confined in their resources and cannot fund high-technology ventures[513]
		Fleming (2003); Schwienbacher (2002)	- VCFs float only high quality investments to protect their reputation[514]

[511] Subrahmanyam/Titman (1999), p. 1075

[512] Cumming/MacIntosh (2001), p. 451f.

[513] Wang/Sim (2001), p. 343 and p. 353; Wright/Robbie/Romanet/Thompson/Joachimsson/Bruining/Herst (1994), p. 94f.

[514] Fleming (2003), p. 9; Schwienbacher (2002), p. 7f.

	Advantages of M&A exits	Cumming/MacIntosh (2001); Wright et al. (1994)	- Private investors' background enhances their understanding of the venture resulting in less information gaps - Private investors benefit from synergies or access to new technologies while public markets consider only the stand-alone value[515]
		Schwienbacher (2001)	- VCFs can bargain higher valuation levels in M&A exits if the venture threatens an incumbent firm's market position[516]
Certification and promotion	VCF's certification	Bygrave/Timmons (1992); Gompers (1996); Megginson/Weiss (1991); Sahlman (1997)	- To preserve their reputation, VCFs avoid to overprice IPOs and to benefit from short-term advantages - The presence of VCFs certifies for IPOs and helps investors overcome informational concerns[517]

[515] Cumming/MacIntosh (2001), p. 556; Wright/Robbie/Romanet/Thompson/Joachimsson/Bruining/Herst (1994), p. 94ff.

[516] Schwienbacher (2001)

[517] Bygrave/Timmons (1992), p. 208; Gompers (1996), p. 153f.; Megginson/Weiss (1991), p. 881; Sahlman (1997), p. 107; see also Neus/Walz (2001), p. 17

		Barry et al. (1990)	- VCF's investment behavior signals the venture's quality - The VCF's decision to (re-) invest represents a costly quality signal; the VCF loses money if the venture fails[518]
		Bradley/Jordan (2002); Lerner (1994a)	- IPOs backed by seasoned VCFs employ more often prestigious underwriters - Prestigious underwriters lower prospective investors' concerns about the issue[519]
	Third-party certification	Baron (1982); Beatty/Ritter (1986); Booth/Smith (1986); Carter/Dark/Singh (1998); Carter/Manaster (1990); Johnson/Miller (1988); McDonald/Fisher (1972); Megginson/Weiss (1991); Neuberger/Hammond (1974)	- The presence of prestigious investment banks provides certification for financing transactions and resolves informational concerns of follow-on investors - More prestigious investment banks provide greater certification[520]
		Beatty (1989); DeAngelo (1981); Megginson/Weiss (1991); Titman/Trueman (1986)	- Auditors provide certification for the IPO-valuation lowering concerns of follow-on investors[521]

518 Barry/Muscarella/Peavy/Vetsuypens (1990), p. 448

519 Bradley/Jordan (2002), p. 601; Lerner (1994a), p. 305, table 4, and p. 314

520 E.g., Baron (1982), p. 955ff.; Beatty/Ritter (1986), p. 214ff.; Booth/Smith (1986), p. 261; Carter/Dark/Singh (1998), p. 285ff.; Carter/Manaster (1990), p. 1062; Johnson/Miller (1988), p. 28; McDonald/Fisher (1972), p. 102; Megginson/Weiss (1991), p. 879; Neuberger/Hammond (1974), p. 172f.

521 E.g., Beatty (1989), p. 694f.; Megginson/Weiss (1991), p. 890f.

		Hsu (2004)	- To provide more certification, VCFs can lease additional reputation from third parties[522]
	VCF's promotion	Habib/Ljungqvist (2001)	- IPO candidates can reduce underpricing by promoting the issue[523] - The benefits from promotion exceed the expenses for reducing information gaps only for deals featuring great information inefficiency[524]
		Relander/Syrjänen/Miettinen (1994)	- VCFs foster M&A exits by tapping their network of private investors - In doing so, the VCF essentially certifies the venture's quality[525]

Table 3: Overview on the exit-related literature

4.2 Methodological Approach

This study pursues the aim of linking the VCF's exit behavior to information asymmetry between inside and outside investors. The predicted relations between these parameters are set out on the basis of a framework. This section elaborates the basic structure of the underlying framework.

4.2.1 Overall Theoretical Framework

This dissertation pursues an empirical research approach. Empirical studies model causal relationships between exogenous factors and endogenous parameters in the form of research hypotheses. These hypotheses are tested on the basis of sample data. In this dissertation, a single hypothesis describes the relationship of one exogenous factor and one endogenous variable so that the direct impact of the

---

[522] Hsu (2004), p. 1805

[523] Habib/Ljungqvist (2001), p. 434f.

[524] Habib/Ljungqvist (2001), p. 455

[525] Relander/Syrjänen/Miettinen (1994), p. 139f.

exogenous factor becomes observable. However, an endogenous variable is typically affected by numerous factors while a single hypothesis captures only one dependency. Moreover, this study contemplates more than one endogenous variable because the VCF's exit strategy is the result of several decisions.[526] Naturally, a single hypothesis cannot encompass this complexity.

In order to describe the emergence of exit strategies as completely as possible, a matrix contrasts both dimensions – the exogenous and endogenous factors. The horizontal axis captures the endogenous parameters whereas the vertical axis lists the exogenous factors. As for the first dimension, the literature exemplifies several origins of information asymmetry. Scholars identify two general sources of information dissimilarity between inside and outside investors: the venture's characteristics and the implications of departures of members of the entrepreneurial management team.[527] A wide research stream also looks into the roles of financial intermediates such as VCFs or investment bankers mitigating information asymmetry through their certification. Besides, the literature analysis and the preceding reasonings inspire the contents of the endogenous dimension. Scholars describe VCFs' exit strategies in terms of timing, exit vehicle and the extent of promotion.[528] Promotion can address the VCF's interactions with prospective investors or the employment of third-parties that certify for the deal.

The matrix, pictured in figure 18, allows for the discussion of every combination of endogenous and exogenous parameters separately. Every discussion results in one hypothesis on how exogenous factors impact endogenous variables. The set of hypotheses represents the research model that is to be validated empirically. Besides providing research hypotheses, the matrix also allows for identifying VCFs' proper reactions to certain types of information asymmetry. The research model offers the VCF four options to include specific information dissimilarities in their exit behavior. The empirical tests will show VCFs' preferred reactions to the five types of information asymmetry. The following tests will validate relevant hypotheses while the remaining options will be rejected. Given this consideration, it is not expected that the entire model will be accepted. The outcomes will rather highlight appropriate reactions of VCFs in certain scenarios.

However, three hypotheses do not stem from information asymmetry reasonings. These hypotheses rather pick up the contradicting results provided in the literature and account for alternative explanations instead of informational concerns of prospective outside investors. These three hypotheses relate:

---

[526] See section 3.2.4

[527] E.g., Bruton/Fried/Hisrich (1997); Bruton/Fried/Hisrich (2000); Fiet/Busenitz/Moesel/Barney (1997); Fredrickson/Hambrick/Baumrin (1988); Sweeting/Wong (1997)

[528] See section 4.1

- The exit's timing to the VCF's seasoning (H 3.1.1)[529]
- The exit vehicle to the VCF's seasoning (H 3.1.2)[530]
- The employment of third-party certification to the VCF's seasoning (3.1.4)[531]

529 Gompers (1996), p. 133ff.; Gompers/Lerner (1999a), p. 30; Milgrom/Roberts (1982), p. 283; Zemke (1995), p. 145f.

530 Gompers (1996), p. 135f.; Wang/Sim (2001), p. 352

531 E.g., Johnson/Miller (1988), p. 20 and p. 28; Logue (1973), p. 100

	Timing	Vehicle	Promotion	3rd-party cert.
Project	- Innovation (H 1.1.1) - Exit stage (H 1.2.1) - Competition (H 1.3.1)	- Innovation (H 1.1.2) - Exit stage (H 1.2.2) - Competition (H 1.3.2)	- Innovation (H 1.1.3) - Exit stage (H 1.2.3) - Competition (H 1.3.3)	- Innovation (H 1.1.4) - Exit stage (H 1.2.4) - Competition (H 1.3.4)
Entre-preneur	- Departures (H 2.1.1)	- Departures (H 2.1.2)	- Departures (H 2.1.3)	- Departures (H 2.1.4)
VCF	- VCF's age (H 3.1.1)	- VCF's age (H 3.1.2)	- VCF's age (H 3.1.3)	- VCF's age (H 3.1.4)

Figure 18: Scheme of hypotheses

4.2.2 Venture Capitalists' Exit Considerations

Section 3.2.4 identifies four major decisions through which VCFs shape their exit strategies: Timing, Exit Vehicle, Promotion and Third-Party Certification. For every transaction, VCFs have to consider the individual parameters of every exit transaction to derive the optimal exit strategy.[532] This section elaborates the general tendencies of the VCF's decisions against the background of changing information costs.

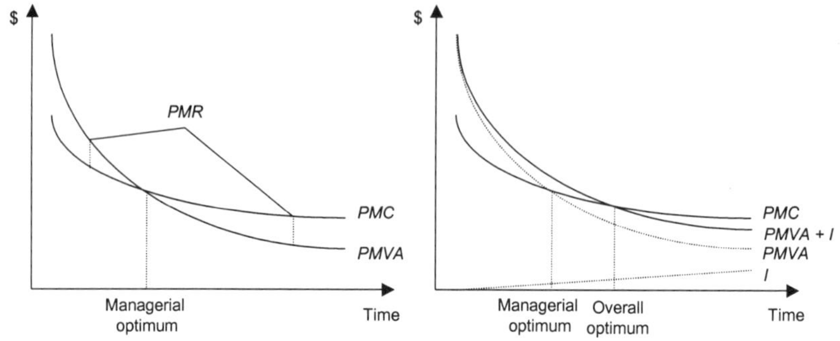

PMC = Projected Marginal Costs; PMVA = Projected Marginal Value Added; PMR = Projected Marginal Return
I = Gains from Improved Information Efficiency

Figure 19: Exit-timing considerations[533]

First, VCFs have to time their exits. Cumming and MacIntosh (2001) set out that the managerial optimum occurs when the projected marginal costs (PMC) of a further commitment to the venture equal the projected marginal value added (PMVA).[534] Thereafter, the VCF's services create no value in excess of the marginal costs anymore. If a VCF exits prior to the managerial optimum, it forgoes the chance of maximizing the proceeds of its involvement. If the VCF exits later, it allocates its resources inefficiently.[535]

In the context of information efficiency, VCFs accrue a specific type of costs upon exit. The more information inefficiency prevails, the more costly and incomplete is the prospective investor's due diligence. Follow-on investors discount their valuation to be compensated for their due diligence efforts and the remaining investment risk. Suppose a venture was not surrounded by information asymmetry at all; the VCF would exit at the Managerial Optimum without considering loses from information asymmetry. If the same venture was suffering from information inefficiency, the VCF's exit would experience discounts. Then, the Managerial Optimum would not represent the optimal solution anymore as it does not include the discounts from in-

---

[532] Further factors are considered as control variables; e.g., for hot issue markets see Ibbotson/Jaffe (1975), p. 1027; Ritter (1984), p. 238f.; see also Chemmanur/Fulghieri (1999), p. 271; Gompers/Lerner (2000), p. 6; Lam (1991), p. 148; Lowry (2003), p. 5; Ljungqvist/Wilhelm (2003), p. 723; Ofek/Richardson (2003), p. 113f.

[533] Based on Cumming/MacIntosh (2001), p. 448

[534] Cumming/MacIntosh (2001), p. 447, consider „all the direct and overhead costs associted with creating value, as well as the opportunity cost associated with alternative deployments of capital".

[535] Cumming/MacIntosh (2001), p. 447f.; Neus/Walz (2001), p. 17

formation inefficiency. As pictured in figure 19, information efficiency – embodied by the I-curve – is the worst at the very beginning of the VC process. Following the discussion in section 1.2, this is why only VCFs provide capital to the venture while alternative sources of funding remain unavailable to the firm. Over time, VCFs improve the venture's credibility and resolve information asymmetries.[536] In the sense of this study, growing information efficiency translates into less discounts respectively higher valuations for the VCF's stakes elevating the PMVA + I curve over the PMVA curve. The more potential for establishing information efficiency exists (I), the more the VCF delays the exits. In the sense of Cumming and MacIntosh's (2001) model, VCFs incorporate higher information efficiency potentials in their exit strategy in that they postpone exits and vice versa to optimize their proceeds as illustrated in figure 19.

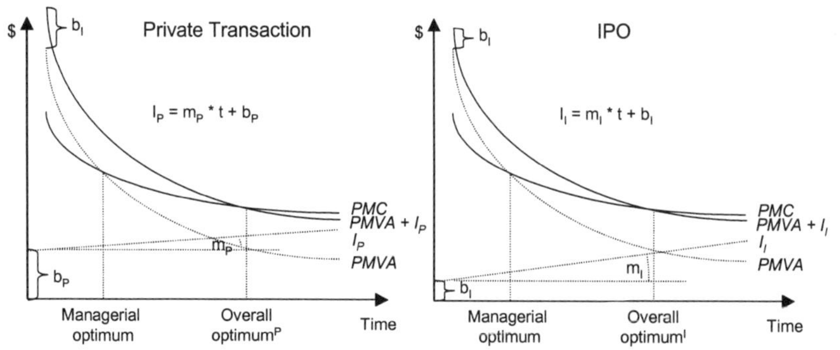

PMC = Projected Marginal Costs; PMVA = Projected Marginal Value Added; PMR = Projected Marginal Return
I = Gains from Improved Information Efficiency

Figure 20: Exit channel considerations

Second, VCFs have to commit to an exit vehicle. Several studies set out that the IPO generally constitutes the value maximizing solution.[537] From an information asymmetry perspective, both, the IPO and the trade sale are yet associated with specific advantages and disadvantages which may alter this perception in varying scenarios. For simplicity, this analysis presumes that if VCFs select the follow-on investor that resolves the information asymmetry surrounding the transaction best, they optimize their proceeds from the exit.[538] The extent of information efficiency as illustrated in figure 20 varies for private and public investors. Every investor's perception of information efficiency over time – as pictured in the I-curve – is characterized by

---

[536] Barry/Muscarella/Peavy/Vetsuypens (1990), p. 448; Bygrave/Timmons (1992), p. 208; Gompers (1996), p. 153f.; Megginson/Weiss (1991), p. 881; Neus/Walz (2001), p. 17; Sahlman (1997), p. 107

[537] E.g., Lam (1991) ; Zingales (1995)

[538] Pagano/Panetta/Zingales (1998), p. 36; Cumming/Fleming (2003), p. 5

two factors: the investor's initial endowment of information (b) and his ability to collect and process information over time (m). In general, the industrial investor's expertise gives him a constant information advantage over public investors; public investor can never establish a similar systematic understanding of the venture's industry, markets and technologies because they do not operate in the venture's industry ($b_p > b_I$).[539] However, capital markets have superior capabilities in acquiring and processing public information; they outnumber private investors, are more likely to find serendipitous information and confer about their findings ($m_I > m_p$).[540] Initially, the private investor capitalizes on his background. Given that the venture releases new information over time, the public investors begin to benefit from their advantages in processing public information only in later periods. Eventually, public investors can reduce their information costs to the same extent as the private investor. This point is characterized by the relative differences in the investor's abilities.

$$t_0 = \frac{(b_I - b_p)}{(m_p - m_I)} = \frac{-\Delta b}{\Delta m} \quad \text{(Equilibrium for the choice of follow-on investors)}$$

Thereafter, the IPO becomes the more information efficient and thus cheaper option. Initially, the VCF's timing decision *t* predetermines the exit vehicle. If the venture has already released information to the public at this point, VCFs are likely to float the venture ($|\Delta m| >> |\Delta b|$). If the venture's information is kept private, the VCF is likely to sell the firm privately ($|\Delta b| >> |\Delta m|$).

However, the occurrence of hot issue markets shifts t_o forward. In hot issue markets, investors tolerate more information asymmetry and impose fewer discounts on the VCF's exit.[541] If the VCF wishes to capitalize on hot issue markets, it is likely to choose the IPO. Besides seeking to optimize the exit's monetary returns, the VCF may as well prioritize to build its reputation. Even though IPOs do not always prove more profitable than trade sales, the VCF's ambition to establish a reputation through visible transactions may prompt it to float most ventures rather than looking out for more efficient alternatives.[542] The VCF's reputation gain may then trade off the loss from facilitating IPOs. While information efficiency results either in an IPO or a private transaction, reputation building narrows the choice down to the IPO.

Third, the VCF has to configure its involvement in the exit process. VCFs that are actively seeking to exit are denoted as involved investors. VCFs that abstain from promoting the exit are considered as passive. Habib and Ljungqvist (2001) argue that VCFs can influence the underpricing – respectively the ex-ante information spreads –

---

[539] Chemmanur/Fulghieri (1999), p. 271; Cumming/MacIntosh (2001), p. 446
[540] Chemmanur/Fulghieri (1999), p. 271
[541] Lowry (2003), p. 5; Ofek/Richardson (2003), p. 113f.; Neus/Walz (2001), p. 17
[542] Gompers (1996), p. 135f.; Wang/Sim (2001), p. 352

through the intensity of their interactions with follow-on investors.[543] By promoting a venture, the VCF essentially resolves information asymmetry and lowers the discounts upon exit while passive VCFs encounter the original information spreads. Yet, VCFs cannot step up their promotion for every venture. Rather, the decision to increase promotion is subject to two considerations. First, the VCF's involvement does not come cheap. Active VCFs incur costs for informing investors. Second, VCFs carry opportunity costs for neglecting other transactions. Given limited resources, the VCF cannot offer the same intensity of commitment to every transaction. If the VCF devotes more attention to one transaction, another transaction automatically receives less. Thus, the VCF has not only to decide on its involvement on the level of an individual venture. Rather it has to consider the whole portfolio of investments in order to allocate its promotion efforts in such way that it maximizes the overall outcome.[544] Provided that the VCF wants to exit two ventures simultaneously, it is likely to allocate more promotion to the venture whose transaction is hampered by information asymmetry.

While the VCF's promotion addresses the question of whether the VCF engages in interactions with outsiders to foster exits at all, VCFs must also decide whether they lease additional certification to overcome information dissimilarities or not. To provide a more effective certification, VCFs can acquire reputation from third parties.[545] Several studies suggest that investors attribute less uncertainty about the fair valuation to transactions backed by well-known thrid-parties while the presence of less prestigious parties does not diminish their concerns so much.[546] Common models outline that investment bankers represent third parties that can provide certification for a transaction and hence resolve informational concerns of follow-on investors.[547] It is argued that investment banks gain reputation through a continuously fairly pricing of transactions. Investors project this pattern to future transactions assuming proper valuations.[548] Had the investment bank overpriced a deal, it would lose its reputation. The investment bank then encounters more suspicious investors in future transactions which demand higher underpricings in the future.[549] Falsely certifying eventually imposes costs on investment banks.[550] Public investors thus as-

---

[543] Habib/Ljungqvist (2001), p. 435

[544] MacMillan/Kulow/Khoylian (1989), p. 37

[545] Hsu (2004), p. 1805

[546] E.g., Baron (1982), p. 955ff.; Beatty/Ritter (1986), p. 214ff.; Booth/Smith (1986), p. 261; Carter/Dark/Singh (1998), p. 285ff.; Carter/Manaster (1990), p. 1062; Johnson/Miller (1988), p. 28; McDonald/Fisher (1972), p. 102; Megginson/Weiss (1991), p. 879; Neuberger/Hammond (1974), p. 172f.

[547] Johnson/Miller (1988), p. 19f.

[548] Beatty/Ritter (1986), p. 214

[549] Logue (1973), p. 92

[550] Booth/Chua (1996), p. 292; Booth/Smith (1990), p. 266ff.; Milgrom/Roberts (1982), p. 283

cribe particular credibility to the statements and certification of prestigious banks.[551] Even though research agrees that if VCFs acquire certification from investment banks they can enhance exits, VCFs must contrast the following trade-off:[552]

- Leasing additional reputation may accelerate the occurrence of information efficiency so that the VCF can exit earlier, access more exit vehicles and reduce its promotion efforts.
- Yet, the reputational capital of investment banks varies. So does the certification they can provide and the fees they demand.[553] Established underwriters charge higher underwriting fees as compared to less established investment banks. Seasoned underwriters also demand a higher initial underpricing lowering the VCF's immediate proceeds at exit.[554] In support of this argumentation, table 4 shows the correlation between high quality underwriters and the fee structure as well as the initial underpricing in the original data sample on which this study is based. However, Carter, Dark and Singh (1998) as well as McDonald and Fisher (1972) show that enlisting prestigious underwriters translates into a superior performance of the issue over a three-year period.[555]

	N	Investment bank's market share	
		Spearman-Rho	*Significance*
Fees	529	0.244	0.000***
IPO First-day-return	1,108	0.143	0.000***

* significant on a 10 % level; ** significant on a 5 % level; *** significant on a 1 % level

Table 4: Impact of the investment banker's quality on the underpricing and fee structure[556]

Consequently, VCFs only employ third-party certification in transactions in which the potential to trade off discounts exceeds the investment bank's fees. If not, the fees for affiliating with prestigious investment banks will not be recouped through reduced information costs. Involving third-party certification then becomes inefficient.

This thesis assumes that VCFs make all four decisions contingent on the three factors – the venture's business, the VC relationship and its current reputation. The research model discusses how VCFs decide in different scenarios.

---

[551] Johnson/Miller (1988), p. 20

[552] Johnson/Miller (1988), p. 19

[553] Carter/Manaster (1990), p. 1051ff.; Megginson/Weiss (1991), p. 900f.

[554] Bradley/Jordan (2002), p. 613; Habib/Ljungqvist (2001), p. 452ff.; Michaely/Shaw (1994), p. 315; see Hsu (2004), p. 1806, for a more general view on the costs of affiliation with third-parties

[555] Carter/Dark/Singh (1998), p. 301f.; McDonald/Fisher (1972), p. 97

[556] The sample comprises data from VC-backed IPOs in the period 1997 to 2002

4.3 The Venture's Business as Source for Information Asymmetries

This section sets out how the venture's business affects the distribution of information upon exit and the impact on the VCF's exit strategy. To fathom the emergence of information dissimilarities more precisely, the venture's business is described by the degree of innovation, its development stage and the extent of competition the venture faces.

4.3.1 Degree of Innovation

VCFs typically fund innovative projects.[557] An innovation generally refers to a new product, a new market, a new technology or combinations of these aspects.[558] The degree of innovation is the lowest if a venture places a new product based on common technologies in an existing market. This setting entails almost no information asymmetry; information about R&D results is observable and the product's market acceptance is predictable since market preferences are apparent. The degree of innovation gradually increases if the venture targets new markets with existing technologies or introduces new technologies into existing markets.[559] The highest degree of innovation occurs if a venture enters a new market with a new technology. The nature of newness impacts the distribution of information in that

- only the entrepreneur has accumulated extensive knowledge about the market, technology or both throughout the invention.[560] In the absence of similar experiences and knowledge, outsiders suffer from information asymmetry.[561]
- the outsider's lack of specific knowledge allows the insider to hide negative information about bad market experiences, technology flaws or both.[562]

Scholars conclude that the more innovative the business is the more information inefficiency prevails between insiders and outsiders.[563] Bradley and Jordan (2002) presume an IPO's underpricing to correlate with the degree of information asymmetry and compare average first-day returns across industries. Consistent with the present argumentation, Bradley and Jordan report a higher underpricing prevailing in innova-

---

[557] Black/Gilson (1998), p. 245; Cumming/MacIntosh (2001), p. 445f.; Gompers (1995), p. 1487; Lam (1991), p. 137

[558] Rothwell (1986), p. 111ff.; Schumpeter (1947), p. 149; for simplicity, the present analysis focuses on these types of innovation and excludes further aspects.

[559] Deeds/Decarolis/Coombs (1997), p. 32

[560] Anand/Galetovic (2000), p. 616; Campbell (1979), p. 915

[561] Baum/Silvermann (2004), p. 415; Bygrave (1988), p. 137; Eisenhardt (1989a), p. 64; Sapienza/Gupta (1994), p. 1618; Schefczyk (2004), p. 67f.

[562] See sections 1.2.2, 1.2.3 and 1.2.4

[563] Bourgeois/Eisenhardt (1988), p. 816; Janney/Folta (2003), p. 362; Schmeisser/Krimphove (2001), p. 87; Weimerskirch (1999), p. 34f.

tive industries than across non-innovative sectors.[564] Table 5 analyzes the first-day-returns of VC-backed IPOs from 1994 to 2003 on the data basis of this dissertation and confirms the elaborations of Bradley and Jordan; the differences between Non-High-Technology and other industries are significant. The so-called High-Technology sectors – including Communication & Media, Computer Related, Life Sciences and Semiconductor ventures – feature higher average first day-returns than the Non-High-Technology sector. Only the Biotechnology and Life Sciences industries are not consistent with this picture.[565] In essence, information disadvantages hamper the outside investor's due diligence and impose information costs on him.

	N	*Mean*	*SD*	*t*-test *p*-value 2.	3.	4.	5.	6.
1. Biotechnology	98	21.44	40.30	0.000***	0.000***	0.123	0.354	0.008***
2. Comm. & Media	206	80.61	104.03		0.003***	0.000***	0.000***	0.001***
3. Computer Related	377	57.34	79.22			0.000***	0.000***	0.058*
4. Life Sciences	146	15.49	19.00				0.432	0.000***
5. Non-High-Tech.	275	17.72	30.94					0.000***
6. Semiconductors	100	41.11	61.12					

* significant on a 10 % level; ** significant on a 5 % level; *** significant on a 1 % level

Table 5: Differences in the first-day-returns in VC-backed IPOs across industries

a) Timing

The consideration of two extreme scenarios underlines the impact of innovations on the exit timing. The least innovative venture places a new product based on common technologies in existing markets. Outside investors can immediately access public information about the venture's technologies and the product's market acceptance. Thus, outsiders hardly suffer from information asymmetry. The most innovative venture enters new markets with new technologies. In this scenario, only the entrepreneur has developed relevant expertise. Due to the newness of the venture's technologies and markets, outside investors cannot access public information for a thorough due diligence. Allen and Gale (1998) confirm that immediately after an innovation occurs, hardly any information and experiences are available to support an outside investor's due diligence.[566] This setting is consequently characterized by the greatest information asymmetry between inside and outside investors as regards both the technology and the markets.[567] Based on this reasoning, Cumming and

---

[564] Bradley/Jordan (2002), p. 613, see also Certo/Daily/Dalton (2001), p. 34; Easley/O'Hara (2004), p. 1578

[565] The exceptional character of Biotechnology ventures is addressed in sections 6.1.2 a) and 6.1.3 a).

[566] Allen/Gale (1998), p. 69f.

[567] Robinson/van Osnabrugge (2001), p. 31

MacIntosh (2001) as well as Shepherd and Zacharakis (2001a) suggest that high-technology ventures generally require longer holding periods than low-technology ventures. Both articles link the VC duration to the venture's industry affiliation reasoning that follow-on investors have to resolve different extents of information asymmetry across sectors.[568] Chemmanur and Fulghieri (1999) argue similarly that more complex technologies require longer holding periods since it takes outside investors more time to accumulate sufficient information to assess the innovation.[569] If a VCF wanted to exit a non-innovative venture and an innovative venture simultaneously, the latter would be more costly.[570] The prospective investor would have to collect more information at higher costs. These costs in turn increase the prospective investor's discounts and lessen the VCF's proceeds.

The longer the venture operates, the more it resolves prospective investors' uncertainties.[571] To resolve the additional information asymmetry and to lower the costs for exiting in the innovative setting to the level of costs for exiting in the non-innovative scenario, the VCF can wait until details about the innovative venture's products, markets and technologies have spread publicly. The following hypothesis picks up this argumentation.

H. 1.1.1 The higher the degree of innovation the longer is the VC holding period.

b) Exit vehicle

A major concern of VCFs addresses the difficulty of outside investors to assess a venture upon exit. If the least innovative venture accomplishes an exit, information about the markets, products and technologies are publicly accessible. However, outside investors can generally not access information on innovative ventures given that no public knowledge exists on the venture's markets, technologies or both.[572] Yet, different groups of follow-on investors possess different abilities to resolve information asymmetry and consequently accrue different information costs.[573] Chemmanur and Fulghieri (1999) demonstrate that the prospective investors' information gaps are contingent on two factors: the investor's ability to collect information and to process it. First, public investors are superior in gathering public information, such as the product's market acceptance for instance, since they outnumber private investors by far.

---

568 Cumming/MacIntosh (2001), p. 446; Shepherd/Zacharakis (2001a), p. 66

569 Chemmanur/Fulghieri (1999), p. 271

570 Cumming/MacIntosh (2001), p. 449; Elango/Fried/Hisrich/Polonchek (1995), p. 159; Hinkel (2001), p. 36; Janney/Folta (2003), p. 364; Schmeisser/Krimphove (2001), p. 87

571 Chemmanur/Fulghieri (1999), p. 252 and p. 255f.; Lam (1991), p. 144f.

572 Booth/Chua (1996), p. 294; Habib/Ljungqvist (2001), p. 433f.; Maksimovic/Pichler (1999), p. 2; Marshall (1998), p. 1081; Petty/Shulman/Bygrave (1994), p. 44; Welch (1989),p. 421f.

573 Cumming/MacIntosh (2001), p. 446

Second, public investors exchange information and confer about their knowledge as opposed to competing private investors.[574] However, internal information about the venture's resources and potentials cannot be found in public unless the venture deliberately releases pertaining details.[575] Unlike public investors, private investors benefit from their experience with similar projects enabling them to establish a basic understanding of the venture's internal circumstances even if the venture is reluctant to disclose information.[576] This distinction implies that public investors suffer from information gaps about intrinsic values more than private investors. But public investors benefit more from public information.[577] If the venture's operations allow for many observations, public investors can capitalize on their advantages and resolve their uncertainty more efficiently than private investors.[578] Conversely, settings that feature high information inefficiency advantage private investors.

VCFs can minimize the follow-on investor's concerns and discounts if they sell innovative ventures that are more difficult to evaluate for outsiders to private investors. For non-innovative ventures, public investors perceive less information gaps and yield lower discounts. VCFs are consequently more likely to float non-innovative ventures than innovative ventures.

H. 1.1.2 The higher the degree of innovation the more likely are trade sales.

c) Promotion

If an exit is impeded because of the prospective investors' shortcomings in assessing the venture's business, VCFs can take actions to improve information efficiency. Habib and Ljungqvist (2001) set out that VCFs can enhance information efficiency in promoting an exit.[579] Relander, Syrjänen and Miettinen's (1994) findings support this notion. They hold that VCFs alleviate prospective investors' concerns in that they circulate information and certify for a transaction. To do so, VCFs tap their networks of financial intermediaries and prospective investors.[580]

The VCF's concerns about reputation and limited resources, however, call for a selective approach. Given that more innovative ventures are more difficult to assess

---

[574] Chemmanur/Fulghieri (1999), p. 271

[575] Bader (1996), p. 147; Bascha (2001), p. 39ff.; Cumming/MacIntosh (2001), p. 453f; Cumming/MacIntosh (2003), p. 514; Kohers/Kohers (2001), p. 36; Relander/Syrjänen/Miettinen (1994), p. 135ff.; Wang/Sim (2001), p. 341

[576] Chemmanur/Fulghieri (1999), p. 271

[577] Cumming/MacIntosh (2003), p. 520; Stoughton/Wong/Zechner (2001), p. 379, explicitly refer to public markets as "uninformed investors"

[578] Chemmanur/Fulghieri (1999), p. 271

[579] Habib/Ljungqvist (2001), p. 434f.

[580] Relander/Syrjänen/Miettinen (1994), p. 139f.

for outside investors, VCFs must engage in a more intense promotion to facilitate their exits. As opposed to highly innovative ventures, low innovative ventures are easier to gauge and impose less information costs on outside investors. Hence, VCFs are assumed to commit more promotion to innovative ventures while they devote fewer efforts to endorse exits of non-innovative ventures.

H. 1.1.3 *The higher the degree of innovation the more the VCF engages in promoting the venture.*

d) Third-party certification

Building on hypothesis 1.1.3, VCFs can also resolve uncertainties in that they lease additional certification from investment bankers. The presence of investment bankers can confirm the correctness of valuations and disperse outside investors' concerns about the venture's valuation. Yet, investors ascribe more credibility to the certification of investment banks with longer track records of fairly priced transactions. In settings of great heterogeneity, seasoned investment banks convey more credible information about proper valuation than less seasoned investment banks.[581] VCFs can virtually choose the extent of third-party certification by selecting a particular investment bank.

However, Habib and Ljungqvist (2001) observe that the benefits from third-party certification only exceed the costs for hiring investment bankers' certification in settings of severe information asymmetry.[582] Given that more innovative ventures feature higher information asymmetry, third-party certification is more likely to be beneficial in withdrawals from innovative ventures than in non-innovative environments. Innovative ventures hence call for a more intense third-party certification than non-innovative ventures.

H. 1.1.4 *The higher the degree of innovation the more third-party certification is required.*

4.3.2 Development Level

Because most ventures are founded on the basis of one product, the firm's development initially follows the life-cycle model of the product itself.[583] This dependency prevails until the venture launches further products or services.[584] If the ven-

---

[581] Booth/Smith (1990), p. 266ff; Carter/Manaster (1990), p. 1051ff.; Certo/Daily/Dalton (2001), p. 41; Cumming/MacIntosh (2003), p. 520; Megginson/Weiss (1991), p. 900f.; Milgrom/Roberts (1982), p. 283

[582] Habib/Ljungqvist (2001), p. 454f.

[583] Engelmann/Juncker/Natusch/Tebroke (2000), p. 25; Schiereck (1973), p. 55

[584] Mellewigt/Witt (2002), p. 84f.; Ruhnka/Young (1987), p. 169; Schween (1996), p. 96

ture's product is surrounded by information asymmetry, the venture is too. The life-cycle model reflects the improvement of information efficiency about the venture's products contingent on the accomplishment of interim goals. At the very beginning, only the entrepreneur accumulates knowledge about the venture's markets and technologies.[585] But the venture has not yet spread information in public. Given their lack of insights, outsiders cannot assess the early stage venture. The outsider's information gap moreover allows the insider to hide negative information about bad market experiences, technology flaws or both.[586] However, throughout its maturity, the venture circulates information about its achievements that is publicly accessible such as successful market tests, the product's successful market introduction and the market's acceptance. The product's market performance essentially conveys information about the market acceptance and the technological quality to outsiders. In doing so, the venture resolves information spreads between inside and outside investors.[587] This analysis picks up the ventures' development level at exit and looks into the consequences on the exit strategy.

a) Timing

Assuming that the VCF wants to exit an early stage and a late stage venture simultaneously, outsiders can access more public information for the later stage venture than for the early stage venture. The venture's transition to higher development levels is triggered by the accomplishment of interim goals such as R&D completion or first revenues.[588] The outside investor can essentially observe the later stage venture's quality on the basis of its market and technological performance. Outside investors, however, suffer from information asymmetry about early stage ventures because they cannot access public information about the venture's performance. Thus, outside investors step up their discounts. Early stage exits are always more costly than later stage exits.

VCFs incorporate the follow-on investors' concerns in their exit timing and exit only ventures that have already accomplished certain stages. The faster a venture passes through the development model, the earlier it arrives at proper exit stages. Moreover, ventures that fulfil the requirements for each stage more quickly emphasize their quality to prospective investors. The extreme opposite are so-called "living dead" investments that virtually remain in an early development stage for ever. All else equal, these ventures eventually require an endless holding period until they

---

[585] Anand/Galetovic (2000), p. 616; Campbell (1979), p. 915

[586] See sections 1.2.2, 1.2.3 and 1.2.4

[587] Janney/Folta (2003), p. 363; Sapienza (1992), p. 12f.; Weimerskirch (1999), p. 34f.; Ruhnka/Young (1991), p. 125ff., report that internal risks decrease with the venture's maturity

[588] Chemmanur/Fulghieri (1999), p. 249f.; Maksimovic/Pichler (2001), p. 460f. and p. 484; Subrahmanyam/Titman (1999), p. 1075

progress to possible exit stages.[589] The venture's pace in progressing to exit levels is thus assumed to negatively correlate with the holding duration.

H. 1.2.1 The faster a venture progresses the earlier the VCF exits.

b) Exit vehicle

Unlike a later stage venture, early stage ventures do not spread information in public. Ventures in early stages concentrate on internal activities such as R&D, establishing organizational structures or building joint ventures with incumbent industrialists. Neither are these activities observable for outside investors nor is the entrepreneur likely to circulate this information in public. In fact, the entrepreneur may rather withhold information to protect his proprietary assets and maintain his competitive advantage.[590] Ventures in later stages launch their products into the market. In doing so, they essentially circulate information in public.[591]

Private and public investors benefit from this development differently.[592] Chemmanur and Fulghieri (1999) demonstrate that private investors can revert to their industry expertise to assess the venture's internal measures while public investors lack relevant industry knowledge.[593] However, once the venture spreads information publicly, public markets begin capitalizing on their superior ability in gathering and processing public information.[594]

If the VCF wants to exit an early stage venture, private investors benefit from their industry background and suffer from less information gaps than public investors. Thus, the private transaction is the more information efficient solution. If the VCF exits a later stage venture, public and private investors can access public information. Yet, public investors can resolve their information gaps even better and discount the transaction less. In later stage exits, the public transaction thus constitutes the value maximizing solution for the VCF.[595]

H. 1.2.2 The earlier the venture's development stage at exit the more likely it will

---

[589] Ruhnka/Feldman/Dean (1992), p. 138f.; Wang/Sim (2001), p. 343; Wright/Robbie/Romanet/Thompson/Joachimsson/Bruining/Herst (1994), p. 103f.

[590] Yosha (1995), p. 3ff.

[591] Chemmanur/Fulghieri (1999), p. 271; Fama/Jensen (1985), p. 117ff.; Lam (1991), p. 148; see Jensen (1986), p. 323, on the monitoring ability of public markets

[592] Cumming/MacIntosh (2001), p. 446

[593] Chemmanur/Fulghieri (1999), p. 271

[594] Bader (1996), p. 147; Bascha (2001), p. 39ff.; Cumming/MacIntosh (2001), p. 453f; Cumming/MacIntosh (2003), p. 514; Kohers/Kohers (2001), p. 36; Relander/Syrjänen/Miettinen (1994), p. 135ff.; Wang/Sim (2001), p. 341

[595] Cumming/Fleming (2003), p. 5

be sold to private investors.

c) Promotion

As previously outlined, new information surfaces once the ventures accomplishes a higher development level. Thus, follow-on investors suffer less informational disadvantages the higher the venture's development level. To overcome prospective investors' information disadvantages in early stage exits, the VCF can engage in promotion. In the sense of Habib and Ljungqvist (2001) and Relander, Syrjänen and Miettinen (1994), the VCF thus supplements investors with internal information to lessen their information disadvantages.[596]

The VCF has to engage in promotion in earlier stages in order to facilitate exits while information asymmetry would otherwise deter investors or cause relatively high discounts. Investors are less likely to be deterred in more information efficient settings in later stage exits and impose fewer discounts. Accordingly, the need for VCFs to promote an exit decreases for later stage ventures. If the VCF wants to exit an early stage and a later stage venture at the same time but is limited in its promotion resources, it will devote more promotion to facilitate the early stage transaction.

H. 1.2.3 *VCFs promote exits of early stage ventures more than later stage divestments.*

d) Third-party certification

The extent of information asymmetry associated which every development level may additionally impact the necessity for third-party certification. Given that higher uncertainties prevail in earlier stages, follow-on investors in general will be more careful when investing. In contrast, later stage exits are accompanied by higher information efficiency allowing investors a more precise due diligence.

In order to diminish prospective investors' information disadvantages upon exits, the VCF can lease additional reputation. Yet, Habib and Ljungqvist (2001) outline that the benefits from the investment banker's certification only trade off the increased fees in settings of severe information asymmetry.[597] Consequently, VCFs are assumed to incur costs for third-party certification in early stage exits – to smooth prospective investors' concerns. Later stage withdrawals, however, do not benefit from the presence of seasoned investment banks so much anymore. Hence, VCFs lease less third-party certification the higher the venture's development level at exit.

---

[596] Habib/Ljungqvist (2001), p. 434f.; Relander/Syrjänen/Miettinen (1994), p. 139f.

[597] Habib/Ljungqvist (2001), p. 455

H. 1.2.4 *VCFs lease more third-party certification for early stage exits than for later stage withdrawals.*

4.3.3 Competitive Environment

Competition also affects the distribution of information. In a competitive setting, ventures are forced to circulate information in order to promote their products over the competitors' products. Simultaneously, rivals produce public information to endorse their products. Conversely, ventures that encounter no competition face less pressure to promote their activities. In fact, they may rather wish to maintain secrecy so that prospective competitors cannot copy their business.[598] Their proprietary knowledge essentially serves as an entry barrier for new competitors and protects their business.[599] Competition consequently translates into greater information efficiency.[600] At any given point in time, ventures in competitive environments are surrounded by higher information efficiency and thus feature fewer discounts through concerned investors than ventures in non-competitive environments.

a) Timing

Public markets and private investors appreciate competition because it generates public information about the venture, the technology and customers' preferences. In non-competitive environments, prospective investors face more information asymmetry and have to step up their discounts. If the VCF exits a venture in a competitive environment and a venture in a non-competitive setting, it would consequently incur fewer discounts in the first transaction. If the VCF wishes to lower the discounts of the latter transaction to the level of the first transaction, it can allow the venture more time to generate public information. Thus, the venture in the non-competitive market can establish a similar degree of information efficiency. VCFs are hence supposed to sell ventures in non-competitive settings later than ventures in competitive settings to avoid the greater discounts.

H. 1.3.1 The more competitive the venture's environment the earlier VCFs exit.

b) Exit vehicle

Given the exit of a non-competitive and a competitive venture, follow-on investors can access different information. The second venture endorses its products over

---

[598] Cumming/MacIntosh (2003), p. 517; Schröder (1992), p. 252; Temple (1999), p. 101f.

[599] Yosha (1995), p. 3ff.

[600] See Elango/Fried/Hisrich/Polonchek (1995), p. 159 and Schwienbacher (2001), p. 2f., for aspects of competition in innovative settings

the rival's products. Thus, the venture spreads information about the product's market and the technologies in public. Ventures in non-competitive environments lack pressure to circulate information in public. Outside investors consequently suffer from the absence of public information and have to commit to a more expensive due diligence.[601]

However, as Chemmanur and Fulghieri (1999) argue, public and private investors have different capabilities of coping with both scenarios. In competitive settings, public investors capitalize on their superiority in gathering and processing public information. The public investors' information disadvantage against insiders are hence lower than the private investors' information gaps in competitive settings. In contrast, private investors employ their industry expertise to perform better due diligence than public markets on ventures that do not have to release information in the absence of rivals.[602] Thus, public finance is cheaper in competitive settings and private funding in non-competitive environments. If a VCF exits a non-competitive venture, the value maximizing solution is the private investor. If a VCF sells a highly competitive venture, public markets will impose fewer discounts on the VCF.

H. 1.3.2 The more competition the venture faces the more likely it will be exited via an IPO.

c) Promotion

If a VCF exits ventures in a non-competitive and a competitive environment simultaneously, the latter exit is less hampered by a general lack of public information. In contrast, the exit of the non-competitive venture happens in a relatively information inefficient setting. The transaction in the non-competitive setting imposes more information asymmetry on prospective investors resulting in higher discounts or a greater likelihood of investors being deterred.

VCFs can engage in promotion to improve information efficiency – particularly in the non-competitive scenario.[603] Given that more innovative ventures are more difficult to assess for outside investors and the VCF can only devote a limited extend of promotion to both exits, VCFs must engage in a more intense promotion to facilitate information inefficient exits and to alleviate severe discounts. In turn, information efficient exits in competitive environments obtain less endorsement.

---

[601] Subrahmanyam/Titman (1999), p. 1065f.

[602] Bascha (2001), p. 39ff.; Chemmanur/Fulghieri (1999), p. 271; Cumming/MacIntosh (2001), p. 453f; Cumming/MacIntosh (2003), p. 514; Kohers/Kohers (2001), p. 36; Relander/Syrjänen/Miettinen (1994), p. 135ff.; Wang/Sim (2001), p. 341

[603] Habib/Ljungqvist (2001), p. 434f.; Relander/Syrjänen/Miettinen (1994), p. 139f.

H. 1.3.3 *The more competitive the venture's environment the less promotion efforts VCFs incur.*

d) Third-party certification

Presuming that competition sets information about the venture free, prospective investors face higher information efficiency in highly competitive settings in comparison to low-competitive environments. Given the presence of competition, VCFs have to incur fewer efforts to resolve information asymmetries. With increasing competition, VCFs consequently need to employ less third-party certification to foster withdrawals. Contrary thereto, low competitive environments feature higher information inefficiency between inside and outside investors. In order to alleviate information spreads, VCFs may have to complement their promotion with third-party certification. Third-party certification then assists the outside investor in discriminating high quality from low quality ventures. In essence, VCFs can make up for lower information efficiency in non-competitive settings in that they employ more third party certification. If competition prevails, the higher degree of information efficiency makes third-party certification redundant.

H. 1.3.4 *The more competitive the venture's environment the less third-party certification VCFs lease.*

4.4 Ex-Ante Uncertainty after Departures of Entrepreneurial Team Members

In the VC context, departures of entrepreneurial team members occur in two variations: as dismissals or as divestments of members of the entrepreneurial team. Both incidents are generally accompanied by a signalling effect that affects outsiders' perception of the venture.[604]

Research frequently looks into the quality of the relationship between the VCF and the entrepreneur.[605] Researchers argue that the quality of the VC relationship impacts the quality of the venture. Sapienza and Gupta (1994) point out that in joining efforts, the VCF and the entrepreneur overcome the venture's initial struggles more effectively.[606] Cable and Shane (1997) argue that the venture's performance can only be optimized if both parties cooperate.[607] Gompers (1995) indirectly supports this reasoning in that he confirms the positive effect of a healthy VC relationship

[604] Janney/Folta (2003), p. 361f.; Keasey/Short (1997), p. 75f.; Marshall (1998), p. 1081
[605] E.g., Cable/Shane (1997); Gorman/Sahlman (1989); Sahlman (1990); Sapienza/Gupta (1994)
[606] Sapienza/Gupta (1994), p. 1620
[607] Cable/Shane (1997), p. 170f.

on the occurrence of IPOs.[608] Yet, the separation of ownership and management causes agency problems. VCFs employ several means to prevent entrepreneurs from disruptive behavior – as outlined in chapter 2.3.2 d). The ultimate threat, however, is the replacement of opportunistic and ineffective members of the entrepreneurial team. If the quality of the VC relationship turns bad, VCFs eventually dismiss ineffective and opportunistic managers.[609] In the absence of observable information by which to judge the cooperation between VCF and entrepreneur, outside investors may interpret a dismissal as an indicator of a malfunctioning VC relationship and for a struggling business concept. The following sections set out how this signal impacts outside investors' perception of the venture's quality and the consequences on the VCF's exit strategy.

In line with research on signalling in capital markets, outside investors look upon the divestment of insiders as an indicator of overvaluation.[610] Since insiders access non-public data, they incorporate more information in their valuation than outsiders.[611] The insider's incentive to withdraw arises when his information advantage prompts him to lower his valuation while the markets' valuation is still unaffected from the private information.[612] Insider trading thus signals that insiders withhold negative information.[613] Given that entrepreneurs usually commit most of their wealth to the venture, they do essentially not diversify their investments. In essence, the entrepreneur's wealth is tied to the venture's success. If the venture fails and cannot return the entrepreneur's investment, the entrepreneur loses his wealth. To preserve his funds, the entrepreneur may withdraw once he detects unfavorable trends while outsiders still look favorably upon the venture. Departures of entrepreneurial team members thus raise information asymmetry concerns of prospective investors.

a) Timing

The comparison of two extreme scenarios shows how departures of entrepreneurial team members impact the VCF's timing strategy. If no departures occur, the follow-on investor has no reason to be concerned about the VC-relationship and/or

---

[608] Gompers (1995), p. 1482ff.

[609] Fiet/Busenitz/Moesel/Barney (1997), p. 349; Fredrickson/Hambrick/Baumrin (1988), p. 255; Oviatt (1988), p. 214; Walsh/Seward (1990), p. 421; Sweeting/Wong (1997), p. 127, report that dismissals occur surprisingly often.

[610] Janney/Folta (2003), p. 361f.

[611] Keasey/Short (1997), p. 75f.

[612] E.g., Lerner (1994b), p. 16; see also Cumming/MacIntosh (2003), p. 517f. for the VCF's divestment; see Bradley/Jordan (2002), p. 597f., for a general model of divestments in IPOs

[613] E.g., Espenlaub/Tonks (1998), p. 1037f.; see also Allen/Faulhaber (1989); Ambarish/Kose/Williams (1987); Constantinides/Grundy (1989); Grinblatt/Hwang (1989); Janney/Folta (2003); Keasey/Sort (1997); Marshall (1998); see Morris (1987) on general impacts of signals on public valuations of securities

insiders being privy about negative information. If, however, members of the entrepreneurial team depart from the investment, the prospective investor must assume either a malfunctioning VC-relationship, information advantages of insiders or both. While the initial scenario does not impact the prospective investors' general information gaps, the second scenario increases his concerns about the reasons and consequences of the departure. In fact, dismissals immediately increase ex-ante uncertainty since failure is obvious and both, the appropriateness of the dismissal and the capabilities of new management members (in case of replacements) are not observable to outside investors. Not until the dismissal has been justified through improved performance is the outside investors' ex-ante uncertainty reduced. In support of this argumentation, Bruton, Fried and Hisrich (1998) find that replacements do not entail immediate changes since the new management cannot respond promptly to the causes of failure; they have to establish an understanding of their new tasks first.[614] Hence, dismissals require the VCF to prove their appropriateness delaying exits in comparison to ventures that avoid dismissals.

Similarly, the negative signal emanating from entrepreneurs' divestments can only be falsified if new information surfaces in the long-term that ascribes the entrepreneurs' divestment to other reasons than awareness of pending negative events. Prospective investors collect such observations and resolve their informational concerns about the divestment's causes over time.

Valuations of ventures that feature departures of inside parties thus suffer from greater discounts. If the VCF wanted to reduce these discounts, it could postpone the exit until the current valuation is confirmed through the disclosure of further information. Ventures that experience no departures can, in turn, be exited earlier given that follow-on investors are relatively less concerned about information dissimilarity.

H. 2.1.1 Departures lead to postponed exits.

b) Exit vehicle

The impact of departures on the follow-on investors' perception of the venture varies across private and public investors. Subrahmanyam and Titman (1999) reason that public markets rely solely on publicly available information while private investors revert to pertinent expertise from related endeavours. Particularly for internal restructurings, Subrahmanyam and Titman demonstrate relatively greater information disadvantages for public investors as compared to private investor.[615] In the absence of a helpful background, public markets must exercise more caution in case of dismiss-

---

[614] Bruton/Fried/Hisrich (1998), p. 46

[615] Subrahmanyam/Titman (1999), p. 1075

als. The private investor's specific industry expertise, however, grants him more insights in the impacts of internal restructuring means such as dismissals. If dismissals occur, public investors add more discounts to their valuation than private investors.

Prospective investors also infer an information advantage of insiders against the public from insider sales. If incumbents stick to their investment, their decision shows confidence in a positive performance of future stock prices.[616] The incumbents' welfare is then tied to the venture's success and warrants their persistent commitment. If entrepreneurs divest from the venture, both public and private investors must assume information disadvantages. However, private investors can still revert to their industry background to assess the venture's internal quality in terms of resources or technologies. Public investors, in contrast, depend solely on public information. While the private investors can track eventual causes for the entrepreneur's divestment with respect to the venture's internal measures, public investors cannot narrow down the entrepreneur's incentive to divest. Public investors must rather assume that the venture has failed in general. The public investors' discounts reflect their impression of a general failure whereas the private investor's enhanced awareness of the divestment's origin allows him to discount selectively.

Given that the public investor's general discount concerns the overall venture, it exceeds the private investor's discount. In consequence, the private transaction is more likely to maximize the proceeds from the exit the more departures occur.

H. 2.1.2 *The occurrence of departures increases the likelihood of private transactions.*

c) Promotion

Departures of venture team members increase information asymmetry because the prospective investor must assume that the departure is either caused by a disruptive management or by insiders capitalizing on information advantages. Yet, if a poor performance prompts the VCF to replace members of the entrepreneurial management team, a possible source of failure may be eliminated. The dismissal then represents a consequence of the VCF's adverse selection upon the initial investment decision and in fact lowers the eventual adverse selection risk of follow-on investors. To avoid additional discounts due to the dismissal, the VCF can convey this information to outside investors through promotion.

Similarly, departures of entrepreneurial team members may be triggered by other events than information advantages. Divestures are frequently motivated by diversifi-

---

616 Bradley/Jordan (2002), p. 597f.; Cumming/MacIntosh (2003), p. 512f.; Lerner (1994b), p. 16; Lin/Smith (1998), p. 242ff.

cation or liquidity considerations if entrepreneurial team members sell stock that forms part of their remuneration. Also, an entrepreneur may be forced to re-allocate his funds to pay back personal debts, to preserve his or his family's health through expensive therapies etc.. If so, the VCF can alleviate outside investors' additional concerns only if it explains the entrepreneur's real motivations to divest from the venture.

These considerations lead to the following comparison. If the VCF exits from two ventures of which one features departures, the withdrawal from the venture that avoids departures is surrounded by relatively greater information efficiency. Habib and Ljungqvist (2001) and Relander, Syrjänen and Miettinen's (1994) show that the VCF can alleviate prospective investors' concerns in that it steps up communication with outsiders to provide additional certification and information.[617] In order to facilitate the exit from the latter investment, the VCF must explain the departure's causes and consequences to prospective investors and close their information gaps with respect to this incident. The VCF thus engages in relatively more promotion to enable exits of ventures that experience departures as compared to investments without departures.

H. 2.1.3 The occurrence of departures prompts the VCF to increase its promotion.

d) Third-party certification

Given that departures of entrepreneurial team members negatively affect the outside investor's assessment of the venture, VCFs have to incorporate them into their promotion strategy. As hypothesized above, VCFs can choose to circulate more information to explain the departure and justify the subsequent valuation. Leasing third-party certification represents a complementary strategy. VCFs can employ third-party certification to increase the credibility of their valuation and mitigate concerns about the reasons that cause entrepreneurs' departures. Presuming greater information asymmetry concerns of follow-on investors in case departures occur, VCFs may counteract these concerns by employing more third-party certification.

H. 2.1.4 The occurrence of departures increases the need for third-party certification.

---

617 Habib/Ljungqvist (2001), p. 434f.; Relander/Syrjänen/Miettinen (1994), p. 139f.

4.5 VC Intermediation as Source of Information Asymmetries

A broad body of literature argues that VC involvement affects investors' perception about the venture.[618] Megginson and Weiss (1991) find that the presence of VCFs certifies for IPOs and helps overcome investors' concerns. Megginson and Weiss set out that VCFs have information advantages over public markets due to their monitoring and involvement in the IPO candidate's decisions. Megginson and Weiss elaborate that certification requires the VCF to possess reputational capital which is costly to acquire. Moreover, Megginson and Weiss presume the present value of lost reputational capital by cheating to be greater than the one-time gain from providing false certification. Thus, VCFs wish to avoid to overprice IPOs and to benefit from short-term advantages.[619] Because of the importance of reputation to the VCF, Megginson and Weiss conclude that the initial offering price of a VC-backed firm is more likely to reflect all available inside information than the valuation of non-VC-backed firms whose investors do not return to the public markets.[620] Bygrave and Timmons (1992) and Sahlman (1997) sustain the notion that prospective investors appreciate VCFs' certification and demand less underpricing for VC-backed IPOs.[621] Gompers (1996) expands the previous findings and observes differences in VCFs' certification. He finds that offerings by seasoned VCFs exhibit less underpricing than those backed by younger VCFs. Given their high reputational capital, seasoned VCFs can alleviate public markets' concerns about overpricing even more than unseasoned VCFs.[622]

In essence, the literature suggests that less seasoned VCFs cannot convey the venture's value with the credibility of an established VCF as they lack certification power.[623] If a venture is backed by a seasoned VCF, prospective investors assume ex-ante less information disadvantages. This study analyzes the consequences of seasoning on VCFs' exit strategies.

a) Timing

Initially, this reasoning implies that seasoning allows VCFs to exit in more information inefficient settings. VC-backing through seasoned VCFs alleviates investors concerns towards early stage ventures and lowers investors' discounts. Section 4.2.2 elaborates that if prospective investors reduce their discounts, the VCF exits closer to

---

[618] E.g., Barry/Muscarella/Peavy/Vetsuypens (1990), p. 448; Bygrave/Timmons (1992), p. 208; Megginson/Weiss (1991), p. 879; Sahlman (1997), p. 107

[619] Megginson/Weiss (1991), p. 881

[620] Megginson/Weiss (1991), p. 879

[621] Bygrave/Timmons (1992), p. 208; Sahlman (1997), p. 107

[622] Gompers (1996), p. 153f.; see also Neus/Walz (2001), p. 17

[623] E.g., Gompers (1996), p. 153f.; Neus/Walz (2001), p. 17

the managerial optimum.[624] In terms of timing, seasoning thus enables VCFs to withdraw earlier.

However, Gompers (1996) makes contradicting observations. Gompers finds that unseasoned VCFs tend to exit earlier than more established VCFs in order to accelerate their reputation building.[625] To gain reputation, younger VCFs even accept the higher discounts for ex-ante uncertainty and information gaps of follow-on investors.[626] Conversely, the matured VCF's reputation has already been established through several transactions; single transactions do not significantly improve seasoned VCFs' reputation anymore. In the absence of the chance to enhance their reputation, seasoned VCFs rather seek to capitalize on reduced information asymmetries in later stage exits. In essence, younger VCFs are assumed to exit their ventures earlier than their seasoned counterparts.

H. 3.1.1 Younger VCFs tend to exit earlier.

b) Exit vehicle

In the sense of grandstanding, Gompers (1996) and Wang and Sim (2001) note that IPOs represent the best way for VCFs to demonstrate their abilities to the public; IPOs are publicly observable while information about private transactions are not always released. Thus, fund investors can derive more information about a VCF's quality from its IPO activities than from its M&A transactions.[627] More seasoned VCFs have, however, fewer incentives to give up proceeds to build their reputation and thus consider both private and public transactions detached from grandstanding. Gompers (1996) and Wang and Sim (2001) consequently hold that unseasoned VCFs accomplish more IPOs in relation to seasoned VCF.[628]

Moreover, through repeatedly successful transactions with private investors, older VCFs possess greater established networks with private investors than their unseasoned counterparts.[629] Because the benefits from future transactions within these networks exceed short-term profits from opportunistic behavior in the actual deal, neither the VCF nor the private investor seek to extract short-term advantages.[630] Long-time relationships essentially help overcome information asymmetries

---

[624] See also Cumming/MacIntosh (2003), p. 516f.
[625] Gompers (1996), p. 135f.
[626] Cumming/MacIntosh (2003), p. 518
[627] Gompers (1996), p. 135f.; Wang/Sim (2001), p. 352
[628] Gompers (1996), p. 136; Wang/Sim (2001), p. 352; see also Lee/Wahal (2002), p. 5f.
[629] Milgrom/Roberts (1982), p. 283
[630] Cable/Shane (1997), p. 163; Soh (2003), p. 728

and increase the effectiveness of the VCF's certification.[631] Thus, private transactions are subject to fewer discounts and consequently more profitable for established VCFs in comparison to younger VCFs. Accordingly, it is suggested that private transactions will be more likely to occur for matured VCFs than for younger ones.

H. 3.1.2 The younger the VCF the more it seeks IPO exits.

c) Promotion

Researchers find that VCFs can transfer reputational capital gained in previous transaction to current deals. In that VCFs tie their reputation and thus their long-term return-potential to the transaction's success, they can resolve follow-on investors' concerns about the venture's quality.[632] However, the impact of VCFs' certification varies across VCFs. Because reputation emerges through repeated transactions, newly established VCFs possess less reputational capital than older ones. A highly regarded VCF's certification is consequently more effective than a less established VCF's.[633] To make up for their lack of certification power, unseasoned VCFs have to get more involved in promoting the venture than seasoned VCFs to push exits.

Furthermore, when – in line with Gompers' (1996) findings – young and unseasoned VCFs want to accelerate exits without awaiting the establishment of an information efficient setting, they have to work against prospective investors' concerns. To resolve the prospective investors' uncertainty, unseasoned VCFs can engage in promotion.[634] Older VCFs in contrast, do not perceive the need to establish their reputation and experience less pressure to push premature exits. Given this fundamental difference in the incentives to exit, young VCFs are expected to engage in more promotion than matured ones.

H. 3.1.3 Younger VCFs incur more promotion efforts than older ones.

d) Third-party certification

Johnson and Miller (1988) and Logue (1973) elaborate that seasoned investment banks only provide certification for less risky transactions.[635] Carter and Manaster conclude that seasoned investment banks are pickier than unseasoned investment

---

[631] Bader (1996), p. 147; Brück (1998), p. 37; Schröder (1992), p. 257; Sorensen/Stuart (2001), p. 1556

[632] Milgrom/Roberts (1982), p. 283; Zemke (1995), p. 145f.

[633] Parkhe (1993), p. 799f.; Baum/Silverman (2004), p. 412

[634] Gompers (1996), p. 133ff.; Gompers/Lerner (1999a), p. 30

[635] Johnson/Miller (1988), p. 20 and p. 28; Logue (1973), p. 100

banks because they wish to preserve their reputation.[636] Megginson and Weiss (1991) summarize that VC-backing is generally appreciated by investment banks. But their findings imply that investment banks do not only revert to VC-backing as a quality indicator but also pay attention to the quality of the involved VCFs. VCFs differ in their seasoning in that inexperienced VCFs have not yet established a reputation for their capabilities in successfully nurturing ventures. This shortcoming restrains their access to top investment banks because the investment banks cannot assess the VCF's skills. Seasoned VCFs in turn are found to have superior access to prestigious investments as their reputation reflects their outstanding ability of nurturing successful ventures.[637] In essence, only established VCFs can employ seasoned investment banks whereas new VCFs have to revert to less seasoned intermediates to enhance their exits.

H. 3.1.4 More seasoned VCFs employ more prestigious investment banks.

4.6 Pre-Tests of the Research Model

The present research model originates solely from the literature and theoretical considerations. Thus, the research model may overlook factors that have not been explored in the literature yet. Moreover, the literature analysis may have missed findings on exit strategies if these findings were not published in the major journals. To complement possible omissions and detect inconsistencies, qualitative pilot-studies were conducted. The insights have already been integrated in the research model above. They are, however, discussed in the following sections.

4.6.1 Qualitative Pilot-Study Approach

Scholars frequently employ qualitative pilot studies in advance to larger surveys.[638] Qualitative pilot studies allow for the examination of causalities that have not been researched in depth before.[639] Yin (1989) points out that qualitative case studies are particularly suitable to research how- and why-questions in a contemporary real life context and to complement conclusions drawn solely from the literature.[640] The results of qualitative pilot studies help strengthen research models and lead to adjustments prior to launching larger surveys.

---

[636] Carter/Manaster (1990), p. 1062

[637] Megginson/Weiss (1991), p. 880 and p. 887

[638] Zikmund (1991), p. 75ff.

[639] Bortz/Döring (1995), p. 362; Eisenhardt (1989b), p. 532ff.; Howorth/Westhead/Wright (2004), p. 516

[640] Yin (1989), p. 13

Scholars discriminate two sources of information to research qualitative case studies: interviews and data collection from public sources. As for this study, the collection of public information suffers from two disadvantages against interviews. First, VCFs are reluctant to release details about their transactions. Second, investigating the literature and other publications does not offer the opportunity to gain insights into the exit approaches of practitioners. These disadvantages disqualify the investigation of public information from being employed in the context of this study. Even though interviews only yield cognitions that are limited to individual experiences of the interviewees, they represent one media to learn from practitioners about their approaches. Interviews are consequently utilized in entrepreneurship research for exploring new themes.[641]

Through interviews, this analysis gained insights from experienced practitioners about the research model's quality and on possible improvements. A semi-structured questionnaire has served as guideline during the interview sessions. Semi-structured interviews allow the interviewer to address all aspects and to probe particularly interesting aspects even if these issues are not foreseen in the interview guideline. Conversely, structured interviews do not allow researchers to explore new insights immediately. The interview guideline consisted of three sections:

- Introducing questions asking the interviewee to describe his approach towards exiting ventures
- Questions addressing the interviewee's involvement in exits, his timing approach and his choice of exit vehicles
- Questions about further strategies that help facilitate exits.

Throughout the interview, the interviewees were encouraged to illustrate their experiences in examples.

4.6.2 Sample Selection

Given the focus of this study on central decisions in the VC process such as exit timing and exit channel, senior VC-managers with extensive expertise in exiting ventures were interviewed. The limited research resources allowed for four interviews to take place. Each interview lasted approximately one hour.

Since the research model addresses differences across VCFs, industries and investment/divestment stages, representatives of VCFs that differ in these respects were interviewed. The first VCF focuses on non-high-tech ventures in later stages. The second VCF funds preferably Communication ventures in early stages. The third VCF targets technology investments at all stages. Initial contacts were established

[641] E.g., Hellmann/Puri (2000); Murray (1996); see also Norton/Tenenbaum (1992), p. 20f.

either by reverting to adjunct faculty members of Babson College, MA, or through recommendation by Professor Andrew Zacharakis who currently serves as the Director of the Arthur M. Blank Center for Entrepreneurship at Babson College. Two interviews were conducted with senior partners of major VCFs in Boston and one interview with a senior investment manager. In addition, a senior investment banker with an outstanding deal flow of VC-backed transactions was interviewed.

4.6.3 Insights From the Pilot-Studies

As regards the introducing questions, interviewees provided examples of successful and unsuccessful transactions. Initially, they were asked to highlight what measures would reflect a transaction's success. Common sense suggested that high return-multiples would characterize successful exit transaction. Interviewees stated that high multiples were, however, only achieved if the venture would perform well and could prove its viability to prospective investors. To quote one interviewee, a successfully exited firm would "expect strong growth, high market shares, cash flows and profits". In advance to unsuccessful transactions, the venture would already experience difficulties to establish a viable business. One interviewee noted that "living dead companies which only deliver penny valuations" could not accomplish successful exits as they could not attract many investors. The lack of competing investors in turn would not afford the VCF with bargaining power and would result in low valuations. In fact, the lack of follow-on investors forces the VCF to join into the first possible transaction. Write-offs were almost always named as examples for unsuccessful exits. In essence, the interviewees related the withdrawal's outcome to the venture's success and to its ability to attract possibly many investors.

The answers regarding the VCF's promotion were consistent with the proposed research model. Only questions centering on grandstanding were spared. On the one hand, the interviewees represented well established firms. Thus, a tendency to grandstand was not expected anyway. On the other hand, it seemed unlikely that VCFs would admit to their opportunistic behavior. Questions about promotion efforts particularly addressed the employment of investment banks and the VCF's interactions with prospective investors. One interviewee set out that the role of investment banks in IPOs was "to look for institutional investors and in M&A transactions to search for private investors".

Above all, identifying the proper exit channel and investor was highlighted as the central task upon exit. Interviewees pointed out that it was essential not only to find one prospective investor but rather to establish competition among investors; one interviewee explained that competition among investors would allow VCFs to capitalize on their bargaining power so that they could obtain the best valuation. The choice of the exit vehicle was also related to timing considerations. Interviewees set out that floating a venture would require the venture to exhibit outstanding track records which would only materialize in later stages. Earlier exits were mostly motivated by an approach of an industrial investor either attracted through the VCF's continuous interactions with incumbent industrials or by the venture's inventions. All three VC managers rejected the notion that hot issue markets would determine the exit's timing. They agreed that timing the market would be too risky considering that it would take more than half a year to launch an IPO. By the end of the preparations, the hot issue market might have vanished. The investment banker, however, outlined that equity valuation levels would indeed play a significant role and that pending hot issue markets would "induce VCFs to accelerate their exit preparations". This was the only aspect in which answers differed. It appeared that VCFs did not like to admit to their market timing.

Interviewees also referred to promotion as a means to facilitate exits. They summarized activities that would help attract and convince prospective investors as promotion efforts. Interviewees exemplified that tapping their network of industrial investors, of intermediates and financial investors would direct attention to the venture. Interviewees stated that their promotion and network activities would enable prospective investors to distinguish high-quality from low quality investments. This notion conforms the certification assumptions in the literature. Promotion efforts were also contingent on the exit vehicle with IPOs requiring far more involvement than private investors. Investment banks were outlined to be a means of promotion as well. One interviewee exemplified that investment banks would establish a valuation approach for the transaction and would communicate this value to follow-on investors in case they could not perform due diligence at similar intensity – for instance in an IPO. Another interviewee explained that investment banks would "virtually extend the VCF's network"; VCFs would revert to investment banks to look out for suitable acquirers and to certify for the venture's quality.

The research model was supported in every interview; the answers in the interview sessions were consistent with the presumed relationships in the research model. Interviewees admitted that a crucial factor for successful exits was that the follow-on investor would resolve his information gaps. The interviewees incorporated this rational in their exit strategy as set out in the research model. Yet, information asymmetry was not always referred to as the only driving force. The interviews revealed two other determinants for exit strategies:

- External approaches of industrial investors would make an exit strategy obsolete.
- The venture's performance if favorable could ease exits or complicate withdrawals in case the venture struggles. "Living dead" investments, for instance,

would require much more attention to achieve exits even if they would feature high information efficiency in that they were obviously stalling.

Another aspect that occurs in the literature was addressed during the interviews. VC research argues that the extent of the entrepreneur's financial commitment constitutes a signal. Whether entrepreneurs devote more or less equity is regarded as an indicator for their perception of the venture's quality.[642] Furthermore, scholars set out that entrepreneurs have fewer incentives to engage in opportunistic actions the closer their wealth is tied to the venture's performance.[643] Consistent with Hellmann (1998) as well as Prasad, Bruton and Vozikas (2000), the interviewees pointed out that the entrepreneur's equity stake would primarily be subject to his own wealth constraints rather than to his inside knowledge. Hellmann argues that if the entrepreneur could raise sufficient capital himself, he would not have to approach a VCF.[644] The entrepreneur's initial investment has thus been eliminated from the research model. Instead, the research model examines the entrepreneur's divestment behavior in advance to the exit to mirror his perception of the venture's progress prior to the transaction.

4.7 Conclusive Remarks

This chapter develops a research model that captures the influence of information asymmetries between the incumbent inside investors and prospective outside investors on VCFs' exit behavior. The general framework is inspired by a thorough literature analysis. Four pilot studies substantiate the assumptions. The framework allows for deriving research hypotheses which become the subject of empirical validation.

The research model consists of 20 research hypotheses generated through contrasting five endogenous variables with four endogenous variables. The exogenous parameters describe possible information asymmetries between incumbent inside and prospective outside investors. The research model sets out how the venture's innovativeness, development stage at exit and the competitiveness of the venture's environment affect the extent of information asymmetry by the time of the VCF's withdrawal. The dimension of exogenous variables also spans exceptional events such as dismissals and divestments of inside investors that raise outside investors' concerns. The exogenous variables finally capture how VCFs' certification resolves

---

[642] E.g., Busentitz/Fiet (1996); Busenitz/Barney (1997), p. 9; Certo/Daily/Dalton (2001), p. 35f.; Inderst/Müller (2004), p. 320; Janney/Folta (2003), p. 364ff.; Leland/Pyle (1977), p. 376; Sapienza/Gupta (1994), p. 1621; Zemke (1995), p. 31

[643] Busenitz/Barney (1997), p. 9; Leland/Pyle (1977), p. 376; Sapienza/Gupta (1994), p. 1621

[644] Hellmann (1998), p. 59; Prasad/Bruton/Vozikas (2000), p. 170

prospective investors' uncertainty. The endogenous variables describe the VCF's exit strategy in terms of timing, exit vehicle, promotion efforts and third-party certification.

To draw terminal conclusions about the model's quality – and on the impact of information asymmetry on the VCF's exit strategy – this model needs to be validated on the basis of empirical data.

5 Research Methodology

This chapter sketches the empirical design that underlies this study. First, it sets out the operationalization of the dependent, independent and control variables. Second, this chapter describes how the data samples are gathered. Thereupon, this part contrasts the data samples and outlines possible shortcomings as regards the survey samples' representativeness. Finally, the empirical methods that are employed are introduced.

5.1 Empirical Design

This section describes the empirical design. It discusses measurement procedures for both the independent and dependent variables and their roots in the literature. Similarly, control variables are introduced which allow for the observation of undesired effects on the endogenous parameters. In addition, this chapter sets out the sources of information which are tapped in order to build the data basis.

5.1.1 Dependent Variables

This section defines how this study operationalizes the dependent variables timing, exit vehicle, promotion and third-party certification. Particularly for the latent dependent variable promotion, this section builds a proper proxy to quantify the occurrence of promotion activities.

a) The exit's timing

The research model incorporates the exit's timing in order to investigate the dynamics of information asymmetry over time. Accordingly, the exit's timing is defined as the length of the VCF's holding period. The VCF's holding period begins with the initial VC-investment and ends with the VCF's withdrawal. Similar approaches are pursued by Cumming and MacIntosh (2001), Wang, Wang and Lu (2002) and Fleming (2003).[645]

The VCF's holding period is measured in months and calculated as the difference between the date of the VCF's initial investment and the date of the exit transaction. Both dates are acquired from VentureXpert.

b) The exit vehicle

The exit vehicle as used in the research model characterizes the different abilities of follow-on investors to resolve information asymmetries. Previous studies dis-

[645] E.g., Cumming/MacIntosh (2001), p. 455ff.; Fleming (2003), p. 14; Wang/Wang/Lu (2002), p. 68

cern up to five exit vehicles. Usually, they refer to exits as events in which the venture (1) fails and goes out of business, (2) is acquired by the management, (3) is acquired by another VC investor or (4) by an industrial investor or (5) is sold to the public markets. Examples for this definition can be found in Cochrane (2001) as well as Cumming and MacIntosh (2003) among others.[646]

This research model draws a simplified distinction between public transactions (IPO) and acquisitions by industrial investors. This dissertation's focus on information spreads between incumbent investors with inside knowledge and prospective outside investors upon exit calls for this simplification. First, some exemplified exit vehicles do not essentially entail information asymmetries between inside and outside investors. In a buyback, the acquiring manager is an inside investor instead of an outsider. He does consequently not suffer from information disadvantages. In a liquidation event, the venture's assets are sold rather than the business. Information asymmetries about the venture's quality do essentially not occur anymore at this stage because the venture has apparently failed.

Second, secondary purchases, buybacks and liquidations occur only in exceptional situations in which neither an IPO nor a private transactions materializes. Ventures that are sold to financial investors or to the incumbent management have usually failed or struggle severely.[647] In fact, the decision for these exit vehicles is motivated by the venture's performance and the lack of alternatives instead of information asymmetry concerns. This dissertation excludes secondary purchases, buybacks and liquidations to eliminate the success bias that underlies the VCF's decision for these exit routes. Rather, this study focuses on the different abilities to resolve information asymmetry that VCFs ascribe to public markets and private industrial investors. These abilities in turn drive the VCF's decision on either exit route. Likewise, most theoretical papers pick up this simplified distinction between IPOs and M&A exits.[648]

Accordingly, the initial public offering is coded as "IPO" and the acquisition through an industrial investor is demarked as "Acquisition". For each transaction, this information is acquired from VentureXpert.

c) The VCF's promotion

The VCF's promotion addresses the question of how VCFs overcome information spreads at exit through interactions with outside parties such prospective investors or intermediates. Usually, VC research looks into interactions between the VCF

---

[646] E.g., Cochrane (2001), p. 8; Cumming/MacIntosh (2003), p. 513ff.; Das/Jagannathan/Sarin (2003), p. 2ff.; Wright/Robbie/Romanet/Thompson/Joachimsson/Bruining/Herst (1994), p. 94f.

[647] See section 3.1.1; Temple (1999), p. 110

[648] E.g., Chemannur/Fulghieri (1999), p. 249f; Subrahmanyam/Titman (1999), p. 1045

and the entrepreneur during the VC process in order to determine the impact of VC-backing on ventures.[649] Therefore, researchers investigate the quantity and quality of the VCF's interactions with the entrepreneur. Sahlman (1990) exemplifies the measuring of the VCF's involvement in its ventures. He counts the number of contacts and quantifies the duration of bilateral communication between the VCFs and the entrepreneur to describe the degree of the VCF's involvement.[650] Sapienza and Gupta (1994) gauge the quality of the interactions using matched responses from a survey addressed to both entrepreneurs and VCFs. Then, they measure the quantity of interactions such as face to face conversations, telephone calls and exchange of written mail.[651]

In the absence of research focussing on the VCF's interactions with prospective outside investors, research has, however, not established an approach to operationalize this issue yet. Only Habib and Ljungqvist (2001) touch this dimension of the VCF's exit behavior; they set out that VCFs resolve prospective investors' uncertainties in that the VCF's managers attend roadshows and meetings.[652] Their example inspires a proxy for measuring the VCF's engagement in interactions with outside parties. Similar to MacMillan, Kulow and Khoylian's (1998) method to quantify the VCF's involvement in the venture during the VC period, it is asked what actions the VCF performs when approaching the exit. In the sense of this study, it is surveyed with whom the VCF interacts to overcome information dissimilarity.[653] This construct is divided into four items: Initially, it is surveyed whether representatives of the VCF attended road shows and/or get involved in the negotiations with underwriters and private investors. The responses indicate whether the VCF devotes resources to endorsing the venture through entering discussions with outside investors. Second, it is asked whether the VCF taps its network to promote the transaction. This question evaluates whether the VCF wishes to revert to its network to facilitate the exit in a trustworthy environment. Third, VCFs may approach investment banks in order to capitalize on third-party certification or to let them looking out for investors. Either way, the VCF's decision to enlist investment banks in advance to the exit exemplifies its willingness to incur costs to overcome information asymmetries.

Every item is surveyed in a single question asking whether the VCF initiates these interactions or not. The information about the VCF's promotion is finally aggregated to one measure that reflects the overall promotion intensity; one point is added for every question that is answered with yes. The maximum value of this measure

---

[649] E.g., Gorman/Sahlman (1989); Sahlman (1990)

[650] Gorman/Sahlman (1989), p. 235f.

[651] Sapienza/Gupta (1994), p. 1624

[652] Habib/Ljungqvist (2001), p. 434f.

[653] MacMillan/Kulow/Khoylian (1988), p. 31

can amount up to four in case the VCF does attend roadshows, negotiations, taps its network and enlists investment banks. The minimum is zero if the VCF initiates no interactions with outside parties. In essence, the proxy mirrors to what extent the VCF engages in endorsing the venture with higher values corresponding to more efforts.

This measure is subject to several shortcomings. First, it cannot account for the intensity at which VCFs engage in one particular interaction. The measure does not differentiate whether a VCF focuses on individual parties and incurs substantial efforts to endorse the venture to this party or whether the VCF confers just briefly about the possibility of a transaction with an outside party. Second, the measure weights each item equally. Hence, the measure cannot account for the different impacts of every item. However, pilot studies have fostered the assumption that this proxy covers the usual approaches VCFs take in advance to an exit and gives a basic idea of the extent of VCFs' promotion efforts. Nevertheless, subsequent research must devote more attention to further develop proper instruments to evaluate how VCFs interact upon exit.

d) Third-party certification

The degree of third-party certification reflects the intensity of external certification the VCF utilizes to resolve information asymmetry. Usually, research views investment banks as providers of third-party certification.[654] Investment bankers get involved either to underwrite an IPO or to facilitate a private transaction. Provided that investment bankers are hired in an exit, their reputation may affect the exit strategy in that the investment bank's certification lessens outside investors' concerns about information dissimilarity.[655]

The most prominent approach to measure the investment banker's certification is exemplified by Megginson and Weiss (1991). They relate an investment banker's reputation to the relative volume of IPOs he underwrites. Initially, Megginson and Weiss compute the cumulative value of all IPOs for the period of their data sample. For every investment bank, Megginson and Weiss add up the total value of those IPOs in which the investment bank was the lead-underwriter. To obtain the relative market share, Megginson and Weiss divide every investment bank's transaction volume by the total value of all IPOs completed during the sample period. Finally, Megginson and Weiss rate investment banks on a scale from 1 to 9 with 9 denoting the

---

[654] E.g., Baron (1982), p. 955ff.; Beatty/Ritter (1986), p. 214ff.; Booth/Smith (1986), p. 261; Carter/Dark/Singh (1998), p. 285ff.; Carter/Manaster (1990), p. 1062; Johnson/Miller (1988), p. 28; McDonald/Fisher (1972), p. 102; Megginson/Weiss (1991), p. 879; Neuberger/Hammond (1974), p. 165

[655] Booth/Smith (1986), p. 261

highest certification power and 1 the least contingent on the bank's overall market share.[656]

Given that IPOs are usually underwritten by several investment banks, Megginson and Weiss contemplate only the lead underwriter's certification power. If an issuing firm names more than one lead underwriter, Megginson and Weiss calculate the mean of the lead underwriters' market shares as the proxy for the extent of third-party certification the IPO obtained.[657] This method is continuous, easy to construct and employed in several succeeding studies.[658]

Information about both, the IPO volume and investment bankers' involvement are acquired from the SDC database. Thereupon, the market shares for the lead-underwriters are calculated and assigned to each transaction. For simplicity, an investment bank's involvement in private transactions is treated similarly. Given that valuations in M&A exits are not always disclosed, the investment bank's reputation from public markets is transferred to the private transaction. Since the major underwriters also lead the M&A league tables, this approach seems appropriate to assess the presence of third-party certification in private transactions too. Table 6 reports the top 15 investment banks and their market shares computed through this procedure. The investment banks are, however, not ranked; instead, this analysis considers their market share as a direct quality indicator.

[656] Megginson/Weiss (1991), p. 887ff.; see also Carter/Manaster (1990), p. 287ff.

[657] Megginson/Weiss (1991), p. 890

[658] E.g., Certo/Daily/Dalton (2001), p. 41; Bradley/Jordan (2002), p. 601

Rank	Name	Total Number of IPOs	Total amount of offerings [mio US$]	Market share
1.	Merrill Lynch	2,310	535,595	3.595 %
2.	Goldman Sachs	1,754	497,292	3.338 %
3.	Morgan Stanley	1,739	442,871	2.973 %
4.	Credit Suisse	1,520	382,329	2.566 %
5.	Salomon Smith Barney	1,353	317,294	2.130 %
6.	Lehman Brothers	1,556	315,604	2.118 %
7.	JP Morgan	798	270,949	1.819 %
8.	Bear Stearns	1,248	263,901	1.771 %
9.	AG Edwards	1,234	251,244	1.686 %
10.	Donaldson Lufkin & Jenrette	1,385	245,631	1.649 %
11.	Deutsche Bank AG	944	228,797	1.536 %
12.	Prudential Securities	1,100	218,334	1,466 %
13.	Legg Mason	967	216,314	1.452 %
14.	Banc of America	633	184,643	1.239 %
15.	Raymond James & Ass.	1,055	174,534	1.172 %
	...			

Table 6: Market shares of the top 15 investment banks in the period of 1998 to 2002

5.1.2 Independent Variables

This section sets out the operationalization of the independent variables that are used in the research model to describe the types of information that are distributed asymmetrically. According to the scheme of hypotheses, the venture's business is decomposed into the degree of innovation, the development level at exit and the extent of competition.

a) Innovation

A firm's innovativeness is a latent variable which is not directly observable. Several different approaches have emerged to assess a firm's degree of innovation. In some studies, the degree of innovation is measured on a five point scale ranging from highly innovative to not innovative. Sapienza (1992), for instance, asks entrepreneurs to gauge the innovativeness of their venture in six different dimensions on five-point scales.[659] Sapienza and Gupta (1994) pick up this methodology and ask entrepreneurs to rate their venture's innovativeness in comparison to the competition on five scales: the venture's technical position, its product design and the process technology. In addition, Sapienza and Gupta seek the entrepreneur's opinion about the venture's position in terms of R&D expenditures and process technology.[660]

---

[659] Sapienza (1992), p. 16f.

[660] Sapienza/Gupta (1994), p. 1625

Bygrave, Timmons and Fast (1984) apply yet another proxy for evaluating ventures' innovativeness on the basis of partial measures. First, Bygrave, Timmons and Fast survey information about the venture's innovativeness regarding technologies inherent in manufacturing processes, components and delivery systems from entrepreneurs. Afterwards, Bygrave, Timmons and Fast aggregate this information to assess the degree of innovation for every venture's production. Second, Bygrave, Timmons and Fast appraise the degree of innovation of the venture's product(s). They ask entrepreneurs, how the specific use of their firm's product differs from the traditional way the product's function is performed. In terms of measuring, Bygrave, Timmons and Fast employ seven point scales for both dimensions. Then, they classify companies that attained a rating of four or higher on the product's and the production's scale as innovative.[661]

Both approaches suffer from two systematic problems. On the one hand, every measure is based on the entrepreneur's opinion and is thus exposed to entrepreneurs overstating the degree of innovation.[662] To exclude this bias, researchers revert to categorizations of industry and businesses performed by third parties. On the other hand, both methods require that a variety of data is collected from entrepreneurs. However, surveying this information from entrepreneurs would expose this study to two low response ratios in sequence. Initially, this study uses a questionnaire to acquire private information from VCFs. If this information had to be complemented with survey data from entrepreneurs, a second questionnaire had to be launched. The second survey, however, has to match the first survey; it can only include those transactions for which VCFs have provided data. The terminal data sample suffers again from a low response ratio. Presuming response rates of 20 % in both inquiries, the final data set would only contain a fraction of 4 % (20 $\%^2$) of the original data sample. In addition, the eventual data sample was likely to be subject to two success biases among other flaws. In fact, both approaches are inappropriate for this study.

Nevertheless, research on the firm's resource base introduces another proxy to measure the venture's degree of innovation. In their study on how innovative companies acquire knowledge, Ranft and Lord (1997) include only those firms that are associated with "high-technology" in the SDC Worldwide M&A database. Their sample comprises of firms from biotechnology, computer equipment, computer software, computer services, electronic and communications industries.[663] Similarly, Kohers and Kohers (2001) identify innovative companies based on their classification codes

---

[661] Bygrave/Timmons/Fast (1984), p. 2; see also Hellman/Puri (2000), p. 965ff.

[662] Hinkel (2001), p. 68

[663] Ranft/Lord (2000), p. 303

as provided by SDC. Their sample firms stem from industries such as biotechnology, chemicals, computers, defence, electronics, communications, medical and pharmaceuticals. Kohers and Kohers argue that these industries comprise more young and innovative firms than other industries.[664] According to Ranft and Lord, this categorization also serves as indicator for the extent of tacit knowledge and ex-ante uncertainty about the firm's business. In this sense, Ranft and Lord observe significantly higher market-to-book ratios for high-technology firms classified as set out above than for the remaining firms.[665]

This analysis presumes that the industry affiliation properly classifies companies according to their products, markets and technologies. Each industry spans rather similar business concepts and encompasses innovations in the same field. The subsequent analysis distinguishes ventures on the basis of the nature of their primary businesses in high-tech (software, communications, electronics, biotechnology and semiconductors) and low technology businesses. It is important to note that this measurement is simplified too. The binary coding does not distinguish between different extents of innovation other than high and low.[666] Information about the ventures' businesses is taken from the VentureXpert. So are the industry affiliations.

b) Development stage at exit

Manifold vocabularies exist demarking stages in the development process of young companies. Sapienza and Gupta (1994) refer to "Pratt's Guide to Venture Capital Sources" and define the following stages: (1) seed, (2) start-up, (3) first stage, (4) re-start, (5) expansion and (6) bridge.[667] Schwienbacher (2002) discerns only an early class which comprises seed and start-up firms, a later class including firms in their development and expansion stages and finally a buyout class.[668] Sapienza (1992) measures a venture's development stage by the current financing stage of the venture. He categorizes ventures from seed to bridge or acquisition levels.[669]

This study follows Sapienza (1992) and measures the venture's development level according to the venture's financing stage. This study presumes that the financing stage of the VCF's last investment corresponds with the venture's development stage at exit. The literature on staged investments stresses that VCFs constrict the venture's budget in order to prevent the entrepreneur from pursuing opportunistic

---

[664] Kohers/Kohers (2001), p. 40; see also Carpenter/Petersen (2002), p. 62
[665] Ranft/Lord (2000), p. 303
[666] Sapienza/Gupta (1994), p. 1625
[667] Sapienza/Gupta (1994), p. 1624f.
[668] Schwienbacher (2002), p. 14
[669] Sapienza (1992), p. 16

strategies. VCFs invest in stages instead of injecting the entire investment at once.[670] In essence, VCFs condition further capital infusions on the completion of interim goals such as the achievement of higher development levels.[671] Thus, the final investment stage virtually represents the venture's development level at exit. Information about the VCF's last investment stage is reported in the VentureXpert data base. The different financing stages as coded in VentureXpert in sequential order are (1) Early Stage, (2) Seed Stage, (3) Start-up, (4) First Stage, (5) Expansion Stage, (6) Second Stage, (7) Third Stage, (8) Bridge Financing, (9) Other Expansion, (10) Acquisition for Expansion, (11) LBO and (14) Open Market Purchase.[672]

c) Competition

In a VC context, only Schwienbacher (2001) and Maksimovic and Pichler (2001) analyze the impact of competition on exit strategies. However, they apply an analytical framework rather than operationalizing competition. Business research in general uses competition measures such as the CR 4 (Concentration Ration) or CR 8 to describe the intensity of rivalry in a market. These concentration measures compute the market share that is taken by the biggest four (CR 4) or eight (CR 8) firms respectively. The purpose of this approach is to analyze the influence of collusion and cartels on firm's marketing strategies.[673] Given the number of VC transactions and the inaccessibility of detailed information about emerging markets, this approach proves not feasible.

Following the earlier argumentation, competition has to reflect whether ventures have to release information about their products in order to prevail in a competitive environment. The degree of competition of the environment is thus determined by the number of rivaling products. Presuming that the number of products positively correlates with the number of competing firms, this study operationalizes the competitiveness of a venture's environment by using the number of competitors as proxy. VentureXpert provides information on the number of competitors associated with each venture.

e) Departures of members of the entrepreneurial team

Departures in a VC context have been investigated in several studies. One research stream contemplates divestments of inside investors.[674] Research on divestments usually focuses on the entrepreneur's divestments subsequent to an IPO. In-

---

[670] E.g., Sahlman (1990), p. 473 and p. 503

[671] Sahlman (1990), p. 506f.

[672] See http://vx.thomsonib.com/NASApp/VxComponent/VXMain.jsp under "glossary"

[673] Huyghebaert/Van de Gucht (2004), p. 671

[674] E.g., Gompers/Lerner (1998), p. 2167

formation about the entrepreneur's behavior after the IPO is collected from SEC filings. The SEC obliges officers, directors and ten percent block holders to disclose all trades in a Form 4 statement no later than the tenth day of the month after the transaction. Five percent block holders are required to disclose changes in their ownership in amended Forms 13d or 13g.[675] In essence, these approaches aim at discovering divestments of entrepreneurs after the going public whereas the present study researches the entrepreneur's behavior prior to the exit. Hence, this approach cannot be employed.

Another research stream looks into dismissals.[676] Dismissals – particularly prior to a public listing – are hardly observable. In the absence of obligations to disclose such incidents before the venture becomes subject to SEC filings, data about dismissals of entrepreneurial team members remain unreported. Insiders represent the only reliable source for information about the occurrence of dismissals. Researchers typically quantify the occurrence of dismissals as follows: VCFs are surveyed about their investments and asked whether dismissals have occurred. If so, VCFs are further asked whether exactly one dismissal or more than one dismissal happened. The answers are translated into the following scale; "0" codes no dismissals, "1" codes one dismissal and "2" codes more than one.[677]

This analysis assumes the latter methodology. VCFs are surveyed whether dismissals or divestments of entrepreneurial team members have occurred throughout the VC holding period. The answers are aggregated into one dummy variable. The dummy is coded "0" if no departure has been reported, "1" for one and "2" for more than one departure.

f) VCF's reputation

In line with VC main stream research, this study incorporates the VCF's reputation.[678] Scholars usually employ the VCF's age to quantify its reputation with fund investors and follow-on investors.[679] In essence, the VCF's age reflects whether the VCF repeatedly accomplishes successful exit transactions over time. In doing so, the VCF establishes a track record that allows outside investors to assess its capabilities. Both, follow-on investors and VC fund investors incorporate the VCF's quality into

---

[675] E.g., Aggarwal/Krigman/Womack (2002), p. 116ff.; Bradley/Jordan/Yi/Roten (2001), p. 468; Gompers/Lerner (1998), p. 2167

[676] E.g., Bruton/Fried/Hisrich (1997); Bruton/Fried/Hisrich (2000); Fiet/Busenitz/Moesel/Barney (1997); Hellmann (1998)

[677] E.g., Bruton/Fried/Hisrich (1997), p. 46f.; Bruton/Fried/Hisrich (2000), p. 71f.; Fiet/Busenitz/Moesel/Barney (1997), p. 356

[678] E.g., see Gompers (1996) on „grandstanding"

[679] E.g., Gompers/Lerner (1999a), p. 30; Lerner (1994a), p. 304

their investment decisions.[680] Given that unsuccessful VCFs will not be able to attract follow-on investors and to raise follow-on funds, the VCF's survival exemplifies the VCF's reputation with investors for successfully nurturing venture investments.[681]

Yet, this proxy only captures the institutional experience of the VCF based on previous transactions. The measure neglects, however, the individual employees' reputation. If VC managers spin off their own VCF from an incumbent investment firm, their track record of VC-related activities is superior to the institutional experience of their new firm.[682] Consequently, the proxy does not entirely reflect the newly founded VCF's seasoning.

Given the common acceptance of the VCF's age as proxy, this study picks up the methodology and collects information about each VCF from VentureXpert. Following Barry, Muscarella, Peavy and Vetsuypens (1990), the analysis assumes the earliest VCF to be the lead investor. Then, the lead VCF's age in years is assigned to the transaction.[683]

5.1.3 Control Variables

In order to isolate the proposed effects, this study accounts for the possibility of alternative explanations. Therefore, the analysis includes other likely determinants on exit strategies that do not correspond with the research focus on information asymmetry. The control variables address the involvement of other third parties than the investment bank, the VC investment's characteristics and external conditions.

a) Third parties' influences

Exit transactions frequently involve third parties that perform specialized tasks on behalf of the VCF or the venture. Besides investment banks, auditors occur frequently. Corporate Finance research holds that the auditor's reputation provides additional third-party certification to financing transactions.[684] In line with certification theory, scholars observe a lower underpricing for issues which are audited by high quality firms and conclude that prestigious auditors help resolve information asymmetry upon IPO.[685] The present analysis considers the impact of the presence of prestigious auditors on the prospective investors' perceptions too. However, dependen-

---

[680] Sorensen/Stuart (2001), p. 1556f.

[681] Gompers/Lerner (2000), p. 64

[682] Gompers/Lerner (2000), p. 66

[683] Barry/Muscarella/Peavy/Vetsuypens (1990), p. 464

[684] E.g., Baron (1982), p. 955ff.; Beatty/Ritter (1986), p. 214ff.; Booth/Smith (1986), p. 261; Carter/Dark/Singh (1998), p. 285ff.; Carter/Manaster (1990), p. 1062; Johnson/Miller (1988), p. 28; McDonald/Fisher (1972), p. 102; Megginson/Weiss (1991), p. 879; Neuberger/Hammond (1974), p. 172f.

[685] E.g., Beatty (1989), p. 694f.; Megginson/Weiss (1991), p. 890f.

cies between the presence of prestigious auditors and VC-backing respectively the enlisting of seasoned investment banks have not been established yet – unlike the relation between underwriters and VCFs. Given that this thesis does not emphasize the role of auditors in particular, only the control variables account for a possible influence of seasoned auditors on the extent of information asymmetry at exit while the research hypotheses omit the auditor's impact.

As for measuring the auditor's quality, this analysis follows the approach of Feltham, Hughes and Simunic (1991). They discern seasoned auditors known as the "Big Eight" auditors and unseasoned firms such as local or small auditors. However, Feltham, Hughes and Simunic's study (1991) does not account for industry dynamics. Since 1991, the big accounting firms have merged so that only four remain today: Deloitte Touche Tohmatsu, Ernest & Young, KPMG and PriceWaterhouse Coopers.[686]

This analysis takes information about the venture's auditors from VentureXpert. Companies audited by one of the Big Four are coded 1 and 0 otherwise.

b) Investment's characteristics

VC research reports that an investment's characteristics may affect the exit as well. Most prominently named characteristics are the investment's size and performance.

Giot and Schwienbacher (2003) find considerable differences in the exit timing across industries. Internet firms in their sample exhibit the fastest IPOs. These observations contradict the findings of Shepherd and Zacharakis (2001a) and the reasoning of Chemmanur and Fulghieri (1999) that underlie the research model.[687] Giot and Schwienbacher attribute their finding to higher investments and the VCF's closer monitoring in these industries which signals quality to prospective investors.[688] Giot and Schwienbacher's discussion provides hints for alternative explanations if the empirical analysis fails to validate hypotheses on the impact of industry related uncertainties on the exit's timing. Given that the VCF's monitoring intensity increases with the number of investment stages, the total investment supposedly correlates with the venture's quality. In essence, Giot and Schwienbacher relate higher investments to a higher likelihood of IPOs and earlier exits.[689] The present analysis must

---

[686] Feltham/Hughes/Simunic (1991), p. 389ff.; Lerner (1994a), p. 306

[687] Chemmanur/Fulghieri (1999), p. 271; Cumming/MacIntosh (2001), p. 446; Shepherd/Zacharakis (2001a), p. 66

[688] Giot/Schwienbacher (2003), p. 3 and p. 13f.; Keasey/Short (1997), p. 75f.; Marshall (1998), p. 1081; see Certo (2003), p. 434, on signalling theory

[689] E.g., Busenitz/Fiet (1996); Busenitz/Fiet/Moesel (2003), p. 11; Gompers (1995), p. 1481ff.; Mason/Harrison (2002), p. 228f.; Wang/Sim (2001), p. 344

consequently control for the individual investment's size as alternative influence. VentureXpert reports every venture's investment's size.

Researchers also relate an investment's performance to the VCF's exit strategy.[690] VCFs are found to carefully select their IPO candidates even if external conditions favor initial public listings. Schwienbacher (2002) and Fleming (2003) argue that VCFs are concerned about their reputation with public markets. In order to preserve their reputation, VCFs only float high quality investments and divest low quality firms to private investors.[691] To account for this dependency, the control variables must include the venture's performance. The IRR concept represents a common approach in empirical studies to measure a single venture's success represents.[692] Return multiples constitute alternative indicators that reflect the venture's success.[693] In the context of this study, return multiples feature two advantages over IRRs. First, a return multiple is not biased by the holding duration.[694] Given that this study considers the holding duration as a separate factor, it is desirable to have a success indicator that does not contain timing aspects itself. Second, return multiples require less information to be computed. Unlike, IRRs cannot be collected from public sources; database such as VentureXpert do not capture all variables that are necessary to compile an IRR. In fact, VCFs withhold information about their IRRs but prove less reluctant to release return multiples.

The return multiples of venture investments are inquired from VCFs on a five point scale. The scale has been developed in consultation with a senior VC manager. The categorizations for every investment's multiple are (1) more than five times of the initial investment, (2) two to five times, (3) a minor gain, less than two times, (4) gained principle investment back and (5) lost money.[695] This proxy roughly reflects the return multiple and meets VCFs' demands for confidentiality about details.[696]

c) External conditions

Scholars emphasize the impact of capital markets on exits as well. Given that asset prices reflect the public markets' optimism about the quality of new issues, the valuation of IPOs is not entirely driven by objective considerations. In fact, investor

---

[690] See section 4.1

[691] Fleming (2003), p. 9; Schwienbacher (2002), p. 7f.

[692] E.g., Fleming (2003), p. 13; Nesbit/Reynolds (1997); Schefczyk (2004)

[693] Fleming (2003), p. 13f.; Das/Jagannathan/Sarin (2003), p. 3

[694] Fleming (2003), p. 13f.

[695] See Hinkel (2001), p. 164, for a similar approach; Fried/Bruton/Hisrich (1998), p. 497, use a seven-point scale to survey the investment's performance

[696] This approach has been tested in pilot studies and has proven its superiority in terms of responses over more detailed questions

optimism can cause price inflations across industries or markets.[697] Subsequent declines are driven by investors growing scepticism after they have become disappointed from too many lemon issues. The occurrence of hot issue markets may reduce the impact of information asymmetry on the VCF's exit strategy since investors become less concerned about information gaps. The present analysis involves the market's valuation levels to control for the impact of investor optimism.

The common approach to discern hot issue markets grounds on the soaring valuation levels for new issues during hot issue periods.[698] Scholars assume the occurrence of hot issue markets if the initial average returns on IPOs in certain periods exceed the overall average of the sample period.[699] A higher average underpricing during a specific period implies higher initial returns and thus hotter markets.

This study pursues a similar approach. Information about IPOs is taken from VentureXpert. Then, monthly averages are calculated and assigned to each exit transaction – irrespectively whether it is an IPO or M&A transaction. This value reflects the equity valuation levels that accompany every exit transaction. It allows comparing the valuation levels across exits in different periods.

5.2 Data Collection

This section reports the data collection. It introduces the sources of data that this study taps and analyzes the representativeness of the data samples. Then, this section discusses the instruments the following chapter applies to validate the research model.

5.2.1 Secondary Data Collection

The data collection embarks on gathering publicly available information on exit transactions in the period from January 1st 1998 to December 31st 2002. The sample of VC-backed IPOs and M&A transactions is taken from VentureXpert. VentureXpert is a subsidiary of Thomson Financial, inc. that provides financial information on VC-investments, buyouts, PE funds and VC funds. VentureXpert claims to cover over 2,300 funds worldwide. Since 1985, it tracks almost every transaction within this focus.[700] The VentureXpert database hence mirrors a virtually complete picture of the VC activities in the U.S. and is assumed to constitute the entire population of exit transactions.

---

[697] Gompers/Lerner (2000), p. 206; Ibbotson/Jaffe (1975), p. 1027; Lowry (2003), p. 5; Ljungqvist/Wilhelm (2003), p. 723; Ofek/Richardson (2003), p. 113f.; Ritter (1984), p. 238f.

[698] E.g., Ibbotson/Jaffee (1975), p. 1027; Wang/Wang/Lu (2002), p. 72

[699] Bradley/Jordan (2002), p. 600; Ritter (1984), p. 216f.

[700] More information on VentureXpert can be found at www.venturexpert.com or www.thomsonfinancial.com.

VentureXpert was used in the Horn Library at Babson College, MA, on May 4th, 2004. By the time of the request, VentureXpert listed 11,856 international VC-backed companies that have filed information on corporate actions such as liquidations, IPOs, LBOs or M&A deals. For the sample period 1998 to 2002, only 3,959 (33.4 %) ventures have reported corporate actions. Out of those corporate actions, 2,825 (71.4 % respectively 23.8 %) ventures have accomplished either an IPO or an M&A transaction.[701] These transactions constitute the original data sample.[702] For each transaction, the following parameters are acquired:

- The company's major industry class and the businesses description
- Corporate actions such as the date of the first VC investment, the company's current situation and the dates of IPOs and acquisitions
- Information about the VC investment such as the number of involved VCFs, number and dates of investment rounds, the actual holding period and the company's stage at the initial investment and at exit
- Information about the involved investment banks and if applicable about the underpricing
- Information about the company's environment such as its auditors and competitors

However, this data sample does not contain all information required to empirically validate the research model. The research model addresses three additional aspects. First, the VCF's interactions with prospective investors and intermediates as it moves towards the exit are not reported. Second, information about the occurrence of departures and third about the investment's performance need to be added. Given that neither ventures nor VCFs publish this information on a regular basis, a primary data collection has to complement the original data sample.

5.2.2 Primary Data Collection

Management research suggests three instruments to raise data that is not provided by financial information systems: documentary analysis, interviews and direct inquiries via questionnaires.[703] Table 7 summarizes the advantages and shortcomings of each method.

---

[701] If the venture is floated but afterwards acquired by a private investor, VentureXpert reports an acquisition of a public company.

[702] VentureXpert refers to the VCF's portfolio companies as companies and to the VCF as "firm".

[703] Schefczyk (2000), p. 244f.

	Documentary analysis	Databases	Direct inquiries	
			Personal interview	Questionnaire
Access to relevant information	- publicly available information	- publicly available information	- detailed, internal information on past transactions	- detailed, internal information on past transactions
Time burden per data set	- depending on the depth of the inquiry	- low	- high, includes scheduling the interview as well as traveling	- low, including pre-contacts and sending the questionnaire
Reliability of the information	- depending on the source and disclosure rules	- partly incorrect	- suffering from reluctance to answer or oblivion in case of past events	- suffering from reluctance to answer or oblivion in case of past events

Table 7: Selection criteria for survey instruments[704]

As for this study, the private character of the missing information limits the application of documentary analysis. Data about the VCF's interactions with prospective investors, intermediates and other inside parties are not publicly accessible; this information is exclusively held by the involved parties.[705]

Interviews allow for the inquiry of private data. Yet, they require substantial resources and time. Every interview takes time to set up, to conduct and to evaluate ex-post. According to those experiences gained in the pilot studies, one interview requires up to six hours of preparations, travelling, conducting and revising depending on the location. Provided that each interviewee discusses on average five transactions, the collection of 150 transactions takes 180 hours. Besides, travelling imposes substantial costs. Because of the limited resources available to this project, interviews do not prove feasible.

To fill the information gap on the VCF's interactions, departures and the venture's performance, a direct inquiry is employed. Direct inquiries via questionnaires are attributed with the same advantages of interviews over documentary analysis. In addition, a survey using a questionnaire bears less efforts and lower costs. As from the addressee's perspective, questionnaires also feature two advantages that are likely to result in a better response ratio than attainable for personal interviews:[706]

- A questionnaire allows the addressee to flexibly determine the day and the time of his response. Fried, Bruton and Hisrich (1998) lay out that VC organizations have flat hierarchies. Senior VCFs have to deal with the daily busi-

[704] According to Schefczyk (2004), p. 246ff.

[705] Lerner (1994a), p. 295

[706] Atteslander (1995), p. 167; Friedrichs (1990), p. 237; Schefczyk (2004), p. 244f.; Stier (1999), p. 198

ness.[707] A flexible and easily accessible questionnaire allows VCFs to use narrow time lags to support independent scientific surveys.

- The addressee can be sure that his input will be kept strictly confidential given that his answers are aggregated by a computer and only reported in this form coupled with widely available secondary data. This approach hopes to collect data on failures without that the addressee must fear to lose his prestige.

Nevertheless, employing a questionnaire to raise data entails two specific problems. On the one hand, one exit transaction never equals another deal. Rather, exit transactions are individual processes involving a multitude of parties, activities and interactions. A standardized questionnaire does not capture the entire range of individuality of each transaction. To ensure highest possible consistency, the questionnaire is pilot tested and improved in discussions with a senior VC manager and with two senior researchers with substantial experiences in empirical analysis and VC research.[708] On the other hand, it is difficult to control for the person who eventually answers the questions. Cases in which the addressee forwards the questionnaire to lower levels in the hierarchy which eventually do not possess the proper information cannot be excluded.[709]

The VentureXpert database discerns 2,006 organizations that have been involved in the 2,825 venture investments during the sample period. Besides profit-oriented and independent VCFs, the sample contains individual investors, venture capital organizations of financial institutions and affiliates of industrial corporations. In several cases, the type and name of the financing organization is not disclosed so that the initial sample includes “undisclosed funds” respectively “undisclosed investors” as well. After excluding the anonymous investors and those organizations that do not meet the condition of being profit-minded and independent, 1,197 (59.7 %) VCFs remain. Out of these firms, 976 exhibit ten or less exit transactions within the period of 1998 to 2002. 135 have accomplished between 11 and 20 exits. Not more then 34 (25) VCFs have withdrawn from up to 30 (40) ventures. 27 VCFs report more than 40 exit transactions.

For each VCF, the information provided on the website has been screened in order to identify senior VC managers that took the lead in VC investments.[710] Pilot studies have fostered the assumption that if addressees recognize transactions they

---

[707] Fired/Bruton/Hisrich (1998), p. 496

[708] Prof. Andrew L. Zacharakis, Acting Director of the Arthur M. Blank Center, Babson College, MA, and Prof. William D. Bygrave, Frederic C. Hamilton Professor for Free Enterprise, Babson College, MA

[709] For a further discussion see Atteslander (1995), p. 168; Stier (1999), p. 198f.

[710] E.g., Norwest Venture Partners (www.nvp.com) or Draper Fisher Juverston (www.dfj.com) list transactions for each of their partners whereas HarbourVest Partners LLC (www.harnbourvest.com) does not provide such information.

are familiar with in the correspondence, they appreciate the previous identification work and are more prone to support the survey. Moreover, this method helps ensure that merely senior managers or employees that are familiar with the transaction provide their insights.[711] Naturally, this approach suffers from a success bias; since VCFs device their websites to promote their track records of successful investments, they are likely to list only successful transactions. Anticipating this bias, the initial letter, follow-up mails and the instructions given in the survey instrument explicitly ask the addressees to provide information on successful as well as on non-successful transactions.

In total, only 105 (8.8 %) VCFs provide sufficient information on their websites. 686 combinations of transactions and senior VC managers are identified this way. Given that most VC investments are syndicated, this data sample only contains 520 (75.8 %) genuine VC investments. Six deals are listed by four different VCFs, 27 deals by three VCFs and 93 by two VCFs. 268 names are connected to on average 2.56 transactions. 20 Managers are found to be involved in more than 5 transactions respectively 43 in more that three deals. Only one exit is identified for 96 individuals.

The questionnaire was set up online to warrant comfortable access and to quicken the answering process. Addressees were contacted four times unless they have provided information before. Initially, a regular letter was sent to invite the addressees to take part in the survey. After two weeks, a reminder was sent via e-mail. Thereupon, voicemails were left about one week later. A terminal follow-up e-mail was sent another week later. Each letter or e-mail contained the link to the online questionnaire and the sample of the addressee's transactions.[712] The survey has collected information on 169 transactions out of 520 identified deals (32.5 %). 47 (17.5 %) VC managers from 40 VCFs (38.1 %) took the survey. Figure 21 reports the distribution of responses. Four addressees declined to participate because their firm's policies forbid them to release information to outsiders.[713]

---

[711] Schefczyk (2004), p. 244

[712] The letter and mails are attached in the appendix. The online questionnaire was accessible under www.babson.edu/vcexits.

[713] Fried/Bruton/Hisrich (1998), p, 496, experience similar difficulties

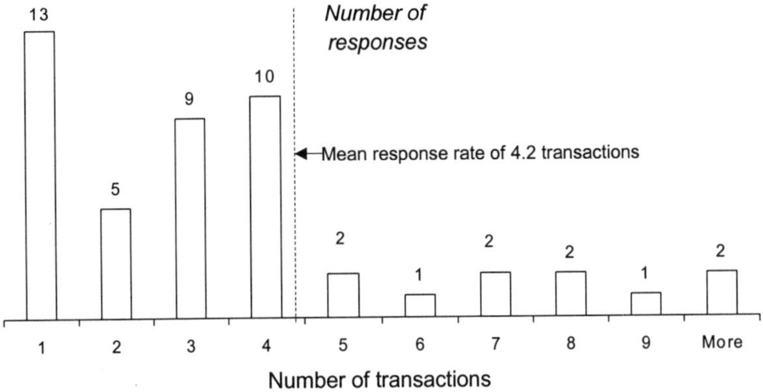

Figure 21: Distribution of responses

5.2.3 Representativeness of the Survey Data

To characterize the survey sample and assess its representativeness, the transactions in the survey sample are compared to the 2,825 transactions taken from VentureXpert. This analysis helps identify biases that may confound the results from the survey sample and skew the conclusions. Both samples are contrasted as regards the origins and characteristics of the exit transactions (represented major industry groups, investment stages, exit vehicles, exit dates and the venture's location) and the attributes of the involved VCFs (total know amount invested by firm and age).

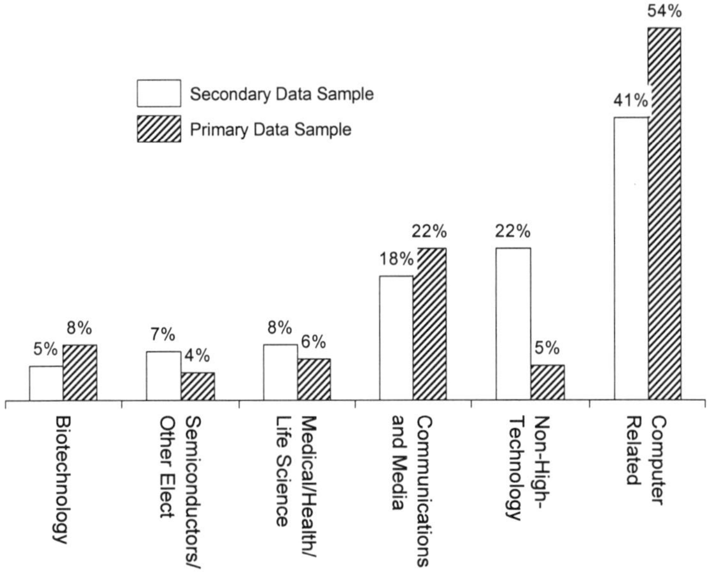

Figure 22: Company major industry affiliations in both data samples

As sketched in figure 22, the survey sample does not exactly resemble the original sample as regards the distribution of industries. In fact, the Pearson χ^2-test yields a χ^2-value of 37.59. Given five degrees of freedom, this value translates into a statistically significant difference of both samples ($p = 0.000$). Although the relative presence of Biotechnology, Semiconductor, Health Care and Communication ventures in both samples does not differ substantially, Non-High-Technology ventures are under-represented and Computer Related firms over-represented in the survey sample. This skewness may emanate from differing perceptions about VC between practitioners and VentureXpert. VentureXpert captures investments in low- and high-technology industries performed by institutional investors.[714] However, the survey instrument and the correspondence with addressees during the survey outline this dissertation's explicit focus on VC. Thus, addressees may have been tempted to provide more information on particularly innovative ventures and neglect low technology sectors. Yet, this bias does not confound later results severely given that the analyses do hardly involve the relative distribution of industries.

---

[714] E.g., Black/Gilson (1998), 245; Cumming/MacIntosh (2001), p. 445f.; Lam (1991), p. 137; these researchers relate VC primarily to the funding of high-technology businesses; see Chandler/Jansen (1992), p. 233, and MacMillan/Siegel/Subbanarasimha (1985), p. 125 for "self-selection-bias"

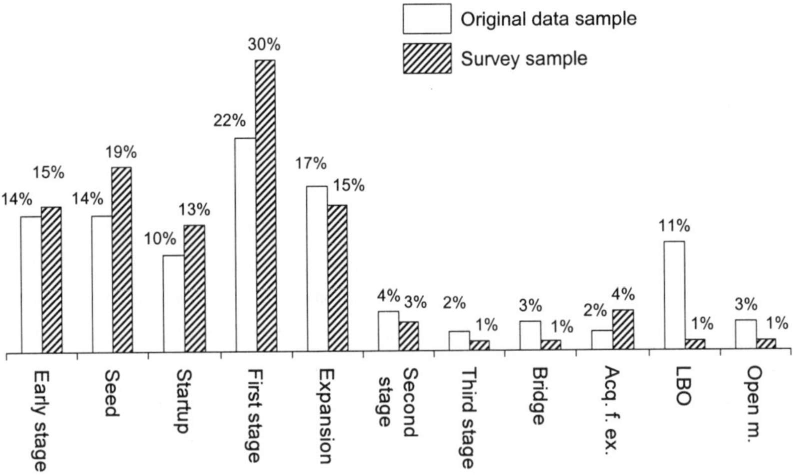

Figure 23: VCFs' entry-stages in both data samples

Both samples do not resemble each other as regards the entry stages; the Pearson χ^2-test delivers a χ^2-value of 134.61 at 11 degrees of freedom; the test confirms the statistically significant difference of both samples at a confidence level of 0.000. Given the focus on VC, early investment stages (Early stage to First stage) dominate in both samples. But the survey sample contains even more early stage investments and fewer later stage investments as compared to the original data sample. Akin to the bias in industry affiliation, this skewness may stem from VCFs' understanding of VC as being a financing option that particularly addresses the funding gaps of early stage ventures. A similar perception prevails in research.[715] Unlike, VentureXpert has a broader focus and spans more later stage investments. The discrepancy may impact the analysis of exit stages in that the average exit stage in the survey sample is shifted forward as well in relation the original data sample. Thus, survey sample exits suffer from relatively higher information dissimilarity as opposed to those transactions in the original data sample. To avoid this bias, the following analyses will draw on the original data sample instead of the survey sample for tests involving the venture's exit stage if possible.

[715] E.g. Black/Gilson (1998), p. 245; Gaida (2002), p. 147; Leitinger/Strohbach/Schöfer/Hummel (2000),p. 89; Levin (2001), p. 1–5; Pfirrmann/Wupperfeld/Lerner (1997), p. 9; Wright/Robbie/Romanet/ Thompson/Joachimsson/Bruining/Herst (1994), p. 84;

	N	IPOs	Private transactions	Total
Original data sample	2,836	27.2 %	72.8 %	100 %
Survey Sample	169	32.5 %	67.5 %	100 %

Table 8: Exit vehicles in both data samples

The distribution of IPOs across both samples seems to differ; the survey sample includes almost 20 % more IPOs than the original data sample and likewise less private transactions. The discrepancy between both samples is, however, not confirmed through the Pearson χ^2-test. The test yields a confidence level of only 0.302. Significant impacts on the outcomes are consequently not expected.

As discussed earlier, surveys in general may be subject to a success bias. Addressees prefer to provide data on successful transactions rather than admitting to mistakes. The literature suggests that only selective ventures are floated while the remainders sold to private investors.[716] Yet, the relative predominance of IPOs in the survey sample is statistically not significant so that both samples reflect a similar distribution. Thus, the survey sample does not suffer from a success bias with respect to the exit vehicle.

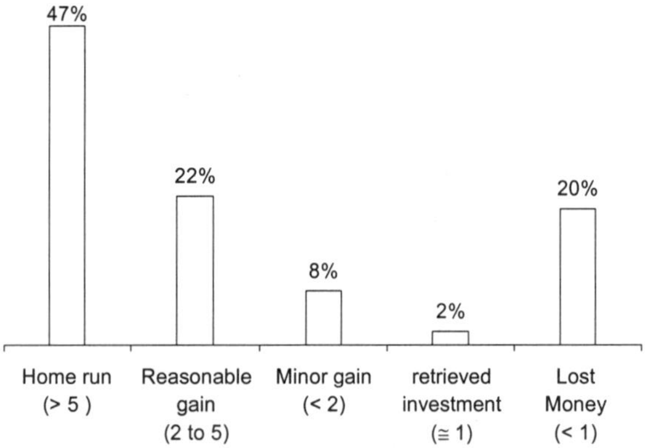

Figure 24: Distribution of investment multiples in the data sample

The analysis of the distribution of return multiples dwells further on the possibility of a success bias. Figure 24 illustrates the distribution of return multiples. The literature reports that usually 20 % of a VCF's investments turn out to be high-flyers whereas nearly 50 % of the surveyed transactions yield extraordinarily high return

[716] E.g., Black/Gilson (1998), p. 260; Fleming (2003), p. 9; Schwienbacher (2002), p. 7f.; see also section 3.1.1

ratios. Only the number of losses roughly complies with the notion in the literature that up to 30 % of the investments fail.[717] This congruence can be ascribed to the fact that the survey instrument explicitly instructs addressees to provide information on unsuccessful ventures as well. Given these instructions together with the success bias leading to an overweight of successful transactions, it appears reasonable that mean outcomes are underrepresented. However, the survey sample makes up for the overweight of successful transactions with a relatively great number of unsuccessful deals. In line with the finding on exit vehicles, both extreme outcomes (good and bad) are represented in the survey sample eliminating a general success bias.

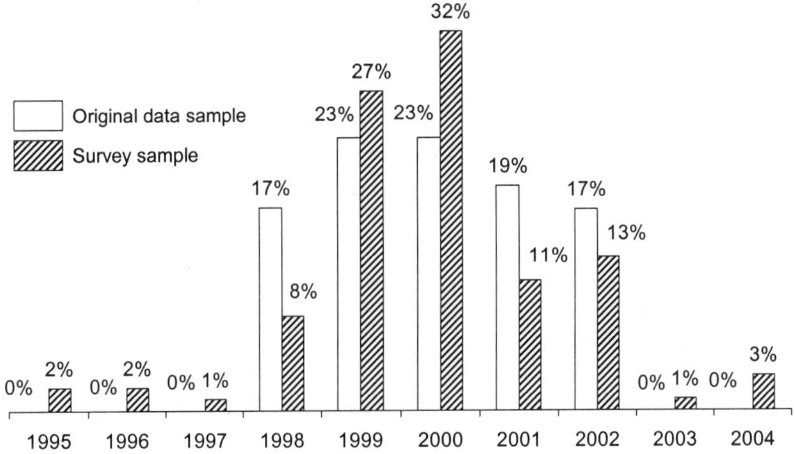

Figure 25: Comparison of exit dates in both data samples

The occurrence of exits peaks in the years 1999 and 2000 in both samples. Overall, the distribution of exits in the original data sample seems to be less punctuated compared to the survey sample. The standard deviation for the original data sample is 1.34 while the survey sample features a standard deviation of only 1.16 (respectively 1.63 if transactions prior 1998 and after 2002 are included). Nevertheless, the comparison of means does not substantiate a significant discrepancy; both means differ only at a confidence level of 0.75 (respectively 0.517 if outliers are included) so that the distribution of exit dates does essentially not differ across both samples. Three reasons may explain the slight differences that become apparent in figure 25:

[717] E.g., Bergemann/Hege (1998), p. 704; Bhide (2000), p. 143; Gompers/Lerner (2000), p. 6; Ruhnka/Young (1991), p. 119

- First, addressees have provided data from extraordinarily successful ventures. Highly profitable exits are more likely to occur if the capital markets allow for high valuation levels – as they did during the hot issue markets in 1999 and 2000. This notion explains the peak in the survey sample for 2000.
- The slight overweight of recent transactions in the survey sample may stem simply from the fact that those transactions are easier to remember. In an attempt to avoid acquiring historical data, the addressees may have preferred to report recent transactions.
- A few addressees were so kind to devote much time to the survey. They completed the survey for all ventures they are familiar with. In doing so, they added transactions from before 1998 and after 2002.

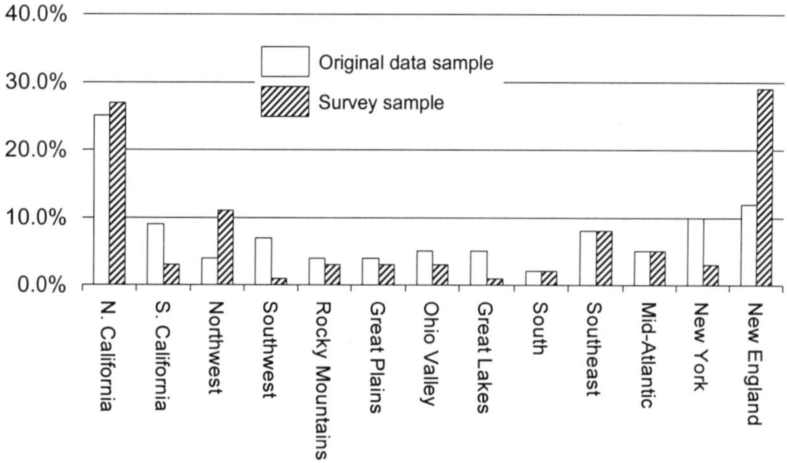

Figure 26: Regional origin of the venture companies

Elango, Fried, Hisrich and Polonchek (1995) and Shepherd and Zacharakis (2001a) among others discern different VC patterns across regions in the United States. Mostly, researchers refer to the Silicon Valley, CA, and to Route 128 around Boston, MA, as regional centres of VC financing in the U.S..[718] In this context, Shepherd and Zacharakis (2001a) exemplify that regional conditions influence the speed to IPO.[719] In their data sample of well above 900 IPOs, Shepherd and Zacharakis find that differences in the environmental conditions affect ventures' progress and thus

---

[718] Elango/Fried/Hisrich/Polonchek (1995), p. 158; Lee/Wahal (2002), p. 2; Shepherd and Zacharakis (2001a), p. 59 and p. 66

[719] Shepherd/Zacharakis (2001a), p. 59

their exit transactions; ventures in the Silicon Valley and around Route 128 accomplish IPOs faster than ventures stemming from other regions.[720] To inform the discussion about a possible bias, the regional origins of ventures in both samples are compared. Figure 26 illustrates that the survey sample contains relatively more transactions from the New England area than the original data sample. In turn, the survey sample captures relatively less transactions in New York and central areas of the U.S.. As for California, both ratios are virtually equal. The Pearson χ^2-test yields a value of 80.49. At 14 degrees of freedom, this value translates into a confidence level of 0.000 for the difference of both samples confirming an overweight of transactions in the Boston area. It is likely that this bias stems from the Babson College's reputation facilitating the data collection in the Boston area. To exclude the impact of this bias, the following analyses will draw on the original data sample if possible instead of the survey sample.

	Mean	2.	3.
1. All identified VCFs	14.3	0.000***	0.001***
2. Contacted VCFs	18.7		0.325
3. Participants	20.3		

* significant on a 10 % level; ** significant on a 5 % level; *** significant on a 1 % level

Table 9: VCFs' ages across samples

The research model does not only incorporate the venture's characteristics in its independent dimension. Additionally, the research model addresses the impact of the VCFs' characteristics on the exit transaction. Hence, the survey sample's representativeness in this respect has to be assessed too. Table 9 reports the test results for differences in VCFs' mean ages across the original data sample, the sample of contacted VCFs and VCFs that have taken the survey. Significant differences occur between the original data sample and the sample of transactions for which senior VC managers were identified as well as between the original data sample and the survey sample. The sample of transactions assigned to VC managers and the survey sample contain significantly older VCFs. The contact sample and the survey sample do, however, not vary significantly. This finding hints at a success bias that already affects the screening of VCFs' websites; seasoned VCF can advertise more successful transactions on their websites than younger firms with fewer exits. Thus, transactions of younger VCFs are more difficult to identify and to ascribe to senior managers.

[720] Shepherd/Zacharakis (2001a), p. 66

	Mean	2.	3.
1. All identified VCFs	299,102	0.000***	0.001***
2. Contacted VCFs	957,788		0.424
3. Participants	817,231		

* significant on a 10 % level; ** significant on a 5 % level; *** significant on a 1 % level

Table 10: VCF's total known amount invested [in 1,000 US$] in all companies

A similar bias becomes evident when contrasting the total known amount invested by the VCFs. Again, VCFs in the original sample are characterized by lower total known amounts invested than those VCFs in the contact sample and in the survey sample. However, the survey sample and the sample of contacted VCFs do not exhibit a significant discrepancy. Table 10 reports these results.

In essence, the survey sample lacks representativeness as regards the participating VCFs. Mostly older and larger VCFs in the New England area have taken the survey. This bias restrains the analysis of the impact of VC-backing. The exit behavior of younger and smaller VCFs is underrepresented so that the observed exit strategies already reflect a certain degree of seasoning. The impact of seasoning can consequently not be isolated entirely so that the survey sample does not allow for quantifying the complete impact of seasoning on exit strategies.

5.3 Employed Statistical Methods

The data samples found the basis for an empirical validation of the research model. This dissertation employs statistical methods to assess the quality of the proposed causalities. This chapter introduces these methods and discusses indicators that assess the outcomes' quality.

5.3.1 Conclusive Statistics and Hypothesis Testing

Testing the research model requires conclusive statistics that allow for a result in a defined confidence level. Initially, a test for significance requires the researcher to specify the proper confidence level α. The confidence level stipulates an interval in which an empirical result is accepted as statistically significant. Thus, errors within a certain margin become tenable and do not automatically lead to a hypothesis' rejection. In Psychology, Business Science and in other domains, researchers customarily denote findings as statistically significant if contradicting results occur in not more that five out of 100 times.[721]

[721] Bamberg/Baur (1998), p. 179ff.; Bohley (1996), p. 567ff.; Bortz (1999), p. 109ff.; Glass/Hopkins (1996), p. 257f.

Two types of mistakes occur in significance tests. On the one hand, a hypothesis is rejected even though it is true. Mistakes of this sort are denoted as α-errors. They occur if the value assigned to α is chosen too small so that only a very narrow array of hypotheses is accepted. On the other hand, a hypothesis may be accepted even though it is false. This so-called β-error originates from a high α value that allows for too many validations. How to determine α depends on the sample's size.[722] Large samples yield already significant results for weak causalities that small samples cannot confirm. A common confidence level in Finance is the 5 % hurdle; results that are robust on this level are accepted. The following table reports the different values and meanings that are oftentimes assigned to α. Given the difference in size between the original and the survey sample, the significance levels are chosen separately. Tests that involve the survey sample call for a confidence level of 10 %. For tests that exclusively draw on the original sample, a significance level of 5 % is set.

Probability for error α in %	Implications
[0; 0.1]	highly significant
(0.1; 1]	well significant
(1; 5]	significant
(5; 10]	roughly significant
> 10	not significant

Table 11: Significance levels and their implications[723]

Conditional on the scaling of the available of data, proper test statistics have to be determined. A variable's scale refers to the variable's definition and measurement procedure. Every scale measurement has other attributes that permit different statistical methods. The four scales of measurement are nominal, ordinal, interval and ratio:[724]

- *Nominal:* Categorical data and numbers that are simply used as identifiers or names represent a nominal scale of measurement. A nominal measurement assigns objects to nominal groups so that all those objects in a singe category are (virtually) equivalent with respect to their attributes. This thesis involves nominal measures for instance with respect to the venture's industry affiliation.
- *Ordinal:* An ordinal scale of measurement represents a ranked series of relationships. Likert-type scales, for instance, are ordinarily scaled. These scales do not provide a measurable quantity but a ranked order from low to high. As

[722] Bortz (1999), p. 124

[723] According to Bühl/Zöfel (1998), p. 111f.; Rüdiger (2000), p. 254; Zöfel (2001), p. 63

[724] Bortz/Döring (1995), p. 64ff.; Glass/Hopkins (1996), p. 7ff.; Zöfel (2001), p. 13ff.

for this thesis, most variables are ordinally scaled, such as Promotion, Exit Stages, etc.

- *Interval:* An interval scale measures quantities and has equal units. Interval scales are used to measure the VC holding period, the investment's size etc.
- *Ratio:* The ratio scale of measurement is similar to the interval scale in that it represents quantity and has equality of units. However, this scale also has an absolute zero with no numbers existing below. Physical measures, for instance, represent ratio data. Physical measures do not occur in this analysis.

Once the variables conjoint in a hypothesis have been defined, the proper test method can be selected. Science has developed a multitude of testing procedures for bi-variate tests of every possible combination of scale measurements. Zöfel (2001) suggests the scheme reported in table 12 to pick the proper test statistic. Zöfel, however, acknowledges that modern statistical software selects suitable tests automatically.

	Nominal	Ordinal	Intervall
Nominal	Cross-classified table with Chi-square	Cross-classified table;Test for different means	Test for different means
Ordinal		Cross-classified table; Spearman rank correlation	Spearman rank correlation; Kendall rank correlation
Intervall			Spearman rank correlation; Pearson correlation

Table 12: Statistical tests contingent on the variables' scales[725]

5.3.2 Regression Analysis and Discriminant Analysis

Besides validating dependencies between two variables, the strength of the suggested relations is analyzed. This method allows researchers to forecast the impact of exogenous factors on endogenous variables. To explore such issues, this study employs regression analysis. Regression analysis is a statistical means for the investigation of the dependency of one variable (Y) on another (X).[726] In a linear regression model, the dependent variable Y is assumed to be a linear function of one or more independent variables plus an error term introduced to account for omissions. A regression analysis with a single explanatory variable is termed "bi-variate regression" while an analysis of several independent variables is referred to as "multi-

---

[725] Zöfel (2001), p. 89

[726] Glass/Hopkins (1996), p. 170; Pedhazur/Schmelkin (1991), p. 371ff.

variate regression".[727] Multi-variate regressions moreover deliver results on interdependencies in the independent variables and allow for the isolation of every variable's impact. The following equation represents the general regression model:

$$Y = \beta_1 X_{i1} + \ldots + \beta_K X_{Ki} + \upsilon_i \qquad \textit{(Linear regression model)}$$

The purpose of regression analysis is to estimate the coefficients β based upon the information contained in the data set. The method of least squares is used to fit the continuous variable Y as a linear function of the predictor variables X_K. The least square method finds the line that minimizes the sum of squared deviations for each point in the sample to the point on the line corresponding to the X-value. Regression model is based on the following assumptions:[728]

- The relationship between X and Y is linear
- The dependent variable must be at least ordinally scaled
- The variance of the error term is constant for all values of the dependent variable X.
- The independent variable is uncorrelated with the error term
- The error term is normally distributed

A common test to measure the goodness for fit of regression models is the R^2 test. This test statistic is equal to one minus the ratio of the sum of squared estimated errors (the deviation of the actual value of the dependent variable from the regression line) to the sum of squared deviations about the mean of the dependent variable. The sum of squared deviations about the regression line is a measure of the extent to which the regression fails to explain the dependent variable. Hence, the R^2 statistic is a measure of the extent to which the total variation of the dependent variable is explained by the regression model. The R^2 statistic ranges between zero and one.[729] A high value of R^2, suggests that the regression model explains the variation in the dependent variable well. Low values indicate the omission of important causal variables raising the possibility that the error term may contain further explanatory factors.[730]

In general, R^2 soars when further independent variables are added to an existing model. For an infinite number of factors, R^2 theoretically attains the maximum value of one. However, if the explained deviation of a new variable is lower than the impact on the model's degree of freedom[731], the model's quality suffers – even though R^2 still grows. To detect this misleading result, researchers introduce the adjusted R^2.

---

[727] Glass/Hopkins (1996), p. 170 and p. 173f.

[728] Glass/Hopkins (1996), p. 170ff.

[729] Hanushek/Jackson (1977), p. 57f.

[730] Brosius (1998), p. 534f.

[731] The degree of freedom goes up since a new variable is added to the model.

The adjusted R^2 accounts for both changes and delivers a measure to assess the model's new quality after complementing a new factor. Adding new factors contributes to the model's quality only if the adjusted R^2 soars. As long as the R^2 exceeds the adjusted R^2, the model neglects important factors.[732]

Regression models oftentimes suffer from collinearity. Collinearity refers to the interrelatedness of exogenous factors. If two or more independent variables correlate with each other, their impact on the dependent variable overlaps. The regression analysis' results thus lose power. To diminish collinearity, the explaining variables have to be disentangled. SPSS automatically measures the Tolerance (respectively the Variance Inflation Factor (VIF)) for each exogenous factor. If the test delivers a Tolerance lower than 0.1, collinearity may exist between at least one pair of exogenous variables. In this case, the variables deserve further attention and some parameters may need to be excluded. The elimination of factors with low Tolerances improves the model's clearness.[733]

The Discriminant Analysis resembles the Regression analysis. Yet, Discriminant Analyses drop the presumption of ordinal or higher scales dependent variables.[734] The Discriminant Analysis classifies a set of predictor variables with the number of classes being determined by the nominal dependent variable. In the first instance, a linear discriminant equation is calculated akin to the regression analysis. The resulting equation is used to compute the theoretical class for every case. The quality of the discriminant model is evaluated on the basis of the class differences. The model has more explanatory power the more the classes differ. The ratio of the between classes sum of squares in relation to the classes' sum of squares yields the Eigenvalue. The Eigenvalue serves as goodness of fit indicator. Higher values indicate a better discrimination between classes. Wilks' lambda constitutes an inverse measure. It is used to test the null hypothesis that the classes feature similar means. The smaller Wilks' lambda becomes, the more doubt cast upon the classes' similarity.[735] The models explanatory power is reflected by the Canonical Correlation. Conversely to Pearson's Correlation Coefficient, the Canonical Correlation measures the relationship between two sets of variables. For the dependent variable with only two values, the squared Canonical Correlation accounts for the percent of variation in the endogenous variable discriminated by the exogenous factors. The model's explanatory power thus increases with higher Canonical Correlation coefficients.[736]

---

[732] Brosius (1998), p. 546ff.

[733] Brosius (1998), p. 563ff.; Pedhazur/Schmelkin (1991), p. 448ff.

[734] E.g., Westhead/Wright (1998) employ discriminant analyses in an entrepreneurship context

[735] Brosius (1998), p. 591ff.; Zöfel (2001), p. 209f.

[736] Brosius (1998), p. 601

5.3.3 Hierarchical Cluster Analysis

The Hierarchical Cluster Analysis represents a procedure for grouping cases with similar properties. These groups are mutually exclusive and – most important – unknown. In contrast to statistical devices that test predefined structures, the purpose of the cluster analysis is to identify new structures. Cluster analysis has proven useful in a variety of management sciences where the identification of groups with similar properties provides meaningful hints for decisions. Marketing research, for instance, employs cluster analyses to combine customers with similar attributes.[737]

The Cluster Analysis always produces groups. At every stage, the combination with the smallest distance is clustered and constitutes a new group. The quality of the agglomeration at each step hence depends on the distances between the joined groups. The number of clusters decreases and similarity amid the each cluster declines with increasing distances. Distances also measure the improvement of each further step. If the distances between two subsequent steps do not increase considerably, the aggregation unites rather similar clusters. With increasing distances, the similarity within the cluster declines.

5.4 Conclusive Remarks

This chapter presents the empirical design and describes the collection of the data samples which underlie the subsequent tests. This study is based on two data samples. The first data sample is taken from a public source and captures virtually all transactions during the sample period. Yet, this data sample does not provide all information that is necessary to empirically validate the research model. Hence, non-public data is complemented throughout an online-survey.

The quality of the data samples eventually determines the quality of the empirical findings. To assess the data-quality, this chapter devotes particular attention to discuss significant differences. The results imply that the survey sample is biased. As regards the investments, the analysis identifies three biases. First, high-technology ventures overweight in the survey sample as compared to the original data sample. Second, VCFs that participate in the survey seem to enter transactions in earlier stages. Finally, the survey sample comprises relatively more exit transactions in the New England area than the original data sample. To alleviate the confounding impact of the survey sample's shortcomings, the following analyses revert to the original data sample instead of the survey sample if possible. Yet, the survey sample does not suffer from a success bias. This shortcoming was anticipated through instructing VCFs to provide information on both successful and unsuccessful exits. In essence,

---

[737] See Anderberg (1973) for a general introduction to cluster analysis; Brosius (1998), p. 691ff.; in a VC context, MacMillan/Kulow/Khoylian (1989) employ cluster analyses

the data sample resembles a parabola with an overweight of both successful and unsuccessful while medium outcomes are underrepresented. Thus, the success is not considered to flaw the empirical findings greatly. Besides, the survey sample is confounded because the participating VCFs are on average more seasoned than the average VCF in the original sample. This bias influences the empirical result in that the analyses cannot capture the impact of seasoning completely but must assume a certain degree of seasoning prevalent in the survey sample.

Given the survey sample's shortcomings, the empirical analysis reverts to the original data sample as often as possible. Moreover, the discussion is alert for the biases.

6 Empirical Analysis

Throughout this section, the research model is tested for its validity on the basis of the survey data sample and the original data sample if applicable. After discussing the research model and the interrelations between the endogenous variables, this section aims at identifying structures in the survey sample that have not been foreseen in the research model but influence the VCF's exit strategy as well. Therefore, an investigative technique – the cluster analysis – is employed.

6.1 Confirmatory Analysis

This section discusses the hypotheses as set out in the research model. It seeks to disclose statistically significant relationships between the suggested independent variables and the VCF's exit options Timing, Exit Vehicle, Promotion and Third-Party Certification. Therefore, this dissertation employs bi-variate and multi-variate tests. Bi-variate tests precede the multi-variate tests as they allow for a focused discussion on the result of every hypothesis with the chance of exploring further combinations of related factors in order to probe the outcome. Every section is concluded with a multi-variate regression analysis that aggregates the independent factors and the control variables into one model providing a more general overview on the structure of influences on the dependent parameters.

Figure 27 summarizes the outcome of the statistical tests for every hypothesis. The figure shows that the research model fits for the VCF's timing strategy and its choice of exit vehicles. For both dimensions, three out of five hypotheses are validated. As regards the VCF's promotion, two hypotheses are accepted while two other assumptions result in significantly contradicting results. The only significant result for third-party certification contradicts the relevant hypothesis; four dependencies do not prove significant. As will be seen in the following discussion, the VCF's decisions on promotion and thrid-party certification mainly depend on the exit vehicle instead of information asymmetry concerns as set out in the research model. IPOs trigger both, greater pormotion efforts and more third-party certification than private transactions. Alternative explanations such as the VCF's investment philosophy and interdependencies between the exit strategy options add substantial explanatory power to the model reflecting that information asymmetry concerns rival with other influences.

The following discussion is organised in a way that allows summarizing the actual impacts on one exit strategy option; for every strategy decision, influences are examined separately and conjointly.

	Timing		Vehicle		Promotion		3rd-party cert.	
Innovation	H 1.1.1	!	H 1.1.2	!	H 1.1.3	!	H 1.1.4	-
Exit stage	H 1.2.1	✓	H 1.2.2	✓	H 1.2.3	-	H 1.2.4	-
Competition	H 1.3.1	-	H 1.3.2	✓	H 1.3.3	!	H 1.3.4	!
Departures	H 2.1.1	✓*	H 2.1.2	✓*	H 2.1.3	✓	H 2.1.4	-
VCF's age	H 3.1.1	✓	H 3.1.2	!	H 3.1.3	✓	H 3.1.4	-

✓ Hypothesis confirmed ! Contradicting outcome - No significant outcome

** Validated ex-post in the multi-variate analysis*

Figure 27: Overview on the outcomes for every hypothesis

6.1.1 The Holding Duration

a) The degree of innovation and industry affiliation

Hypothesis 1.1.1 argues that later exits increase information efficiency; yet, newness may moderate this relationship in that the time it takes to accomplish information efficiency increases with the degree of innovation. At any given time, highly innovative ventures require more time to resolve prospective investors' uncertainty since they impose more information spreads about the business on outsiders. Table 13 reports the test results on the basis of the original data sample.

		N	*Mean*	*SD*	*t*-test *p*-value
Holding duration	Non-innovative	530	64.00	58.98	0.000***
	Innovative	2,127	48.82	47.68	
Exit stages	Non-innovative	488	8.82	3.39	0.000***
	Innovative	1,961	6.85	2.79	
Financing rounds	Non-innovative	583	2.43	2.24	0.000***
	Innovative	2,182	3.65	2.65	

* significant on a 10 % level; ** significant on a 5 % level; *** significant on a 1 % level
[1] [mil. US$]

Table 13: Industry affiliation vs. timing considerations

The test reveals highly significant differences between non-innovative and innovative industries as regards the holding duration, the number of exit stages and financing rounds. The mean VC holding period of non-innovative ventures significantly tops the average VC duration of innovative ventures. This finding contradicts hypothesis 1.1.1 and leads to its initial rejection. In fact, the first test suggests that either innovative ventures require less time to resolve information asymmetry or information dissimilarities are resolved differently across industries. To further explore this observation, an extra test researches the mean VC holding duration across the six industry groups.

	N	*Mean*	*SD*	*t*-test *p*-value 2.	3.	4.	5.	6.
1. Biotechnology	127	65.20	49.83	0.000***	0.000***	0.582	0.794	0.979
2. Comm. & Media	493	43.05	41.77		0.933	0.000***	0.000***	0.000***
3. Computer Related	1,120	43.24	43.06			0.000***	0.000***	0.000***
4. Life Sciences	208	68.31	50.33				0.322	0.632
5. Non-High-Tech.	534	63.72	58.86					0.755
6. Semiconductors	179	65.39	69.12					

* significant on a 10 % level; ** significant on a 5 % level; *** significant on a 1 % level

Table 14: Industry affiliation vs. holding duration

Table 14 essentially discerns two clusters by their mean holding periods. Ventures in Communication and Media and Computer Related sectors remain in the VCF's portfolio for 43 months while ventures in other industries are exited after 20 more months (over 30 % more). The discrepancy between these two groups proves significant for almost every combination. The same pattern emerges when contrasting the holding periods across industries for IPO exits and M&A exits. For M&A transactions, all differences between either Communication, Media or Computer sectors and the remaining industries prove significant at p = 0.000. The comparisons for IPO exits are slightly less significant on 5 % levels. Only, Semiconductor IPOs do not require significantly longer holding periods than Communication and Media and Computer Related IPOs. In fact, Semiconductor IPOs range between the relatively short holding periods of Communication and Media and Computer Related ventures and the relatively long holding periods in the remaining sectors. But Semiconductor IPOs do not significantly differ from IPOs in any other group. Nevertheless, the clustering of Communication and Media and Computer Related ventures on the one hand and other ventures on the other hand remains robust even if the exit vehicle's impact is excluded. Conversely to the initial test's outcome, table 14 does not report significant differences between high and low tech ventures anymore but rather between these two categories. Given that both groups comprise so-called innovative sectors, a general relationship between information efficiency about the business with the holding duration must be declined.

The observed clusters in IPO exits inspire an alternative reasoning to hypothesis 1.1.1 on the impact of hot issue markets. The data sample's period from 1998 to 2002 coincides with the most recent hot issue markets for internet and communication companies. Ljungqvist and Wilhelm (2003) and Chang (2004) observe in support of this argumentation a "dot-com" bubble for internet related companies from 1996 to 2000. During this period, internet-IPOs obtained higher valuation levels than other issues.[738] Akin, Gompers and Lerner (2000) report hot issue markets in "recent years" particularly for computer related businesses and internet ventures.[739] The comparison of average first-day returns across industries sustains this notion; Communication and Media and Computer Related ventures experience the highest returns on the first day of trading, significantly surpassing the average initial proceeds in the remaining sectors.[740] The significantly shorter holding periods for Communication and Media and Computer Related ventures reflect that the market's optimism towards these industries eases VCFs' floatations of ventures in these sectors. Given the presence of hot issue markets, the VCF's exit timing is not determined by managerial considerations or transaction costs anymore but rather by exit opportunities for Communication and Media and Computer Related ventures. The occurrence of particularly appealing equity valuation levels in the Computer Related and Communication and Media sector thus allows VCFs to shorten the holding duration of ventures without giving up returns. Lerner's (1994a) conclusions support this argumentation;

---

[738] Ljungqvist/Wilhelm (2003), p. 727ff., and p. 738, table 5; see also Chang (2004), p. 722ff.

[739] Gompers/Lerner (2000), p. 206

[740] See table 5

Lerner shows that VCFs can time their exits to capitalize on hot markets.[741] Likewise, section 6.1.1 f) reports that equity valuation levels impact the VCF's timing decision. Given the absence of a comparable hype for the remaining industries, IPO exits in the Computer Related and Communication and Media sectors require relatively shorter holding periods

This argumentation also holds against the exit stage as shown in table 15. The comparison of the average exit stages across industries confirms that Computer Related and Communication and Media ventures are withdrawn significantly earlier in their development process than ventures in other industries. Non-High-Technology ventures on average accomplish exits in the latest stage – throughout the Bridge and the Other Expansion stage – given that they experience lower equity valuation levels.

	N	*Mean*	*SD*	*t*-test *p*-value 2.	3.	4.	5.	6.
1. Biotechnology	105	7.15	3.11	0.625	0.027**	0.167	0.000***	0.905
2. Comm. & Media	444	7.00	2.76		0.003***	0.003***	0.000***	0.682
3. Computer Related	1,050	6.55	2.60			0.000***	0.000***	0.012**
4. Life Sciences	194	7.76	3.23				0.000***	0.048**
5. Non-High-Tech.	488	8.82	3.39					0.000***
6. Semiconductors	168	7.11	2.99					

* significant on a 10 % level; ** significant on a 5 % level; *** significant on a 1 % level

Table 15: Industry affiliation vs. exit stages

While this rationale explains the difference between Computer Related and Communication and Media IPOs and IPOs in the remaining sectors, it is still unclear why Non-High-Technology ventures are not exited earlier than Semiconductor ventures for example. The finding on significant differences in the number of financing rounds across industries – as reported in table 13 – points at another possible explanation: Innovative ventures may experience earlier exits because of superior supervision. Innovative ventures are found to receive almost 50 % more financing rounds than non-innovative ventures. The implementation of more investment stages translates into a more intense monitoring with VCFs reviewing their involvement more often. As the VCF's investment decision at every stage signals the investment's quality, more investment rounds improve the outside investors' perceptions about the venture's quality.[742] The significantly lower holding periods in combination with more stages even amplifies the monitoring intensity for innovative ventures.[743]

---

[741] Lerner (1994a), p. 300; Wang/Sim (2001), p. 342

[742] Barry/Muscarella/Peavy/Vetsuypens (1990), p. 501; Cornelli/Yosha (2003), p. 1; Giot/Schwienbacher (2003), p. 11; Gompers (1995), p. 1487; Gompers/Lerner (2000), p. 164; Gorman/Sahlman (1989), p. 238; Lam (1991), p. 139; Leland/Pyle (1977), p. 371

[743] See Gompers (1995), p. 1482ff. for similar findings and conclusions

Another test confirms this argumentation. If the VCF's monitoring is more intense for ventures that are exited earlier, a negative correlation between the monitoring intensity and the holding duration must sustain the interrelatedness. In fact, the Monitoring Intensity[744] and the Holding Period correlate with a Pearson's r of –0.282 at a significance level of 0.000.[745] The highly significant and negative correlation suggest that ventures that receive a more intense supervision as operationalized by financing rounds over time can accomplish exits earlier. A less rigorous monitoring in turn delays the VCF's withdrawal.

In essence, hypothesis 1.1.1 bears some substance in that exits of innovative ventures appear more difficult. These difficulties result from information asymmetries about the venture's innovations. That is why innovative ventures are monitored more closely and depend more on hot issue markets. Nevertheless, VCFs do not adjust the exit timing as predicted; they rather resolve prospective investors' uncertainties through their investment behavior and exploit IPO hypes to accomplish exits.

b) Development level

Hypothesis 1.2.1 reasons that the holding duration decreases the faster the venture progresses. If a venture progresses to higher development stages earlier, it establishes track records and gains visibility faster. Quick progress enables prospective investors to resolve their uncertainties sooner. Table 16 reports the correlation analysis' outcome.

	N	Development pace	
		Pearson's r	*Significance*
Holding Duration	2,196	-0.176	0.000***
Monitoring Intensity	2,195	0.338	0.000***

* significant on a 10 % level; ** significant on a 5 % level; *** significant on a 1 % level

Table 16: Development pace vs. timing[746]

According to the test result, the speed in accomplishing higher development levels negatively correlates with the holding duration at a high confidence level. Separate tests for the correlation between Holding Duration and Development Pace for IPO exits and M&A transactions deliver similar correlation coefficients (–0.208 in

[744] The Monitoring Intensity equals the Number of Financing Rounds divided by the Holding Period in Months.

[745] N = 2,661

[746] Development Pace is equals the Number of Stages the venture has taken during the VC process plus one (to capture those investments that do not progress at all) divided by the Holding Duration in Months.

IPOs and –0.161 in M&A exits; both significant at p = 0.000). Regardless of the terminal development level and the exit vehicle, faster progressing ventures achieve exits earlier. The assumption that a higher pace establishes information efficiency earlier and quickens exits is thus validated. The test's outcome is also consistent with prior results; a higher development pace is accomplished through a more intense supervision. The correlation between the Monitoring Intensity and the Development Pace proves highly significant as reported in table 16.

c) Competition

Hypothesis 1.3.1 posits a positive relationship between the competitiveness of the venture's environment and the holding duration. It is presumed that competition forces ventures to release more information. Thus, competition improves information efficiency and allows for earlier exits. Table 17 analyzes the correlation.

	N	No. of competitors	
		Pearson's r	*Significance*
Holding duration	2,651	0.027	0.166
Exit stage	2,449	0.136	0.000***

* significant on a 10 % level; ** significant on a 5 % level; *** significant on a 1 % level

Table 17: Competition vs. holding duration

The number of competitors is not found to determine the holding duration significantly. Ventures in highly competitive settings are neither exited earlier nor later than ventures in non-competitive environments. The same notion applies for non-competitive settings. Even if the moderation of the exit vehicle is excluded, no significant correlation between Holding Duration and No. of Competitors materializes. The confidence level for private transactions is 0.111 and 0.569 for IPOs. Hypothesis 1.3.1 is thus rejected.

Hypothesis 1.3.1 also implies earlier stage exits for competitive settings. If rivalry forces ventures to release details about their business, information efficiency is established in earlier development stages. In fact, the analysis finds a positive correlation between the exit stage and the number of competitors. In highly competitive settings, ventures are withdrawn later while non competitive settings accelerate exits. Again, this finding contradicts the assumptions in hypothesis 1.3.1; hypothesis 1.3.1 is rejected. Yet, the significantly positive correlation points at an alternative explanation. First, IPO candidates are found to feature more competitors.[747] In the context of the choice of exit vehicles, competition improves information efficiency within a sector

[747] See section 6.1.2 c)

advantaging public finance over private finance. Second, VCFs select their IPO candidates carefully; only later stage investments are floated while ventures that stall in earlier stages are sold privately.[748] This indirect connection reflects the origin of the present outcome and allows for rejecting a direct causality.

Both findings suggest that information asymmetry does neither determine the holding duration nor directly impact the exit stage as set out in hypothesis 1.3.1. Rather, the selection of proper exit vehicles for competitive and non-competitive settings translates into a decision about the exit stage. Nevertheless, this selection is driven by informational concerns.

d) Departures of entrepreneurial team members

Hypothesis 2.1.1 argues that departures evoke additional concerns of prospective investors. In consequence, VCFs have to stick to ventures longer until uncertainties produced by departures are resolved through the surfacing of new information. Table 18 shows the test results.[749]

	N	No. of departures	
		Pearson's r	*Significance*
Holding duration	164	-0.025	0.749
Exit stage	161	0.113	0.154

* significant on a 10 % level; ** significant on a 5 % level; *** significant on a 1 % level

Table 18: Timing vs. departures

In fact, it appears that departures have virtually no impact on the holding duration. First, the correlation coefficient varies only slightly from zero. Second, this correlation is not significant. Separate tests for IPO exits and private transactions deliver similar results; the correlation between Holding Duration and Number of Departures is not significant at $p = 0.622$ for private transactions respectively 0.593 for IPO exits. VCFs essentially time their exits regardless whether departures have occurred or not. Hypothesis 2.1.1 is thus rejected.

The rejection is also robust against the exit stage. Given this result, the occurrence of departures has no influence on the VCF's timing strategy. VCFs do not await the venture's progress to a higher development stages to alleviate prospective investors' concerns about departures.

---

[748] See section 6.1.2 f); see also Fleming (2003), p. 9; Schwienbacher (2002), p. 7f.

[749] Based on the survey sample

e) The VCF's certification ability

Hypothesis 3.1.1 accounts for the grandstanding phenomenon. Younger VCFs are supposed to exit earlier than older VCFs. Table 19 reports the result.

	N	VCF's age	
		Pearson's r	*Significance*
Holding duration	2,526	0.303	0.000***
Exit stage	2,316	0.152	0.000***
No. of stages	2,080	0.308	0.000***
Financing rounds	2,577	0.374	0.000***
Development pace	2,080	0.068	0.002***

* significant on a 10 % level; ** significant on a 5 % level; *** significant on a 1 % level

Table 19: VCF's age vs. holding duration

The positive correlation between the VCF's age and the holding duration proves highly significant. Younger VCFs evidently exit earlier than their older peers. The test confirms the grandstanding phenomenon and highlights the greater importance unseasoned VCFs ascribe to reputation building in comparison to establishing information efficiency at exit.[750] Separate tests for private transactions and IPOs show that Gompers' grandstanding hypothesis applies to both exit vehicles alike. For 1,869 private transactions, the correlation between the VCF's age and the holding period amounts to 0.334 at p = 0.000. Likewise, the analysis of 657 IPOs delivers a Pearson's r of 0.246 at p = 0.000. Hypothesis 3.1.1 is thus sustained.

Hypothesis 3.1.1 also holds against the exit stage, the number of investment stages and the number of financing rounds. All parameters soar with the VCF's seasoning. This finding sustains the notion that unseasoned VCFs hustle their ventures into exits. But they do not try to accelerate withdrawals in that they step up monitoring or seek to improve the venture's development pace. In essence, younger VCFs seem to contribute less to the fledging of their portfolios and yet exit earlier. Given the high correlation coefficient, grandstanding turns out to be an elementary factor that determines the timing strategy substantially.

f) Control variables

Besides the proposed causalities centering on information dissimilarities between inside and outside investors, further factors may determine the VCF's holding duration. Table 20 reports the test results for significant differences across nominally scaled variables.

---

[750] Gompers (1996), p. 135f.

	N	Mean	SD	t-test p-value
Non-leading auditor	50	75.52	53.19	0.000***
Leading auditor	1,604	54.95	47.31	
Private transaction	1,975	54.16	53.28	0.000***
Public transaction	686	45.04	40.61	
No external approach	93	57.28	55.51	0.451[1]
External approach	71	49.63	74.21	

* significant on a 10 % level; ** significant on a 5 % level; *** significant on a 1 % level

[1] Based on the survey sample

Table 20: Nominal control variables vs. holding duration

Holding periods vary contingent on the auditors and exit vehicles. Ventures that enlist big four auditors are on average exited more than one year before ventures with less prestigious auditors. This finding is consistent with the combination of two causal relations. On the one hand, IPO candidates are exited earlier. On the other hand, IPOs require the VCF to hire more prestigious auditors to certify for the correctness of financial statements than private transactions do.[751] Thus, auditors and holding duration are indirectly connected through the chosen exit vehicle. In addition, this finding may reflect the positive influence of the auditor's third-party certification on prospective investors' uncertainties; VCFs can capitalize on big four auditors providing certification for financial statements in that ventures are exited earlier. Separate tests for IPO exits and M&A transactions sustain the finding that prestigious auditors accelerate exits. It remains, however, open whether the auditor's presence triggers sooner exits or whether the employment of prestigious auditors is the consequence of investments' characteristics which at the same time promote earlier exits. The regression analysis dwells on this question.

Ventures that eventually undergo a private transaction remain longer in the VCF's portfolio. This significant distinction may mirror VCFs' ambitions to try a floatation first. If the VCF cannot place the venture in public markets, it follows up on alternative strategies such as private transactions.[752] Whether an external investor approaches the VCF or not does not significantly impact the holding duration. Only a slight tendency towards earlier exits in case of an approach is observable. Both aspects receive further attention in the following part.

---

[751] See section 6.1.2 f)

[752] Section 3.1.1 a) sets out the advantages of IPOs over private transactions; e.g., Chang (2004), p. 723; Lam (1991), p. 96; Wang/Sim (2001), p. 343 and p. 353; Zingales (1995), p. 425f.

The remaining scaled control variables exert almost no significant influence on the holding duration. Only the public market's condition six to nine month in advance to the exit affects the holding duration slightly. The relation between equity valuation levels and the holding duration confirms that investors' tolerate earlier exits in hot issue market periods.[753] This finding is also consistent with Lerner's (1994a) conclusion that VCFs try to time their exits so that they capitalize on hot issue markets.[754] Moreover, hot issue markets shorten the VC duration given the strong influence of equity valuation levels on the choice of the exit vehicle and in turn the exit vehicle's impact on the timing decision.[755] The fact that this test only yields a significant result for the market's state six to nine months prior to the exit accounts for the long preparation period for IPO exits. In essence, VCFs must decide on a floatation six months before the initial listing to complete the preparations in time. The correlation analyses' results are presented in table 21.

	N	Holding duration	
		Pearson's r	*Significance*
Third-party certification	563	-0.063	0.136
Promotion	163	-0.084	0.286[1]
First-day returns upon exit	2,661	0.027	0.158
Initial returns 3-6 months in advance	2,661	-0.011	0.568
Initial returns 6-9 months in advance	2,661	-0.043	0.028**
Performance	165	-0.020	0.796[1]
Investment's size	2,661	-0.014	0.468

* significant on a 10 % level; ** significant on a 5 % level; *** significant on a 1 % level

[1] Based on the survey sample

Table 21: Scaled control variables vs. holding duration

g) Regression model

The regression analysis extends the insights on the determinants on the VCF's timing decision in that it allows for a direct comparison of the impact of the exogenous variables. Initially, all factors are integrated in one regression model. Yet, as sketched in section 5.3.2, inflating the regression equation with too many independent variables does not prove a proper way to step up the equation's quality. Rather, the analysis must identify the driving factors. The analysis starts with an all-covering regression model and tests eliminations of single factors for their impact on the adjusted R^2. If the elimination of a particular factor results in an increasing adjusted R^2, the factor is removed and the test series begins again for the remaining parameters.

[753] Ofek/Richardson (2003), p. 113f.; see also Lowry (2003), p. 5

[754] Lerner (1994a), p. 294

[755] See section 6.1.2 f)

This procedure is repeated until the adjusted R^2 peaks. Table 22 reports the individual steps and the regression analysis' results on the basis of the survey sample.

Steps	1.	2.	3.	4.	5.	6.	7.	8.	9.
R^2	.350**	.469***	.469***	.468***	.467***	.465***	.375***	.372***	.365***
Adjusted R^2	.201	.398	.404	.409	.414	.417	.336	.338	.335
	Std. Beta								
1. High-Tech	-.091	-.491	-.492	-.489	-.487	-.483	-.383	-.378	-.370
2. Bio-Tech	.034	-.008	-	-	-	-	-	-	-
3. Competition	.171	-.017	-.016	-	-	-	-	-	-
4. Departures	.065	.082	.083	.081	.086	.080	.108	.107	.094
5. VCF's age	-.019	-.083	-.084	-.084	-.090	-.093	-.059	-	-
6. Auditor quality	.050	.022	.022	.021	.023	.023	-	-	-
7. Investment bank	-.041	-	-	-	-	-	-	-	-
8. Promotion	-.037	-.142	-.143	-.144	-.139	-.151	-.125	-.115	-.119
9. Exit vehicle	-.230	-.107	-.108	-.113	-.104	-.094	-.082	-.087	-.066
10. First day return	.165	.053	.054	.051	.050	.052	.045	.042	.058
11. External approach	-.264	-.058	-.058	-.058	-.057	-	-	-	-
12. V.'s performance	-.072	-.150	-.149	-.149	-.141	-.133	-.093	-.092	-
13. Investment size	.064	.041	.040	.037	-	-	-	-	-
14. Monitoring intensity	-.444	-.377	-.376	-.375	-.369	-.363	-.379	-.373	-.385

* significant on a 10 % level; ** significant on a 5 % level; *** significant on a 1 % level

Table 22: Regression analysis of the holding duration

The adjusted R^2 peaks in the sixth step. For this equation, the Durbin-Watson value amounts to 1.558. In comparison to subsequent models, this value deviates considerably from the optimal value of 2. But according to Brosius (1998), a Durbin-Watson value within the interval of 1.5 to 2.5 fulfils the basic requirements for excluding autocorrelation concerns.[756] Given that the Tolerance of each independent variable equals or tops 0.852 (all VIFs are smaller than 1.18), the final regression model does not suffer from considerable collinearity. The Condition Index of 25.04, however, suggests some collinearity concerns. The regression analysis detects three major interdependencies among the exogenous factors:

- In line with Schwienbacher's (2002) and Fleming's (2003) reasoning on the VCF's selection of high quality firms for IPO exits,[757] the performance of IPO candidates correlates with the likelihood for floatations.[758]
- The Exit Vehicle impacts the choice of auditors with public transactions involving more frequently prestigious auditors.[759]

[756] Brosius (1998), p. 561

[757] Fleming (2003), p. 7f.; Schwienbacher (2002), p. 9

[758] See section 6.1.2 f)

- Given these findings, it appears reasonable that the performance and the auditor's quality are also interrelated.

In order to alleviate collinearity concerns, the least significant of these three critical factors are sequentially eliminated until collinearity indicators become tolerable. First, the Auditor Quality is removed since its beta coefficient features a significance of only 0.299 versus 0.371 for Performance and 0.413 for Exit Vehicle. In result, the Durbin-Watson value soars to 1.808. VIF values equal or stay below 1.162. The Condition index slumps to 18.684. The declining collinearity confirms the earlier assumption that the auditor's reputation does not shorten the VC duration but rather correlates with factors that impact the VC duration.[760] After this step, the impact of the elimination of each factor is calculated again. The test sequence suggests that the elimination of the VCF's age improves the adjusted R^2 and hence the model's quality. The Condition Index declines to 16.029 with all other quality measures remaining virtually constant. Since the Condition Index still exceeds 15, SPSS recommends a further elimination. Again the significance levels of the critical factors exit vehicle and performance are contrasted; the absolute significance of the beta coefficient of Performance is lower than the significance of the beta coefficient of the Exit Vehicle (0.220 versus 0.237). Performance is consequently removed. This elimination lowers the Condition Index to 14.567 which is below the critical value of 15. Even though slight concerns about collinearity remain, excluding further factors does not translate into a considerably improved model anymore; both, the adjusted R^2 and the R^2 slump substantially with only few improvements in the Condition Index or the VIFs. Model nine is consequently adopted as terminal regression equation.

For the final equation, the R^2 amounts to 0.365 accompanied by an adjusted R^2 of 0.335 (92 %). Including only six out of 14 factors (43 %), the terminal regression explains roughly 37 % of the holding duration's variance. As the adjusted R^2 comes close to the R^2, the regression model captures most influences and reflects a roughly accurate picture of the impact on the VCF's holding duration.

Model nine includes two out of originally five variables that describe information asymmetry upon exit. The removals of Biotech affiliation and Competition conform earlier findings. So does the presence of the high-tech dummy. But the elimination of the VCF's age and the presence of departures strike. Even though the previous correlation analysis confirms grandstanding, the VCF's age does not prevail in the final regression equation. It rather appears that the VCF's age impacts the holding duration only indirectly because the coefficients of several parameters – including the Exit Vehicle and Promotion – alter substantially from model eight to model nine. Section

---

[759] See section 6.1.2 f)

[760] See section 6.1.2 f)

6.1.2 f) reflects the impact of the VCF's age on the Exit Vehicle and section 6.1.3 f) sustains a relation between Promotion and the VCF's age. Against this background, the regression analysis does not lead to an ex-post rejection of the influence of the VCF's seasoning. The analysis rather confirms that seasoning determines the holding period in many ways.

The presence of departures featuring a positive coefficient is consistent with hypothesis 2.1.1. Hypothesis 2.1.1 argues that departures increase prospective investors' uncertainty. Such incidents require VCFs to delay exits until the additional uncertainty is resolved over time. The regression model isolates the impact of departures and detaches overlaying factors while the correlation analysis does not account for other influences. Given the present finding, hypothesis 2.1.1 is validated ex post.

As regards the control variables, the final regression equation mostly confirms earlier findings. The auditor quality is excluded for reasons set out above. While promotion is previously found not to shorten the holding period, it prevails in the regression model. According to the negative coefficient, VCFs can accelerate exits if they increase information efficiency through promotion. Or, longer holding periods reduce the need for promotion because the firm has more time to mature and establish a track record. The impact of hot issue markets is oppositional to the original finding in the bi-variate test. The preceding analysis suggests a negative correlation between the initial returns two quarters in advance to the exit and the holding duration whereas the coefficient in the present regression analysis is positive. The initial finding complies with the notion that VCFs center exits on hot issue markets to capitalize on investor-optimism and IPO dynamics.[761] The antagonism between the initial and the present finding originates from the moderation of the Exit Vehicle. First, the exit vehicle is found to heavily depend on the equity capital market's condition; hot issue markets spur IPOs.[762] Second, IPO exits require significantly shorter holding periods.[763] Given the low impact of hot issue markets on the timing in the prior bi-variate test,[764] it seems that the slightly positive coefficient for hot issue markets alleviates the influence that hot issue markets exert indirectly through the exit vehicle. In essence, collinearity confounds both, the earlier and the present finding. However, given that hot issue markets foster the occurrence of IPOs and IPOs feature shorter holding periods, the consistent bi-variate finding is adopted as final conclusion.

In essence, three categories of factors remain. First, the VCF's investment strategy – its investment focus and monitoring behavior – impacts the holding duration.

---

[761] E.g., Gompers/Lerner (2000), p. 206; Ibbotson/Jaffe (1975), p. 1027; Lowry (2003), p. 5; Ofek/Richardson (2003), p. 113f.; Ritter (1984), p. 238f.

[762] See sections 6.1.2 f) and 6.1.2 g)

[763] See section 6.1.1 f)

[764] See section 6.1.1 f)

Industry affiliation delivers the overall strongest coefficient. Akin to the preceding findings, innovative ventures accomplish exits earlier so that the timing is already predetermined by the VCF's investment focus. The monitoring intensity ranks second on impact on the holding duration. Consistent with earlier results, a closer monitoring shortens the holding duration. Given that VCFs supervise high-technology ventures more intensively, the investment strategy accounts for most of the found variance in the holding duration. Second, the exit strategy options prejudice the VC duration. Consistent with earlier findings, IPO exits are accomplished earlier while private exits only constitute the next best alternative if the venture cannot be floated. Private transactions thus occur if an IPO does not materialize. A raise in Promotion also shortens the holding duration. However, Promotion ranks third and the exit vehicle only sixth as regards the impacts so that the overall influence of the exit strategy stands back behind the investment strategy. Third, exceptional incidents affect the holding duration. Departures extend the holding period because they initially increase prospective investors' concerns about the venture's quality. Departures ranked fourth and constitute the weakest influence.

Information asymmetry reasonings underlie the regression equation only partly. Departures require longer holding periods as presumed in hypothesis 2.1.1. Besides, Promotion affects the holding period in that it helps establish information efficiency for earlier exits. In fact, the regression equation emphasizes the importance of the VCF's investment approach on the VC duration. VCFs work against investment risks and uncertainties of prospective investors with more intense monitoring. The increased monitoring translates into a higher development pace and more quality signals to outside investors. Thus, a more intense supervision generally enables earlier exits without that the VCF has to incorporate information asymmetries in its exit behavior.

Interestingly, hot issue markets – though popularly exemplified as the most important determinant – have a relatively low direct impact on the VCF's timing strategy.[765] The market's influence rather seems to concern the exit vehicle.[766]

6.1.2 Exit Vehicle

a) The degree of innovation and industry affiliation

Hypothesis 1.1.2 sets out that private investors suffer less information disadvantages in relation to public investors the more innovative the venture is. Non-innovative ventures, in turn, encounter higher information efficiency in public markets.

---

[765] E.g., Giot/Schwienbacher (2003), p. 7; Lerner (1994a), p. 294; Shepherd/Zacharakis (2001a), p. 66; Wang/Sim (2001), p. 342

[766] See section 6.1.2 f)

In an attempt to minimize discounts from information asymmetry, VCFs are assumed to sell innovative ventures to private investors and non-innovative ventures to public investors. Table 23 shows the cross table comparison for the original data sample.

	Acquisition	Went Public	Total
Non-innovative	473	142	615
Innovative	1,591	630	2,221
Total	2,064	772	2,836
Pearson $\chi2$	0.009***		
Phi	0.049		

* significant on a 10 % level; ** significant on a 5 % level; *** significant on a 1 % level

Table 23: Innovation vs. exit vehicles

In fact, 76.9 % of the non-innovative ventures undergo an acquisition as opposed to only 71.6 % of the innovative ventures. In contrast to the expectation in hypothesis 1.1.2, non-innovative ventures are sold more frequently to private investors while innovative ventures are more often floated. The χ^2-test sustains this finding but accounts for the small difference with a weak Phi. Hypothesis 1.1.2 is thus rejected. Information efficiency either plays a subordinated role in the VCF's decision on exit vehicles or the agglomeration of innovative industries is misguiding. An extra test explores differences across industries. The results are given in table 24.

	N	*IPO frequency*	*Pearson χ^2* 2.	3.	4.	5.	6.
1. Biotechnology	133	42.9 %	0.008***	0.000***	0.033**	0.000***	0.002***
2. Comm. & Media	518	30.7 %		0.022**	0.770	0.004***	0.239
3. Computer Related	1,153	25.3 %			0.042**	0.298	0.826
4. Life Sciences	233	31.8 %				0.010***	0.206
5. Non-High-Tech.	615	23.1 %					0.402
6. Semiconductors	184	26.1 %					

* significant on a 10 % level; ** significant on a 5 % level; *** significant on a 1 % level

Table 24: Industry affiliation vs. exit vehicles

The cross-industry comparison shows that Biotechnology ventures are floated most frequently; Biotechnology ventures stand out significantly in relation to every other sector. Life Sciences ventures rank second but do not significantly differ from Semiconductors and Computer Related ventures. Non-High-Technology ventures exhibit the least IPO frequency. Communication and Media ventures range amid Life Science and Semiconductor ventures. This picture initially sustains the rejection of hypothesis 1.1.2.

The exceptional position that Biotechnology and Life Sciences take can be explained in two ways – both argumentations ground on the specific characteristics of Biotechnology and Life Science ventures in comparison to other sectors. First, the peak complies with Gompers' (1995) reasoning. Gompers sets out that Biotechnology and Life Sciences ventures require more follow-on funding than ventures in other industries. Lerner (1994a) concurs; he elaborates that Biotechnology ventures accomplish exits long before they earn revenues whereas other ventures generally accomplish profits by the time of the VCF's withdrawal. Unlike other ventures, Biotechnology ventures still consume great amounts of capital after the VCF has exited.[767] Gompers argues that capital requirements of Biotechnology and Life Science ventures eventually exceed the resources of private investors. However, the public markets' funding ability is virtually unlimited. Following Gompers (1995), the significantly higher IPO ratio for Biotechnology and Life Science ventures stems from the Biotechnology and Life Sciences ventures' greater capital requirements narrowing the choice of exit vehicles down to the IPO.[768]

Second, Lerner (1994a) demonstrate that Biotechnology and Life Science ventures entail considerably higher investment risks for prospective investors given the absence of profitable products, still prevailing R&D risks and an unforeseeable commercial take-off at exit.[769] Section 2.3.1 discusses private investors' motivations to acquire a venture, such as gaining access to new technologies, markets or human resources.[770] Biotechnology or Life Science ventures are relatively less likely to appeal to a private investor than other ventures because of their lack of readily developed products, market shares or brand names upon exit. Biotechnology or Life Science ventures are more likely to attract public investors seeking high-risk-high-return investments and portfolio diversification. While M&A exits are impeded by the lack of investors, VCFs may well find public investors for Biotechnology or Life Science offerings. The higher IPO ratio for Biotechnology or Life Science ventures thus originates from different expectations of investors towards the venture.

The scheme for the remaining industries resembles the underpricing scheme as shown in table 5. This similarity evokes an alternative explanation to hypothesis 1.1.2. In line with the literature, the occurrence of hot issue markets appears to foster IPO activities. Scholars argue that a general optimism makes public markets ignoring investment risks. Investor optimism then translates into hot issue markets with sky-

---

767 Lerner (1994a), p. 294

768 Gompers (1995), p. 1474f., table 4; Wang/Sim (2001), p. 343 and p. 353

769 Lerner (1994a), p. 294; Lerner/Shane/Tsai (2003), p. 412f. and p. 417ff.

770 E.g., Achleitner (1999), p. 140; Alvarez/Barney (2001), p. 139f.; Blonigan/Taylor (2000), p. 50ff.; Cable/Shane (1997), p. 144; Cumming/MacIntosh (2003), p. 514; Frick/Torres (2002), p. 114; Gaughan (1999), p. 133; Lane/Salk/Lyles (2001), p. 1141ff.; Merrifield (1988), p. 172; Picot (1998), p. 11; Ranft/Lord (2000), p. 296

rocketing first-day returns.[771] In essence, investor optimism allows VCFs to exit more easily while achieving higher valuations.[772] As reported in section 6.1.1 a), scholars observe hot issue markets particularly in Communication and Media and Internet sectors.[773] The observations in table 5 on the average underpricing of IPOs within the data sample shows that this reasoning applies to the original data sample too. As a consequence of the impact of hot issue markets on the occurrence of IPOs and the observation that Communication and Media and Computer Related ventures experience the hottest markets in comparison to the remaining industries, Communication and Media and Computer Related must exhibit higher IPO ratios. In essence, table 24 demonstrates that VCFs capitalize on the investors' optimism and the overall high equity valuations in that they accomplish more IPOs in hot sectors than in cold sectors. This reasoning is consistent with the literature on the impact of hot issue markets on the VCF's choice of exit vehicles.[774]

	N	*Mean*	*SD*	*t*-test *p*-value
Acquisition	2,008	3.25	2.64	0.000***
IPO	757	3.78	2.50	

* significant on a 10 % level; ** significant on a 5 % level; *** significant on a 1 % level

Table 25: Number of financing rounds in IPOs and M&A exits

The finding on the impact of the number of financing rounds on the exit's timing across industries points at another possible explanation. Innovative ventures may accomplish more IPOs than non-innovative ventures because VCFs devote more attention to innovative ventures. Sapienza and Gupta (1994) set out that innovative ventures impose more risks on the VCF. Thus, VCFs monitor the progress of innovative ventures more closely.[775] Gompers (1995) as well as Wang and Sim (2001) show that the closer monitoring enhances the VCF's decision making throughout the investment process. VCFs can abandon failing ventures earlier if they get more involved in the venture. Thus, the ratio of exited ventures which eventually fulfil the requirements of an IPO increases.[776] Table 25 reports that IPO candidates in general

---

[771] Lowry (2003), p. 5; Ofek/Richardson (2003), p. 113f.; see also Ibbotson/Jaffe (1975), p. 1027; Ritter (1984), p. 238f.

[772] Chang (2004), p. 721f.; Lowry (2003), p. 5

[773] Gompers/Lerner (2000), p. 206; Lerner (1994a), p. 300; Ljungqvist/Wilhelm (2003), p. 727ff. and p. 738, table 5; Wang/Sim (2001), p. 342

[774] E.g., Giot/Schwienbacher (2003), p. 7; Shepherd/Zacharakis (2001a), p. 66

[775] Sapienza/Gupta (1994), p. 1620

[776] Barry/Muscarella/Peavy/Vetsuypens (1990), p. 501; Cornelli/Yosha (2003), p. 1; Giot/Schwienbacher (2003), p. 11; Gompers (1995), p. 1487; Gompers/Lerner (2000), p. 164; Gorman/Sahlman (1989), p. 238; Lam (1991), p. 139; Leland/Pyle (1977), p. 371

receive 16 % more financing rounds. The higher IPO ratio for innovative ventures as compared to non-innovative ventures thus stems from differences in VCFs' investment approaches across these industries as well.

The assumptions on the impact of information efficiency on the choice of exit vehicles are misleading. VCFs appear to be well aware of the public markets' constraints in evaluating innovative businesses. But VCFs overcome the public investors' concerns in that they exploit times of increasing investor-optimism for particular industries and improve their selection of IPO candidates. Sectors that experience no investor optimism and receive lower attention from the VCF exhibit a lower IPO rate. This discussion underlines the influence of potential investors' concerns in exit strategies yet differently than originally assumed.

b) Development level

Hypothesis 1.2.2 posits a dependency between the exit vehicle and the exit stage. It is assumed that early stage exits encounter more information inefficiency than later stage exits. In case of early stage exits, private investors capitalize on their background and thus experience relatively fewer information disadvantages as compared to public investors. In later stage exits, the public investors' superior ability to benefit from public information helps their due diligence. Later stage exits thus increase the likelihood of IPOs whereas private transactions are more pronounced in early stage exits. Table 26 compares both exit vehicles regarding the mean exit stage.

	N	*Mean*	*SD*	*t*-test *p*-value
Acquisition	1,886	7.09	3.12	0.000***
IPO	563	7.77	2.62	

* significant on a 10 % level; ** significant on a 5 % level; *** significant on a 1 % level

Table 26: Exit stage vs. exit vehicle

The comparison of means yields a highly significant difference. IPOs are more likely to occur in later stages while private transactions materialize more frequently in early stage exits. Ventures that are floated have on average entered the Third Stage while private transactions already occur in the Second Stage. The result conforms hypothesis 1.2.2 and sustains the argumentation. To deepen this notion, the IPO frequency is calculated for each exit stage separately, as shown in table 27.

	N	IPO frequency	Pearson χ^2	Cramer's V
1. Early stage	101	7.9 %		
2. Seed	36	5.6 %		
3. Startup	56	14.3 %		
4. First Stage	250	12.1 %		
5. Expansion	793	25.2 %		
6. Second st.	275	20.4 %	0.000***	0.772
7. Third stage	186	24.7 %		
8. Bridge	291	40.5 %		
9. Other exp.	4	75.0 %		
10. Acq. f. ex.	73	19.2 %		
11. LBO	206	24.8 %		
12. Open m.	176	23.9 %		

* significant on a 10 % level; ** significant on a 5 % level; *** significant on a 1 % level

Table 27: IPO frequency across exit stages

Table 27 provides further insights. The IPO frequency basically increases with later exit stages. The overall increasing tendency sustains hypothesis 1.2.2 again; later exit stages attract more public investors in relation to earlier stages. But the distribution does not resemble a linear relation. Table 27 rather shows several sequential peaks. The IPO frequency culminates for the first time in the Start-up stage and lastly in the LBO stage. The overall summit occurs in the Other Expansion respectively the Bridge stage. The lowest IPO frequency is calculated for the Seed stage where the ratio of IPO exits is more than ten times lower in comparison to the overall maximum.

However, the occurrence of peaks does not comply with the presumption of a steady decline of information asymmetry throughout the venture's development process. Apart from the generally soaring tendency, every peak needs to be contemplated separately to fathom its emergence. Fleming (2003) argues that VCFs only float their best ventures because they fear that bad IPOs distress their reputation.[777] If a company fulfils the VCF's expectations, it is likely to be floated. Few ventures prove their quality in early stages and can accomplish IPOs in these stages while the private sales of struggling ventures dominate at this time. Most ventures require more development levels to fulfil the VCFs requirement's for an IPO. The soaring IPO frequency in advance to every peak visualizes this selection process. The eventual occurrence of peaks in the IPO ratio in particular stages is consistent with Cumming and MacIntosh's (2003) notion on VCFs' timing decisions. Cumming and MacIntosh

---

[777] Fleming (2003), p. 9; Gompers/Lerner (1998), p. 2162; Schwienbacher (2002), p. 7f.

stress that every VCF reaches a managerial optimum for its commitment to a single venture. Cumming and MacIntosh argue that VCFs achieve optimal exits at this point while a further commitment becomes inefficient.[778] A single peak essentially represents the ultimate exit stage for a group of similar VCFs. The occurrence of several peaks implies that the cost-return ratios vary across VCFs;[779] early stage investors focus on emerging ventures and have to exit in the Expansion stage while later stage investors exits must occur on the Bridge/Other Expansion stage at the latest. Thus, different peaks characterize the multiple investment emphases – such as early stage and later stage VC – in the VC market in the U.S.. The discussion for hypothesis 1.2.1 points out that VCFs even incur underpricing to facilitate exits during these stages in order to avoid a further commitment.

Hypothesis 1.2.2 is basically validated; VCFs incorporate concerns about information asymmetry across different development stages in their decision on the exit vehicle. Besides, the VCF's investment focus determines the exit vehicle.

c) Competition

Hypothesis 1.3.2 elaborates on a dependency of the exit vehicle on the degree of competition. Since competition forces ventures to release more information about their products, competitive settings feature higher information efficiency. In competitive settings, public investors capitalize on their superior processing of public information while non-competitive settings favor the private investor who generates information from his pertinent expertise. Table 28 compares both exit vehicles in this respect.

	N	*Mean*	*SD*	*t*-test *p*-value
Acquisition	2,055	1.36	4.30	0.000***
IPO	770	8.31	7.38	

* significant on a 10 % level; ** significant on a 5 % level; *** significant on a 1 % level

Table 28: Competition vs. exit vehicle

The comparison of means shows that IPO candidates encounter on average six times more competitors than ventures that are sold privately. This discrepancy is highly significant and validates hypothesis 1.3.2. The test confirms the assumption on the impact of competition on the exit vehicle.

---

[778] Cumming/MacIntosh (2003), p. 447f.; Neus/Walz (2001), p. 17

[779] Researchers draw a distinction between early stage investors (VCFs) and later stage investors (Private Equity); e.g. Barry/Muscarella/Peavy/Vetsuypens (1990), p. 448; Black/Gilson (1998), p. 245; Gaida (2002), p. 147; Leitinger/Strohbach/Schöfer/Hummel (2000),p. 89; Levin (2001), p. 1–5; Pfirrmann/Wupperfeld/Lerner (1997), p. 9; Wright/Robbie/Romanet/Thompson/Joachimsson/Bruining/ Herst (1994), p. 84;

d) Departures of entrepreneurial team members

Hypothesis 2.1.2 posits that the occurrence of departures increases the likelihood of M&A exits. The occurrence of departures initially imposes uncertainty on prospective investors about the venture's quality and its valuation. Because private investors capitalize on their industry experience, they can generate information to appraise the causes and consequences of changes in the ownership structure more accurately than public investors. Public investors must consequently assume more general problems and impose relatively greater discounts on the exit than private investors. The results for the survey sample are given in following table.

	Acquisition	Went Public	Total
No departures	69	34	103
One departure	23	9	32
More departures	21	12	33
Total	113	55	168
Significance (Pearson χ^2)		0.775	
Cramer's V		0.055	

* significant on a 10 % level; ** significant on a 5 % level; *** significant on a 1 % level

Table 29: Departures vs. exit vehicle

61 % of the private transactions and 62 % of the IPOs are not preceded by departures. 20 % of the acquisitions feature one departure as opposed to only 15 % for floatations. Accordingly, the ratio for more than one departure in IPOs (22 %) surpasses the ratio in M&A transactions (19 %). Given this distribution and the narrow differences, the cross table test does not support a significant dependency; the occurrence of departures has no significant impact on the choice of exit vehicles.

Conversely to the predictions, departures do not reduce chances for an IPO. In fact, replacements prior to IPOs may not only be triggered by a disruptive management but rather by the necessity to comply with public market's expectations towards newly listed companies. IPO candidates must exhibit experienced management teams. This goes back to the notion that entrepreneurs possess the skills to set up a business but not to manage the concerns of a public company anymore.[780] Hence, IPO candidates may complement their management team with experienced CFOs or CEOs and essentially replace the entrepreneur-CEO. The entrepreneur then assumes another position such as board member or overseeing R&D activities.[781]

[780] See section 2.1.2; see also Picot/Schneider/Laub (1989), p. 366 and p. 381f.

[781] Petty/Bygrave/Shulman (1992), p. 47

Against the background of this argumentation, departures do not per se signal struggles but are generally accepted in advance to fundamental changes in ventures' ownership structures. The survey instrument does not account for the difference between assigning the entrepreneur to other responsibilities and dismissing him because of opportunistic behavior. In this respect, the survey sample does not allow for an ultimate conclusion on the impact of dismissals and divestures on the VCF's exit strategy prior to the exit.

e) The VCF's certification ability

Hypothesis 3.1.2 accounts for unseasoned VCFs' grandstanding ambitions. It is argued that since young VCFs wish to build their reputation, they are more likely to accomplish visible exit transactions such as IPOs. Unlike, seasoned VCFs are assumed to weight both exit vehicles more equally. The comparison of means is reported in table 30.

	N	*Mean*	*SD*	*t*-test *p*-value
Acquisition	1,882	24.62	11.66	0.000***
IPO	695	26.82	11.51	

* significant on a 10 % level; ** significant on a 5 % level; *** significant on a 1 % level

Table 30: VCF's age vs. exit vehicle

In fact, a highly significant dependency exists between the VCF's age and the exit vehicle. IPO exits involve more seasoned VCFs while private transactions outweigh among younger VCFs. This finding does, however, not comply with hypothesis 3.1.2. Hypothesis 3.1.2 is thus rejected. Moreover, Wang and Sim's (2001) finding from the VC market in Singapore that unseasoned VCFs accomplish more IPOs to enhance grandstanding is rejected for the U.S. market.[782]

The literature suggests an alternative reasoning. According to Megginson and Weiss (1991), capital markets discern IPOs backed by seasoned and unseasoned VCFs. Consistent with Barry, Muscarella, Peavy and Vetsuypens (1990), Megginson and Weiss observe that capital markets appreciate the backing of more seasoned VCFs. The presence of seasoned VCFs translates into less underpricing in the long run. Given that capital markets are sensitive to the VCF's quality, unseasoned VCFs cannot simply increase the IPO frequency without suffering from severe consequences. If unseasoned VCFs float ventures, the market requires more underpricing

[782] Wang/Sim (2001), p. 352

in relation to IPOs of seasoned VCFs.[783] Quotations thus prove more costly for unseasoned VCFs so that their reputation building becomes too expensive. If the unseasoned VCF avoids higher underpricing, the IPO may not succeed and harm the VCF's reputation instead. In essence, IPO exits appear not to constitute a mean for unseasoned VCFs to build their reputation. Conversely, the capital markets' trust in issues backed by seasoned VCFs translates into less information costs. The results imply that seasoning leads to direct cost advantages in IPOs for older VCFs in relation to young VCFs. The finding on seasoning allowing older VCFs to achieve more floatations complies with the findings in the literature.[784]

f) Control variables

This section contrasts the VCF's decision on exit vehicles against other possible influences. Initially, the exit vehicle's dependency on nominal factors is tested. Table 31 reports the results.

	Acquisition	Went Public	Total	Significance (Pearson χ^2)	Phi
Non-leading auditor	40	10	50	0.000***	0.288
Leading auditor	942	562	1,504		
Total	982	572	1,554		
External approach	55	19	74	0.083*[1]	-0.134
No external approach	58	36	94		
Total	113	55	168		

* significant on a 10 % level; ** significant on a 5 % level; *** significant on a 1 % level

Table 31: Nominal control variables vs. exit vehicle

The test reveals a significant difference as regards the presence of leading auditors. Even though leading auditors are present in almost every transaction, the ratio for non-leading auditors in private transactions (4.1 %) more than doubles the ratio of public transactions (1.8 %). This finding underlines the notion that IPOs require far more certification in comparison to M&A deals.[785] Considering this, the presence of leading auditors does not represent an exogenous factor but rather an endogenous factor contingent on the chosen exit vehicle. It will thus be excluded in the regression analysis.

---

[783] E.g., Gompers (1996), p. 153f.; Neus/Walz (2001), p. 17

[784] Barry, Muscarella, Peavy and Vetsuypens (1990), p. 448f.; Gompers (1996), p. 153f.; Hsu (2004), p. 1834; Megginson/Weiss (1991), p. 881

[785] See section 6.1.4 f)

The occurrence of private investors affects the VCF's choice of exit vehicles at a low confidence level. If an exit transaction is initiated by an industrial investor, the venture is more likely to be sold privately. Yet, more than one fourth of those ventures that experience an external approach are floated in spite of the occurrence of a private investor. This finding underlines that VCFs do not blindly pursue the first exit option but rather balance their choices carefully. In the sense of Montgomery, Thomas and Kamath (1984), VCFs pursue definite divestment strategies that eventually lead to higher valuations than reactionary divestures on short term opportunities because of the thorough matching of the venture with follow-on investors' expectations.[786] Thus, an IPO in the long term may be more profitable than the private sale to the interested industrialist.

	N	*Mean*	*SD*	*t*-test *p*-value
Investment bank				
Acquisition	559	1.53	1.22	0.000***
IPO	546	2.66	0.87	
Investment size				
Acquisition	1,888	28.78	56,239	0.000***
IPO	709	71.73	160,796	
Performance				
Acquisition	114	2.52	1.68	0.001***[1]
IPO	55	1.67	0.96	
First-day returns upon exit				
Acquisition	2,063	38.54	35.95	0.000***
IPO	772	59.63	37.89	
Initial returns 3-6 months in advance				
Acquisition	2,063	41.22	39.75	0.000***
IPO	772	62.10	39.38	
Initial returns 6-9 months in advance				
Acquisition	2,063	49.56	43.44	0.000***
IPO	772	75.03	43.89	

* significant on a 10 % level; ** significant on a 5 % level; *** significant on a 1 % level

[1] Based on the survey sample

Table 32: Scaled control variables vs. exit vehicle

Akin to the presence of leading auditors, IPOs also feature more prestigious investment banks in comparison to M&A transactions. While IPOs are almost always

[786] Montgomery/Thomas/Kamath (1984), p. 831; see also Brück (1998), p. 16; Duhaime/Patton (1980), p. 46

underwritten by one of the top three investment banks, private transactions are only accompanied by on average one of the top 11 advisors. Exhibiting top investment banks appears to be a prerequisite for IPOs whereas an M&A transaction requires far less third-party certification.

IPO candidates receive roughly 2.5 times more capital than ventures that are sold privately. The result complies with the notion given in the literature. On the one hand, IPO candidates must have a reasonable size to catch the public markets' attention. IPO candidates are consequently selected according to their size.[787] On the other hand, the total investment also correlates with the number of financing rounds resulting in a more intense monitoring of IPO candidates.[788] Earlier findings confirm that a closer monitoring results in higher chances for an IPO exit.[789]

The performance of IPO candidates significantly exceeds the performance of ventures that are sold privately. This result conforms Black and Gilson's (1998) notion that VCFs float well performing in order to reward the entrepreneur for his commitment.[790] In addition, this finding underlines VCFs' reputational concerns. VCFs carefully select the ventures they float in order to protect their reputation.[791] In contrast, the trade sale represents a more universal exit vehicle applicable in a multitude of circumstances, for instance, to medium performing or smaller investments.[792]

The highly significant finding for the public market's condition emphasizes the importance of high equity valuation levels for the occurrence of IPOs. This finding holds for the markets' states during the floatation, one quarter and two quarters in advance. The test underlines the impact of hot issue markets in the VCF's decision to initiate an IPO. However, preparing the IPO and filing with the SEC usually takes half a year so that the equity valuation levels by the time of the exit decision prompt the VCF to float the venture. This result confirms the conclusions of Lerner (1994a) and Wang and Sim (2001) that VCFs time their IPOs contingent on hot issue markets.[793]

g) Discriminant analysis

Given that the exit vehicle can only be operationalized in a nominal variable rather than a scaled measure, this multi-variate analysis employs a discriminant analysis instead of a regression model. The discriminant model assigns the value 1 to IPO exits and 0 to M&A transactions. The development procedure, however, re-

---

[787] Higashide/Birley (2002), p. 61; Mikkelson/Partch/Shah (1997), p. 284; Schwienbacher (2002), p. 5
[788] Gompers (1995), p. 1487; Mason/Harrison (2002), p. 228
[789] See section 6.1.2 a)
[790] Black/Gilson (1998), p. 260
[791] Fleming (2003), p. 9; Gompers/Lerner (1998), p. 2162; Schwienbacher (2002), p. 7f.
[792] Schwienbacher (2002), p. 24
[793] Lerner (1994a), p. 300; Wang/Sim (2001), p. 342

sembles the procedure in which the regression model above is derived. Only, the aim is now to maximize the Eigenvalue.[794] Table 33 reports the steps for the survey sample.

Steps	1.	2.	3.	4.
Eigenvalue	.483	.499	.503	.503
Wilks' Lambda	.674***	.667***	.665***	.666***
	Std. Coefficients			
1. High-Tech	.132	.121	.116	.115
2. Bio-Tech	.144	.158	.156	.154
3. Exit stage	.407	.392	.392	.391
4. Competition	.694	.674	.669	.670
5. Departures	-.140	-.137	-.141	-.143
6. VCF's age	.086	.057	.059	.060
7. First day return upon exit	-.073	-	-	-
8. First day return 1Q ahead	.063	.031	.024	-
9. First day return 2Qs ahead	.333	.341	.343	.360
10. External approach	-.295	-.273	-.268	-.268
11. V.'s performance	-.301	-.311	-.311	-.312
12. Rounds	-.030	-.031	-	-
13. Investment size	.234	.240	.238	.240

* significant on a 10 % level; ** significant on a 5 % level; *** significant on a 1 % level

Table 33: Exit vehicle discriminant analysis

The model fits best for step 3 – after the removal of just two variables. Equation four exhibits almost the same fit parameters but eliminates the duplication of the impact of first-day returns. Given that the model fit suffers only marginally, model four is adopted as terminal discriminant equation. The Eigenvalue of 0.503 confirms that the model possesses substantial discriminating power. With a Wilks' Lambda of 0.666 and a χ^2-value of 56.598, the model is highly significant. In fact, the model classifies 78.1 % of the transactions correctly. The squared Canonical Correlation coefficient amounts to 0.345 so that approximately 35 % of the variance in the Exit Vehicle is explained.

The terminal model eliminates only three variables out of seven control variables. All factors describing information asymmetry upon exit prevail. The terminal model virtually equals the preceding tests. The final equation only differs in one instance.

[794] Westhead/Wright (1998), p. 194f. pursue a similar approach

Departures prevail even though their impact is neglected in the previous test and potential shortcomings with respect to measurement were discovered. Nevertheless, the discriminant model appears to isolate the impact of Departures in that it separates other factors that overlay the bi-variate test.[795] Considering the negative beta-coefficient, hypothesis 2.1.2 is validated ex-post; the occurrence of departures raises scepticism of public investors and hampers IPO exits.

The remaining parameters describe two dimensions of the exit transaction: the venture's characteristics and the external conditions at exit. The venture's characteristics cluster the two strongest factors (and others) competition and exit stage. Competition attains by far the highest coefficient. In line with the earlier finding, the likelihood of IPOs increases with the extent of competition the venture encounters. The exit stage ranks second confirming that a certain development level constitutes a general prerequisite for IPOs. Earlier stages either indicate that the venture struggles to achieve progress or that the venture did not have enough time to establish track records. In line with the earlier finding, early stage exits more likely result in private transactions. The coefficient of the venture's performance confirms the importance of a viable financial concept as a condition for IPOs; without having proven its financial viability, a venture is more likely to be sold privately. A relatively low impact is measured for the venture's industry affiliation. Both, high-technology affiliation and biotech affiliation increase chances for an IPO exit. Likewise, departures reduce chances for an IPO. Yet, the impact of departures is the second least underlining the low importance. The VCF's age represents the weakest factor. The greater certification power older VCFs have impacts the IPO frequency only marginally. This outcome is consistent with the preceding finding; IPOs are launched by VCFs that are on average only 8.9 % older than those selling their ventures privately.[796]

External conditions address the second cluster of influences. Even though the impact of the public market's equity valuation level represents a strong influence and conforms the literature,[797] the effect on the choice of the exit vehicles ranks only third and stands back behind the impact of the businesses characteristics. As expected, external exit initiatives foster private transactions. Akin to the preceding test, the relatively low coefficient implies that an external approach does not automatically trigger an M&A deal. Overall, the impact of the external factors is lower in relation to the im-

---

[795] Departures respectively dismissals occur less frequently in ventures that exhibit a bad performance. This relationship is roughly significant for the survey sample ($p = 0.063$; $r = 0.144$). The contradiction of the assumption that dismissals occur in struggling ventures points at shortcomings in the survey sample. Simultaneously, bad performance lowers the venture's prospects for an IPO. In the bi-variate test, this chain of dependencies overlays the direct impact of dismissals and flaws the result.

[796] See section 6.1.2 e)

[797] E.g., Giot/Schwienbacher (2003), p. 7; Lerner (1994a), p. 294; Shepherd/Zacharakis (2001a), p. 66; Wang/Sim (2001), p. 342

pact of the venture's characteristics. This comparison rejects the common notion that hot issue markets solely account for the occurrence of IPOs regardless of the venture; in fact, rivalry and the venture's development level constitute even stronger determinants.

The finding that Exit Stage, Performance and Departures matter, confirms the role of information asymmetry as set out in the hypotheses. The outstanding influence of competition highlights that prospective investors capitalize on rivalry between ventures and the resulting improvements in sectoral information efficiency. Hot issue markets play a substantial role as well; VCFs literally use the exit vehicle decision to capitalize on investor optimism translating into lower information asymmetry per se.

6.1.3 Promotion

a) The degree of innovation and industry affiliation

Hypothesis 1.1.3 relates the VCF's promotion to the degree of innovation. The hypothesis predicts that outsiders incur difficulties evaluating the venture the higher the degree of innovation. VCFs must devote more efforts to overcome the new investors' information gaps in order to facilitate exits for innovative ventures than for non-innovative firms. Table 34 compares the differences in promotion between non-innovative and innovative ventures.

	N	*Mean*	*SD*	*t*-test *p*-value
Non-innovative	8	1.75	1.04	0.341
Innovative	159	2.08	0.96	

* significant on a 10 % level; ** significant on a 5 % level; *** significant on a 1 % level

Table 34: Innovation vs. promotion

The mean Promotion for innovative ventures exceeds the average for non-innovative ventures. Yet, the difference proves not significant. Even separate tests for IPO exits and M&A exits do not deliver significant differences.[798] As the VCF's promotion is most likely not influenced by the venture's innovativeness, hypothesis 1.1.3 is initially rejected. The outcome suggests, however, a general tendency across industries. An extra test decomposes the relation between industry affiliation and promotion efforts; table 35 reports the results.

[798] p = 0.712 for IPOs (innovative ventures: N = 54; Mean = 2.3; SD = 0.79; non-innovative ventures: N = 1; Mean = 2.00); p = 0.520 for M&A exits (innovative ventures: N = 105; Mean = 1.97; SD = 1.02; non-innovative ventures: N = 7; Mean = 1.71; SD = 1.11)

	N	Mean	SD	t-test p-value 2.	3.	4.	5.	6.
1. Biotechnology	14	2.50	0.73	0.100*	0.099*	0.722	0.065*	0.054*
2. Comm. & Media	38	1.97	1.06		0.670	0.233	0.594	0.555
3. Computer Related	90	2.06	0.95			0.265	0.390	0.363
4. Life Sciences	10	2.40	0.49				0.101	0.073*
5. Non-High-Tech.	8	1.75	0.97					0.946
6. Semiconductors	7	1.71	0.88					

* significant on a 10 % level; ** significant on a 5 % level; *** significant on a 1 % level

Table 35: Industry affiliation vs. promotion

According to table 35, Biotechnology and the Life-Science ventures receive the most promotion. Computer Related and Communication and Media ventures rank third and fourth only slightly surpassing Non-High-Technology and Semiconductor ventures. Even though hypothesis 1.1.3 is initially rejected, the closer examination discovers roughly significant differences between Biotechnology/Life Sciences industries and the remaining sectors. Differences among the other industries prove not significant. This comparison shows on the one hand that Biotechnology and Life Science exits stand out as they did in previous tests.[799] On the other hand, table 35 reports essentially no differences in the VCF's promotion efforts across industries other than Biotechnology and Life Sciences. This insight inspires a separate discussion of this finding.

First, the ranking of average promotion efforts across industries other than Biotechnology and Life Science is scrutinized. The industry ranking in table 35 roughly reflects the distribution of underpricing across industries as reported in table 5. Non-High-Technology and Semiconductor IPOs exhibit the lowest underpricing and they receive the least promotion. IPOs in the Communication and Media sector significantly top the underpricing of IPOs in every other sector; they also receive more promotion. Given that underpricing mirrors the extent of information asymmetry between inside and outside investors,[800] information dissimilarity upon exit calls for more promotion. This outcome is consistent with the presumptions underlying hypothesis 1.1.3 except that the survey sample does not allow for significant conclusions. The fact that the outcome does not prove significant may rather stem from shortcomings in the data sample or in the operationalization of Promotion.

Second, Biotechnology and Life Sciences ventures take a special status akin to the findings on the exit stage and the IPO frequency.[801] In the sense of hypothesis

[799] See section 6.1.2 a)

[800] Bradley/Jordan (2002), p. 613, see also Certo/Daily/Dalton (2001), p. 34; Easley/O'Hara (2004), p. 1578

[801] See section 6.1.2 b)

1.1.3, the Biotechnology/Life Science's peak in promotion efforts originates from higher information asymmetry and ex-ante uncertainty.[802] Even though the significant lower underpricing for Biotechnology and Life Science IPOs does initially not support the presumption on higher information spreads, research provides a variety of reasons why these two sectors impose exceptional uncertainties on investors. But the underpricing of Biotechnology and Life Science IPOs may not appropriately reflect the extent of information asymmetry that prevails in these sectors upon exit. Lerner (1994a) observes that the Biotechnology sector represents the only industry in which IPOs are frequently accomplished before the venture is profitable. In fact, only one Biotech venture within the survey sample exhibits profits by the time of the exit (out f both IPO exits and M&A transactions). Lerner observes that biotechnology ventures in comparison to other sectors remain longer in the R&D stage and often launch products only one decade after their foundation.[803] Moreover, Lerner outlines that VC funding solely flows into R&D activities instead of tangible assets such as plants, infrastructure etc.. These investments bear consequently no transferable value in case of failure so that investments cannot be retrieved.[804] Lerner, Shane and Tsai (2003) conclude in this sense that Biotechnology investments resemble a gamble with exceptionally high risks in relation to other sectors.[805] In this context, hypothesis 1.1.3 is well suited to explain the variance in promotion between Biotech and Life Science and other sectors. The results suggest that VCFs step up their promotion efforts for Biotechnology ventures accounting for the relatively higher uncertainties and risks. Against this background, hypothesis 1.1.3 is validated at a roughly significant level.

Even though hypothesis 1.1.3 cannot be sustained entirely on the basis of the survey data, it applies to some combinations so that the fundamental validity is sustained. Information dissimilarities about the venture's innovativeness require the VCF to engage in Promotion. In turn, Promotion enables exits in information inefficient settings. Yet, this discussion challenges further research on the VCF's Promotion.

b) Development levels

Hypothesis 1.2.3 assumes differences in Promotion across exit stages. The model suggests that exits at later stages reduce the need for the VCF's involvement since information efficiency increases. In fact, the exit stage and Promotion correlate at a Pearson's r of 0.169 with a confidence level of 0.033 for 160 transactions. The test shows that Promotion significantly increases with later stages. The result, how-

---

[802] See also Bourgeois/Eisenhardt (1988), p. 816; Bradley/Jordan (2002), p. 613; Certo/Daily/Dalton (2001), p. 34; Janney/Folta (2003), p. 2003), p. 362

[803] Lerner (1994a), p. 294

[804] Lerner (1994a), p. 294

[805] Lerner/Shane/Tsai (2003), p. 412f. and p. 417ff.

ever, implies that early stage exits receive significantly less promotion than later stage exits. Given this outcome, hypothesis 1.2.3 is initially rejected.

Instead of confirming that VCFs supply prospective investors with information for earlier stage exits, the finding points at an alternative causal relationship. It appears that VCFs use Promotion to comply with their increasing exit-ambitions in later stages. The finding suggests a further analysis of the mean promotion efforts for each exit stage. However, the survey sample does not contain enough transactions to provide robust results; the data sample includes just one exit transaction for the Seed, the Acquisition for Expansion, the LBO and the Open Market Purchase stage. Only four out of 12 exit stages occur more than ten times in the survey sample. Instead, VCFs' ambitions to enforce exits across different development levels are approximated by the underpricing of VC-backed IPOs given that the original data sample contains far more observations to draw on. In general, corporate finance research argues that issuers deliberately underprice offerings to facilitate IPOs.[806] Issuers choose a valuation that is likely to be surpassed by the market on the first day of trading. Underpricing creates an incentive for public investors to subscribe to the offer.[807] Yet, underpricing translates into a wealth loss for incumbents the more they divest in the IPO.[808] Akin to Promotion, a deliberate underpricing imposes costs on the VCF and is only justified if the transaction's ultimate outcome makes up for the additional costs. Underpricing and Promotion thus share characteristics that help approximate a theory on the dependency of the VCFs' exiting efforts on the exit stage. Table 36 contrasts the average underpricing across exit stages.

[806] E.g., Easley/O'Hara (2004), p. 1578

[807] Certo/Daily/Dalton (2001), p. 34; Petty/Shulman/Bygrave (1994), p. 44; Welch (1989), p. 421

[808] Franzke (2001), p. 10ff.; Habib/Ljungqvist (2001), p. 454f.

				t-test										
				p-value										
	N	*Mean*	*SD*	2.	3.	4.	5.	6.	7.	8.	9.	10	11.	12.
1. Early stage	4	42.50	23.99	0.396	0.385	0.332	0.585	0.607	0.587	0.387	0.761	0.912	0.231	0.318
2. Seed	1	69.00	-		0.202	0.298	0.968	0.957	0.907	0.850	0.961	0.484	0.167	0.830
3. Startup	5	27.22	25.02			0.702	0.274	0.404	0.272	0.201	0.523	0.529	0.717	0.141
4. First Stage	17	18.95	45.20				0.026**	0.079*	0.022**	0.009***	0.307	0.448	0.824	0.004***
5. Expansion	166	65.63	84.26					0.516	0.756	0.044**	0.928	0.603	0.007***	0.166
6. Second St.	45	76.04	128.32						0.522	0.511	0.865	0.634	0.031**	0.634
7. Third Stage	37	61.02	66.57							0.134	0.987	0.597	0.005***	0.148
8. Bridge	102	89.52	107.63								0.704	0.431	0.001***	0.973
9. Other Exp.	2	60.20	118.23									0.781	0.189	0.669
10. Acq. f. Ex.	3	40.17	29.32										0.355	0.365
11. LBO	28	21.55	32.82											0.000***
12. Open M.	31	80.80	89.86											

* significant on a 10 % level; ** significant on a 5 % level; *** significant on a 1 % level

Table 36: Underpricing across exit stages

Table 36 shows no general tendency for the underpricing across exit stages. A regression analysis delivers a standardized beta coefficient of only 0.049 at a low confidence level of 0.299. A significantly positive relationship is thus rejected. In fact, table 36 pictures a highly scattered pattern of underpricing across exits stages; a similar picture emerges for Promotion across exit stages, yet less significant. First-day returns upon exit neither increase continuously nor decrease throughout the venture's development but the underpricing culminates several times. The overall peak occurs in the Bridge stage. Further peaks are observable in the Seed stage, Second stage and the Open Market Purchase stage. Underpricing in the First Stage and the LBO stage is significantly lower than in almost every other stage.

Initially, the absence of a continuous relation between underpricing and the exit stage is striking. The very basic discussion provided in chapter 2.1.1 elaborates that higher development levels disperse uncertainties about the venture. Given that underpricing emanates from outside investors' uncertainty about an issue, it must steadily decline the later the exit stage.[809] However, this pattern is not observable in table 36.

The pattern pictured in table 36 rather resembles the findings for the IPO frequency across exit stages as illustrated in table 27. Akin to the underpricing, the IPO frequency peaks in the Expansion stage and in the Bridge or Other Expansion stage. The finding that VCFs incur more underpricing to facilitate IPOs in certain stages appears to be consistent with the argumentation in section 6.1.1 b). Section 6.1.1 b) sets out a relationship between the venture's development and the exit stage. Well performing ventures accomplish IPOs already in early stages. If a venture matures slower, VCFs can only exit in later development stages. However, as section 6.1.1 b) elaborates, VCFs desire to divest in stages in which a further commitment to the venture is more costly than beneficial.[810] Thus, VCFs incur more efforts and allow for more underpricing for ventures that have not been exited in this terminal stage. The increasing underpricing in advance to every peak illustrates this reasoning with the summit representing the terminal stage. Moreover, section 6.1.1 b) discerns VCFs with different investment emphases; their different investment emphases explain the occurrence of several peaks. The first peak characterizes exits of VCFs with an early stage focus while the second peak is attributed to later stage VCFs. Against this background, table 36 shows that VCFs use underpricing to center their IPO activities on those stages that allow for a managerially optimal exit. VCFs may employ Promotion alike given its fundamental similarity to the underpricing concept. The survey sample does, however, not allow for a significant support.

The overall tendency to raise Promotion in later stages hints at a further explanation. Giot and Schwienbacher (2003) outline that if ventures have not been exited up to a certain point they become more difficult to withdraw. Giot and Schwienbacher refer to such firms as "living dead" investments picking up Ruhnka, Feldman and Dean's (1992) labelling for companies that neither fail nor produce attractive profits. These ventures progress to higher development levels but they cannot attract follow-on investors.[811] Wright, Robbie, Romanet, Thompson, Joachimsson, Bruining and

---

809 E.g., Bradley/Jordan (2002), p. 613; Certo/Daily/Dalton (2001), p. 34

810 See Cumming/MacIntosh (2003), p. 447f.; Neus/Walz (2001), p. 17

811 Giot/Schwienbacher (2003), p. 3; Ruhnka/Feldman/Dean (1992), p. 138f. and p. 147f.; see also Inderst/Müller (2004), p. 321

Herst (1994) observe similar patterns in the MBO market in UK and report that later exits become more difficult. They stress that after the highfliers are withdrawn in the first place, only low performing ventures remain to be disposed.[812] Instead of reflecting the VCF's intention to overcome information asymmetry, the slightly positive correlation between Promotion and the development level suggest that VCFs must endorse later stage exits in order to enhance their exits while the highfliers do not require much support.

The result sustains the presumption that VCFs utilize Promotion to enhance exits. Yet, promotion is not triggered by information dissimilarities. The VCF's investment focus forces it to withdraw at certain stages and thus drives Promotion and Underpricing decisions.

c) Competition

Hypothesis 1.3.3 proposes that Promotion is less pronounced in competitive environments. Competition is presumed to increase information efficiency since competitive ventures have to release more information to promote their products over the rivals' products. Because competition supplies prospective investors with additional information, VCFs have to engage less in Promotion. The correlation analysis delivers a Pearson's r of 0.186 for 167 transactions. The result is highly significant at p = 0.016.

The test finds a highly significant correlation between the number of competitors and Promotion. Yet, the correlation is positive as opposed to the assumption of a negative relationship. The outcome shows that the conjecture on the VCF's increasing efforts to resolve uncertainty in less competitive settings does not apply. Given this result, hypothesis 1.3.3 is not validated at this point. In fact, VCFs turn out to engage more in Promotion the more competitive the venture's environment is.

Akin to the discussion on hypothesis 1.2.2, this outcome challenges the assumption that Promotion is systematically driven by information inefficiency. The result inspires an alternative explanation. Exits in general require the VCF to attract prospective investors. Competition is operationalized by the number of firms that offer similar products. Higher competition in a product market correlates with a higher number of firms – particularly in emerging markets in which companies offer only one product. Competition for customers thus translates into rivalry for follow-on investors since more firms are likely to require funding. In competitive settings, exits are hampered because prospective investors face a larger number of – from their perspective rather homogenous – investments opportunities. In consequence, VCFs have to endorse their ventures to investors in order facilitate their withdrawal. Merton (1987) under-

[812] Wright/Robbie/Romanet/Thompson/Joachimsson/Bruining/Herst (1994), p. 97

lines the importance of investors' knowledge of a particular investment opportunity for its financing costs. Merton demonstrates that a stock's initial market performance correlates with the number of investors aware of the issue.[813] Increasing the private and the public markets' awareness through Promotion thus bears value for exits in competitive settings. The finding on the impact of Competition on Promotion reflects that VCFs alert investors about their ventures to succeed in competitive settings. VC investments in low competitive sectors in turn require less promotion to attract follow-on capital. If investors pursue investments in less competitive sectors, their screening is likely to target the venture sooner or later. Given low rivalry for follow-on capital, exits require the VCF to incur less promotion to distinguish the venture as compared to highly competitive settings.

Furthermore, the outcome substantiates interdependencies between the VCF's exit strategy options. The test for hypothesis 1.3.2 suggests that IPO candidates feature significantly more rivals than ventures that undergo M&A transactions; IPO candidates face six times more competitors. Simultaneously, public transactions receive almost 17 % more Promotion in relation to private transactions.[814] The difference is highly significant. Since IPOs are more likely in information efficient settings as indicated by competition, rivalry indirectly requires the VCF to engage in Promotion. This argumentation also sustains the first notion; public markets see numerous IPOs while private investors focus on a strategic fit with only few ventures. The IPO thus requires the VCF to distinguish the venture and endorse it to public investors.

In essence, Promotion does not serve as a means to overcome information asymmetries in early stage exits. It rather allows the VCF to attract follow-on capital in settings where the follow-on investor can choose between numerous investment opportunities.

d) Departures of entrepreneurial team members

Hypothesis 2.1.3 relates the extent of promotion to the occurrence of departures of members of the entrepreneurial team. It is argued that departures send negative signals about the VC relationship and insiders' information advantages raising prospective investors' suspiciousness. VCFs are required to supplement relevant information to alleviate prospective investors' concerns. Thus, VCFs supposedly engage more in promotion if departures occur. The correlation analysis computes a Pearson's r of 0.227 at a confidence level of 0.003 for 167 transactions. The significant correlation prevails in separate tests only for private transactions (Pear-

[813] Merton (1987), p. 487ff., see also Subrahmanyam/Titman (1999), p. 1047

[814] See section 6.1.2 f)

son's r = 0.259 at p = 0.006) whereas the correlation in IPOs proves only roughly significant (Pearson's r = 0.153 at p = 0.089).

Indeed, the occurrence of dismissals correlates significantly with Promotion. Hypothesis 2.1.3 is hence accepted. Moreover, the overall Pearson's *r* represents the strongest correlation coefficient for Promotion so far. This preliminary result suggests that promotion is highly driven by exceptional circumstances such as departures rather than by continuous conditions such as industry affiliation.

e) The VCF's certification ability

Hypothesis 3.1.3 elaborates that seasoned VCFs possess more certification power in comparison to unseasoned VCFs. At a similar intensity, the seasoned VCFs' promotion is consequently more effective than the unseasoned VCF's promotion. Hypothesis 3.1.3 captures this notion in proposing a negative correlation between the VCFs' seasoning and promotion intensity. For 167 transactions, the Pearson correlation coefficient between both variables is –0.206 at a significance level of 0.008. The result prevails even after separating IPO exits (Pearson's r = -0.322 at p = 0.016) and private exits (Pearson's r = -0.173 at p = 0.068).

The test of hypothesis 3.1.3 yields a highly significant and negative correlation between the VCF's age and its promotion efforts. The result supports hypothesis 3.1.3. Hypothesis 3.1.3 seems to possess even more explanatory power for IPO exits while the correlation for private exits is lower and proves only roughly significant. This notion is consistent with the finding that private transactions receive less promotion anyway. Thus, the variance in promotion in private transactions is less affected by the VCF's seasoning. Moreover, the absolute Pearson's *r* represents the second highest correlation result observed so far. The individual investment's characteristics are not attributed with similarly strong influences making seasoning an important factor.

This result sustains previous findings on the different abilities of VCFs to overcome information spreads at exit.[815] The negative correlation suggests that unseasoned VCFs' promotion is less effective than seasoned VCFs' promotion. Inexperienced VCFs thus have to incur more promotion efforts if they want to accomplish the same outcome. Over time, the growing reputation improves unseasoned VCFs' certification power increasing the effectiveness of their promotion. This conclusion also complies with the findings of Barry et al. (1990) that unseasoned VCFs must underprice their offerings more to facilitate exits.[816]

---

[815] E.g., Gompers (1996), p. 153f.; Lerner (1994a), p. 305; Barry/Muscarella/Peavy/Vetsuypens (1990), p. 448

[816] Barry/Muscarella/Peavy/Vetsuypens (1990), p. 469f.

Furthermore, the outcome resembles Gompers' (1996) findings on grandstanding.[817] The result indicates that unseasoned VCFs utilize Promotion to quicken their reputation building given that they engage more in promotion.

f) Control variables

Several other parameters are introduced to control for alternative explanations. Table 37 summarizes the test results for the nominal scaled variable Auditor-Reputation, Exit Vehicle and External Approach.

	N	*Mean*	*SD*	*t*-test *p*-value
Non-leading Auditor	10	1.5	1.08	0.080*
Leading Auditor	115	2.10	0.90	
Acquisition	112	1.96	1.02	0.033**
Went Public	55	2.29	0.79	
External approach	94	1.93	0.90	0.031**
No external approach	73	2.25	1.01	

* significant on a 10 % level; ** significant on a 5 % level; *** significant on a 1 % level

Table 37: Nominal control variables vs. promotion

Promotion efforts differ between ventures that are accompanied by leading auditors and ventures with non-leading auditors on a 10 % confidence level. Transactions that are promoted more intensely also feature more distinguished auditors. It appears that VCFs complement their promotion efforts with certification of seasoned auditors. This observation, however, originates from the dependency of both parameters on the chosen exit vehicle. Leading auditors are less frequently in private transaction and, as will be demonstrated next, public transactions require far more promotion. In fact, the occurrence of more promotion and prestigious auditors coincide in IPO exits.

The exit vehicle decision drives promotion efforts. The difference between public and private transactions is significant with IPOs receiving substantially more promotion. The reason for this result lies in the nature of public markets. Chemmanur and Fulghieri (2001) argue that public finance becomes cheaper than private finance once sufficient information about the venture is publicly available.[818] If a VCF desires to tap the public markets and to capitalize on their superior capability to procure and process public information, it must release information. Promotion constitutes a means to provide public investors with information. Private finance, however, is ad-

[817] Gompers (1996), p. 135f.

[818] Chemmanur/Fulghieri (1999), p. 249f., see also Subrahmanyam/Titman (1999), p. 1047

vantageous if prospective investors can access only little public information. Private transactions become unfavorable if the VCF improves information efficiency through promoting the venture so that M&A transactions are naturally accompanied by less promotion. Hence, IPOs require the VCF to engage in Promotion.

External approaches significantly reduce promotion efforts. External approaches occur in the form of industrial investors wishing to acquire the venture. It seems reasonable that if an external investor shows interest in an acquisition, the VCF is not required to resolve his information gaps anymore. Rather, the prospective investor has already gathered appealing information about the venture. This information eventually prompts the acquirer to initiate a transaction. Accordingly, Promotion drops for 14 % in case an industrial investor approaches the VCF.

	N	VCF's promotion	
		Pearson's r	*Significance*
Investment Bank's reputation	99	-0.101	0.320
Investment's size	167	0.173	0.026**[1]
Performance	167	0.077	0.325
First-day returns upon exit	165	-0.060	0.447
Initial returns 3-6 months in advance	165	0.008	0.916
Initial returns 6-9 months in advance	165	0.116	0.137

* significant on a 10 % level; ** significant on a 5 % level; *** significant on a 1 % level

[1] Spearman-Rho has been used instead of Pearson's r

Table 38: Scaled control variables vs. promotion[819]

Table 38 reports the tests for the impacts of scaled control variables on Promotion. Controlling for the investment banker's reputation delivers a negative correlation. Yet, the correlation is not significance so that an impact of investment bankers on promotion is initially rejected.

The investment's size correlates significantly with the VCF's promotion. The notion that larger investments entail more promotion is attributed to the impact of the investment size on the choice of exit vehicles.[820] VCFs stipulate investment stages contingent on the venture's progress. If a venture stalls, it will not receive further investments. If the venture progresses, it obtains further capital infusions. Hence, the number of financing rounds correlates with the investment's total size which in turn indicates its quality.[821] Moreover, VCFs are known to float only their best ventures to

[819] The impacts of equity valuation levels have already been contemplated in hypothesis 1.1.2

[820] See section 6.1.2 f)

[821] See section 2.3.2; e.g. ; Admati/Pfleiderer (1994), p. 371f.; Cornelli/Yosha (2003), p. 1; Bergemann/Hege (1998), p. 704; Busenitz/Fiet (1996); Gifford (1997), p. 459; Gompers (1995), p. 1461; Sahlman (1990), p. 507

preserve their reputation.[822] IPO exits in turn require more promotion as set out above so that the investment size indirectly determines the extent of promotion.

The venture's overall performance has not proven to correlate significantly with the VCF's promotion. Neither do low performing ventures receive more nor well performing ventures less promotion. Promotion thus appears not to be a measure to enforce exits of low performing ventures.

The analysis of the first-day returns yields no significant correlations. The extent of the VCFs' promotion activities is obviously not driven by the states of public markets; neither do VCFs incur fewer efforts in hot issue markets nor more efforts in cold issue markets. In fact, VCFs keep interacting with outsiders at a constant intensity irrespective of investor optimism, scepticism or IPO waves. VCFs do not even increase their efforts to center their exits on peaking stock markets as suggested by Lerner (1994a) and Wang and Sim (2001).[823] Whether and how they capitalize on high first day returns may rather be determined by other strategy options.

g) Regression model to explain the VCF's promotion

To compare the factors affecting promotion and to isolate the major determinants, a regression model is developed on the basis of the survey sample. The analysis proceeds in the common manner. Table 39 reports the individual steps.

---

[822] Fleming (2003), p. 9; Gompers/Lerner (1998), p. 2162; Schwienbacher (2002), p. 7f.

[823] Lerner (1994a), p. 300; Wang/Sim (2001), p. 341

Steps	*1.*	*2.*	*3.*	*4.*	*5.*	*6.*	*7.*	*8:*	*9:*	*10.*
R^2	.339***	.344***	.364***	.366***	.366***	.364***	.361***	.354***	.352***	.343***
Adjusted R^2	.203	.236	.269	.285	.293	.299	.304	.307	.309	.308
	Std. Beta									
1. High-Tech	.006	-.048	-.055	-.065	-.076	-.080	-.087	-.087	-.092	-
2. Bio-Tech	.161	.106	.114	.092	.091	.085	.083	.080	-	-
3. Exit stage	-.159	-.051	-.049	-	-	-	-	-	-	-
4. Financing rounds	.195	.176	.170	.156	.160	.147	.160	.156	.149	.140
5. Competition	.110	.033	.029	.033	-	-	-	-	-	-
6. Departures	.025	.060	.063	.053	.058	.053	-	-	-	-
7. VCF's age	-.300	-.359	-.385	-.419	-.416	-.402	-.406	-.411	-.411	-.402
8. First day return	-.100	-.038	-	-	-	-	-	-	-	-
9. Auditor quality	.088	-	-	-	-	-	-	-	-	-
10. Investment bank	-.244	-.224	-.192	-.155	-.154	-.161	-.155	-.151	-.149	-.153
11. Exit vehicle	.186	.229	.225	.196	.205	.199	.198	.194	.218	.226
12. External approach	.194	.226	.240	.226	.229	.218	.226	.229	.230	.227
13. V.'s performance	.106	.026	.024	.075	.072	.064	.064	-	-	-
14. Investment size	-.009	-.002	-.011	-.052	-.053	-	-	-	-	-

* significant on a 10 % level; ** significant on a 5 % level; *** significant on a 1 % level

Table 39: Regression analysis of the VCF's promotion

Step nine represents the final regression model. Thereafter, the model's quality suffers from the elimination of further variables. The Durbin-Watson value for the terminal model surpasses 1.8 and is close enough to 2 to eliminate autocorrelation concerns. The Tolerance of each independent variable exceeds 0.8 by far (all VIFs are smaller than 1.2) so that collinearity is a marginal concern. Even though the Condition Index stays well below 30 it amounts up to 20.7. Given this value, collinearity cannot be excluded completely. Two pairs of variables seem particularly critical:

- The exit vehicle affects the extent of third-party certification in that IPOs feature significantly more prestigious investment banks.[824]
- Approaches of private investors more often result in private transactions. Out of 74 approaches, 55 (74 %) acquisitions materialize while only 62 % of those transactions without an external approach lead to an M&A exit. The cross table sustains this argumentation exhibiting a Pearson χ^2 of 2.996. At one degree of freedom, the relationship is roughly significant with p equalling 0.099.

Yet, excluding one of these factors weakens the model. If the Exit Vehicle is removed, the Condition Index improves only slightly to 19.39 (minus 6.3 %) while the R^2 falls below 0.31 (minus 11.6 %). A similar result occurs, if the External Approach is taken out; the Condition Index declines only marginally to 19.789 (minus 4.4 %) while R^2 sinks to 0.301 (minus 14.7 %). Eliminating Third-Party Certification reduces the Condition Index to 14.095 (minus 31.9 %) but similarly distresses R^2 to 0.134 (minus 62 %). Given these choices, the analysis accepts equation nine as the final model and proceeds with increased sensitivity for interactions between these factors.

The R^2 of the final regression of 0.352 stands for 35 % of the variation of the VCF's promotion that is explained by the model. The regression model's fit peaks for only six variables out of fourteen (43 %). The adjust R^2 soars from 0.203 for the initial model to 0.309 in the final regression. Since R^2 exceeds the adjusted R^2, the model still fails to capture at least one more determinant. Yet, the adjusted R^2 is 12 % less than the R^2. Thus, the terminal model provides a roughly accurate picture of the determinants of the VCF's promotion efforts.

The model excludes five significant dependencies established throughout the hypotheses tests: the exit stage, the extent of competition, the occurrence of dismissals, auditors and the investment size. Even though the terminal model does not contradict the previous findings, these factors seem to dilute the regression model more than they contribute to it. However, the purged variables are mostly represented through other variables; these collinearities become apparent in the changes of the remaining coefficients during the transformation to higher steps:

- The Exit Stage is removed. Yet, it appears that the number of rounds the venture receives captures the exit stage's impact. The correlation analysis based on the survey sample exhibits a Pearson's *r* of 0.230 at a confidence level of 0.004.[825] Ventures that progress to higher development levels obtain more funds while the VCF abandons stalling ventures to minimize losses. As set out in section 6.1.3 b), the VCF must exit in certain stages to avoid becoming inefficient. Thus, promotion efforts increase the more rounds the venture receives.

---

[824] This finding is further discussed in sections 6.1.2 f) and section 6.1.4 f).

[825] For the original sample, Pearson's *r* is 0.146 at a confidence level of 0.000, N = 2,449

The changes in step four also indicate that eliminating the exit stage increases the impact of the VCF's certification and the impact of performance on the VCF's promotion. First, this finding hints at the venture's performance serving as alternative proxy for the venture's progress instead of the exit stage with high performances indicating a later stages and less uncertainty. Second, the VCF's certification seems to make up for at whatever exit stage the venture is terminated, all else equal. This correlation proves, however, not significant in a separate test.

- Despite the earlier finding, the model eliminates the extent of competition. In consistency with the argumentation for hypothesis 1.3.3, the exit vehicle incorporates the rivalry of the venture's environment; comparing the mean number of competitors between private and public transactions delivers a highly significant difference.[826] On the other hand, the elimination of competition amplifies the impact of the technology affiliation. The comparison of means yields a significant difference; non-high-technology ventures face far more competition than high-technology ventures (on average 7.44 vs. 3.35 at a confidence level of 0.057).
- The elimination of departures increases the impact of the industry affiliation, the number of financing rounds and the importance of the external approach. Yet, none of these correlations prove significant in isolated test. Thus, the finding for hypothesis 2.1.3 is not revised at this stage.
- The auditor quality remains indirectly represented through the exit vehicle.[827]
- The investment size indirectly impacts promotion efforts through the number of rounds (Pearson's r of 0.509 at a significance level of 0.000)[828] and through the VCF's age (Pearson's r of –0.160 at a significance level of 0.038).

The remaining factors mostly correspond to the previous findings. The VCF's age represents the major determinant with almost twice as much impact on Promotion as the second strongest determinant External Approach and the Exit Vehicle, ranked third. In comparison, the Industry Affiliation, the Number of Rounds and the Investment Bank constitute relatively weak factors. The overall picture conforms Gompers (1996) and others who underline the importance of the VCF's certification ability upon the exit strategy.[829] The model also complies with Habib and Ljungqvist (2001); more seasoned investment banks make up for less promotion whereas less

---

[826] See section 6.1.2 c)

[827] See previous discussion for control variables

[828] For the original data sample: Pearson's r is 0.135 at a confidence level of 0.000, N = 2,765.

[829] E.g., Gompers (1996), p. 153f.; Barry/Muscarella/Peavy/Vetsuypens (1990), p. 448; Neus/Walz (2001), p. 17

seasoned investment banks require the VCF to increase its involvement.[830] Even though the negative relationship is not significant in the preceding test for hypothesis 1.1.3, the industry affiliation's impact on Promotion prevails. The coefficient implies that high-technology ventures obtain less Promotion than Non-High-Technology ventures. This finding grounds on two earlier results. First, high-technology ventures are more likely to accomplish an IPO which in turn requires more Promotion.[831] Second, Biotech ventures are promoted more than other ventures.[832] In support of this argumentation, table 39 reports that the impact of the industry affiliation soars with the elimination of the Biotech dummy. Accounting for the earlier findings on weak impacts, the coefficient for industry affiliation is the lowest over the whole model.

The regression analysis accounts for the initiative of prospective private investors. If the VCF is not approached by private investors, it has to increase promotion by almost one fourth to facilitate exits. Two extreme scenarios impact the extent of Promotion by almost 50 %. Given the approach of external investors, VCFs reduce their promotion while their decision for an IPO in the absence of a private investor's approach requires 23 % more Promotion effort. This divergence underlines the importance of the exit strategy for promotion again.

The regression model outlines the importance of two determinants for the VCF's promotion efforts. First, the VCF's certification power drives promotion. Second, the exit vehicle prejudices Promotion. As outlined in the discussion for control variables, IPOs require the VCF to improve information efficiency in public markets. Most factors that prevail in the terminal model, such as External Approach or Investment Banks, are related to the exit vehicle. Against the initial assumptions, information asymmetry at exit explains only the coefficient of the VCF's Age.

6.1.4 Third-Party Certification

a) The degree of innovation and industry affiliation

Hypothesis 1.1.4 predicts a correlation between the extent of third-party certification and the degree of innovation. The hypothesis sets out that the valuation spreads between inside and outside investors differ more for innovative ventures increasing the necessity for additional certification. Table 40 renders the test's results for the original data sample of VC-backed transactions.

---

[830] Habib/Ljungqvist (2001), p. 453

[831] See sections 6.1.2 a) and 6.1.3f)

[832] See section 6.1.3 a)

	N	Mean	SD	t-test p-value
Non-innovative	224	1.870	1.29	0.004***
Innovative	881	2.14	1,18	

* significant on a 10 % level; ** significant on a 5 % level; *** significant on a 1 % level

Table 40: Innovation vs. third-party certification

The means of both categories differ substantially with innovative ventures enlisting more seasoned investment banks. The test initially sustains hypothesis 1.1.4. Non-innovative ventures hire on average a top eight investment bank while the innovative venture's choice is essentially narrowed down to a top four investment bank.

		N	Mean	SD	t-test p-value
Private Transactions	Non-innovative	146	1.45	1.23	0.352
	Innovative	413	1.56	1.21	
IPOs	Non-innovative	78	2.69	0.98	0.738
	Innovative	468	2.65	0.85	

* significant on a 10 % level; ** significant on a 5 % level; *** significant on a 1 % level

Table 41: Third-party certification across exit vehicles and industries

To gain deeper insights in the effects of industry affiliation on the involvement of investment banks, the analysis is deepened in two dimensions. First, the impact of the exit vehicle is eliminated in that separate tests are performed for third-party certification in innovative and non-innovative IPOs and M&A transactions. According to table 41, the significant differences between innovative and non-innovative ventures vanish after the industry's effect is isolated from the exit vehicle. Innovative M&A transactions involve more prestigious investment banks but this difference proves not significant. IPOs even seem to invert the presumptions although this result is not significant either. Given these findings, hypothesis 1.1.4 is rejected. The initial result rather seems to be flawed because innovative ventures are more often floated and the IPO requires more third-party certification than the private transaction.[833] The initial result thus reflects the impact of the exit vehicle instead of the influence of the degree of innovation. To further investigate the occurrence of the initial result, table 42 analyzes the average market shares of investment banks for exits across industries.

[833] See section 6.1.2 a) and 6.1.2 f)

	N	*Mean*	*SD*	*t*-test *p*-value 2.	3.	4.	5.	6.
1. Biotechnology	69	2.44	1.00	0.567	0.019**	0.002***	0.001***	0.001***
2. Comm. & Media	227	2.35	1.15		0.006***	0.001***	0.000***	0.001***
3. Computer Related	410	2.09	1.18			0.168	0.041**	0.070*
4. Life Sciences	102	1.91	1.16				0.852	0.603
5. Non-High-Tech.	224	1.88	1.29					0.696
6. Semiconductors	73	1.81	1.26					

* significant on a 10 % level; ** significant on a 5 % level; *** significant on a 1 % level

Table 42: Industry affiliation vs. third-party certification

Ten out of 15 combinations prove significantly different. The test may raise the question whether individual investment banks are drawn to certain industries. Yet, the fact that the mean market shares across all industries exceed 1.8 confirms the presence of at least one out of the top eight investment banks in almost every transaction. However, evidence for an industry focus of these bulge bracket banks is neither given on their homepages nor does the literature report such emphases. Rather, the comparison of mean investment bankers' reputation across industries delivers a basic ranking for the general need for prestigious investment banks. Biotechnology and Communication ventures require significantly more third-party certification than transactions in other industries. Transactions within the Biotechnology or Communication and Media sector involve on average one of the top four investment banks. Computer Related ventures also hire more seasoned investment bankers than ventures in the Non-High-Technology or Semiconductor industry. But Computer Related ventures do not significantly differ from Life Science ventures. Given that almost all innovative industries require more third-party certification, hypothesis 1.1.4 appears to bear some substance when comparing industry affiliations. However, not all differences prove significant and Semiconductor ventures contradict the general presumption of hypothesis 1.1.4. Again, the pattern in table 42 basically complies with the results for the IPO frequency across industries with higher IPO frequencies increasing third-party certification.[834] Biotechnology ventures lead both comparisons while Non-High-Technology and Semiconductor ventures rank last as regards the IPO frequency and the extent of third-party certification. Because the IPO frequency confounds this analysis, the subsequent tests separate the exit vehicles again and contrast the occurrence of third-party certification across industries.

[834] See section 6.1.2 a)

	N	*Mean*	*SD*	*t*-test *p*-value 2.	3.	4.	5.	6.
1. Biotechnology	45	2.68	0.81	0.190	0.430	0.192	0.966	0.993
2. Comm. & Media	121	2.87	0.81		0.002***	0.003***	0.163	0.229
3. Computer Related	216	2.57	0.89			0.429	0.317	0.485
4. Life Sciences	51	2.46	0.84				0.172	0.228
5. Non-High-Tech.	78	2.69	0.98					0.962
6. Semiconductors	35	2.68	0.81					

* significant on a 10 % level; ** significant on a 5 % level; *** significant on a 1 % level

Table 43: Third-party certification in IPOs across industries

The analysis of third-party certification in IPOs across industries delivers only two significant differences. Thus, table 43 resembles the earlier finding in table 41 that third-party certification in IPOs does not vary significantly across industries. In fact, only Communication & Media ventures stand out and surpass Computer Related and Life Science ventures at a considerable confidence level. Table 43 ranks Non-High-Technology IPOs second after Communication and Media ventures. Non-High-Technology IPOs tend to involve more prestigious investment bankers than Computer Related, Biotechnology, Life Science or Semiconductor ventures. The observed pattern does not resemble any other patterns found in this dissertation. Rather, the high level of underwriters' prestige and the absence of significant differences highlight VCFs' decisions to employ top four underwriters to ensure the issue's success regardless of the issue's characteristics.

	N	*Mean*	*SD*	*t*-test 2.	3.	4.	5.	6.
1. Biotechnology	24	1.99	1.18	0.410	0.102	0.033**	0.047**	0.001***
2. Comm. & Media	106	1.76	1.20		0.151	0.046**	0.044**	0.001***
3. Computer Related	194	1.55	1.23			0.309	0.444	0.012**
4. Life Sciences	51	1.35	1.17				0.642	0.156
5. Non-High-Tech.	146	1.44	1.23					0.047**
6. Semiconductors	38	1.01	1.04					

* significant on a 10 % level; ** significant on a 5 % level; *** significant on a 1 % level

Table 44: Third-party certification in M&A exits across industries

Table 44 contrasts the presence of third-party certification in M&A transactions across industries. Conversely to the IPO scheme, eight out of 15 combinations vary significantly. Biotechnology mergers rank first and significantly surpass Life Sciences, Non-High-Technology and Semiconductor deals. Communication & Media ventures come in second place and differ significantly from transactions in the same industries as Biotechnology exits do. Computer Related and Non-High-Technology ventures hire on average more prestigious investment banks than Semiconductor ventures. In essence, hypothesis 1.1.4 explains the differences between Non-High-Technology and Biotechnology respectively Communication & Media transactions and thus bears some value in M&A transactions.

Hypothesis 1.1.4 does, however, not apply for the observation that Semiconductor ventures receive significantly less third-party certification in M&A transactions and slightly less in IPOs. The present finding allows for several speculations. The fact that Semiconductor M&A transactions involve less prestigious investment banks indicates that prospective investors suffer less uncertainty. The first reasoning contradicts the finding that Semiconductor IPOs are significantly more underpriced – twice as much as Non-High-Technology IPOs. In terms of Habib and Ljungqvist (2001), this severe discrepancy would justify more third-party certification for Semiconductor ventures.[835] Despite this, VCFs do not hire more prestigious investment banks. The finding also contradicts the literature that holds that investment banks avoid backing risky transactions to protect their reputation.[836] The comparison shows that investment banks certify for other innovative industries that feature an even higher average underpricing.[837] The investment bank's selection thus fails to explain this finding.

This dissertation observes similar patterns for hypothesis 1.1.1. Even though innovative venture were initially assumed to impose more uncertainty on prospective investors, they accomplished exits earlier than non-innovative ventures because of VCFs' closer supervision of innovative firms. The literature on VC contains several articles sustaining the positive impact of monitoring on prospective investors' perception of the venture.[838] A comparison of means implies that supervision accounts for the present observation too:[839]

- Semiconductor IPO receive significantly more investment rounds than Non-High-Technology IPOs (Ø = 3.31, N = 48 versus Ø = 2.56, N = 137 at a confidence level of 0.037).
- Semiconductor M&A exits receive significantly more investment rounds than Non-High-Technology M&A deals (Ø = 3.66, N = 135 versus Ø = 2.39, N = 446 at a confidence level of 0.000).

In essence, it appears that the presence of investment bankers depends mostly on the exit vehicle. Besides, VCFs resolve prospective investors' uncertainty already during the investment period in that they monitor high-technology ventures more

---

[835] Habib/Ljungqvist (2001), p. 435

[836] Carter/Manaster (1990), p. 1062; Johnson/Miller (1988), p. 20 and p. 28; Logue (1973), p. 100; Megginson/Weiss (1991), p. 880 and p. 887

[837] See table 5 for average underpricing across industries

[838] E.g., Barry/Muscarella/Peavy/Vetsuypens (1990), p. 501; Cornelli/Yosha (2003), p. 1; Giot/Schwienbacher (2003), p. 11; Gompers (1995), p. 1487; Gompers/Lerner (2000), p. 164; Gorman/Sahlman (1989), p. 238

[839] This finding does not apply for other combinations among high-technology industries; see also Habib/Ljungqvist (2001), p. 452

closely. Hypothesis 1.1.4 bears some value, given that it explains six significant differences across industries for M&A exits. The greater information asymmetries associated with high-technology industries call for more third-party certification; VCFs thus hire more prestigious investment bankers to facilitate private transaction in high-technology industries in comparison to low technology sectors.

b) Development levels

Hypothesis 1.2.4 holds that since investors associate early stage exits with more information asymmetries, VCFs are more likely to lease additional certification. The test results are given in table 45.

	N	Third-party certification	
		Pearson's r	*Significance*
Exit stage	937	0.008	0.799
Holding duration	1,076	-0.072	0.019***
Financing rounds	1,084	0.087	0.004***

* significant on a 10 % level; ** significant on a 5 % level; *** significant on a 1 % level

Table 45: Exit stages vs. third-party certification

Both, the marginal correlation coefficient between Exit Stage and Third-Party Certification and the low confidence level lead to the rejection of hypothesis 1.2.4. Given this result, VCFs do not incorporate the dynamics of information efficiency over time in their third-party certification strategy. The separate test for the presence of prestigious investment banks in M&A exits complies with the initial finding.

However, the test for IPO exits contradicts this notion; Pearson's r amounts to 0.098 at p = 0.042 for 435 transactions.[840] VCFs lease more third-party certification in later stage IPOs than in early stage IPOs. This finding rejects the notion that VCFs hire investment bankers to facilitate difficult exits. In fact, the literature contradicts the assumption that VCFs can access prestigious underwriters for all transaction. Researchers argue that investment banks carefully select the transactions they back in order to protect their reputation.[841] In line with Habib and Ljungqvist (2001), VCFs can only access third-party certification for ventures that fulfil the investment bank's requirements for instance with respect to the issue's size.[842] The positive correlations between the exit stage and the extent of third-party certification in IPO exits underline this reasoning; given that later stage investments become bigger, VCFs can access

[840] In line with the initial finding, acquisitions deliver no significant results; Pearson's r amounts to only 0.012 at a confidence level of 0.780.

[841] E.g., Johnson/Miller (1988), p. 20 and p. 28; Logue (1973), p. 100

[842] Habib/Ljungqvist (2001), p. 452

more seasoned investment banks. The observed positive correlation between the number of financing rounds and third-party certification confirms the argumentation that the investment's size enhances the VCF's access to prestigious underwriters.

Table 45 relates another variable that capture timing aspects to the occurrence of third-party certification. Even though hypothesis 1.2.4 is not validated in the context of exit stages, its assumption applies to the holding duration. The test yields a significant negative correlation. The more time the VCF spends on nurturing the venture and the more time the venture has to establish track records, the less third-party certification is required for the exit. The finding complies with the literature. In line with Barry et al. (1990), hypothesis 1.2.4 holds; prospective investors appreciate the VCF's contribution holds as risk reducing which in turn lowers the necessity for additional certification.[843]

The test series shows that if a VCF floats two ventures simultaneously, the larger IPO is more likely to involve prestigious underwriters. If the VCF exits two ventures of similar sizes, the younger one is likely to be backed by more prestigious investment banks. Only the last finding is consistent with hypothesis 1.2.4 while the prior findings hint at other causalities than information asymmetry.

c) Competition

Hypothesis 1.3.4 proposes a relation between the extent of competition and the occurrence of third party certification. Competition prompts ventures to promote their products and to release information. Prospective investors can access more public information in competitive settings. Given more competition, exits require less certification as opposed to non-competitive settings. The correlation analysis establishes a significant relation between the investment bank's market share and the number of competitors. For 1,100 public and private transactions, Pearson's r amounts to 0.251 at a confidence level of 0.000. Yet, the direction does not correspond to hypothesis 1.3.4. Rather, third-party certification significantly soars with an increasing number of competitors.

The strong correlation between the number of competitors and the market share of the investment banks points at an alternative explanation. In highly competitive environments, public finance becomes cheaper.[844] Moreover, an IPO calls for more third-party certification.[845] Thus, competition indirectly increases the need for third-party certification. The finding that competition increases the likelihood for IPOs confirms the impact of competition on information efficiency. However, the strong interre-

---

[843] Barry/Muscarella/Peavy/Vetsuypens (1990), p. 448 and p. 469f.

[844] See section 6.1.2 c)

[845] Subrahmanyam/Titman (1999), p. 1047

lations bewteen competition and the exit vehicle as well as between the exit vehicle and third-party certification flaw this test and do not allow for a conclusion on hypothesis 1.3.4 at this point. In essence, this finding emphasizes the dominance of the exit vehicle decision over the decision for third-party certification. VCFs first decide on how they adjust the exit vehicle to information asymmetry before they lease third-party certification in accordance to the exit vehicle.

Separate tests are performed to eliminate the impact of the exit vehicle. For private transactions, the number of competitors and the extent of third-party certification do not correlate significantly (Pearson's r = 0.056; N = 555; p = 0.190). In IPOs, the number of competitors even increases the need for third-party certification. For 545 IPOs, the correlation analysis delivers a Spearman's Rho of 0.128 at a confidence level of 0.003. Hypothesis 1.3.4 is thus rejected. In fact, this finding supports the reasoning of section 6.1.3 c). Ventures' competition for customers translates into rivalry for public capital. In public transactions, VCFs must distinguish their IPO from other IPOs. The results show that VCFs employ prestigious underwriters to distinguish their issues from other IPOs and to attract follow-on funding the more competitive the venture's environment is.

d) Departures of entrepreneurial team members

Hypothesis 2.1.4 reasons that VCFs lease more third-party certification the more departures occur. Through adding external certification, VCFs wish to work against the negative signals emitted by dismissals or insider sales. The correlation analysis delivers a Pearson's r of 0.121 for 99 transactions which proves not significant. Even when repeating the test for IPOs and private transactions separately, a significant correlation does not occur; the confidence level for the correlation between third-party certification and departures for private transactions amounts to 0.243 and to 0.819 for IPOs.

The outcome shows no significant correlation between exits subsequent to departures and exits without departures and the employment of third-party certification. The result does not validate hypothesis 2.1.4. While the test of hypothesis 2.1.3 confirms that VCFs step up their promotion to facilitate exits, they do not add significantly more third-party certification to work against additional information asymmetries caused by departures. Habib and Ljungqvist (2001) argue that hiring more seasoned and hence expensive investment banks is only justified in settings of severe information asymmetry.[846] Given the present finding, it rather appears that dismissals do not increase prospective investors' suspiciousness to an extent that justifies the employment of more seasoned investment banks.

---

[846] Habin/Ljungqvist (2001), p. 435ff.

e) The VCF's certification ability

Hypothesis 3.1.4 predicts a correlation between the VCF's reputation and the accessibility of top investment banks. In an attempt to maintain their reputation, investment banks are assumed to join only seasoned VCFs rather than unseasoned VCFs. Pearson's *r* for the correlation of the VCF's age and Third-Party Certification amounts to virtually zero at a confidence level of 0.777. Given this result, seasoned investment banks neither appear more frequently in transactions backed by older VCFs nor in exits of younger VCFs. Hypothesis 3.1.4 is thus rejected.

However, the strong correlation between the VCF's choice of exit vehicles and third-party certification calls for a separate contemplation for each exit route. As for private transactions, the initial finding is sustained. The correlation does not become significant; Pearson's r barely exceeds 0.052 and the result's significance amounts to only 0.241. Third-party certification in M&A exits seems to be independent from the VCF's seasoning. When isolating IPOs, the VCF's age and the extent of third-party certification correlate with a Pearson's r of 0.105 at a confidence level of 0.016. The latter result matches the findings of Megginson and Weiss (1991) that more seasoned VCFs employ more seasoned investment banks in IPOs.[847] This finding validates hypothesis 3.1.4 for IPO exits.

The absence of a significant correlation in private transactions, however, complies with later findings that private transactions do generally not require as much third-party certification as IPOs do.[848] Section 6.1.4 f) sets forth that private investors are less receptive for public information than public investors.[849] Private transactions cannot benefit as much from third-party certification as IPOs can. Thus, the private transaction does not require prestigious investment bankers. The comparison of mean market shares of investment bankers in IPOs and private transactions sustains this notion. The mean market share of an investment bank that backs a private transaction is almost 43 % lower than the average market share of underwriters in IPOs. This finding shows that less seasoned investment banks do not carefully chose those private transactions they back. In fact, low-level third-party certification is available to all M&A exits and for every VCF. The finding also implies that prestigious investment bankers mostly occur in IPOs where the VCF's pre-selection of IPO candidates warrants a certain level of quality.

---

[847] Megginson/Weiss (1991), p. 883; see also Bradley and Jordan (2002), p. 601

[848] See section 6.1.4 f)

[849] Subrahmanyam/Titman (1999), p. 1047

f) Control variables

This section contrasts the occurrence of third-party certification against several control variables. The first test investigates the impact of nominal scaled variables such as the auditor's reputation, the exit vehicle and external approaches through private investors on the extent of third-party certification. The results are reported in table 46.

	N	*Mean*	*SD*	*t*-test *p*-value
Non-leading auditor	10	1.73	1.07	0.147
Leading auditor	788	2.26	1.15	
Private transaction	559	1.53	1.22	0.000***
Public transaction	546	2.66	0.88	
No external approach	60	2.05	1.04	0.050**[1]
External approach	39	1.64	0.98	

* significant on a 10 % level; ** significant on a 5 % level; *** significant on a 1 % level

[1] Based on the survey sample

Table 46: Nominal control variables vs. third-party certification

Ventures audited by one of the big four firms do not significantly vary from ventures audited by smaller firms as regards the presence of prestigious investment banks. The choice of auditors is consequently not linked to the presence of investment banks. This finding is particularly interesting against the background that IPOs feature both – better auditors and more seasoned investment banks. Given this indirect linkage, the actual finding seems to be flawed by the low ratio of non-leading auditors limiting the test's scope. The test does hence not allow for a terminal conclusion.

The employment of investment banks dependents on the choice of exit vehicles. While private transactions are accompanied on average by one of the top twelve advisors, IPOs are underwritten by top four banks. As reasoned earlier, public finance becomes only cheaper when information about the venture spreads publicly. Otherwise, private funding proves more efficient.[850] To facilitate IPOs, VCFs engage in promotion and circulate information. Habib and Ljungqvist (2001) argue that involving seasoned investment bankers represents one strategy of promoting a venture and

[850] Subrahmanyam/Titman (1999), p. 1047

releasing information about the quality of the valuation.[851] The finding that IPOs feature more seasoned investment banks validates this reasoning.

In case of an external approach, third-party certification is less required. The fact that external approaches foster the chances for a private transaction, which in turn involves less third-party certification, explains this outcome.

	N	VCF's promotion	
		Pearson's r	*Significance*
Investment's size	1,105	0.144	0.000***
Performance	169	0.023	0.821[1]
First-day returns upon exit	1,105	0.075	0.012**
Initial returns 3-6 months in advance	1,105	0.107	0.000***
Initial returns 6-9 months in advance	1,105	0.127	0.000***

* significant on a 10 % level; ** significant on a 5 % level; *** significant on a 1 % level

[1] Based on the survey sample

Table 47: Scaled control variables vs. third-party certification

Second, the impact of the ordinal scaled control variables on the extent of third-party certification is researched. Table 47 renders the results for the investment size and the venture's performance.[852] In accordance with Johnson and Miller (1988), larger transactions are more likely to attract seasoned investment bankers.[853] Yet, the extent of third-party certification is not related to the venture's performance. Investment banks do obviously not decline backing unprofitable ventures. This finding contradicts the literature that argues that prestigious investment banks only engage in low risk transactions in order to protect their reputation.[854]

The analysis also reveals significant correlations between the equity markets' states and the employment of investment banks.[855] Because higher first day returns prompt more IPOs,[856] the demand for third-party certification increases as well. This finding is robust for the quarter in which the transaction is actually accomplished as well as for the two preceding quarters.

---

[851] Habib/Ljungqvist (1998), p. 434f.

[852] The relation between the investment bank and the VCF's promotion has already been discussed in the previous section.

[853] Johnson/Miller (1988), p. 20

[854] Carter/Manaster (1990), p. 1062; Johnson/Miller (1988), p. 20 and p. 28; Logue (1973), p. 100; Megginson/Weiss (1991), p. 880 and p. 887

[855] Since IPOs require several months of preparation, the equity valuations prior to the initial floatation may influence the VCF's decision to enlist prestigious investment banks as well.

[856] See section 6.1.2 f)

g) Regression model

This section develops the regression model for the extent of third-party certification on the basis of the survey sample. Table 48 reports the elimination sequence and the final model.

Steps	1.	2.	3.	4.	5.	6.	7.	8.
R^2	.299**	.320***	.329***	.329***	.328***	.323***	.318***	.302***
Adjusted R^2	.143	.209	.219	.228	.236	.241	.245	.235
	Std. Beta							
1. High-Tech	.057	-.025	-.024	-	-	-	-	-
2. Bio-Tech	.044	.040	.042	.040	-	-	-	-
3. Exit stage	-.055	-.005	-.006	-.007	.012	.017	.017	.041
4. Financing rounds	.165	.156	.157	.154	.147	.142	.157	.206
5. Duration	-.147	-.145	-.145	-.143	-.145	-.151	-.149	-.158
6. Competition	.187	.133	.133	.139	.140	.150	.164	.164
7. Dismissals	.035	.083	.083	.082	.078	.075	-	-
8. VCF's age	.077	.073	.073	.075	.079	-	-	-
9. Auditor quality	-.042	-	-	-	-	-	-	-
10. Promotion	-.265	-.232	-.233	-.231	-.227	-.258	-.254	-.239
11. Exit vehicle	.229	.253	.254	.253	.260	.262	.254	.272
12. First day return	-.277	-.227	-.227	-.230	-.236	-.234	-.243	-.256
13. External approach	-.180	-.205	-.204	-.205	-.208	-.200	-.195	-.170
14. V.'s performance	.080	-.008	-	-	-	-	-	-
15. Investment size	.135	.160	.158	.157	.159	.136	.148	-

* significant on a 10 % level; ** significant on a 5 % level; *** significant on a 1 % level

Table 48: Regression analysis of third-party certification

As regards the model's quality, the control parameters yield no reason for concern. The Durbin Watson value amounts to 1.929 and is close to the optimal value of 2. Each remaining factor features a Tolerance of at least 0.75 (all VIFs are smaller than 1.34). The Condition Index comes close to 10 (11.221). Autocorrelation and collinearity are hence excluded. With a terminal R^2 of 0.318, the regression model explains roughly 32 % of the variance of third-party certification. The adjusted R^2 amounts to 0.245 which is more than twice as much as the initial value. Yet, the discrepancy between R^2 and the adjusted R^2 (23 %) implies that at least one important determinant is omitted. Out of the original 15 factors, nine determinants remain (60 %).

Four remaining factors stem from conjectures on the impact of information asymmetry on the extent of third party certification. The elimination of Departures and the VCF's Age complies with earlier findings. The beta coefficients for the holding duration, competition and the number of financing rounds conform earlier findings as well. As for the control variables, only the auditors' quality and the venture's performance are suspended. The auditors' quality is captured in the factor exit vehicle with IPOs featuring more frequently high quality auditors. The elimination of the venture's performance complies with earlier finding that varying performances do not affect the VCF's promotion. As for this section, performance is not found to impact the employment of more or less seasoned investment banks. Again, the notion that VCFs and investment banks ascribe less importance to the venture's overall performance is sustained.

The control variables add substantial explanatory power to the model. They contain the four strongest factors with the exit vehicle and the VCF's promotion equally weighted. In line with earlier findings, seasoned investment banks appear to substitute the VCF's promotion. IPOs step up the necessity for high quality investment banks in comparison to private transactions. In this sense, the occurrence of external investors diminishes the need for third-party certification. First-day returns constitute the third strongest factor.

As opposed to earlier findings in the control section, first-day returns now reduce the necessity for third-party certification. This antagonism originates from neglecting the role of exit vehicles in the bi-variate controlling test. Since the IPO frequency soars in hot issue markets and IPOs also require more third-party certification, the bi-variate test confirms a relation between first-day returns and third-party certification.[857] The regression analysis, however, accounts for the occurrence of IPOs separately and purges the indirect relation between investment banks and initial returns. The regression analysis shows that investor optimism during hot issue markets tends to lessen public markets' sensitivity for investment risks and decreases the need for third-party certification.[858]

The regression analysis outlines three facets. First, the exit strategy matters. The Exit Vehicle impacts the presence of investment banks. In line with earlier findings, IPOs require more certification than M&A transactions. The occurrence of external investors even decreases the necessity for seasoned investment banks since less information about the venture's quality need to be conveyed. These findings show that public markets are more sensitive to certification than private investors. The result also confirms the importance of Promotion as a mean to resolve uncertainty; Promotion substitutes third-party certification. Second, size matters. The employment of seasoned investment banks increases with the investment size, the development

---

[857] See section 6.1.2 f)

[858] Lowry (2003), p. 5; Ofek/Richardson (2003), p. 113f.; see also Ibbotson/Jaffe (1975), p. 1027; Ritter (1984), p. 238f.

level and the number of financing rounds. This finding reflects the investment bankers' ambitions to engage only in less risky transactions in order to preserve their reputation.[859] Third, the necessity for third-party certification depends on the market's attitude towards new issues. If the markets tolerate more uncertainties, third-party certification is less frequently employed. If the market faces more choices as pictured in higher competition, VCFs use third-party certification to distinguish their venture over rivaling IPOs.

In essence, this section asserts that the exit vehicle determines whether investment bankers are hired or not. Information asymmetries due to the venture stand back behind the exit vehicle's influence and the transactions volume. The research hypotheses and thus the information asymmetry framework do not fit well to explain the involvement of seasoned investment bankers given that the control variables contribute most of the explanatory power.

6.2 Explorative Analysis

While the previous tests only validate predefined structures, this section aims at discovering further unpredicted dependencies that may exist in the data sample. To detect unforeseen structures and to extend the understanding of the emergence of exit strategies, this section employs a cluster analysis. This chapter first reports the agglomeration schedule. Second, it researches selected structures.[860]

6.2.1 Agglomeration Schedule

Until now, this study researches VCFs' exit behavior as far as it has previously been set out. The study's research model centers on information asymmetries between incumbent inside investors and prospective outside investors and their impact on the VCF's exit strategies. Rationality suggests that other factors or combinations of factors determine VCFs' exit behavior as well. That the research model fails to capture systematic determinants is indicated by the results of the regression analyses; the models on Promotion, Third-Party Certification and Holding Duration exhibit considerably lower adjusted R^2s as compared to the R^2s. This discrepancy hints at shortcomings in the coverage of factors or structures. For instance, the exit strategy may be determined by factors concerning the VCF's investment behavior as suggested by Giot and Schwienbacher (2003).[861] Besides, exit strategy options may also occur in different combinations in comparable settings which are not foreseen by the

---

[859] E.g., Johnson/Miller (1988), p 20 and p. 28; Logue (1973), p. 100, this finding is consistent with Habib/Ljungqvist (2001), p. 452f.

[860] MacMillan/Kulow/Khoylian (1989), p. 38f., note that this type of exploratory research does not always allow for terminal conclusions. Hence, insignificant findings should be given careful consideration too.

[861] Giot/Schwienbacher (2003), p. 3

linear test methods employed in the confirming analyses. Thus, it is not researched yet. For example, one group of VCFs may opt to float ventures in information inefficient settings and overcome investors' concern through great promotion efforts and the employment of seasoned underwriters. At the same time, another group of VCFs accounts for similar information asymmetries in that it sells ventures privately and abstains from promotion. To test for the existence of unforeseen influences and structures, this section performs a cluster analysis.

The cluster analysis involves the three exit strategy dimensions Exit Vehicle, VCF's promotion and Third-Party-Certification. Regarding the timing decision, one modification is made in accordance to the previous findings. The preceding tests show that the VCFs' timing decision can be further divided into a decision on the exit stage and on the actual equity valuation level by the time of the withdrawal. VCFs may want to center exits on hot issue markets or consider information dissimilarities due to the venture's development stage when deciding on the timing strategy.[862] The use of both parameters allows for a more concise contemplation of the VCF's motives to time exits than the holding period. The following analysis substitutes the strategy dimension timing by the VCF's decision about the exit stage and the first-day-returns.

The agglomeration schedule reports that the cluster analysis involves 93 cases out of originally 169 (55 %).[863] Accordingly, the analysis proceeds in 92 steps. The last step combines the remaining two clusters with a distance of 16,194 (N_1 = 79; N_2 = 14). The distance increases the less clusters remain. In fact, the distance can never decrease throughout the cluster procedure. A decreasing distance would imply that the chance to merge more similar clusters was omitted in favor for merging a less similar combination. The relative changes in the distances throughout the analysis indicate the quality of the resulting clusters. If the distance between two steps soars only marginally, the clusters that are united hardly differ in their consistency. If the distance rises substantially, two rather unrelated clusters are combined. Figure 28 illustrates the absolute distances and the relative changes in the distance after every step.

[862] See sections 6.1.1 f) and 6.1.2 b)

[863] This discrepancy stems from the unavailability of information particularly for the presence of third-party certification in private transactions.

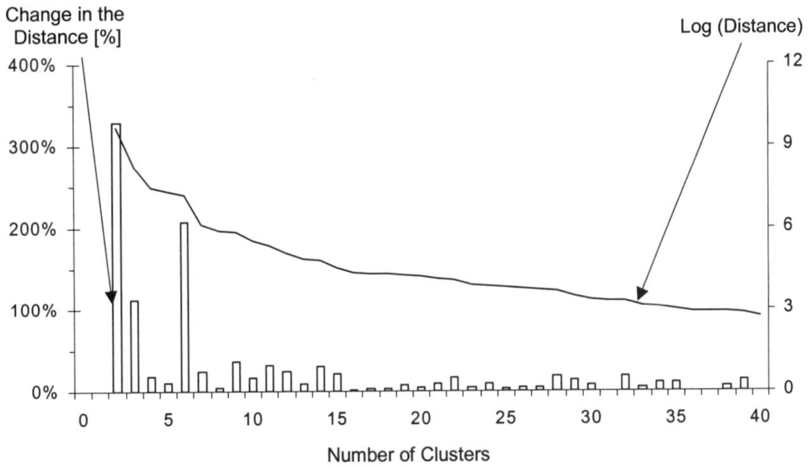

Figure 28: Agglomeration schedule and relative changes in distances

Figure 28 allows for important insights in the cluster procedure and guides the following analysis. The analysis of all clusters after every step multiplies the efforts but adds only marginal explanatory value. Particularly those steps in which rather similar clusters are merged do not provide further information on the differences between the clusters. Only those steps, in which groups with significant distances are combined, show a fundamental progress in the analysis. As pictured in figure 28, major steps are the last step, the second to least step and the fifth to least step that reduces the number of clusters from six to five. Prior to these stages, clusters with relatively high similarities are grouped. The following analysis focuses explicitly on the structure prior to these steps.

However, the cluster analysis begins to dilute at stage six. In general, the cluster analysis aggregates the distances of all parameters of a transaction and contrasts the aggregated distance with other transactions. Thus, only one outlying parameter can cause the separation of a single transaction from other rather similar transactions. The outlying parameter delays the transaction's proper classification and essentially isolates single transactions throughout the procedure. At stage six, the discrepancy between natural clusters and outlier-clusters becomes apparent. The largest cluster contains 50 transactions and the second largest comprises 20. The first cluster already constitutes the basis for cluster 1 to which the second cluster is merged in the third least step. Section 6.2.3 addresses this stage. The final cluster 2 emerges out of the remaining three clusters at stage six with six, one and seven transactions. Particularly the one transaction which is only included in step four exemplifies how outliers puzzle the analysis; this transaction happens at particularly high equity valuation levels (almost 50 % higher first-day returns than for the remaining ventures). All three clusters only differ on the basis of their underpricing but resemble each other in every other dimension. Given that the final cluster 2 unites transactions with exaggerated first-day returns and that cluster 2 transactions occur in a narrow time window of only two months, a further distinction between cluster 2's sub-clusters misguides the analysis; VCFs can neither anticipate the short-term peaks in the first-day returns nor initiate exits during this short period. To capture the most general structures rather than flawed clusters, the following discussion centers on the last two stages.

6.2.2 Characteristics of the Final Two Clusters

The different exit approaches in the final two clusters are compared for every exit strategy dimension separately. Table 49 reports how the two final clusters equal each other and how they differ.

		N	*Mean*	*SD*	*t*-test *p*-value
Promotion	Cluster 1	79	2.09	0.95	0.842
	Cluster 2	14	2.14	0.95	
Third-party certification	Cluster 1	79	1.96	1.04	0.417
	Cluster 2	14	1.71	1.05	
Exit stage	Cluster 1	79	8.41	3.50	0.924
	Cluster 2	14	8.50	2.85	
First-day returns	Cluster 1	79	43.3	30.76	0.000***
	Cluster 2	14	165.15	20.44	
IPO frequency	Cluster 1	79	51.9 %	-	0.582[1]
	Cluster 2	14	50.0 %	-	

* significant on a 10 % level; ** significant on a 5 % level; *** significant on a 1 % level

[1] Significance of the χ^2-test

Table 49: Differences in the final two clusters

Both clusters resemble each other in every respect except for the average first-day returns at exit. Exits in the second cluster receive slightly more promotion but faintly less third-party certification than exits in the first cluster. This finding is consistent with the previous insight on the trade-off between Third-Party Certification and Promotion.[864] Cluster 2 exits are marginally less likely to be floated. Exit transactions

[864] See section 6.1.3 f)

in the second cluster materialize in environments that are relatively more underpriced in comparison to first cluster withdrawals. The comparison of mean exit dates between both clusters shows that cluster 2 exits occur four months earlier in the year 1999 than cluster 1 exits. Cluster 2 exits essentially benefit more from investor optimism than cluster 1 exits.

To determine whether this finding reflects an underlying structure, the VCFs' and the investments' characteristics across both clusters are analyzed. Out of 40 participating VCFs, 25 are exclusively represented in cluster 1 and only one VCF in cluster 2. The latter VCF is about 25 years old and has experiences in almost 70 investments[865] while the 25 VCFs of cluster 1 average 20.5 years respectively 177.1 transactions. Five more VCFs have half or more of those companies for which they provide information merged in cluster 2. Their experience includes a mean of 64.5 investments at an average age of 17.3 years. If the these five investments are exclusively assigned to cluster 2, the six VCFs in cluster 2 prove not significantly older or younger than cluster 1 VCFs but have on average invested in less firms. The difference in investments is roughly significant at a confidence level of 0.059. However, the comparison of VCFs in both clusters is difficult given that only one VCF is precisely assigned to cluster two. Moreover, the analysis is based on survey data that captures only a fraction of VCFs' investment activities; on average, participants provide information on 4.2 ventures as opposed to a total mean experience of 159 transactions per VCF. Thus, the clustering is hardly representative. The notion that emerges from this analysis holds that less experienced (as regards the track record of previous investments) VCFs are more likely to center their exits on hot issue markets. This finding directly contradicts Lerner's (1994a) results.[866] Given other results in the literature and the insufficient data quality, no conclusion is drawn on different exit approaches of VCFs at this point.

Second, the analysis looks into individual investments' characteristics. Cluster 2 includes only high-technology ventures as opposed to two (3 %) non-high-technology ventures in cluster 1. Cluster 1 also embraces Biotechnology (9 %), Communication & Media (29 %), Computer Related (52 %), Life Sciences (6 %) and Semiconductor ventures (1 %) whereas cluster 2 spans Biotechnology (21 %), Communication & Media (29 %) and Computer Related (50 %) ventures. While cluster 1 includes all sectors and thus unites several first-day return levels, cluster 2 centers on particularly underpriced industries.[867] The observed difference in the underpricing stems at least partly from the differences in industry affiliation between both clusters. Yet, both data

---

[865] Details are spared so that the participant is not revealed.

[866] Lerner (1994a), p. 306

[867] See table 5

samples feature rather similar ratios for the highly underpriced industries Computer Related and Communication & Media. The impact of the additional Non-High-Technology and Semiconductor ventures in cluster 1 is hence unlikely to cause the total difference in first-day returns of almost 400 %.

The question arises why VCFs exit some ventures (cluster 2) at more favorable conditions than others while it would be desirable for all investments to be divested during hot issue markets? Table 50 reports that the investments' characteristics vary in only two respects. Cluster 2 ventures receive significantly more investment rounds and are monitored more intensively. A further analysis of the original data sample shows that the Monitoring Intensity[868] and the Number of Rounds[869] significantly correlate with the average equity valuation levels at exit. These findings relate the equity valuation levels at exit to VCFs' supervision's quality; the results highlight that a more intense supervision enables the VCF to better time withdrawals.

		Mean	*SD*	*t*-test *p*-value
Competition	Cluster 1	4.70	7.00	0.239
	Cluster 2	7.14	7.78	
Departures	Cluster 1	0.58	0.81	0.725
	Cluster 2	0.50	0.76	
Size	Cluster 1	44,676	46,895	0.257
	Cluster 2	60,916	60,666	
Rounds	Cluster 1	3.92	1.72	0.001***
	Cluster 2	5.79	2.86	
Monitoring intensity	Cluster 1	0.93	0.49	0.033**
	Cluster 2	1.27	0.56	

* significant on a 10 % level; ** significant on a 5 % level;
*** significant on a 1 % level

Table 50: Ventures' differences across the last two clusters

Cluster analysis of survey data by MacMillan, Kulow and Khoylian (1989) finds differences among VCFs with respect to their behavior during the VC process. MacMillan, Kulow and Khoylian identify three distinctive investment patterns labelled "laissez faire", "moderate" and "close tracker". The laissez faire approach differs from the close tracker approach in that the latter VCFs get far more involved in the ven-

868 Pearson's r = 0.178 at p = 0.036; n = 140 for the survey sample; respectively Pearson's r = 0.085; p = 0.000; n = 2,661 for the original data sample

869 Pearson's r = 0.206 at p = 0.009; n = 158 for the survey sample; respectively Pearson's r = 0.079; p = 0.000; n = 2,764 for the original data sample

ture's decision making. However, MacMillan, Kulow and Khoylian do not find differences as regards returns between these groups.[870] Several papers also suggest that VCFs seek to center their exits on hot issue markets but with diverse success.[871] Lerner (1994a) attributes this difference to seasoning. He argues that seasoned VCFs have better capabilities in executing exit transactions. But Lerner fails to empirically substantiate this reasoning.[872] The present finding on different monitoring intensities relates the findings of MacMillan, Kulow and Khoylian to Lerner. First, the clusters imply that VCFs pursue different investment approaches. While MacMillan, Kulow and Khoylian cannot detect consequences that result from different approaches, this analysis shows that a closer monitoring enables VCFs to exit in periods of higher equity valuation levels and thus reap greater profits. Lerner's findings on differences in VCFs' abilities to center exits on hot issue markets are sustained additionally. The correlation analysis for the syndicate's lead VCF's age and the average equity valuation levels yields a Pearson correlation of 0.123 for 2,576 transactions. This finding proves significant at a 0.000 level. Second, the VCF's age correlates with the number of financing rounds. For 2,080 transactions, Pearson's r amounts to 0.308 at a confidence level of 0.000. Third, a greater number of financing rounds allows VCFs to time their exits more accurately. The correlation analysis between the average equity valuation levels and the number of rounds delivers a Pearson's r of 0.141 at a confidence level of 0.000 for 2,195 exits.

This analysis establishes a new relationship between the VCF's seasoning and its exit strategy. Consistent with Lerner (1994a), it shows that seasoned VCFs become better able to center exits on hot issue markets. This advantage stems at least partly from differences in the supervision across seasoned VCFs and unseasoned VCFs instead of from reputation advantages as suggested by Neus and Walz (2001).[873] More intensely involved VCFs may, for instance, overlook the venture's environment more closely and detect exit opportunities faster. Their seasoning then enables VCFs to perform the exit preparations quicker and hit the hot issue market more accurately. Given the time difference between both clusters, seasoning appears to afford VCFs with an advantage of four months over unseasoned VCFs. Unseasoned VCFs, however, do not monitor their investments as closely. Thus, they fail to study newly emerging information and eventually are less precise in timing the market.

---

870 MacMillan/Kulow/Khoylian (1989), p. 35ff.; see Wall/Smith (1997), p. 11f. for a similar reasoning

871 E.g., Giot/Schwienbacher (2003), p. 7; Shepherd/Zacharakis (2001a), p. 66; Wang/Sim (2001), p. 342

872 Lerner (1994a), p. 300f. and p. 311

873 Neus/Walz (2001), p. 17

6.2.3 Characteristics of the Final Three Clusters

In the third step, cluster 1 is merged out of the two clusters 1.1 (N = 52) and 1.2 (N = 27). Table 51 shows in which items the two sub-clusters vary among each other and from cluster 2.

Cluster 2	Promotion	Third-party certification	Exit stage	First-day returns	IPO frequency[1]
Cluster 1 (differences inbetween)	0.512	0.117	0.201	0.000***	0.119
Cluster 1.1	0.711	0.201	0.807	0.000***	0.517
Cluster 1.2	0.894	0.982	0.382	0.000***	0.320

* significant on a 10 % level; ** significant on a 5 % level; *** significant on a 1 % level

[1] Significance of the χ^2-test

Table 51: Differences in the final three clusters' exit strategies

Again, the main difference between the clusters is drawn in the mean underpricing. Cluster 1.1 exhibits the least mean underpricing while cluster 2 features the highest underpricing. Cluster 1.2 ranges amid cluster 1.1 and cluster 2 in respect to underpricing. The differences in underpricing are highly significant. In line with the finding in section 6.2.2, the higher underpricing in cluster 1.2 as compared to cluster 1.1 stems from earlier exit dates; cluster 1.2 and cluster 2 transactions occur about 6 (cluster 1.2) or 4 (cluster 2) months before cluster 1.1 withdrawals. Both, cluster 1.2 and 2, coincide with peaking stock markets in early 1999 whereas cluster 1.1 exits happen after the market has reviewed its valuation levels. Further differences originate from the IPO frequency. In line with the findings from section 6.1.2 f), higher equity valuation levels prompt a higher IPO frequency in cluster 1.2 in relation to cluster 1.1. Since IPOs require more third-party certification,[874] the occurrence of more IPO raises the need for third-party certification in cluster 1.2 exits over cluster 1.1 exits. Even though the results prove not significant, they feature a relatively high confidence level given the explorative character of this analysis.

The differences between cluster 1.1 and 1.2 may originate from the VCF's characteristics. 18 VCF are exclusively merged in cluster 1.1 and five in cluster 1.2. According to table 52, VCFs do not differ significantly. Yet, the comparison suggests a general tendency in that seasoned VCFs exit at higher equity valuation levels; cluster 1.2 VCFs are on average older and exhibit a longer track record than cluster 1.1 VCFs. This finding matches Lerner's (1994a) conclusion that seasoning increases VCFs' abilities to time hot issue markets.[875] This clustering is also consistent with the outcome of section 6.1.2 e) that seasoned VCFs float on average more ventures than

[874] See section 6.1.3 f)

[875] Lerner (1994a), p. 306

their unseasoned counter parts. In essence, seasoned VCFs can bring forward the exit for six months enabling them to capitalize on higher valuation levels while unseasoned VCFs are less precise in timing their exits.

		Mean	*SD*	*t*-test *p*-value
VCF's age	Cluster 1.1	18.28	7.04	0.224
	Cluster 1.2	23.20	10.28	
VCF's # of investments	Cluster 1.1	139.61	132.78	0.730
	Cluster 1.2	162.20	97.74	
Total amount of invested capital	Cluster 1.1	855,211	1,176,052	0.932
	Cluster 1.2	807,827	625,392	

* significant on a 10 % level; ** significant on a 5 % level;
*** significant on a 1 % level

Table 52: Ventures' differences across the last three clusters

Furthermore, the existence of clusters 1.1 and 1.2 may be explained by the investments' characteristics. Cluster 1.1 unites ventures from all industries (Biotechnology 13 %, Communication & Media 21 %, Computer Related 54 %, Life Science 6 %, Non-High-Technology 4 % and Semiconductors 2 %) while cluster 1.2 consists of only Communication & Media (44 %), Computer Related (48 %) and Life Science (7 %) ventures. Thus, cluster 1.1 and cluster 1.2 are not congruent so that the difference in the underpricing is at least partly ascribed to different industry emphases; cluster 1.1 focuses on more underpriced industries. The consistence of cluster 1.2, however, roughly equals the consistence of cluster 2. Similar to section 6.2.2, the higher average underpricing in cluster 1.1 emanates at least partly from the different consistencies of cluster 1.1 and 1.2. But again, the different consistencies do not account for the entire spread in underpricing of 400 % between cluster 1.1 and cluster 1.2.

As reported in table 53, no further significant differences distinguish clusters 1.1 and 1.2 from cluster 2 besides the monitoring intensity. Significant differences between clusters 1.1 and cluster 2 occur in the number of rounds and in the monitoring intensity. These findings resemble the results provided in section 6.2.2; a superior monitoring enables cluster 2 exits to hit hot issue markets more precisely. In addition to the number of rounds and the monitoring intensity, Cluster 1.2 ventures receive less capital than cluster 2 investments. It appears reasonable that the investment size generally increases with the number of rounds. However, cluster 2 investments are not significantly greater than cluster 1.1 exits even though they receive more rounds. This finding stems from the fact that Biotechnology ventures, which are more frequent in cluster 1.1, and which are found to require higher investments regardless of the number of rounds they receive. In essence, differences in the ventures originate from different monitoring approaches. But at this level, they do not explain the different timing strategies anymore.

Cluster 2	Competition	Departures	Size	Rounds	Monitoring intensity
Cluster 1 (differences inbetween)	0.436	0.834	0.148	0.166	0.335
Cluster 1.1	0.197	0.688	0.504	0.001***	0.026**
Cluster 1.2	0.494	0.838	0.085*	0.046**	0.154

* significant on a 10 % level; ** significant on a 5 % level; *** significant on a 1 % level

Table 53: Differences in the final three clusters' characteristics

In fact, the investment's characteristics do not account for the differences in the underpricing across all three clusters except for the VCF's involvement. After all, it appears that the monitoring intensity allows VCFs to time exits more accurately. However, the terminal clusters 1.2 and 2 mostly differ because of the skyrocketing equity valuation levels. As set out in section 6.2.1, the substantial differences in the equity valuation levels puzzle the clustering process. At level three, the clusters begin to vary in just one factor that shows a great variance over time – the underpricing. The present clusters reflect the dramatic changes in the first-day returns but do not isolate different exit strategies.

6.2.4 Contributions of the Cluster Analysis

This dissertation reverts to cluster analysis to detect unforeseen structures that impact VCF's exit strategies. Initially, the cluster analysis establishes a new relation between already known parameters; the analysis shows first, that the VCF's involvement during the holding period affects the exit timing. A deeper involvement gives the VCF more knowledge about exit opportunities and the venture's condition. The VCF's closer supervision translates into more flexibility to time exits and capitalize on hot issue markets. The fact, that cluster 1 does not span more or less IPOs shows that more involved VCFs can also time their M&A activities in accordance to hot issue markets. The pricing of M&A transactions is oftentimes determined by comparable public transactions or by benchmarks with public companies. Hot issue markets thus result in higher valuations for private transactions too. Second, the analysis conforms Lerner's (1994a) findings that seasoning allows VCFs to time hot issue markets more accurately. However, the analysis finds what Lerner's finding does not reflect; the fact that seasoned VCFs tend to be more involved in their ventures improves their market timing besides their elevated credibility based on their superior reputation.[876] Separate tests on the basis of the original data sample prove the validity of these relationships.

In essence, the cluster analysis relates the VCF's abilities to hit hot issue markets to its seasoning and additionally to its investment philosophy. Nevertheless, these dependencies are mostly covered by the previous regression analysis. Table 54 shows that the regression models' qualities remain unaffected if structures detected by the cluster analysis are added as exogenous variables; the models for Promotion, Timing and Exit Vehicle suggest the immediate elimination of the cluster affiliation.

Only, the third-party certification model improves significantly. Table 54 reports a slight tendency for Promotion to contribute to the regression models in earlier stages. Yet, this tendency originates from the characteristics of the measurements for Third-Party Certification and Promotion. Promotion is operationalized on a scale with only 5 units and thus in fact represents a clustering.[877] The earlier the cluster analysis' stage, the more the clusters resemble the transactions' extents of Promotion. Eventually, the clustering builds groups in which transactions do not vary with respect to promotion anymore. A similar reasoning explains the findings for third-party certification. Even though the measurement does initially not constitute a ranked order, the top investment banks occur in almost every transaction.[878] Thus, the deals are clustered according to the individual investment banks' presence. These results become meaningless and do not contribute to the present thesis.

The cluster analysis does consequently not add explanatory power to the terminal regression models anymore. This tendency suggests that the cluster analysis' results are already incorporated in the final models. Adding the cluster affiliation rather dilutes the models instead of improving their fit. In essence, clusters of VCFs pursuing different exit strategies are not discovered. The research model complemented by the control variables represents an accurate picture of the emergence of exit strategies. Discrepancies in the adjusted R^2s and the R^2s during the regression analyses may in fact only stem from shortcomings of the data basis.

---

[876] Lerner (1994a), p. 306

[877] 0 to 4; see section 5.1.3 b)

[878] See section 6.1.4

Stage	Impacts on the explained variances of...			
	Promotion[1]	Third-party certification[1]	Timing[1]	Exit vehicle[2]
0	.309	.245	.335	.345
...				
84	.284	.291	.176	.226
85	.276	.285	.181	.227
86	.276	.258	.173	.220
87	.283	.236	.180	.233
88	.277	.238	.172	.220
89	.277	.235	.173	.220
90	.277	.255	.175	.222
91	.284	.245	.206	.221
92				

[1] adjusted R^2 [2] Squared Canonical Correlation

Table 54: Cluster analysis' impact on the regression models

7 Conclusion and Implications

This chapter summarizes the findings of the present study. It sets out the implications from a scientific perspective and for practical use. Then, this chapter identifies the weaknesses and limitations of the present analysis. Finally, it addresses further need for research emanating from this dissertation.

7.1 General Conclusions

This dissertation asks whether and how information asymmetries between inside parties and prospective outside investors affect VCFs' exit strategies. The study embarks on the assumption that information asymmetries exist throughout every exit transaction and impose information costs on potential investors. These information costs either deter prospective investors or prompt them to discount their valuation to be compensated for their due diligence efforts and their enhanced investment risk. Information asymmetries thus hamper VCFs' exits and distress their returns. This dissertation identifies common approaches of how VCFs cope with information dissimilarity at exit. Given that these exit patterns are adopted permanently across all VCFs, these strategies are likely to constitute general exit approaches that have proven successful over time. Had these patterns not proven successful, they would not have prevailed and were not validated in the empirical analysis.

This dissertation develops a research model on the basis of the literature, advancements of theoretical models and pilot studies. The research model contrasts five types of information asymmetry prospective investors' encounter upon exit with the VCF's exit strategy. The VCF's exit strategy is described as the combination of four decisions: the exit's timing, the exit vehicle, promotion and third-party certification. The analysis sets out 20 research hypotheses on how VCFs integrate the prospective investors' informational concerns in their exit strategy.

The research model provides the basis for the empirical validation. Bi-variate tests validate six (30 %) research hypotheses. Multi-variate analyses substantiate two (10 %) more hypotheses. Thus, information asymmetry in fact changes VCFs' exit behavior! The tests furthermore establish an understanding of how information dissimilarity between inside investors and outside investors impacts the VCF's exit strategy. VCFs are found to react to the greater information dissimilarities in early stage exits in comparison to later stage divestments in two ways. First, VCFs allow the venture more time to gain visibility and to alleviate information spreads about its progress.[879] Second, VCFs capitalize on private investors' superior abilities to resolve

---

[879] See section 6.1.1. b)

their uncertainty in early stage exits based on their industry expertise. In turn, VCFs exploit public investors' greater skills in gathering and processing public information in later stage exits.[880] Similarly, VCFs benefit from higher information efficiency in competitive settings in that they float more ventures whereas VCFs prefer private transactions in low-competitive – and thus information inefficient – environments.[881] These findings empirically sustain Chemmanur and Fulghieri's (1999) and Subrahmanyam and Titman's (1999) theoretical work on the different abilities of public and private investors to resolve information asymmetry. Departures affect VCFs' timing decisions and their promotion efforts. If departures occur, VCFs are forced to postpone exits to alleviate the negative signals about information spreads and bad VC relationships emanating from insider divestments. At the same time, a departure induces VCFs to work against investors' concerns in that they engage in more interactions with outsiders.[882] The occurrence of departures moreover lowers the venture's prospects for an IPO. Overall, prestigious VCFs suffer less from investors' uncertainty. Their reputational capital allows them to tap public markets more often and lessens investors' scepticism facilitating exits in earlier stages.[883] Besides, seasoning essentially substitutes for promotion efforts at exit.[884] The remaining hypotheses are not validated. In general, VCFs do not incorporate higher uncertainties that surround more innovative ventures in their exit strategy. Only in the riskiest sectors Biotechnology and Life Science do VCFs incur significantly more promotion than in other industries to convince new investors.[885] Moreover, VCFs do not use third-party certification to overcome prospective investors' uncertainties.[886] The contribution of this global approach comparing five different types of information asymmetry with four exit strategy options becomes evident in VCFs' different reactions to all types of information dissimilarities. Focused peer review journal publications are restrained in their length; peer review articles must narrow their focus to only few combinations of uncertainty and exit strategy options and miss the global perspective.[887] This dissertation shows what facets of their exit behavior VCFs adjust to what types of information asymmetry.

This dissertation's global approach also complements the literature in that it demonstrates the interrelatedness of single exit decisions. Given their restricted

[880] See section 6.1.2 b)

[881] See section 6.1.2 c)

[882] See section 6.1.3 d)

[883] See section 6.1.1 e) and section 6.1.2 e)

[884] See section 6.1.3 e)

[885] See sections 6.1.1 a), 6.1.2 a), 6.1.3 a) and 6.1.4 a)

[886] See section 6.1.4

[887] E.g., Cumming/MacIntosh (2001) focus exclusively on the exit's timing; Cumming/MacIntosh (2003) emphasize only partial exits as means to overcome information dissimilarity in exits.

length, peer review articles cannot research these interdependencies unless they explicitly focus on this theme. In fact, no article has looked into interdependencies of VCFs' exit strategy decisions yet. The analyses of interdependencies in the regression models in section 6.1 capture the relationships of the VCF's decisions. Strong ties exist between the choice of exit vehicle and both the average first-day returns and the venture's exit stage. Promotion decisions depend on the chosen exit vehicle and the timing dimension; the decision to float a venture calls for a stepping up of both promotion efforts and third-party certification. Hot issue markets reduce the need for third-party certification while the VCF's promotion efforts remain unaffected. However, in the absence of hot issue markets the VCF has to involve more prestigious investment banks to overcome investors' concerns. Only, the exit stage does not appear to affect VCFs' interactions with outsiders and investor optimism has not influence on the VCF's promotion efforts. Figure 29 illustrates the standardized beta coefficients that emerge in the terminal regression models. Given these strong interdependencies, VCFs are restrained in their choice of exit strategies. In fact, their exit strategies have to consider internal and external conditions which predetermine the exit stage, the chance to exploit hot issue markets and eventually the exit vehicle as set out above. These conditions in turn trigger the VCF's promotion efforts and call for more or less third-party certification.

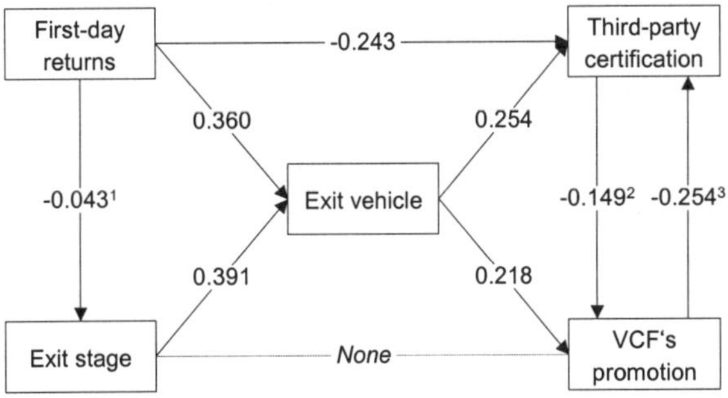

[1] Pearson'r between the holding duration and the initial returns 6-9 months in advance to the exit
[2] Promotion as dependent variable, section 6.1.3 g)
[3] Third-party certification as dependent variable, section 6.1.4 g)

Figure 29: Interdependencies of exit decisions[888]

---

[888] The purpose of this analysis would suggest the use of a structural equation model (SEM). However, the application of software based SEMs is subject to several limitations: 1) at least 15 cases per predictor, 2) normally distributed data and 3) normality for the relations between parameters; see Bentler/Chou (1987), p. 83ff.; the present survey sample provides only 99 complete transactions. Yet, for eight predictors, the analysis would require at least 120 transactions. Besides, neither are the data normally distributed nor are their relationships. Thus, meaningful SEMs cannot be applied on the survey sample.

This dissertation furthermore contributes to research on VCFs' exits in that it delves into a dimension of the VCF's exit strategy that has not received much attention yet. Promotion constitutes a means of supplying prospective investors with information. It helps resolve information disadvantages of prospective outside investors. This thesis researches whether and when VCFs use promotion to improve information efficiency. Upon exit, VCFs can engage in promotion in two different ways. First, the VCF can interact with outside parties to circulate information about the venture's quality. So far, only Habib and Ljungqvist (2001) exemplify the VCF's interactions with potential investors and deal facilitators in advance to the exit.[889] The present dissertation creates the first proxy to operationalize this dimension. The intensity of the VCF's promotion efforts is approximated in that its interactions with outsiders that aim at facilitating an exit are quantified and aggregated into one measure. The empirical results assert that VCFs engage in significantly more promotion interactions, if prospective investors suffer from uncertainties either about the VC relationship or about divestments of entrepreneurial team members. Moreover, the comparison of promotion efforts across exit vehicles substantiates Chemmanur and Fulghieri's (2001) theoretical reasoning. Chemmanur and Fulghieri outline that public finance becomes cheaper than private finance if sufficient information about the venture circulates in public.[890] The more the VCF desires to capitalize on the public market's superior capability to procure and process public information, the more it must enhance information efficiency. In essence, promotion constitutes a means to improve information efficiency in public markets. Accordingly, VCFs engage in more promotion in IPOs as opposed to M&A exits. The findings even suggest that VCFs can improve prospects for an IPO through greater promotion efforts while neglecting promotion is likely to lead to M&A exits.[891] Promotion is found to be affected by the VCF's seasoning. Unseasoned VCFs use promotion to make up for their lack of certification and facilitate exits.[892] In context of Gompers' (1996) grandstanding hypothesis for instance, young VCFs use promotion to enforce early exits that accelerate their reputation building process.[893]

Second, this dissertation researches VCFs' employment of investment banks. In line with Habib and Ljungqvist (2001), this thesis finds that VCFs do not use third-party certification to reduce information asymmetry as set out in the research model. The costs for hiring prestigious investment banks appear to trade off the benefits of improved information efficiency. Hiring prestigious investment banks becomes ineffi-

---

[889] Habib/Ljungqvist (2001), p. 434f.

[890] Chemmanur/Fulghieri (1999), p. 249f., see also Subrahmanyam/Titman (1999), p. 1047

[891] See section 6.1.2 f)

[892] See section 6.1.2 e)

[893] Gompers (1996), p. 134

cient from an informational point of view.[894] However, this thesis goes beyond Habib and Ljungqvist's focus. It looks into the differences in third-party certification between public and private transactions. The results show that the VCF's decision on the exit vehicle drives promotion efforts.[895] If VCFs wish to exploit the public market's superior ability to transform public information into less uncertainty, VCFs have to circulate information. Akin to promotion, third-party certification provides public investors with additional information and resolves information asymmetries. The results exemplify that seasoned investment banks are hired particularly to help resolve the prospective investors' uncertainty about an IPO while prestigious investment bankers' contributions do not recoup their costs in private transactions.

In total, six (30 %) research hypotheses lead to non-significant results. In the sense of Popper's critical rationalism, the non-significant results are the only findings that allow for general conclusions. First, this dissertation provides evidence that no general dependencies exist between the exit's timing and the competitiveness of the venture's environment as measured by the number of rivals.[896] Second, section 6.1.3 b) finds that the VCF's promotion efforts do not vary across exit stages neglecting the impact of the dynamics of information asymmetry over development stages. Furthermore, the present analysis reveals that third-party certification remains unaffected by information asymmetries due to the venture's industry affiliation, its maturity upon exit, departures and the VCF's certification ability. According to Popper, these conclusions guide further research; they allow researchers to focus on other causalities given that evidence exist that contradict these hypotheses. The following sections, however, set out that the results call for improvements in the methodology and inspire further research.

Six relationships emerge that contradict the initial assumptions. The contradictions assert that information asymmetries rival with other factors in shaping the VCF's exit strategy. First, the VCF's investment focus and its philosophy towards nurturing ventures predetermine exit strategies during the VC process. This dissertation discerns early and later stage VCFs; both types differ in the typical entry stage and in the costs they incur by nurturing ventures. Early stage VCFs center particularly on young ventures in the Early or Seed stages;[897] they exit their highfliers around the Expansion stage. At this stage, the early stage VCF's contributions do not add marginal value in excess of the marginal costs anymore so that a further commitment becomes inefficient. If ventures stall, this managerial optimum is already reached in earlier stages given that promoting the firm to higher levels becomes more expen-

---

[894] Habib/Ljungqvist (2001), p. 452ff.

[895] Chemmanur/Fulghieri (1999), p. 249f., see also Subrahmanyam/Titman (1999), p. 1047

[896] See section 6.1.1 c)

[897] See section 5.2.3 and section 6.1.2 b)

sive. This thesis finds that this selection process affects the occurrence of IPOs in that IPOs become more likely in later stages. Thus, this thesis empirically sustains the notion of Fleming (2003) and Schwienbacher (2002). They hold that VCFs float only their best ventures to protect their reputation.[898] This pattern also applies to later stage investors. Later stage investors enter investments in the First/Expansion stage and divest their best ventures in the Bridge/Other Expansion stage.[899] Besides the VCF's investment focus, its philosophy towards supervising the venture impacts the exit strategy. The analysis shows that closer monitoring and more financing rounds shorten the holding period.[900] Moreover, the cluster analysis suggests that an intense monitoring enables VCFs to center their exits more precisely on peaking equity valuation levels.[901] This finding also relates to Lerner (1994a) who observes that seasoning enables VCFs to exit more precisely in hot issue markets.[902] This analysis extends Lerner's findings in that it relates the monitoring intensity to the VCF's seasoning; seasoned VCFs get more involved than unseasoned VCFs.[903] Their higher commitment in turn enhances seasoned VCFs' market timing.[904]

Second, this dissertation confirms the common notion that hot issue markets impact VCFs' exit strategies.[905] The results show that VCFs take advantage of soaring investor optimism[906] in that they bring exits forward[907] and foster more IPOs.[908] Interestingly, hot issue markets – though popularly exemplified as the most important determinant – have a comparably lower impact on timing decisions than the VCF's monitoring for instance.[909] The market's foremost influence concerns the exit vehicle. Yet, VCFs can benefit more from periods of high equity valuation levels if they impose a close supervision making them more proficient in centering exits on hot issue markets.[910]

Third, this dissertation underlines that the VCF's certification as sketched by Barry et al. (1990) or Megginson and Weiss (1991) impacts exit strategies substan-

---

[898] Fleming (2003), p. 9; Schwienbacher (2002), p. 7f.

[899] See section 6.1.2 b)

[900] See section 6.1.1 a) and b)

[901] See section 6.2.2 and 6.2.3

[902] Lerner (1994a), p. 306

[903] See section 6.2.2

[904] See section 6.2.2

[905] E.g., Giot/Schwienbacher (2003), p. 7; Lerner (1994a), p. 294; Shepherd/Zacharakis (2001a), p. 66; Wang/Sim (2001), p. 342

[906] Lowry (2003), p. 5; Ibbotson/Jaffe (1975), p. 1027; Ofek/Richardson (2003), p. 113f.; Ritter (1984), p. 238f.

[907] See section 6.1.1 f)

[908] See section 6.1.2 f)

[909] See section 6.1.1 g)

[910] See section 6.2.2

tially. Seasoned VCFs possess more credibility and thus are more likely to tap public markets.[911] This thesis also confirms grandstanding ambitions of unseasoned VCFs.[912] The results relate grandstanding to certification; unseasoned VCFs have to engage in more promotion in order to make up for their lack of certification power and to accelerate grandstanding.[913]

7.2 Practical Implications

This dissertation shows that general patterns exist for exiting ventures across different scenarios. These strategies are found to be general usage. If VCFs constantly pursue other approaches than recommended by the present findings, their exits are likely to suffer from competitive disadvantages in comparison to other VCFs. Such competitive disadvantages can occur in the form of

- higher transaction costs and worsened returns given that the VCF does not minimize informational costs upon exit.
- lack of follow-on investors because the VCF does not select those investors that suffer from the least information costs.

Exit scenarios are characterized by the venture's innovativeness, the exit stage, the environment's competitiveness, the occurrence of departures and the VCF's seasoning. Exit scenarios are partly predetermined once a VCF enters a particular investment. When advancing towards the exit, the VCF cannot change the venture's industry affiliation, the competitiveness of the venture's environment or its seasoning anymore. Hence, the exit strategy is somewhat predetermined by the venture's business, its industry affiliation and the VCF's characteristics. The present results increase VCFs' awareness of the consequences on exit prospects when they commit to investments. This dissertation elaborates that committing to Biotechnology or Life Science investments as opposed to investments in other industries requires VCFs to

- allow the venture more time to mature given that R&D processes, product admittance etc. take longer for Biotechnology and Life Science ventures.[914]
- work towards an IPO exit given that the venture is likely to require growth capital in excess of private investors' resources.[915]
- incur more promotion efforts to convince investors given that Biotechnology and Life Science ventures are still associated with substantial uncertainties and risks by the time of the VCF's exit.[916]

---

[911] See section 6.1.2 e)

[912] See section 6.1.1 e)

[913] See sections 6.1.1 e) and 6.1.3 e)

[914] See section 6.1.1 a)

[915] See section 6.1.2 a)

- incur relatively more costs for third-party certification to facilitate M&A exits.[917]

The findings on the venture's industry affiliation also show that exits of Computer Related and Communication and Media ventures are far more dependent on hot issue markets than withdrawals in the Semiconductor and Non-High-Technology sectors. Computer Related and Communication and Media transactions feature a higher mean underpricing indicating greater information concerns of public investors than for other industries.[918] If VCFs want to tap public markets with Computer Related and Communication and Media ventures, they should try to capitalize on investor optimism and center exits on hot issue markets.[919] Conversely, Semiconductor and Non-High-Technology ventures appear to be less affected from information spreads between incumbent and prospective outside investors.[920] Thus, Semiconductor and Non-High-Technology investments call for a less intense monitoring already during the VC period and upon exit.[921] Overall, investments in Semiconductor and Non-High-Technology ventures bear relatively more certainty that an exit will materialize given greater information efficiency and lower dependency on hot issue markets in these industries. In essence, the general liquidity of Semiconductor and Non-High-Technology ventures is not as constrained by information asymmetry as investments in other sectors. Yet, Semiconductor and Non-High-Technology exits capitalize less on hot issue markets; they have not experienced similar hot issue markets as Computer Related ventures for instance. Figure 30 illustrates these recommendations.

---

[916] See section 6.1.3 a)

[917] See section 6.1.4 a)

[918] See section 4.1.2

[919] See section 6.1.1 a)

[920] See section 4.1.2

[921] See sections 6.1.1 a) and 6.1.1 b)

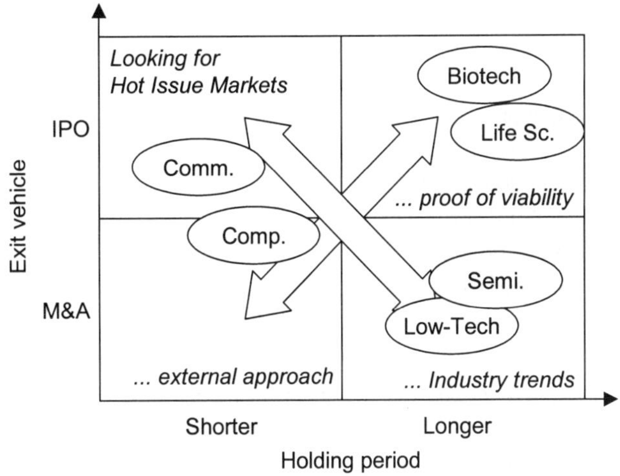

Figure 30: Recommeded exit strategies

The analysis set forth that competition fosters IPOs. However, competition for customers also serves as an indicator for the extent of rivalry for follow-on capital exacerbating exits. This dissertation concludes that competition exposes follow-on investors to numerous – from their perspective – rather homogenous investment opportunities. To attract their attention, VCFs are forced to engage in interactions with prospective investors and to distinguish the venture from other capital seeking firms.[922] To reduce promotion costs caused by competition, VCFs should consider scheduling their withdrawals ahead of follow-on funding initiatives of rivals.

The proper exit strategy becomes even more important for unseasoned VCFs. Seasoned VCFs have established a reputation for fairly priced exits; their presence resolves prospective investors' uncertainties. Conversely, unseasoned VCFs are attributed with less certification power hampering their exit initiatives and exposing them to greater discounts. The lack of reputation particularly pertains the choice of exit vehicles; if unseasoned VCFs wish to bring their ventures public – for instance to accelerate their reputation building – they must incur more underpricing and promotion efforts.[923] To avoid the pitfall of unseasoned IPOs, young VCFs should give private transactions stronger consideration than IPOs. This way, they minimize their losses from information asymmetry and can improve the fund's performance which in turn impresses fund investors. IPO exits may simply be too expensive for new VCFs and their effect on reputation may not trade off the transactions costs. Overall, repu-

[922] See section 6.1.3 c) and 6.1.4 c)

[923] See section 6.1.3 e)

tation is found to be an important asset given that it reduces information costs at exits. Seasoned VCFs can access a greater variety of exit strategies because they possess higher credibility. Thus, they can adjust their exit behavior more effectively to asymmetric information and minimize costs from information dissimilarity upon exit. In the long-term, young VCFs can grow certification power in that they build a track record of successful transactions, if they do not engage in damaging activities such as grandstanding. Both, unseasoned and seasoned VCFs should make it one of their foremost goals to preserve and improve their reputation to cash in on their credibility. One way to of building and maintaining credibility – particularly for young VCFs – is promoting fairly valued exits and increase visibility through successful interactions with private investors, capital markets and service providers.

Besides these exogenous exit scenarios, VCFs can also influence the exit's circumstances with respect to the venture's development stage and departures. The models for timing and exit vehicle show that VCFs have to promote their investments to higher development levels if they want to minimize information costs. The venture's chances for an IPO exit soar in later development stages too. If a VCF does not need to float ventures early for reasons of reputation building or fund performance, for instance, it should allow the venture more time to accomplish higher development levels. Yet, nurturing the venture to this degree of maturity can sometimes proof more costly than selling it to private investors. The results show that if ventures stall, the VCF would be better of divesting in earlier stages and targeting private investors. Enforcing an IPO does consequently not prove viable if the venture does not fulfil the basic requirements. For these situations, VCFs should give M&A exits serious consideration.

If entrepreneurial team members depart from the venture, the VCF must be alert to the negative signal this incident sends to prospective investors. This dissertation finds that departures require VCFs to delay exits and strengthen their interactions with outsiders in order to resolve the additional uncertainties the dismissal produces. Moreover, departures reduce the likelihood for an IPO exit; private investors will be better able to understand the causes and consequences of the departures and thus discount the venture's valuation less. If VCFs have an exit plan that foresees a particular exit timing, they may want to avoid disturbing incidents such as dismissals or divestments of entrepreneurial team members to preserve prospects for successful exits.

Finally, if VCFs seek to capitalize on periods of elevated investor optimism, they should step up their monitoring intensity. In doing so, they inform themselves better about the venture's internal and external conditions. In peaking stock markets, VCFs can transform their enhanced knowledge into a greater ability to center exits on peaking markets. VCFs that abstain from a close supervision risk forgoing chances to exploit hot issue markets. Eventually, they may lack those “home-runs” that account for the phenomenal returns of VCFs in hot issue markets.

If VCFs incorporate prospective investors’ information disadvantages into their exit strategies in the way set out above, they can improve their proceeds. Understanding the interplay of these variables thus helps VCFs to optimize their performance. This dissertation offers VCFs a benchmark for their approach to exiting ventures.

7.3 Limitations

As does all research, this dissertation suffers from limitations. Limitations originate from this dissertation’s focus, the data basis and the methodologies. The thesis’ focus raises two kinds of concerns. First, the dissertation embraces information asymmetries and their consequences for the VCF’s exit behavior. Throughout the analysis, it becomes evident that information asymmetry explains only a portion of the variances in the VCF’s exit strategy options. However, the analysis discusses further determinants only if they emanate from the discussions of contradicting results. The focus on information asymmetry restrains this study in researching further influences and their interplay with the present findings. Second, this thesis describes the VCFs’ exit strategy only in terms of timing, exit vehicle, promotion and third-party certification. Even though the results of four pilot studies imply that these dimensions capture most of the VCF’s pre-exit decisions, behavior patterns that are neither mentioned in interviews nor missed in the literature analysis may exist. For instance, VCFs can deliberately effectuate information asymmetry in order to facilitate exits. VCFs are, however, not expected to admit to this behavior and the literature does not discuss the VCF’s window dressing upon exit. This thesis does consequently not account for these influences on the present findings.

This thesis validates its findings on the basis of empirical data. This approach exposes the findings to the typical criticism of Popper’s rationalism.[924] Because the data samples constitute only a fraction of the whole population, this dissertation cannot draw compelling conclusions and generalize its assumptions. Nowhere is this shortcoming more obvious than in those tests that use the survey sample. For instance, the analysis in chapter 5.2.3 concludes that the survey sample suffers from several biases; most importantly, it contains transactions backed by more seasoned VCFs in the Boston area presumably because the Babson College, MA, is backing this study. The survey sample thus does not fulfil the most basic requirement for an

---

[924] See section 1.4

empirical analysis of constituting a random sample drawn from the whole population in question.[925] The validated hypotheses can consequently not be generalized.

The survey sample moreover suffers from shortcomings with respect to the operationalization of parameters. The survey instrument uses Likert-scale measurements and dichotomous choice questions to build the data sample. This approach generally reduces the informational content of answers in that differences within a group cannot be detected. Particularly the operationalization of the investment's success is subject to this limitation. Findings that deliver only small differences or correlations between success clusters may not prove significant due to this shortcoming.[926] The operationalization of departures experiences similar constraints. To cope with these shortcomings, this analysis lowers the confidence level for tests involving survey data. In essence, the findings that emanate from survey data are exposed to β-errors; given a roughly significant relation, hypotheses are validated even though they may in fact be wrong.[927]

The study develops a new method to operationalize the extent of the VCF's interactions with outsiders upon exit. The proxy converts answers to four dichotomous questions into a numeric value. However, this measurement is subject to several shortcomings limiting its explanatory power. On the one hand, the proxy does not account for the intensity of single interactions. On the other hand, it ascribes similar weight to every sub-item and does not differentiate between more or less important interactions. The measurement thus indicates a low involvement even though VCFs may incur substantial efforts to communicate the venture's advantages to a few investors. Or, the proxy delivers a high value although the VCF confers only briefly with several outside parties.

Finally, this dissertation operationalizes the extent of third-party certification in that it computes the involved investment banker's market share. This measurement is proposed in several other articles.[928] Nevertheless, this measure captures only one facet of a transactions' third-party certification through investment bankers. Usually, IPOs – and sometimes M&A deals too – involve more than one investment bank. This study does, however, not question, what characterizes transactions that feature more than one investment bank. Furthermore, the present method does not capture whether investment bankers specialize in certain industries, for instance, in which their certification bears more value.

---

[925] Bentler/Chou (1987), p. 85

[926] E.g., sections 6.1.1 f) or 6.1.3 f)

[927] E.g., sections 6.1.3 a), 6.1.3 e) and 6.2.3

[928] E.g., Carter/Manaster (1990), p. 287ff.; Megginson/Weiss (1991), p. 887ff.

7.4 Further Research

The present thesis inspires several points of origin for further research. At the same time, it offers chances to drop research in certain areas given that the present results contradict general theories in the sense of Popper. Unless, researchers add to the theoretical background or improve the methodology, they can abstain from looking into dependencies between the exit's timing or the VCF's promotion efforts and the dynamics of information asymmetry as measured by the venture's holding duration. Improvements in this respect would have to address the operationalization of information asymmetries throughout the venture's development level as well as of the measurement of Promotion as set out below. In addition, VCF's employment of third-party certification remains unaffected by information asymmetries due to the venture's industry affiliation, its maturity upon exit, departures and the VCF's certification ability. A promising advancement of the present model constitutes the development of a more detailed research model involving the concerns and abilities of investment banks. Yet, this dissertation mostly excludes the investment bank's perspective.

In general, the present dissertation looks into exits by taking the perspective of VCFs. In addition, at least two more perspectives on exits exist: the entrepreneur's and the fund investors'. While this dissertation identifies diverging interests of VCFs and entrepreneurs upon exit and investigates the impact of departures on the transaction, research needs to look into the consequences of conflicts between entrepreneurs and VCFs on the transaction's parameters. Further research will have to contrast transactions supported by the entrepreneur against exits that are initiated by the VCF without the entrepreneur's approval. Highlighting the impact of the entrepreneur's attitude towards the exit on the transactions outcome provides VCFs with important information on how to improve profitability and prevent damages in their reputation. Research will also have to involve the fund investors' perspective. This thesis acknowledges that VCFs depend on the fund investors' satisfaction with the financial outcome of previous funds. However, this thesis and current research neglects preferences of fund investors regarding the methods and timing of VCFs' exits. This thesis assumes that fund-investors do not influence the VCF's decisions in this respect. However, the occurrence of hot issue markets may induce fund investors to force VCFs into IPO exits and to distribute shares instead of cash. Conversely, cold issue markets may make fund investors to force the VCF into more M&A transactions to return cash instead of securities. How the fund investors affect the VCF's exit behavior is still to be asked.

Further inspirations emanate from the combination of this thesis's findings and its shortcomings. The foremost themes will expand the dissertation's emphasis on information asymmetry by focusing on other theories than information asymmetry and identifying further determinants on the four exit strategy options. This dissertation uses control variables to identify other influences than informational concerns. The results show the VCF's investment philosophy plays a significant role. Given the focus on information dissimilarity, the analysis does not systematically capture factors related to, for instance, the investment approach. Research will have to pick up the results provided in this dissertation and expand the findings on the VCF's investment strategy to provide further information on how to prepare successful exits. The second theme will extend the contemplation of the VCF's exit behavior. This dissertation involves only four dimensions of the VCF's exit behavior. Yet, the literature provides further strategies of how VCFs can manage information asymmetries at exit (e.g., partial exits) or exploit information advantage (e.g., through window dressing).[929] This dissertation exemplifies the impacts of dismissals but does not ask whether VCFs should withhold dismissals deliberately to avoid negative signals. Research will have to pick up these issues to provide further exit strategies to VCFs and inform both, VCFs and follow-on investors on the possibilities and consequences of window-dressing in VC exits.

This study also founds the basis for a research strand of how VCFs promote their exits. The analysis first considers the VCF's interactions with outsiders when advancing the exit. The hypotheses on this topic are rather general. So is the measurement approach. Further research will have to pick up the ideas and deepen the understanding of promotion efforts across investments and VCFs. Second, this thesis picks up the idea of third-party certification as a promotion means. Yet, the present analysis fails to find determinants on the extent of third-party certification other than the exit vehicle. Further research will have to delve into the factors that drive the occurrence of third-party certification in exits. Third, this dissertation emphasizes the lack of proper proxies to quantify promotion efforts. Throughout the analysis, a new scale is created that allows measuring the number of interactions that VCFs initiate to facilitate withdrawals. Yet, as set out in section 5.1.1, this method suffers from several shortcomings. Further analyses should pick up the experiences with this proxy as reported in this thesis and develop more concise approaches.

Beyond that, this thesis finds different exit approaches across industries without that a global reasoning explains these observations. For instance, this thesis finds that the underpricing varies significantly across almost all industries – irrespective whether they are high- or low technology industries.[930] The discussion of results also reveals that the average holding duration differs among high-technology industries. At the same time, mean VC durations are equal in some high-technology and low-

---

[929] E.g., Bascha (2001), p. 61f.; Cornelli/Yosha (2003), p. 2

[930] See table 5

technology industries.[931] These observations imply that investigating the unique characteristics of industries could contribute to the understanding of financing transactions (exit transactions and possibly entry decisions of VCFs). Further research thus should dwell on characteristics of the most frequent industry groups in which VCFs operate researching the differences and their consequences on the transaction's set up.

Finally, this dissertation allows for adopting the assumptions on how transaction costs affect divestment strategies in Corporate Finance research. Whether divestments are executed in a VC context or in a corporate environment, information asymmetry always exists and distresses the proceeds of incumbent investors. However, the difference between both settings stems form the fact that VCFs are experienced in executing transactions and do not depend on the venture/business unit in the long term. Conversely, corporations need to consider internal dependencies and consequences on business strategies. After all, VCFs are more flexible in selling ventures so that this analysis comes to somewhat restrained conclusions from the perspective of corporations. The question of how corporations improve proceeds from divestments through managing information asymmetry draws on this analysis by adopting the fractions of the research models and particularly extending dimensions such as competition etc..

7.5 Closing Words

After all, this dissertation demonstrates that information asymmetry between incumbent inside investors and prospective outside investors hampers the VCF's exit. The dissertation identifies common strategies of how VCFs overcome this obstacle. In the process of analyzing the interplay between information asymmetry and exit patterns, this dissertation establishes a general understanding of determinants of VCFs' exit decisions. The analysis concludes that information costs require VCFs to carefully consider the dynamics of information spreads over time and select proper follow-on investors. To smooth the exit, VCFs can improve information efficiency through promotion activities. If VCFs follow the recommendations given in this dissertation, they can improve their profitability.

---

[931] See section 6.1.1 a); for further examples, see section 6.1.2 a) and 6.1.3 a)

References

Achleitner, Ann-Kristin (1999): Handbuch Investment Banking. Wiesbaden: Gabler.

Admati, Anat R./Pfleiderer, Paul (1994): Robust Financial Contracting and the Role of Venture Capitalists. In: Journal of Finance, 49 (2), p. 371-402.

Aggarwal, Rajesh K./Krigman, Laurie/Womack, Kent L. (2002): Strategic IPO underpricing, information momentum, and lockup expiration selling. In: Journal of Financial Economics, 66 (1), p. 105-137.

Aghion, Philippe/Bolton, Patrick/Tirole, Jean (2000): Exit Options in Corporate Finance: Liquidity versus Incentives. Working Paper: University College London.

Akerlof, George A. (1970): The Market for Lemons: Quality Uncertainty and the Market Mechanisms. In: Quarterly Journal of Economics, 84 (3), p. 488-500.

Albach, Horst/Hunsdiek, Detlef/Kokalj, Ljuba (1986): Finanzieren mit Risikokapital. Stuttgart: Poeschel.

Allen, Franklin/Faulhaber, Gerald R. (1989): Signaling by underpricing in the IPO market. In: Journal of Financial Economics, 23 (2), p. 303-323.

Allen, Franklin/Gale, Douglas (1998): Diversity of Option and Financing of New Technologies. In: Journal of Financial Intermediation, 8 (1-2), p. 68-89.

Alvarez, Sharon A./Barney, Jay B. (2001): How entrepreneurial firms can benefit from alliances with large partners. In: Academy of Management Executive, 15 (1), p. 139-148.

Alvarez, Sharon A./Busenitz, Lowell W. (2001): The entrepreneurship of resource-based theory. In: Journal of Management, 27 (6), p. 755-775.

Ambarish, Ramasastry/Kose, John/Williams, Joseph (1987): Efficient Signalling with Dividends and Investments. In: Journal of Finance, 42 (2), p. 321-343.

Ambrose, Brent W./Winters, Drew B. (1992): Does an Industry Effect Exist for Leveraged Buyouts? In: Financial Management, 21 (1), p. 89-101.

Amihud, Yakov/Lev, Baruch (1981): Risk Reduction as a Managerial Motive for Conglomerate Mergers. In: Bell Journal of Economics, 12 (2), p. 605-617.

Amit, Raphael/Brander, James/Zott, Christoph (1998): Why do venture capital firms exist? Theory and Canadian Evidence. In: Journal of Business Venturing, 13 (6), p. 441-466.

Amit, Raphael/Glosten, Lawrence/Muller, Eitan (1990): Does venture capital foster the most promising entrepreneurial firms? In: California Management Review, 32 (3), p. 102-111.

Anand, Bharat N./Galetovic, Alexander (2000): Weak property rights and hold-up in R&D. In: Journal of Economics & Management Strategy, 9 (4), p. 615-642.

Anderberg, Michael R. (1973): Cluster Analysis for Applications, New York: Academic Press.

Anderson, Erin (1985): The Salesperson as outside Agent or Employee: A Transaction Cost Analysis. In: Marketing Science, 4 (3), p. 234-254.

Ang, James S./Cole, Rebel A./Lin, James Wuh (2000): Agency Costs and Ownership Structure. In: Journal of Finance, 55 (1), p. 81-106.

Argawal, Anup/Mandelker, Gershon N. (1987): Managerial Incentives and Corporate Investment and Financing Decisions. In: Journal of Finance, 42 (4), p. 823-837.

Arzac, Enrique R. (2001): On the Capital Structure of Leveraged Buyouts. In: Financial Management, 21 (1), p. 16-26.

Atteslander, Peter (1995): Methoden der empirischen Sozialforschung. 8th edition. Berlin: de Gruyter.

Bader, Hanspeter (1996): Private Equity als Anlagekategorie - Theorie, Praxis und Portfoliomanagement für institutionelle Investoren. Stuttgart: Haupt.

Bagley, Constance E./Dauchy, Craig E. (1997): The Entrepreneur's Guide to Business Law. Palo Alto: South-Western Publishers.

Baier, Wolfgang (1996): Marketing und Finanzierung junger Technologieunternehmen. Wiesbaden: Gabler.

Baker, Malcom/Gompers, Paul A. (1999): Executive Ownership and Control in Newly Public Firms: The Role of Venture Capitalists. Working Paper: Harvard Business School.

Baker, Malcom/Gompers, Paul A. (2001): The Determinants of Board Structure at the Initial Public Offering. Working Paper: Harvard Business School.

Bamberg, Günter/Baur, Franz (1998): Statistik. 10th edition. München: Oldenbourg.

Barnea, Amir/Haugen, Robert A./Senbet, Lemma W. (1981): Market Imperfections, Agency Problems, and Capital Structure: A Review. In: Financial Management, 10 (2), p. 7-22.

Barney, Jay B. (1991): Firm Resources and Sustained Competitive Advantage. In: Journal of Management, 17 (1), p. 99-120.

Barney, Jay B./Busenitz, Lowell W./Fiet, James O./Moesel, Douglas D. (1994): The relationship between venture capitalists and managers in new firms: Determinants of contractual covenants. In: Managerial Finance, 20 (1), p. 19-30.

Baron, David P. (1982): A Model of the Demand for Investment Banking Advising and Distribution Services for New Issues. In: Journal of Finance, 37 (4), p. 955-976.

Barron, David D. (1984): A Survey of U.S. and Canadian Tax Exempt Funds' Involvement in Venture Capital. New York: Venture Capital Research Service.

Barry, Christopher B. (1989): Initial Public Offering Underpricing: The Issuer's View - A Comment. In: Journal of Finance, 44 (4), p. 1099-1103.

Barry, Christopher B. (1994): New Directions in Research on Venture Capital Finance. In: Financial Management, 23 (3), p. 3-15.

Barry, Christopher B./Muscarella, Chris J./Peavy, John W./Vetsuypens, Michael R. (1990): The role of venture capital in the creation of public companies. In: Journal of Financial Economics, 27 (2), p. 447-471.

Bartlett, Joseph W. (1999): Fundamentals of venture capital. Lanham, MD: Madison.

Bascha, Andreas (2001): Hybride Beteiligungsformen bei Venture Capital. Wiesbaden: Dt. Univ.-Verl..

Bästlein, Hanno (1997): Zur Feindlichkeit öffentlicher Übernahmeangebote: eine ökonomische Betrachtung von Ursachen und Auswirkungen unter besonderer Berücksichtigung der deutschen Situation. Frankfurt a. M.: Peter Lang Verlag.

Bauer, Christoph (1995): Risikomessung. In: Gerke, Wolfgang/Steiner, Manfred (eds.): Handwörterbuch des Bank- und Finanzwesens. 2nd edition. Stuttgart:: Schäffer-Poeschel, p. 1657-1665.

Baum, Joel C./Silverman, Brian S. (2004): Picking winners or building them: Alliance, intellectual, and human capital as selection criteria in venture financing and performance of biotechnology start-ups. In: Journal of Business Venturing, 19 (3), p. 411-436.

Beatty, Randolph P. (1989): Auditor Reputation and the Pricing of Initial Public Offerings. In: Accounting Review, 64 (4), p. 693-699.

Beatty, Randolph P./Ritter, Jay R. (1986): Investment banking, reputation, and the underpricing of initial public offerings. In: Journal of Financial Economics, 15 (1-2), p. 213-232.

Bell, Markus G. (2001): Venture Capital-Finanzierung durch Wandelanleihen. Frankfurt a.M.: Lang.

Benjamin, Gerald A./Margulis, Joel (2000): Angel Financing: How to Find and Invest in Private Equity. New York: Wiley & Sons.

Benston, George J./Smith, Clifford W. (1976): A Transaction Cost Approach of the Theory of Financial Intermediation. In: Journal of Finance, 31 (2), p. 215-231.

Bentler, Peter M./Chou, Chih-Ping (1987): Practical issues in structural modelling. In: Sociological Methods and Research, 16 (1), p. 78-117.

Benton, Lee F./Gunderson, Robert V./Robinson, Julie M. (1997): Portfolio Company Investments: High Technology Corporations. In: Halloran, Michael J. (ed.): Venture Capital and Public Offering Negotiation. 3rd edition. Aspen Publishers, chapters 6-8.

Bergemann, Dirk/Hege, Ulrich (1998): Venture capital financing, moral hazard, and learning. In: Journal of Banking & Finance, 22 (6-8), p. 703-735.

Berger, Allen N./Udell, Gregory F. (1998): The economics of small business finance: The roles of equity and debt markets in the financial growth cycle. In: Journal of Banking & Finance, 22 (6-8), p. 613-673.

Berglöf, Erik (1994): A Control Theory of Venture Capital Finance. In: The Journal of Law, Economics & Organization, 10, p. 247-267.

Bergström, Clas/Högfeldt, Peter/Westin, Andreas (1995): The Role of Venture Capital in Initial Public Offerings: An Explorative Comparison of U.S. and Swedish Evidence. In: Annual Research Series on International Business and Finance, p. 153-158.

Betsch, Oskar/Groh Alexander P./Lohmann, Lutz G. (1998): Corporate Finance - Unternehmensbewertung, M&A und innovative Kapitalmarktfinanzierung. München: Vahlen.

Bhide, Amar V. (1992): Bootstrap Finance: The Art of Start-ups. In: Harvard Business Review, 70 (6), p. 109-117.

Bhide, Amar V. (2000): The Origin and Evolution of New Businesses. New York: Oxford University Press.

Birmingham, Carolyn/Busenitz, Lowell W./Arthurs, Jonathan D. (2003): The escalation of commitment by venture capitalists in reinvestment decisions. In: Venture Capital, X (X), p. 2-14.

Black, Bernard S./Gilson, Ronald J. (1998): Venture Capital and the structure of capital markets: banks versus stock markets. In: Journal of Financial Economics, 47 (3), p. 243-277.

Blake, Jonathan (1999): Structuring Venture Capital Funds for Investment: The Legal Dimension. In: Bygrave, William D./Hay, Michael/Peeters, Jos B. (Ed.):The Venture Capital Handbook. London: Financial Times Prentice Hall, p. 79-93.

Bleackley, Mike E./Hay, Michael (1994): Management Buy-outs and the Economic Cycle: The Pattern and Determinants of Activity. In: Bygrave, William D./Hay, Michael/Peeters, Jos B. (Ed.): Realizing Investment Value. London: Pitman Publishing, p. 110-131.

Blonigen, Bruce A./Taylor, Christopher T. (2000): R&D intensity and acquisitions in high technology industries: evidence from the US electronic and electrical equipment industries. In: Journal of Industrial Economics, 48 (1), p. 47-70.

Blum, Ulrich (1994): Volkswirtschaftslehre. 2nd. Edition. München: Oldenbourg.

Bohley, Peter (1996): Statistik - Einführendes Lehrbuch für Wirtschafts- und Sozialwissenschaften. 6th edition. München: Oldenbourg.

Bolton, Patrick/von Thadden, Ernst-Ludwig (1998): Blocks, Liquidity, and Corporate Control. In: Journal of Finance, 53 (1), p. 1-25.

Boocock, Grahame/Woods, Margaret (1998): The Evaluation Criteria used by Venture Capitalists: Evidence from a UK Venture Fund. In: International Small Business Journal, 16 (1), p. 36-57.

Booth, James R./Chua, Lena (1996): Ownership dispersion, costly information, and IPO underpricing. In: Journal of Financial Economics, 41 (2), p. 291-310.

Booth, James R./Smith, Richard L. (1986): Capital Raising, Underwriting and the Certification Hypothesis. In: Journal of Financial Economics, 15 (1-2), p. 261-281.

Bortz, Jürgen (1999): Statistik für Sozialwissenschaftler. 5th edition. Berlin: Springer.

Bortz, Jürgen/Döring, Nicola (1995): Forschungsmethoden und Evaluation für Sozialwissenschaftler. 2nd edition, Berlin: Springer.

Bourgeois, L. J./Eisenhardt, Kathleen M. (1988): Strategic decision processes in high velocity environments: Four cases in the microcomputer industry. In: Management Science, 34 (7), p. 816-835.

Bovaird, Chris (1990): Introduction to Venture Capital Finance. London: Pitman.

Bowden, Roger J. (1994): Bargaining, size, and return in venture capital funds. In: Journal of Business Venturing, 9 (4), p. 307-330.

Bradley, Daniel J./Jordan, Bradford D. (2002): Partial Adjustment to Public Information and IPO Underpricing. In: Journal of Financial and Quantitative Analysis, 37 (4), p. 595-616.

Bradley, Daniel J./Jordan, Bradford D./Yi, Ha-Chin/Roten, Ivan C. (2001): Venture capital and IPO lockup expiration: An empirical analysis. In: The Journal of Financial Research, 24 (4), p. 465-492.

Brander, James A./Amit, Raphael/Antweiler, Werner (2002): Venture-capital syndication: improved venture selection vs. the value-added hypothesis. In: Journal of Economics & Management Strategy, 11 (3), p. 423-452.

Bratton, William W. (2002): Venture capital on the downside: preferred stock and corporate control. In: Michigan Law Review, 100 (5), p. 891-945.

Brav, Alon/Gompers, Paul A. (1997): Myth or Reality? The Long-Run Underperformance of Initial Public Offerings: Evidence from Venture and Non-venture Capital-Backed Companies. In: Journal of Finance, 52 (5), p. 1791-1821.

Brav, Alon/Gompers, Paul A. (2003): The role of lockups in initial public offerings. In: Review of Financial Studies, 16 (1), p. 1-29.

Brettel, Malte (2002): Entscheidungskriterien von Venture Capitalists. In: Die Betriebswirtschaft, 3, p. 305-325.

Breuer, Rolf E. (1997): Venture Capital - besseres Umfeld ist notwendig. In: Die Bank, 6, p. 324-329.

Brigham, Eugene F. (1985): Financial Management. 4th edition. New York: Dryden Press.

Brophy, David J. (1992): Financing the New Venture: A Report on Recent Research. In: Sexton, Donald L./Kasarda, John D. (eds.): The State of the art Entrepreneurship. Boston: PWS-Kent Publishing Company. p. 387ff..

Brosius, Felix (1998): SPSS 8 Professionelle Statistik unter Windows. CD-ROM, mitp.

Brück, Marco (1998): Beteiligung an Unternehmen - Desinvestition und Lösung von Engagements. Bamberg: Difo-Druck.

Brühl, Volker (2001): Risikokapitalgeber als strategische Partner. In: M&A Review, 4, p. 156-161

Bruno, Albert V./Tyebjee, Tyzoon T. (1985): The entrepreneur's search for capital. In: Journal of Business Venturing, 1 (1), p. 61-74.

Bruton, Garry D./Fried, Vance H./Hisrich, Robert D. (1997): Venture Capitalist and CEO Dismissal. In: Entrepreneurship Theory and Practice, 21 (3), p. 41-54.

Bruton, Garry D./Fried, Vance H./Hisrich, Robert D. (2000): CEO Dismissal in Venture-Backed Firms: Further Evidence From an Agency Perspective. In: Entrepreneurship Theory and Practice, 24 (4), p. 69-77.

Burns, Ian (2003): UK Venture Capital: The Exit Crises. In: Credit Control, 24 (1), p. 29-32.

Büschgen, Hans E. (1985): Venture Capital - Der deutsche Ansatz. In: Die Bank, 25, p. 220-227.

Busenitz, Lowell W./Barney, Jay B. (1997): Differences between entrepreneurs and managers in large organizations: Biases and heuristics in strategic decision-making. In: Journal of Business Venturing, 12 (1), p. 9-30.

Busenitz, Lowell W./Fiet, James O./Moesel, Douglas D. (2003): Signaling in venture capitalist-new venture team funding decisions: do they indicate long-term venture outcomes? Working Paper: University of Oklahoma.

Busentitz, Lowell W./Fiet, James O. (1996): The effects of early stage venture capital actions on venture disposition. In: Journal of Entrepreneurial & Small Business Finance, 5 (2), p. 97-115. (HTML-copy applied)

Bygrave, William D. (1987): Syndicated Investments by Venture Capital Firms: A Networking Perspective. In: Journal of Business Venturing, 2 (2), p. 139-154.

Bygrave, William D. (1988): The structure of the investment networks of venture capital firms. In: Journal of Business Venturing, 3 (2), p. 137-157.

Bygrave, William D. (1992): Venture Capital Returns in the 1980s. In: Sexton, Donald L./Kasarda, John D. (eds.): The State of the art Entrepreneurship. Boston: PWS-Kent Publishing Company. p. 438ff..

Bygrave, William D. (1994): Rates of Return from Venture Capital. Bygrave, William D./Hay, Michael/Peeters, Jos B. (Ed.): Realizing Investment Value. London: Pitman Publishing, p. 12-38.

Bygrave, William D. (1997): The portable MBA in entrepreneurship. 2nd edition. New York: Wiley.

Bygrave, William D./Fast, Norman/Khoylian, Roubina/Vincent, Linda/Yue, William (1989): Early rates of return of 131 venture capital funds started in 1978-1984. In: Journal of Business Venturing, 4 (2), p. 93-105

Bygrave, William D./Hay, Michael/Peeters, Jos B. (1994): Realizing Investment Value. London: Pitman Publishing.

Bygrave, William D./Stein, Michael (1989): A time to buy and a time to sell: A study of venture investments in 77 companies that went public. In: Churchill, Neil C. (ed.): Frontiers of Entrepreneurship Research. Wellesley: Babson College, p. 288-303

Bygrave, William D./Timmons, Jeffry (1999): Venture capital: predictions and outcomes. Venture Capital at the Crossroads and Realizing Investment Value revisited. In: Wright, Mike/Robbie, Ken (eds.): Management Buy-outs and Venture Capital. Cheltenham: Elgar, p. 38-56.

Bygrave, William D./Timmons, Jeffry A. (1992): Venture Capital at the Crossroads. Boston: Harvard Business School Press.

Bygrave, William D./Timmons, Jeffry A./Fast, Norman D. (1984): Seed and start-up investing in technological companies. In: Hornaday, John A./Tarpley, Fred/Timmons, Jeffry A./Vesper, Karl H. (eds.): Frontiers of Entrepreneurship Research. Wellesley: Center for Entrepreneurial Studies, Babson College. p. 1-17.

Cable, Daniel M./Shane, Scott (1997): A prisoner's dilemma approach to entrepreneur - venture capitalist relationships. In: Academy of Management Review, 22 (1), p. 142-176.

Campbell, Tim S. (1979): Optimal Investment Financing Decisions and the Value of Confidentially. In: Journal of Finance, 14 (5), p. 913-924.

Carpenter, Robert E./Petersen, Bruce C. (2002): Capital market imperfections, high-tech investment, and new equity finance. In: The Economic Journal, 112 (February), p. 54-72.

Carter, Richard B./Dark, Frederick H./Singh, Ajaj K. (1998): Underwriter Reputation, Initial Returns, and the Long-Run Performance of IPO stocks. In: Journal of Finance, 53 (1), p. 285-311.

Carter, Richard/Manaster, Steven (1990): Initial public offerings and underwriter reputation. In: Journal of Finance, 45 (4), p. 1045-1067.

Cassar, Gavin (2004): The financing of business start-ups. In Journal of Business Venturing, 19 (2), p. 261-283.

Certo, S. Trevis (2003): Influencing initial public offering investors with prestige: signaling with board structures. In: Academy of Management Review, 28 (3), p. 432-446.

Certo, S. Trevis/Daily, Catherine M./Dalton, Dan R. (2001): Signaling the firm value through board structure: An investigation of initial public offerings. In: Entrepreneurship Theory and Practice, 26 (2), p. 33-50.

Chan, Yuk-Shee (1983): On the Positive Role of Financial Intermediation in Allocation of Venture Capital in a Market with Imperfect Information. In: Journal of Finance, 38 (5), p. 1543-1568.

Chandler, Gaylen N./Jansen Erik (1992): The founder's self-assessed competence and venture performance. In: Journal of Business Venturing, 7 (3), p. 223-236.

Chang, Sea Jin (2004): Venture capital financing, strategic alliances, and the initial public offerings of Internet start-ups. In: Journal of Business Venturing, 19 (5), p. 721-741.

Chemmanur, Thomas J./Fulghieri, Paolo (1999): A Theory of the Going-Public Decision. In: Review of Financial Studies, 12 (2), p. 249-279.

Chiampou, Gregory F./Kallett, Joel J. (1989): Risk/return profile of venture capital. In: Journal of Business Venturing, 4 (1), p. 1-10.

Chmielewicz, Klaus (1970): Die Formalstruktur der Entscheidung. In: Zeitschrift für Betriebswirtschaft, 40, p. 239-268.

Christen, Daniel V. (1991): Anlagen in Venture Capital-Fonds. Stuttgart: Haupt.

Coase, Ronald H. (1984): The new institutional economics. In: Journal of Institutional and Theoretical Economics, 140, p. 229-231.

Cochrane, John H. (2001): The Risk and Return of Venture Capital. Working Paper: University of Chicago.

Constantinides, George M./Grundy, Bruce D. (1989): Optimal Investment with Stock Repurchase and Financing as Signals. In: Review of Financial Studies, 2 (4), p. 445-465.

Cornell, Bradford/Shapiro, Alan C. (1988): Financing corporate growth. In: Journal of Applied Corporate Finance, 1 (Summer), p. 6-22.

Cornelli, Francesca/Yosha, Oved (2003): Stage Financing and the Role of Convertible Securities. In: Review of Economic Studies, 70 (1), p. 1-32.

Cowie, Harry (1999): Venture Capital in Europe. London: Federal Trust for Education and Research.

Cumming, Douglas J. (2002): Contracts and Exits in Venture Capital Finance. Working Paper: University of Alberta.

Cumming, Douglas J. (2004): Adverse Selection and Capital Structure: Evidence from Venture Capital. Working Paper: University of Alberta.

Cumming, Douglas J./MacIntosh, Jeffrey G. (2001): Venture capital investment duration in Canada and the United States. In: Journal of Multinational Financial Management, 11 (4-5), p. 445-463.

Cumming, Douglas J./MacIntosh, Jeffrey G. (2003): A cross-country comparison of full and partial exits. In: Journal of Banking & Finance, 27 (3), p. 511-548.

Cumming, Douglas/Fleming, Grant (2003): A law and finance analysis of venture capital exits in emerging markets. Working Paper: University of Alberta.

Das, Sanjiv R./Jagannathan, Murali/Sarin, Atulya (2003): Private Equity Returns: An Empirical Examination of the Exit of Venture-Backed Companies. In: Journal of Investment Management, 1 (1), p. 1-26.

Davila, Antonio/Foster, George/Gupta, Mahendra (2003): Venture capital financing and the growth of startup firms. In: Journal of Business Venturing, 18 (6), p. 689-708.

DeAngelo, Linda Elizabeth (1981): Auditor independence, 'low ballig', and disclosure regulation. In: Journal of Accounting and Economics, 3 (2), p. 113-127.

Deeds, David L./Decarolis, Dona/Coombs, Joseph E. (1997): The impact of firm-specific capabilities on the amount of capital raised in an initial public offering: Evidence from the biotechnology industry. In: Journal of Business Venturing, 12 (1), p. 31-46.

Demsetz, Harold/Lehn, Kenneth (1985): The Structure of Corporate Ownership: Causes and Consequences. In: Journal of Political Economy, 93 (6), p. 1155-1177.

Denis, David J./Denis, Diane K./Sarin, Atulya (1999): Agency theory and the influence of equity ownership structure of corporate diversification strategies. In: Strategic Management Journal, 20 (11), p. 1071-1076.

Diamond, Douglas D. (1985): Optimal Release of Information By Firms. In: Journal of Finance, 40 (4), p. 1071 - 1094.

Dieckhaus, Oliver-Till (1993): Beteiligungscontrolling auf Basis des Beteiligungslebenszyklus. In: Zeitschrift für Planung, 2 (2), p. 163-190.

Dominguez, John R. (1974): Venture Capital. Lexington, Massachusetts: Heath.

Dotzler, Fred (2001): What Do Venture Capitalists Really Do, and Where They Learn to Do It? In: Journal of Private Equity, 5 (1), p. 6-12.

D'Souza, Patrik (2000): Automatic Conversion in Venture Capital Finance. Ludwig-Maximillians-Universität München: Working Paper.

Duhaime, Irene M./Patton, G. Richard (1980): Selling Off. In: The Wharton Magazin, Winter 1980, p. 43-47.

Easley, David/O'Hara, Maureen (2004): Information and the Cost of Capital. In: Journal of Finance, 59 (4), p. 1553-1583.

Eisele, Florian/Habermann, Markus/Oesterle, Ralf (2002): Die Beteiligungskriterien für eine Venture-Capital-Finanzierung: eine empirische Analyse der phasenbezogenen Bedeutung. Tübingen: Eberhard-Karls-Universität.

Eisenhardt, Kathleen M. (1985): Control: Organizational and economic approaches. In: Management Science, 31 (2), p. 134-149.

Eisenhardt, Kathleen M. (1989a): Agency Theory: An Assessment and Review. In: Academy of Management Review, 14 (1), p. 57-74.

Eisenhardt, Kathleen M. (1989b): Building Theories from Case Study Research. In: Academy of Management Review, 14 (4), p. 532-550.

Eisenhardt, Kathleen M./Schoonhoven, Claudia B. (1990): Organizational Growth: Linking Founding Team, Strategy, Environment, and Growth among U.S. Semiconductor Ventures. In: Administrative Science Quarterly, 35 (3), p. 504-529.

Elango, Balasubramanian/Fried, Vance H./Hisrich, Robert D./Polonchek, Amy (1995): How Venture Capital Firms Differ. In: Journal of Business Venturing, 10 (2), p. 157-179.

Elitzur, Ramy/Gavious, Arieh (2003): Contracting, signaling and moral hazard: a model of entrepreneurs, 'angles,' and venture capitalists. In: Journal of Business Venturing, 18 (6), p. 709-725.

Emrey, Kenneth (2003): Private Equity Risk and Reward: Assessing the Stale Pricing Problem. In: Journal of Private Equity, 6 (2), p. 43-50.

Engelmann, Andree/Junker, Klaus/Natusch, Ingo/Tebroke, Hermann-Josef (2000): Moderne Unternehmensfinanzierung: Risikokapital für Unternehmensgründungen und -wachstum. Frankfurt a.M.: Knapp.

Espenlaub, Susanne/Tonks, Ian (1998): Post-IPO directors' sales and reissuing activity: an empirical test of IPO signalling models. In: Journal of Business Finance & Accounting, 25 (9-10), p. 1037-1079.

European Venture Capital Association (1996): A Survey of Venture Capital and Private Equity in Europe. EVCA, Belgium.

European Venture Capital Association (2003): EVCA Guidelines. Download: www.evca.com/pdf/Guidelines2003.

Fama, Eugene F. (1978): The Effects of a Firm's Investment and Financing Decisions on the Welfare of Its Security Holders. In: American Economic Review, 68 (3), p. 272-284.

Fama, Eugene F. (1980): Agency Problems and the Theory of the Firm. In: Journal of Political Economy, 88 (2), p. 288-307.

Fama, Eugene F./Jensen, Michael C. (1983): Separation of Ownership and Control. In: Journal of Law and Economics, 26, p. 301-325.

Fama, Eugene F./Jensen, Michael C. (1985): Organisation Forms and Investment Decisions. In: Journal of Financial Economics, 14 (1), p. 101-119.

Fassin, Yves/Lewis, Churchill (1994): IPO Markets in Europe and the United States: Principle and Practice. In: Bygrave, William D./Hay, Michael/Peeters, Jos B. (Ed.): Realizing Investment Value. London: Pitman Publishing, p. 39-63.

Feltham, Gerald A./Hughes, John S./Simunic, Dan A. (1991): Empirical assessment of the auditor quality on the valuation of new issues. In: Journal of Accounting and Economics, 14 (4), p. 375-399.

Field, Laura C./Hanka, Gordon (2001): The Expiration of IPO Share Lockups. In: Journal of Finance, 56 (2), p. 471-500.

Fiet, James O. (1995): Risk avoidance strategies in venture capital markets. In: Journal of Management Studies, 32 (4), p. 551-574.

Fiet, James O./Busenitz, Lowell W./Moesel, Douglas D./Barney, Jay B. (1997): Theoretical Perspectives on the dismissal of new venture team members. In: Journal of Business Venturing, 12 (5), p. 347-366.

Finn, Peter B. (2002): Structuring a Start-up Company for Venture Capital Financing. In: Journal of Biolaw and Business, 5 (3), p. 5-33.

Fischer, Lutz (1987): Problemfelder und Perspektiven der Finanzierung durch Venture Capital in der Bundesrepublik Deutschland. In: Die Betriebswirtschaftslehre, 47 (1), p. 8-32.

Fleming, Grant (2003): Venture Capital Returns in Australia. Working Paper: Australian National University.

Florida, Richard/Smith, Donald (1990): Venture Capital, Innovation and Economic Development. In: Economic Development Quarterly, 4 (4), p. 345-360.

Florida, Richard/Smith, Donald (1993): Venture Capital and Industrial Competitiveness. A Research Report to the U.S. Economic Development Administration. Pittsburgh 1993.

Franzke, Stefanie A. (2001): Underpricing of Venture-Backed and Non Venture-Backed IPOs: Germany's Neuer Markt. Working Paper, Center for Financial Studies, University of Frankfurt.

Fredrickson, James W./Hambrick, Donald C./Baumrin, Sara (1988): A model of CEO dismissal. In: Academy of Management Review, 13 (2), p. 255-270.

Fried, Vance H./Bruton, Garry D./Hisrich, Robert D. (1998): Strategy and the board of directors in venture capital-backed firms. In: Journal of Business Venturing, 13 (6), p. 493-503.

Fried, Vance H./Hisrich, Robert D. (1988): Venture Capital Research: past, present, and future. In: Entrepreneurship Theory and Practice, 13 (1), p. 15-28.

Fried, Vance H./Hisrich, Robert D. (1994): Toward a model of venture capital investment decision making. In: Financial Management, 23 (3), p. 28-37.

Friedrichs, Jürgen (1990): Methoden der empirischen Sozialforschung. 14th edition. Opladen: Westdt. Verl..

Gaida, Michael (2002): Venture-Capital in Deutschland und den USA - Finanzierung von Start-ups im Gefüge von Staat, Banken und Börsen. Wiesbaden: Dt. Univ.-Verl..

Galbraith, Jay R. (1973): Designing complex organizations. Reading: Addison-Wesley.

Gaughan, Patrick A. (1999): Mergers, Acquisitions, and Corporate Restructurings. 2ed edition. New York: Wiley & Sons.

Gerke, Wolfgang (1993): Informationsasymmetrien am Markt für Beteiligungen an mittelständischen Unternehmen. In: Gebhardt, Günther (ed.): Handbuch des Finanzmanagements. München: Beck, p. 619-640.

Gerpott, Torsten J. (1994): Abschied von der Spitze. In: Zeitschrift für betriebswirtschaftliche Forschung, 46, p. 4-31.

Gerpott, Torsten J. (1999): Strategisches Technologie- und Innovationsmanagement. Stuttgart: Schäffer-Poeschel.

Gifford, Sharon (1997): Limited attention and the role of the venture capitalist. In: Journal of Business Venturing, 12 (6), p. 459-482.

Gillner, Giso (84): Venture Capital: Leitfaden für die Praxis. Hannover: SLW.

Gilson, Ronald J./Schizer, David. M. (2002): Understanding Venture Capital Structure: A Tax Explanation for Convertible Preferred Stock. Working Paper: Columbia University.

Giot, Pierre/Schwienbacher, Armin (2003): IPOs, trade sales and liquidations: modelling venture capitalist exits using survival analysis. Working Paper: University of Namur.

Gladstone, David (1988): Venture Capital Handbook. Englewood-Cliffs: Prentice Hall.

Gladstone, David/Gladstone, Laura (2002): Venture Capital Handbook - An Entrepreneurs Guide to Raising Venture Capital. Englewood-Cliffs: Prentice-Hall.

Glass, Gene V./Hopkins, Kenneth D. (1996): Statistical methods in education and psychology. 3rd edition. Needham: Simon & Schuster.

Golder, Stanley C. (1984): Structuring and pricing the financing. In: Pratt, Stanley E. (ed.): Pratt's Guide to venture capital sources. 8th edition. Wellesley: Venture Economics, p. 47-56.

Golland, Frank (2000): Equity Mezzanine Capital. In: Finanz Betrieb, 2, p. 34-39.

Gompers, Paul A. (1994): The Rise and Fall of Venture Capital. In: Business and Economic History, 23, p. 1-24.

Gompers, Paul A. (1995): Optimal Investment, Monitoring, and the Staging of Venture Capital. In: Journal of Finance, 50 (5), p. 1461-1489.

Gompers, Paul A. (1996): Grandstanding in the venture capital industry. In: Journal of Financial Economics, 42 (1), p. 133-156.

Gompers, Paul A./Lerner, Josh (1996): The use of covenants: an empirical analysis of venture partnership agreements. In: Journal of Law and Economics, 39 (2), p. 463-498.

Gompers, Paul A./Lerner, Josh (1998): Venture Capital Distributions: Short-Run and Long-Run Reactions. In: Journal of Finance, 53 (6), p. 2161-2183.

Gompers, Paul A./Lerner, Josh (1999a): An analysis of compensation in the U.S. venture capital partnership. In: Journal of Financial Economics, 51 (1), p. 3-44.

Gompers, Paul A./Lerner, Josh (1999b): The Determinants of Corporate Venture Capital Success: Organized Structure, Incentives, and Complementarities. In: Morek, Randal K. (ed.): Concentrated Corporate Ownership. Chicago: University of Chicago Press.

Gompers, Paul A./Lerner, Josh (2000): The Venture Capital Cycle. Cambridge, Mass; London: MIT Press.

Gompers, Paul A./Lerner, Josh (2001a): The Venture Capital Revolution. In: Journal of Economic Perspectives, 15 (2), p. 145-168.

Gompers, Paul A./Lerner, Josh (2001b): The Money of Invention - How Venture Capital Creates Wealth. Boston: Harvard Business School Press.

Gorman, Michael/Sahlman, William A. (1989): What do venture capitalists do? In: Journal of Business Venturing, 4 (4), p. 231-248.

Graf, Steffen/Gruber, Alfred (2001): Intermediationsfunktionen bei Private Equity Investitionen. In: M&A Review, 11, p. 504-509.

Grinblatt, Mark/Hwang, Chuan Y. (1989): Signalling and the Pricing of New Issues. In: Journal of Finance, 44 (2), p. 393-420.

Grossman, Sanford J./Hart, Oliver D. (1988): One share - one vote and the market for corporate control. In: Journal of Financial Economics, 20 (1-2), p. 175-202.

Grüning, Rudolf/Heckner, Frank/Zeus, Anja (1996): Methoden zur Identifikation strategischer Erfolgsfaktoren. In: Die Unternehmung, 1, p. 3-12.

Gupta, Anil K./Sapienza, Harry J. (1992): Determinants of venture capital firms' preferences regarding the industry diversity and geographic scope of their investments. In: Journal of Business Venturing, 7 (5), p. 347-362.

Habib, Michael A./Ljungqvist, Alexander P. (2001): Underpricing and Entrepreneurial Wealth Losses in IPOs: Theory and Evidence. In: Review of Financial Studies, 14 (2), p. 433-458.

Haenecke, Henrik (2002): Methodenorientierte Systematisierung der Kritik an der Erfolgsforschung. In: Zeitschrift für Betriebswirtschaft, 2, p. 165-183.

Hanushek, Eric A./John E. Jackson (1977): Statistical Methods for Social Scientists. New York: Academic Press.

Harris, Timothy J. (2002): Bridge Financing over Troubled Water. In: Journal of Private Equity, 6 (1), p. 59-60.

Hartmann-Wendels, Thomas (1987): Venture Capital aus finanzierungstheoretischer Sicht. In Zeitschrift für betriebswirtschaftliche Forschung, 39, p. 16-30.

Harvey, Michael G./Lusch, Robert F. (1995): Expanding the nature and scope of due diligence. In: Journal of Business Venturing, 10 (1), p. 5-22.

Hax, Herbert (1964): Investitions- und Finanzplanung mit Hilfe der linearen Programmierung. In: Zeitschrift für Bbetriebswirtschaftslehre, 16, p. 430-446.

Hax, Herbert (1991): Theorie der Unternehmung - Information, Anreize und Vertragsgestaltung. In: Ordelheide, Dieter (ed.): Betriebswirtschaftslehre und ökonomische Theorie. Stuttgart: Poeschel, p. 51-72.

Hayek, Friedrich A. (1945): The Use of Knowledge in Society. In: American Economic Review, 35 (4), p. 519-530.

Heitzer, Bernd (2000): Finanzierung junger innovativer Unternehmen durch Venture Capital-Gesellschaften. Köln: Eul.

Hellmann, Thomas (1998): The allocation of control rights in venture capital contracts. In: RAND Journal of Economics, 29 (1), p. 57-76.

Hellmann, Thomas (2000): IPOs, Acquisitions and the Use of Convertible Securities in Venture Capital. Working Paper: Stanford University.

Hellmann, Thomas/Puri, Manju (2000): The Interaction between Product Market and Financing Strategy: The Role of Venture Capital. In: Review of Financial Studies, 13 (4), p. 959-984.

Heyde, Wolfgang/Laudel, Gerd/Pleschak, Franz/Sabisch, Helmut (1991): Innovationen in Industrieunternehmen:Prozesse, Entscheidungen und Methoden. Wiesbaden: Gabler.

Higashide, Hironori/Birley, Sue (2002): The consequences of conflict between the venture capitalists and the entrepreneurial team in the United Kingdom from the perspective of the venture capitalist. In: Journal of Business Venturing, 17 (1), p. 59-81.

Hinkel, Knud (2001): Erfolgsfaktoren von Frühphasenfinanzierungen durch Wagniskapitalgesellschaften. Wiesbaden: Dt. Univ.-Verl..

Hirsch, Seev (1967): Location of Industry and International Competitiveness. Oxford: Oxford University Press.

Hoang, Ha/Antoncic, Bostjan (2003): Network-based research in entrepreneurship - A critical review. In: Journal of Business Venturing, 18 (2), p. 165-187.

Howorth, Carole A. (2001): Small Firm's Demand for Finance: A Research Note. In: International Small Business Journal, 19 (4), p. 78-86.

Howorth, Carole/Westhead, Paul/Wright, Mike (2004): Buyouts, information asymmetry and the family management dyad. In: Journal of Business Venturing, 19 (4), p. 509-534.

Hsu, David H. (2000): Do Venture Capitalists Affect Commercialization Strategies in Start-ups? Working Paper: MIT.

Hsu, David H. (2004): What Do Entrepreneurs Pay for Venture Capital Affiliation. In: Journal of Finance, 59 (4), p. 1805-1844.

Huntsman, Blaine/Hoben, James P. (1980): Investment in New Enterprise: Some Empirical Observations on Risk, Return, and Market Structure. In: Financial Management, 9 (2), p. 44-51.

Huyghebaert, Nancy/Van de Gucht, Linda M. (2004): Incumbent strategic behavior in financial markets and the exit of entrepreneurial start-ups. In: Strategic Management Journal, 25 (7), p. 669-688.

Ibbotson, Roger G./Jaffee, Jeffrey F. (1975): "Hot Issue" Markets. In: Journal of Finance, 30 (4), p. 1027-1042.

Ibbotson, Roger G./Sindelar, Jody L./Ritter, Jay R. (1988): Initial Public Offerings. In: Journal of Applied Corporate Finance, 1 (2), p. 37-45.

Illenberger, Stephan M./Berlage, Jan S. (1991): Verfahrenswahl beim Unternehmenskauf. In: Die Bank, 8, p. 441-445.

Inderst, Roman/Müller, Holger M. (2004): The effect of capital market characteristics on the value of start-up firms. In: Journal of Financial Economics, 72 (2), p. 319-356.

Irvine, Paul J. (2003): The incremental impact of analyst initiation of coverage. In: Journal of Corporate Finance, 9 (4), p. 431-451.

Ivanova, Ana/Tzvetkova, Rossitza (2001): Exit-Strategien bei Private Equity Investments. In: Grünbichler, Andreas/Graf, Stefan/Gruber, Alfred (eds.): Private Equity und Hedge Funds. Frankfurt a.M.: Frankfurter Allgemeine Buch. p. 165-185.

Jain, Bharat A. (1999): Predictors of performance of venture capitalist-backed organizations. In: Journal of Business Research, 52, p. 223-233.

Jakoby, Stephan (2000): Erfolgsfaktoren von Management Buyouts in Deutschland. Köln: Eul.

Janney, Jay J./Folta, Timothy B. (2003): Signaling through private equity placements and its impact on the valuation of biotechnology firms. In: Journal of Business Venturing, 18 (3), p. 361-380.

Jeng, Leslie A./Wells, Philippe C. (2000): The determinants of venture capital funding: evidence across countries. In: Journal of Corporate Finance, 6 (3), p. 241-289.

Jenkinson, Tim/Ljungqvist, Alexander P. (2001): Going Public: The Theory and Evidence on How Companies Raise Equity Finance. 2nd edition. Oxford: Oxford University Press.

Jensen, Michael C. (1983): Organization Theory and Methodology. In: Accounting Review, 58 (2), p. 319-339.

Jensen, Michael C. (1986): Agency Costs of Free Cash Flow, Corporate Finance, and Takeovers. In: American Economic Review, 76 (2), p. 323-329.

Jensen, Michael C. (1988): Takeovers: Their Causes and Consequences. In: Journal of Economic Perspectives, 2 (1), S. 21-48.

Jensen, Michael C./Meckling, William H. (1976): The theory of the firm: Managerial behavior, agency costs, and ownership structure. In: Journal of Financial Economics, 3 (4), p. 305-360.

Johnson, James M./Miller, Robert E. (1988): Investment Banker Prestige and Underpricing of Initial Public Offerings. In: Financial Management, 17 (2), p. 19-29.

Jordan, Judith/Lowe, Julian/Taylor, Peter (1998): Strategy and financial policy in UK small firms. In: Journal of Business Finance and Accounting, 25 (1/2), p. 1-27.

Kanniainen, Vesa/Keuschnigg, Christian (2000): The Optimal Portfolio of Start-Up Firms in Venture Capital Finance. Working Paper: Center for Economics Studies, München.

Kaplan, Steven N./Ruback, Richard S. (1996): The Market Pricing of Cash Flow Forecasts: Discounted Cash Flow vs. The Method of "Comparables". In: Journal of Applied Corporate Finance, 8 (4), p. 45-60.

Kaplan, Steven N./Strömberg, Per (2003): Financial Contracting Theory Meets the Real World: An Empirical Analysis of Venture Capital Contracts. In: Review of Economics Studies, 70 (2), p. 281-315.

Kaplan, Steven N./Strömberg, Per (2004): Characteristics, Contracts, and Actions: Evidence from Venture Capitalist Analyses. In: Journal of Finance, 59 (5), p. 2177-2210.

Keasey, Kevin/Sort, Helen (1997): Equity retention and initial public offerings: the influence of signalling and entrenchment effects. In: Applied Financial Economics, 7 (1), p. 75-85.

Keeley, Robert H./Punjabi, Snajeev (1996): Valuation of early-stage ventures: Option valuation models vs. Traditional approaches. In: Journal of Entrepreneurial & Small Business Finance, 5 (2), p. 114-138.

Keren, Gideon/Raub, Werner (1993): Resolving Social Conflicts Through Hostage Posting: Theoretical and Empirical Considerations. In: Journal of Experimental Psychology: General, 122 (4), p. 429-448.

Kirilenko, Andrei A. (2001): Valuation and Control in Venture Finance. In: Journal of Finance, 56 (2), p. 565-587.

Kirzner, Israel M. (1997): Entrepreneurial Discovery and the Competitive Market Process: An Austrian Approach. In: Journal of Economic Literature, 35 (1), p. 60-85.

Kleiman, Robert T./Shulman, Joel M. (1992): The risk-return attributes of publicly traded venture capital: Implications for investors and public policy. In: Journal of Business Venturing, 7 (3), p. 195-208.

Klemm, H. Alexander (1988): Die Finanzierung und Betreuung von Innovationsvorhaben durch Venture Capital Gesellschaften. Frankfurt a.M.: Lang.

Knight, James A. (1998): Value Based Management: Developing a Systematic Approach to Creating Shareholder Value. New York: McGraw-Hill.

Koeplin, John/Sarin, Atulya/Shapiro, Alan C. (2000): The Private Company Discount. In: Journal of Applied Corporate Finance, 12 (4), p. 94-101.

Kohers, Ninon/Kohers, Theodor (2001): Takeovers of Technology Firms: Expectations vs. Reality. In: Financial Management, 30 (3), p. 35-54.

Kortum, Samuel/Lerner, Josh (2000): Assessing the contribution of venture capital to innovation. In: RAND Journal of Economics, 31 (4), p. 674-692.

Kosnik, Rita D. (1987): Greenmail: A Study of Board Performance and Corporate Governance. In: Administrative Science Quarterly, 32 (2), p. 163-185.

Kotovitz, Yoszef (1987): Moral Hazard. In: Eatwell, John/Milgate, Murray/Newman, Peter (Eds): The New Palgrave - A Dictionary of Economics. London: Macmaillan Press, p. 549-551.

Kreps, David M. (1990): A Course in Microeconomic Theory. Princeton, NJ: Princeton University Press.

Kulicke, Marianne/Müller, Emmanuel (1994): Renditen von Venture-Capital-Gesellschaften - Eine Literaturauswertung zum amerikanischen und europäischen Venture-Capital-Markt. Karlsruhe: FhG-ISI.

Kunz, Roger M./Angel, James J. (1996): Factors Affecting the Value of the Stock Voting Right: Evidence from the Swiss Equity Market. In: Financial Management, 25 (3), p. 7-20.

Lam, Swee-Sum (1991): Venture capital financing: A conceptual framework. In: Journal of Business Finance & Accounting, 18 (2), p. 137-149.

Lane, Peter J./Salk, Jane E./Lyles, Marjorie A. (2001): Absorptive Capacity, and Performance in International Joint Ventures. In: Strategic Management Journal, 22 (12), p. 1139-1161.

Langer, Lutz U./Thiele, Michael (2001): Akquisitionen durch am Neuen Markt notierte Unternehmen. In: M&A Review, 6, p. 250-257.

Lasfer, M. Ameziane/Melnik, Arie/Thomas, Dylan C. (2003): Short-term reaction of stock markets in stressful circumstances. In: Journal of Banking & Finance, 27 (10), p. 1959-1977.

Lee, Peggy M./Wahal, Sunil (2002): Grandstanding, Certification and the Underpricing of Venture Capital Backed IPOs. Working Paper: Emroy University.

Leidecker, Joel K./Bruno, Albert V. (1984): The Identification and Use of Critical Success Factors. In: Long Range Planning, 17 (1), p. 23-32.

Leitinger, Roland/Strohbach, Hannes/Schöfer, Peter/Hummel, Markus (2000): Venture Capital und Börsengänge: von der Produktidee zum internationalen Nischenspezialisten. Wien: MANZ-Verlag.

Leland, Hayne E./Pyle, David H. (1977): Informational Asymmetries, Financial Structure, and Financial Intermediation. In: Journal of Finance, 32 (2), p. 371-387.

Leleux, Benoît F. (1998): Resource Maps And Financing Ecotypes: A Visual Approach To Resourcing The Entrepreneurial Business. In: Babson Entrepreneurial Review, Spring/Summer, p. 23-33.

Leleux, Benoît F./Manigart, Sophie (1994): Initial Public Offerings: Pricing and Performance. In: Bygrave, William D./Hay, Michael/Peeters, Jos B. (Ed.): Realizing Investment Value. London: Pitman Publishing, p. 132-162.

Lerner, Josh (1994a): Venture capitalists and the decision to go public. In: Journal of Financial Economics, 35 (3), p. 293-316.

Lerner, Josh (1994b): The syndication of venture capital investments. In: Financial Management, 23 (3), p. 16-27.

Lerner, Josh/Shane, Hilary/Tsai, Alexander (2003): Do equity financing cycles matter? Evidence from biotechnology alliances. In: Journal of Financial Economics, 67 (3), p. 411-446.

Lessat, Vera/Hemer, Joachim/Eckerle, Tobias H. (1999): Beteiligungskapital und technologieorientierte Unternehmensgründung. Markt – Finanzierung – Rahmenbedingungen. Wiesbaden: Gabler.

Levin, Jack S. (2001): Structuring Venture Capital, Private Equity, and Entrepreneurial Transactions. Frederick: Aspen Publishers.

Lewis, William W./Linden, Lawrence H. (1990): A New Mission for Corporate Technology. In: Sloan Management Review, 31 (4), p. 57-67.

Lin, Timothy H. (1996): The Certification Role of Large Block Shareholders in Initial Public Offerings: The Case of Venture Capitalists. In: Quarterly Journal of Business & Economics, 35 (2), p. 55-65.

Lin, Timothy H./Smith, Richard L. (1998): Insider reputation and selling decisions: the unwinding of venture capital investments during equity IPOs. In: Journal of Corporate Finance, 4 (3), p. 241-263.

Ljungqvist, Alexander/Wilhelm, William J. (2003): IPO Pricing in the Dot-com Bubble. In: Journal of Finance, 58 (2), p. 723-752.

Logue, Dennis E. (1973): On the Pricing of Unseasoned Equity Issues. In: Journal of Financial and Quantitative Analysis, 8 (1), p. 91-103.

Lorenz, Tony (1989): Venture Capital Today. 2nd edition. New York: Woodhead-Faulkner.

Lowry, Michelle (2003): Why does IPO volume fluctuate so much? In: Journal of Financial Economics, 67 (1), p. 3-40.

MacMillan, Ian C./Kulow, David M./Khoylian, Roubina (1989): Venture capitalists' involvement in their investments: Extent and performance. In: Journal of Business Venturing, 4 (1), p. 27-47.

MacMillan, Ian C./Siegel, Robin/Subbanarasimha, P. N. (1985): Criteria used by venture capitalists to evaluate new venture proposals. In: Journal of Business Venturing, 1 (1), p. 119-128.

Maksimovic, Vojislav/Pichler, Pegaret (1999): Private versus Public Offerings: Optimal Selling Mechanisms with Adverse Selection. Working Paper: University of Maryland and Boston College.

Maksimovic, Vojislav/Pichler, Pegaret (2001): Technological Innovation and Initial Public Offerings. In: Review of Financial Studies, 14 (2), p. 459-494.

Manigart, Sophie/Baeyens, Katleen/Hyfte, Wim van (2002): The survival of venture capital backed companies. In: Venture Capital, 4 (2), p. 103-124.

Manigart, Sophie/De Waele, Koen/Wright, Mike/Robbie, Ken/Desbrières, Philippe/Sapienza, Harry J./Beekman, Amy (2002): Determinants of required return in venture capital investments: a five-country study. In: Journal of Business Venturing, 17 (4), p. 291-312.

Marinell, Gerhard (1990): Multivariate Verfahren. München:Oldenbourg.

Marshall, Andrew P. (1998): Discussion of post-IPO directors' sales and reissuing activity: an empirical test of IPO signalling models. In: Journal of Business Finance & Accounting, 25 (9/10), p. 1081-1088.

Martin, John D./Petty, J. William (1983): An Analysis of the Performance of Publicly Traded Venture Capital Companies. In: Journal of Financial and Qualitative Analysis, 18 (3), p. 401-410.

Mason, Colin M./Harrison, Richard T. (2002): Is it worth it? The rates of return from informal venture capital investments. In: Journal of Business Venturing, 17 (3), p. 211-236.

Matz, Christoph (2002): Wettbewerbsentwicklung im deutschen Private-Equity-Markt: Strategieoptionen für Beteiligungskapitalgesellschaften. Wiesbaden: Deut. Univ.-Verlag.

McDonald, J. G./Fisher, A. K. (1972): New-Issue Stock Price Behavior. In: Journal of Finance, 27 (1), p. 97-102.

Megginson, William L./Mull, Frederick H. (1991): Financial characteristics and financing decisions of venture capital backed firms. Paper presented at the Small Business Finance Conference, Florida, April 1991.

Megginson, William L./Weiss, Kathleen A. (1991): Venture Capitalists Certification in Initial Public Offerings. In: Journal of Finance, 46 (3), p. 879-903.

Mellewigt, Thomas/Witt, Peter (2002): Die Bedeutung des Vorgründungsprozesses für die Evolution von Unternehmen: Stand der empirischen Forschung. In: Zeitschrift für Betriebswirtschaftslehre, 72, p. 81-110.

Merkle, Erich (1984): Venture Capital als Instrument des Technologiemanagements. In: Betriebs-Berater, 39, p. 1060-1064.

Merrifield, D. Bruce (1988): Industrial survival via management technology. In: Journal of Business Venturing, 3 (3), p. 171-185.

Merton, Robert C. (1987): A Simple Model of Capital Market Equilibrium with Incomplete Information. In: Journal of Finance, 42 (3), p. 483-510.

Merton, Robert C. (1995): A Functional Perspective of Financial Intermediation. In: Financial Management, 24 (2), p. 23-41.

Michaely, Roni/Shaw, Wayne H. (1994): The Pricing of Initial Public Offerings: Tests of Adverse Selection and Signaling Theories. In: The Review of Financial Studies, 7 (2), p. 279-319.

Mikkelson, Wayne H./Partch, M. Megan/Shah, Kshitij (1997): Ownership and operating performance of companies that go public. In: Journal of Financial Economics, 44 (3), p. 281-307.

Milgrom, Paul/Roberts, John (1982): Predation, Reputation, and Entry Deterrence. In: Journal of Economic Theory, 27 (2), p. 280-312.

Minniti, Maria (2004): Entrepreneurial alertness and asymmetric information in a spin-glass model. In: Journal of Business Venturing, 19 (5), p. 637-658.

Mirrlees, James A. (1997): Information and Incentives: The Economics of Carrots and Sticks. In: The Economic Journal, 107 (444), S. 1311-1329.

Misirli, Osman (1988): Venture-Capital-Gesellschaften als Intermediäre auf dem Kapitalmarkt. Köln: Eul.

Modigliani, Franco/Miller, Merton H. (1958): The Cost of Capital, Corporation Finance and the Theory of Investment. In: American Economic Review, 48 (3), p. 261-297.

Montgomery, Cynthia A./Thomas, Ann R./Kamath, Rajan (1984): Divestiture, Market Valuation, and Strategy. In: Academy of Management Journal, 27 (4), p. 830-840.

Morris, Richard D. (1987): Signalling, Agency Theory and Accounting Policy Choice. In: Journal of Business Research, 18 (69), p. 47-56.

Mull, Rick H. (1994): Venture capital, private firms, and the capital acquisition process. In: Journal of Entrepreneurial & Small Business Finance, 3 (3), p. 229-248. (HTML-copy applied)

Murray, Gordon C. (1994): The Second 'Equity Gap': Exit Problems for Seed and Early Stage Venture Capitalists and Their Investee Companies. In: International Small Business Journal, 12 (4), p. 59-76.

Murray, Gordon C. (1996): A synthesis of six exploratory, European case studies of successfully exited, venture capital-financed, new-technology-based firms. In: Entrepreneurship Theory and Practice, 20 (4), p. 41-60.

Myers, Steward C. (2001): Capital Structure. In: Journal of Economic Perspectives, 15 (2), p. 81-102.

Myers, Steward C./Majluf, Nicolas S. (1984): Corporate financing and investment decisions when firms have information that investors do not have. In: Journal of Financial Economics, 13 (2), p. 187-221.

National Venture Capital Association (1998): Mergers & Acquisitions Pick Up Slack as Preferred Exit Strategy. www.nvca.com, 11/24/1998, Newark.

National Venture Capital Association (2002a): National Venture Capital Association Yearbook 2002. Newark: Venture Economics.

National Venture Capital Association (2002b): Venture-Backed Exit Activity Remains Limited Due to Depressed Valuations and Continued Market Volatility. www.nvca.com, 11/18/2002, Newark.

National Venture Capital Association (2003): Number of venture-backed companies acquired in the first quarter of 2003 declined to 1996 levels. New York: NVCA-Note, 05/13/2003.

Nesbitt, Stephen L/Reynolds, Hal W. (1997): Benchmarks for private market investments. In: Journal of Portfolio Management, 23 (4), p. 85-91. (HTML-copy applied)

Neuberger, Brian M./Hammond, Carl T. (1974): A Study of Underwriters' Experience with Unseasoned New Issues. In: Journal of Financial and Quantitative Analysis, 9 (2), p. 165-177.

Neus, Werner/Walz, Uwe (2001): Exit Timing of Venture Capitalists in the Course of an Initial Public Offering. Working Paper: Unversität Tübingen.

Nevermann, Helga/Falk, Dieter (1986): Venture Capital - Ein betriebswirtschaftlicher und steuerlicher Vergleich zwischen den USA und der Bundesrepublik Deutschland. Baden Baden: Nomos.

Norton, Edgar/Tenenbaum, Bernhard H. (1992): Factors affecting the structure of U.S. venture capital deals. In: Journal of Small Business Management, 30 (3), p. 20-29.

Norton, Edgar/Tenenbaum, Bernhard H. (1993a): Specialization versus diversification as a venture capital investment strategy. In: Journal of Business Venturing, 8 (5), p. 431-442.

Norton, Edgar/Tenenbaum, Bernhard H. (1993b): The effects of venture capitalists' characteristics on the structure of the venture capital deal. In: Journal of Small Business Management, 31 (4), p. 32-41.

O'Brien, Patricia/Bhushan, Ravi (1990): Analyst Following and Institutional Ownership. In: Journal of Accounting Research, 28 Supplement, p. 55-76.

Ofek, Eli/Richardson, Matthew (2003): DotCom Mania: The Rise and Fall of Internet Stock Prices. In: Journal of Finance, 58 (3), p. 1113-1137.

Osareh, Farideh (1996a): Bibliometrics, Citation Analysis and Co-Citation Analysis - A review of Literature I. In: Libri, 46, p. 149-158.

Osareh, Farideh (1996b): Bibliometrics, Citation Analysis and Co-Citation Analysis - A review of Literature I. In: Libri, 46, p. 217-225.

Oviatt, Benjamin M. (1988): Agency and transaction costs perspectives on the manager-shareholder relationship: Incentives for congruent interests. In: Academy of Management Review, 13 (2), p. 214-225.

Pagano, Marco/Panetta, Fabio/Zingales, Luigi (1998): Why Do Companies Go Public? An Empirical Analysis. In: Journal of Finance, 53 (1), p. 27-64.

Pagano, Marco/Röell, Ailsa (1998): The Choice of Stock Ownership Structure: Agency Costs, Monitoring, and the Decision to Go Public. In: Quarterly Journal of Economics, 113 (1), p. 187-225.

Pape, Ulrich/Beyer, Stephan (2001): Venture Capital als Finanzierungsalternative innovativer Wachstumsunternehmen. In: Finanz Betrieb, 3 (11), p. 627-638.

Parkhe, Arvind (1993): Strategic alliance structuring: A game theoretic and transaction cost examination of interfirm cooperation. In: Academy of Management Journal, 36 (4), p. 794-829.

Pedhazur, Elazar J./Schmelkin, Liora Pedhazur (1991): Measurement, design, and analysis: an integrated approach. Hillsdale: Erlbaum Associates.

Perlitz, Manfred/Peske, Thorsten/Schüffel, Patrick (1999): Einsatz von Investitionsbewertungsmethoden bei deutschen Venture-Capital Unternehmen - eine empirische Untersuchung. Universität Mannheim, Arbeitspapier Nr. 6.

Perridon, Louis/Steiner, Manfred (1997): Finanzwirtschaft der Unternehmung. 9th edition. München: Vahlen.

Perrow, Charles (1986): Complex Organizations: A Critical Essay. New York: Random House.

Petty, J. William/Bygrave, William D./Shulman, Joel M. (1992): Harvesting the entrepreneurial venture: A time for creating value. In: Journal of Applied Corporate Finance, 7 (1), p. 48-58.

Petty, J. William/Shulman, Joel/Bygrave, William D. (1994): Mergers and Acquisitions: A Means of Harvesting the Venture. In: Managerial Finance, 20 (1), p. 43-52.

Pfirrmann, Oliver/Wupperfeld, Udo/Lerner, Josh (1997): Venture Capital and new technology based firms: an US-German comparison. Heidelberg: Physica.

Picot, Arnold (1991): Ökonomische Theorien der Organisation - Ein Überblick über neuere Ansätze und deren betriebswirtschaftliches Anwendungspotential. In: Ordelheide, Dieter (ed): Betriebswirtschaftslehre und ökonomische Theorie. Stuttgart: Poeschel, p. 143-169.

Picot, Arnold/Dietl, Helmut/Franck, Egon (1999): Organisation - eine ökonomische Perspetive. Stuttgart: Schäffer-Poeschel.

Picot, Arnold/Laub, Ulf/Schneider, Dietram (1989): Innovative Unternehmensgründungen - eine ökonomische Analyse. Berlin: Springer.

Picot, Gerhard (1998): Unternehmenskauf und Restrukturierung. 2nd edition. München: C.H. Beck.

Picot, Gerhard (2000): Mergers & Acquisitions: Planung, Durchführung, Integration. Stuttgart: Schäffer-Poeschel.

Pleschak, Franz/Sabisch, Helmut (1996): Innovationsmanagement. Stuttgart: Schäffer-Poeschel.

Pogue, Michael (1991): Financing the MBO: A Complex Issue? In: Management Decision, 29 (2), p. 58-62.

Popper, Karl R. (1994): Logik der Forschung. 10th edition. Tübingen: Mohr.

Potter, William Gray (1988): "Of making many books there is no end": Bibliometrics and Libraries. In: Journal of Academic Librarianship, 14 (9), p. 238a-238c (insert between p. 238 and 239)

Prasad, Dev/Bruton, Garry D./Vozikis, George (2000): Signaling value to business angles: the proportion of the entrepreneur's net worth invested in a new venture as a decision signal. In: Venture Capital, 2 (3), p. 167-182.

Prester, Melanie (2002): Exit-Strategien deutscher Venture Capital Gesellschaften. Münster: LIT.

Räbel, Dieter (1986): Venture Capital als Instrument für Innovationsfinanzierung - Eine kritische Analyse unter besonderer Berücksichtigung des Projektbewertungsproblems. Köln: Deutscher Wirtschaftsdienst.

Rajan, Raghuram G. (1992): Insiders and Outsiders: The Choice between Informed and Arm's-Length Debt. In: Journal of Finance, 47 (4), p. 1367-1400.

Rajan, Raghuram/Servaes, Henry (1997): Analyst Following of Initial Public Offerings. In: Journal of Finance, 52 (2), p. 507-529.

Ranft, Annette L./Lord, Michael D. (2000): Acquiring new knowledge: the role of retaining human capital in acquisitions of high-tech firms. In: Journal of High Technology Management Research, 11 (2), p. 295-319.

Ravasi, Davide/Marchisio, Gaia (2003): Going Public and the Enrichment of a Supportive Network. In: Small Business Economics, 21 (4), p. 381-395.

Relander, Kaj-Erik/Syrjänen, Antti-Pekka/Miettinen, Asko (1994): Analysis of the Trade Sale as a Venture Capital Exit Route. In: Bygrave, William D./Hay, Michael/Peeters, Jos B. (Ed.): Realizing Investment Value. London: Pitman Publishing, p. 132-162.

Reynolds, Paul D./Hay, Michael/Bygrave, William D./Camp, S. Michael/Autio, Erkko (2000): Global Entrepreneurship Monitor - Executive Report. Kaufman Center for Entrepreneurial Leadership.

Reynolds, Paul D./Hay, Michael/Bygrave, William D./Camp, S. Michael/Autio, Erkko (2001): Global Entrepreneurship Monitor - Executive Report. Kaufman Center for Entrepreneurial Leadership.

Richter, Rudolf/Furubotn, Eirik G. (1996): Neue Institutionenökonomik - Eine Einführung und kritische Würdigung. Tübingen: Mohr.

Ripperger, Tanja (1998): Ökonomik des Vertrauens: Analyse eines Organisationsprinzips. Tübingen: Mohr Siebeck.

Riquelme, Hernán/Watson, John (2002): Do Venture Capitalists' Implicit Theories on New Business Success/Failure have Empirical Validity? In: International Small Business Journal, 20 (4), p. 395-418.

Ritter, Jay R. (1984): The "Hot Issue" Markets of 1980. In: Journal of Business, 57 (2), p. 215-240.

Ritter, Jay R. (1987): The Cost of Going Public. In: Journal of Financial Economics, 19 (2), p. 269-281.

Robinson, Robert J./Osnabrugge, Mark van (2001): Do Venture Capitalists Behave Differently When Investing in High-Tech Ventures? In: Journal of Private Equity, 4 (3), p. 31-42.

Roesner, Günter (1968): Möglichkeiten und Grenzen einer Verbesserung der Eigenkapitalausstattung kleiner und mittlerer Unternehmungen mit Hilfe von erwerbswirtschaftlich ausgerichteten Kapitalbeteiligungsgesellschaften. Frankfurt.

Ross, Stephan A. (1973): The Economic Theory of Agency: The Principal's Problem. In: American Economic Review, 63 (2), p. 134-139.

Ross, Stephan A. (1977): The determination of financial structure: the incentive signalling approach. In: Bell Journal of Economics, 8 (1), p. 23-40.

Ross, Stephan A./Westerfield. Randolph/Jaffe, Jeffrey/Jordan, Bradford (1996): Corporate Finance. 4th edition. Chicago: McGraw-Hill.

Rothschild, Michael/Stiglitz, Joseph (1976): Equilibrium in Competitive Insurance Markets: An Essay on the Economics of Imperfect Information. In: Quarterly Journal of Economics, 90 (4), p. 629-649.

Rothwell, Roy (1986): Innovation and Re-Innovation - A Role for the Users. In: Journal of Marketing Management, 2 (2), p. 109-123.

Rüdiger, Mathias (2000): Forschung und Entwicklung als Dienstleistung: Grundlagen und Erfolgsbedingungen der Vertragsforschung. Wiesbaden: Dt. Univ.-Verl.

Ruhnka, John C./Feldman, Howard D./Dean, Thomas J. (1992): The "living dead" phenomenon in venture capital investments. In: Journal of Business Venturing, 7 (2), p. 137-155.

Ruhnka, John C./Young, John E. (1987): A venture capital model of the development process for new ventures. In: Journal of Business Venturing, 2 (2), p. 167-184.

Ruhnka, John C./Young, John E. (1991): Some hypotheses about risk in venture capital investing. In: Journal of Business Venturing, 6 (2), p. 115-133.

Ruppen, Daniel A. (2001): Corporate Governance bei Venture Capital-finanzierten Unternehmen. St. Gallen: D-Druck-Spescha.

Sacirbey, Omar (2000): Market Forces New Exit Strategies. In: IPO Reporter, 24 (19), p. 3.

Sah, Raaj K./Stiglitz, Joseph E. (1986): The Architecture of Economic Systems: Hierarchies and Polyarchies. In: American Economic Review, 76 (4), p. 716-727.

Sahlman, William A. (1988): Aspects of financial contracting in venture capital. In: Journal of Applied Corporate Finance, 1 (2), p. 23-36.

Sahlman, William A. (1990): The structure and governance of venture-capital organizations. In: Journal of Financial Economics, 27 (2), p. 473-521.

Sahlman, William A. (1997): How to write a great business plan. In: Harvard Business Manager, 75 (July-August), p. 98-108.

Salop, Joanne/Salop, Steven (1976): Self-Selection and Turnover in the Labor Market. In: Quarterly Journal of Economics, 90 (4), p. 619-627.

Sapienza, Harry J. (1992): When do venture capitalists add value? In: Journal of Business Venturing, 7 (1), p. 9-27.

Sapienza, Harry J./Gupta, Anil K. (1994): Impact of agency risks and task uncertainty on venture capitalist–CEO interaction. In: Academy of Management Journal, 37 (6), p. 1618-1632.

Schefczyk, Michael (2004): Erfolgsstrategien deutscher Venture Capital Gesellschaften. 3rd edition. Stuttgart: Schäfer-Poeschel.

Schefczyk, Michael/Gerpot, Torsten J. (2001): Qualifications and turnover of managers and venture-financed firm performance. In: Journal of Business Venturing, 16 (2), p. 145-163.

Schierenbeck, Henner (1973): Beteiligungsentscheidungen - Betriebswirtschaftliche Grundlagen des Erwerbs und der Veräußerung von Unternehmensbeteiligungen. Berlin: Dunker & Humblot.

Schilit, W. Keith (1991): Dream Makers and Deal Breakers. New Jersey: Prentice Hall.

Schmeisser, Wilhelm/Krimphove, Dieter (2001): Vom Gründungsmanagement zum neuen Markt - Strategien für technologieorientierte kleine und mittlere Unternehmen. Wiesbaden: Gabler.

Schmidt, Klaus M. (2003): Convertible Securities and Venture Capital Finance. In: Journal of Finance, 58 (3), p. 1139-1166.

Schmidt, Reinhard H. (1985): Venture-Capital aus der Sicht der Finanzierungstheorie. In: Betriebswirtschaftliche Forschung und Praxis, 5, p. 421-437.

Schmidtke, Axel (1985): Die Praxis des Venture-Capital-Geschäftes. Landsberg a. Lech: Moderne Industrie.

Schneider, Dieter (1992): Investition, Finanzierung und Besteuerung. 7th edition. Wiesbaden: Gabler.

Schröder, Christoph (1992): Strategien und Management von Beteiligungsgesellschaften: ein Einblick in Organisationsstrukturen und Entscheidungsprozesse von institutionellen Eigenkapitalinvestoren. Baden-Baden: Nomos.

Schulz, Paul (2003): Pseudo Market Timing and the Long-Run Underperformance of IPOs. In: Journal of Finance, 58 (2), p. 483-518.

Schumpeter, Joseph A. (1939): Business Cycles: A Theoretical, Historical and Statistical Analysis of the Capitalist Process. New York: McGraw-Hill.

Schumpeter, Joseph A. (1947): The Creative Response in Economic History. In: Journal of Economic History, 7 (2), p. 149-159.

Schween, Karsten (1996): Corporate Venture Capital: Risikofinanzierung deutscher Industrieunternehmen. Wiesbaden: Gabler.

Schweitzer, Urs (1999): Vertragstheorie. Tübingen: Mohr Siebeck.

Schwienbacher, Armin (2001): Innovation and Venture Capital Exits. Working Paper: University of Namur.

Schwienbacher, Armin (2002): An empirical analysis of venture capital exits in Europe and in the United States. Working Paper: University of Namur.

Seppä, Tuukka J./Laamanen, Tomi (2001): Valuation of venture capital investments: empirical evidence. In: R&D Management, 31 (2), p. 215-230.

Sharpe, Steven A. (1990): Asymmetric Information, Bank Lending, and Implicit Contracts: A Stylized Model of Customer Relationships. In: Journal of Finance, 45 (4), p. 1069-1087.

Sharpe, William F. (1964): Capital Asset Prices: A Theory of Market Equilibrium under Conditions of Risk. In: Journal of Finance, 19 (3), p. 425-442.

Shepherd, Dean A./Zacharakis, Andrew L. (2001a): Speed to Initial Public Offering of VC-Backed Companies. In: Entrepreneurship Theory and Practice, 25 (3), p. 59-69.

Shepherd, Dean A./Zacharakis, Andrew L. (2001b): The venture capitalist-entrepreneur relationship: control trust and confidence in co-operative behavior. In: Venture Capital, 3 (2), p. 129-149.

Sherling, Clive (1999): Deal Structuring and Pricing. In: Bygrave, William D./Hay, Michael/Peeters, Jos B. (Eds.): The Venture Capital Handbook. London: Financial Times Prentice Hall, p. 163-182.

Sidler, Sonja (1997): Risikokapitalfinanzierung von Jungunternehmen. 2nd edition. Stuttgart: Haupt.

Siegert, Theo (1991): Franz Haniel & Cie.: Akquisitionspolitik. In: Rudolph, Bernd (ed.): Unternehmerische Finanzierung: corporate finance im Spannungsfeld von Banken und Industrie. Frankfurt a.M.: Knapp, p. 27-51.

Simon, Hermann/Ebel, Bernhard/Pohl, Alexander (2002): Investor Marketing. In: Zeitschrift für Betriebswirtschaft, 72 (2), p. 117-140.

Soh, Pek-Hooi (2003): The role of networking alliances in information acquisition and its implications for new product performance. In: Journal of Business Venturing, 18 (6), p. 727-744.

Sohl, Jeffrey E. (2003): The U.S. Angel and Venture Capital Market: Recent Trends and Developments. In: Journal of Private Equity, 6 (2), p. 7-17.

Sorensen, Olav/Stuart, Toby E. (2001): Syndication Networks and the Spatial Distribution of Venture Capital Investments. In: American Journal of Sociology, 106 (6), p. 1546-1588.

Spekman, Robert E./Forbes, Theodore M./Isabella, Lynn A./MacAvoy, Thomas C. (1998): Alliance management: A view from the past and a look to the future. In: Journal of Management Studies, 35 (6), p. 747-772.

Spence, Michael (1973): Job Market Signaling. In: Quarterly Journal of Economics, 87 (3), p. 355-374.

Spremann, Klaus (1990): Asymmetrische Information. In: Zeitschrift für Betriebswirtschaftslehre, 60, p. 561-586.

Stähler, Patrick (2001): Geschäftsmodelle in der digitalen Ökonomie. Köln: Eul.

Steier, Lloyd/Greenwood, Royston (1995): Venture capitalist relationships in the deal structuring and post-investment stages of new firm creation. In: Journal of Management Studies, 32 (3), p. 337-357.

Steinmann, Horst (1978): Die Betriebswirtschaftslehre als normative Handlungswissenschaft. In: Steinmann, Horst (ed.): Betriebswirtschaftslehre als normative Handlungswissenschhaft - zur Bedeutung der konstruktiven Wissenschaftstheorie für die Betriebsweitschaftslehre. Wiesbaden: Gabler, p. 73-102.

Stevens, James P. (1996): Applied multivariate statistics for the social sciences. Mahwah: Lawrence Erlbaum Publishers.

Stier, Winfried (1999): Empirische Forschungsmethoden. 2ed. Edition. Berlin: Springer.

Stiglitz, Joseph E. (1985): Credit Markets and the Control of Capital. In: Journal of Money, Credit and Banking, 17 (2), p. 133-152.

Stoughton, Neal M./Wong, Kit Pong/Zechner, Josef (2001): IPOs and Product Quality. In: Journal of Business, 74 (3), p. 375-408.

Subrahmanyam, Avanidhar/Titman, Sheridan (1999): The Going-Public Decision and the Development of Financial Markets. In: Journal of Finance, 54 (3), p. 1045-1082.

Sweeting, R. C./Wong C. F. (1997): A UK 'hands-off' venture capital firm and the handling of post-investment investor-investee relationships. In: Journal of Management Studies, 34 (1), p. 125-152.

Temple, Peter (1999): Private Equity - Examining the new conglomerates of European business. New York: John Wiley & Sons, Inc.

Thakor, Anjan V. (1989): Competitive Equilibrium with Type Convergence in an Asymmetrically Informed Market. In: Review of Financial Studies, 2 (1), p. 49-71.

Tichy, Noel M. (1981): Networks in Organizations. In: Nystrom, Paul C./Startbuck, William H. (eds.): Handbook of Organizational Design. New York: Oxford University Press, p. 203-224.

Timmons, Jeffry A./Bygrave, William D. (1986): Venture capital's role in financing innovation for economic growth. In: Journal of Business Venturing, 1 (2), p. 161-176.

Timmons, Jeffry A./Muzyka, Daniel F./Stevenson, Howard H./Bygrave, William D. (1987): Opportunity Recognition: The Core of Entrepreneurship. In: Churchill, Neil C. (ed.): Frontiers of Entrepreneurship Research. Wellesley: Babson College, p. 109-123.

Titman, Sheridan (2002): The Modigliani and Miller Theorem and the Integration of Financial Markets. In: Financial Management, 22 (March), p. 101-115.

Titman, Sheridan/Trueman, Brett (1986): Information Quality and the Valuation of New Issues. In: Journal of Accounting and Economics, 8 (2), p. 159-172.

Trester, Jeffrey J. (1998): Venture capital contracting under asymmetric information. In: Journal of Banking & Finance, 22 (6-8), p. 675-699.

Tykvová, Tereza (2003): The decision of Venture Capitalists on Timing and Extent of IPOs. Working Paper: Zentrum für Europäische Wirtschaftsforschung.

Ulrich, Hans (1981): Die Betriebswirtschaftslehre als anwendungsorientierte Sozialwissenschaft. In: Geist, Manfred N. (ed.): Die Führung des Betriebes. Stuttgart: Schäffer-Poeschel, p. 1-25.

Vernon, Raymond (1966): International Investment and International Trade in the Product Cycle. In: Quarterly Journal of Economics, 80 (2), p. 190-207.

Wall, John/Smith, Julian (1997): Better Exits. Survey edited by the Exit Committee of the European Venture Capital Association.

Walsh, James P./Seward, James K. (1990): On the efficiency of internal and external corporate control mechanisms. In: Academy of Management Review, 15 (3), p. 421-458.

Wang, Clement K./Sim, Valerie Y. L. (2001): Exit strategies of venture-backed companies in Singapore. In: Venture Capital, 3 (4), p. 337-358.

Wang, Kangmao/Wang, Clement K./Lu, Qing (2002): Differences in performance of independent and finance-affiliated venture capital firms. In: Journal of Financial Research, 25 (1), p. 59-80.

Weimerskirch, Pierre (1999): Finanzierungsdesign bei Venture-Capital-Verträgen. 2nd edition. Wiesbaden: Dt. Univ.-Verl.

Weitenauer, Wolfgang (2000): Handbuch Venture Capital - Von der Innovation zum Börsengang. München: Beck.

Welch, Ivo (1989): Seasoned Offerings, Imitation Costs, and the Underpricing of Initial Public Offerings. In: Journal of Finance, 44 (2), p. 421-449.

Westhead, Paul/Wright, Mike (1998): Novice, portfolio, and serial founders: are thy different? - Evidence from new production firm registrations 1980 - 88. In: Journal of Business Venturing, 13 (3), p. 173-204.

Willard, Gary E./Krueger, David A./Feeser, Henry R. (1992): In order to grow, must a founder go: A comparison of performance between founder and non-founder managed high-growth manufacturing firms. In: Journal of Business Venturing, 7 (3), p. 171-251.

Williamson, Oliver E. (1988): Corporate Finance and Corporate Governance. In: Journal of Finance, 43 (3), p. 567-591.

Williamson, Oliver E. (1990): Die ökonomischen Institutionen des Kapitalismus. Tübingen: Mohr.

Witt, Peter/Schmidt, Tobias (2002): Venture Capital, Börsengänge und Beteiligungsexits. In: Finanz Betrieb, 4 (12), p. 752-756.

Wrede, Thomas (1987): Venture Capital: das US-amerikanische Modell und seine Umsetzung in der Bundesrepublik Deutschland. Köln: Eul.

Wright, Mike/Chiplin, Brian/Thompson, Steve/Robbie, Ken (1990): Realizations of venture capital investments: the case of management buy-outs in the UK. In: Service Industries Journal, 10 (3), p. 499 - 520.

Wright, Mike/Hoskisson, Robert E./Busenitz, Lowell W. (2000): Entrepreneurial growth through privatization: the upside of management buyouts. In: Academy of Managament Review, 25 (3), p. 591-600.

Wright, Mike/Hoskisson, Robert E./Busentitz, Lowell W./Dial, Jay (2001): Finance and management buyouts: agency versus entrepreneurship perspectives. In: Venture Capital, 3 (3), p. 239-261.

Wright, Mike/Robbie, Ken/Ennew, Christine (1997): Venture Capitalists and Serial Entrepreneurs. In: Journal of Business Venturing, 12 (3), p. 229-247.

Wright, Mike/Robbie, Ken/Romanet, Yves/Thompson, Steve/Joachimsson, Robert/Bruining, Robert/Herst, Arthur (1994): Harvesting, Longevity and the Life Cycle of Management Buy-outs and Buy-ins: A Four-Country Study. In: Bygrave, William D./Hay, Michael/Peeters, Jos B. (Ed.): Realizing Investment Value. London: Pitman Publishing, p. 82-109.

Wupperfeld, Udo (1994): Strategien und Management von Beteiligungsgesellschaften im deutschen Seed-Capital-Markt. Karlsruhe: Fraunhofer-Institut.

Yin, Robert K. (1989): Case Study Research Design and Methods. London: Sage Publications.

Yosha, Oved (1995): Information Disclosure Costs and the Choice of Financing Source. In: Journal of Financial Intermediation, 4 (1), p. 3-20.

Zacharakis, Andrew L./Shepherd, Dean A./Coombs, Joseph E. (2003): The development of venture-capital-backed internet companies - An ecosystem perspective. In: Journal of Business Venturing, 18 (2), p. 217-231.

Zemke, Ingo (1995): Die Unternehmensverfassung von Beteiligungskapital-Gesellschaften: Analyse des institutionellen Designs deutscher Venture-Capital-Gesellschaften. Wiesbaden: Gabler.

Zider, Bob (1998): How venture capital works. In: Harvard Business Review, November-December, p. 131-139.

Zikmund, William G. (1991): Business Research Methods. London: Dryden Press.

Zingales, Luigi (1995): Insider ownership and the decision to go public. In: Review of Economic Studies, 62 (212), p. 425-448.

Zöfel, Peter (2001): Statistik - ein Begleitbuch zur Computergestützten Anwendung. München: Addison-Wesley.

Appendices

A.1 Semi-Structured Questionnaire for Pilot Studies

Introductive Questions

1. Please give an example of a company that you exited successfully?
2. Also, please give an example of a company that was unsuccessfully exited?
3. Who are the parties involved and what are their particular interests when approaching the exit?

Basic questions regarding exit-strategies

4. Please specify your basic approach in preparing and accomplishing an exit?
5. How deep do you get involved in the exit's preparations? What contacts are you approaching and what information are you gathering?
6. Please explain your timing approach? When do you strive to exit in respect to the company's development level and how do you exploit external conditions? Did you experience any resistance from the entrepreneur?
7. What would you consider as further scopes and dimensions to adjust exit strategies to individual investments?

Specific questions regarding accomplished exits

8. Think back to a successful exit that you accomplished recently. Why did you consider this transaction successful?
9. Please describe the business briefly?
10. What kind of information did the investor (acquirer, investment banker, etc.) want as you worked with them to close the deal? How did you provide that information?
11. Did the project's nature (degree of innovation, development level, sector or competition) hinder communication? How did you cope with that?
12. Did it seem to you that the entrepreneur withheld important information? Was his behavior cooperative, did he fear the exit and did you perceive any opportunistic considerations? If so, which? How did you cope with that?
13. What would you regard as particular advantage of your involvement for the exit – from the perspective of the venture and the follow-on investors?
14. Did you experience any mistakes or failure during the exit? What did you learn?

A.2 Online Survey

A.2.1 Interface

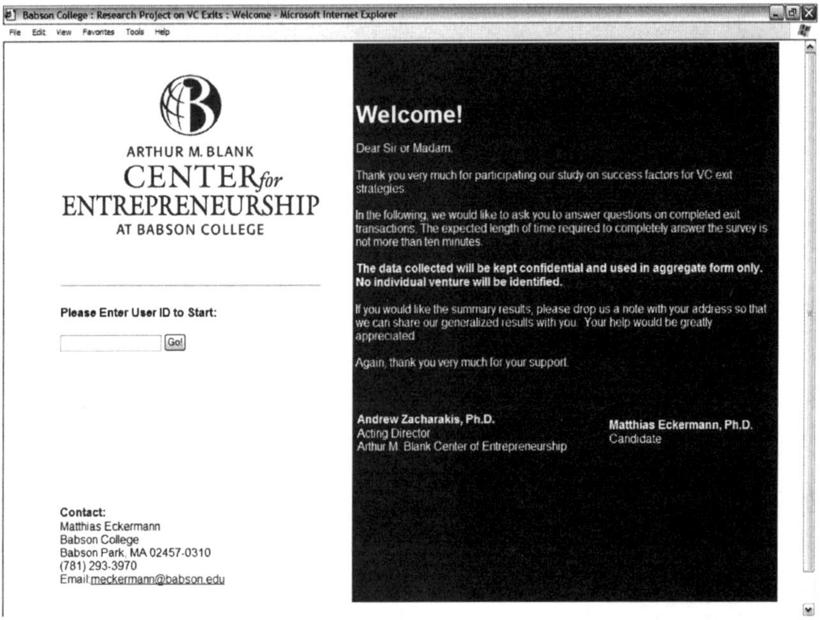

Figure 31: Interface

A.2.2 Instructions

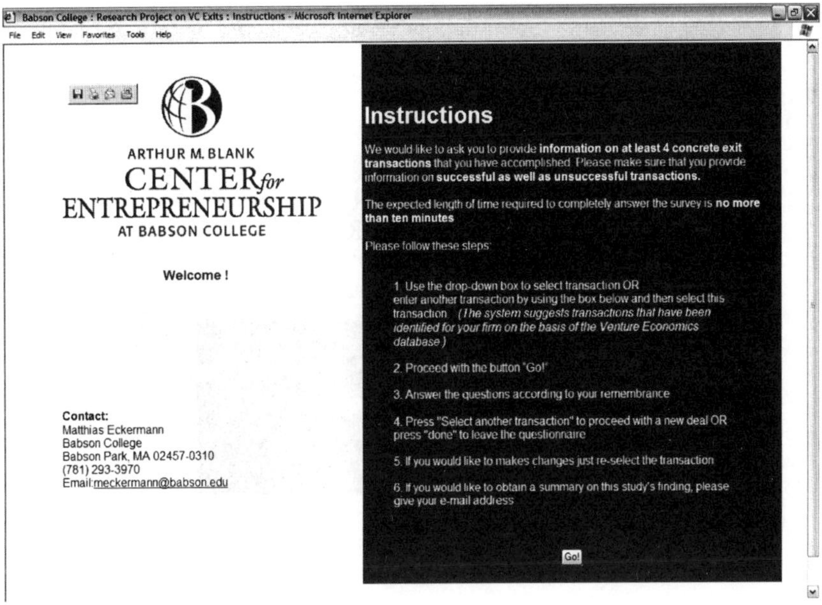

Figure 32: Instructions

A.2.3 Selection-Menu

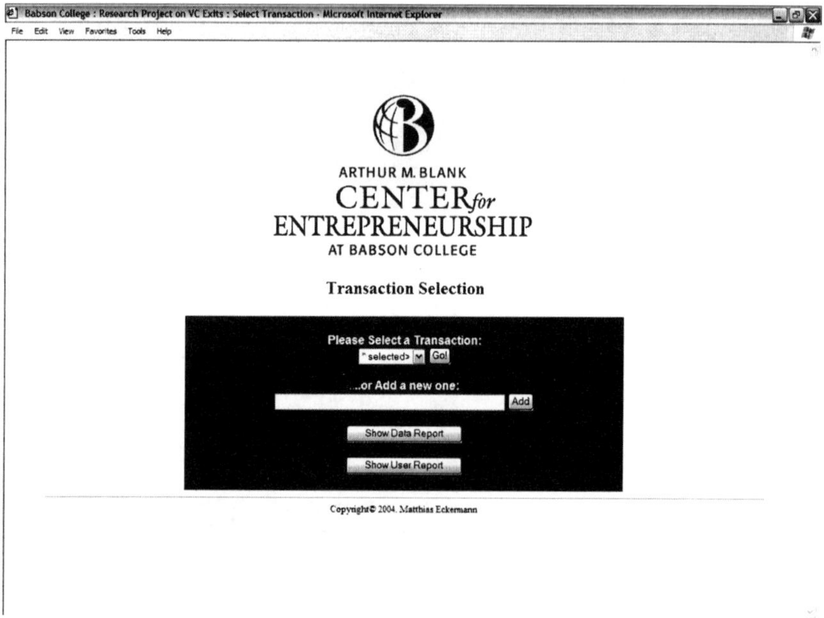

Figure 33: Selection-Menu

A.2.4 Questionnaire

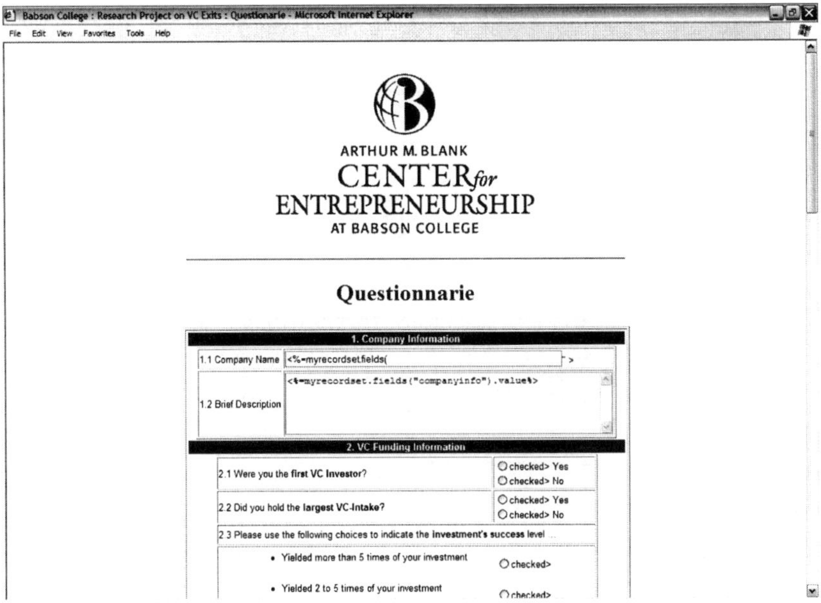

Figure 34: Questionnaire - First Page

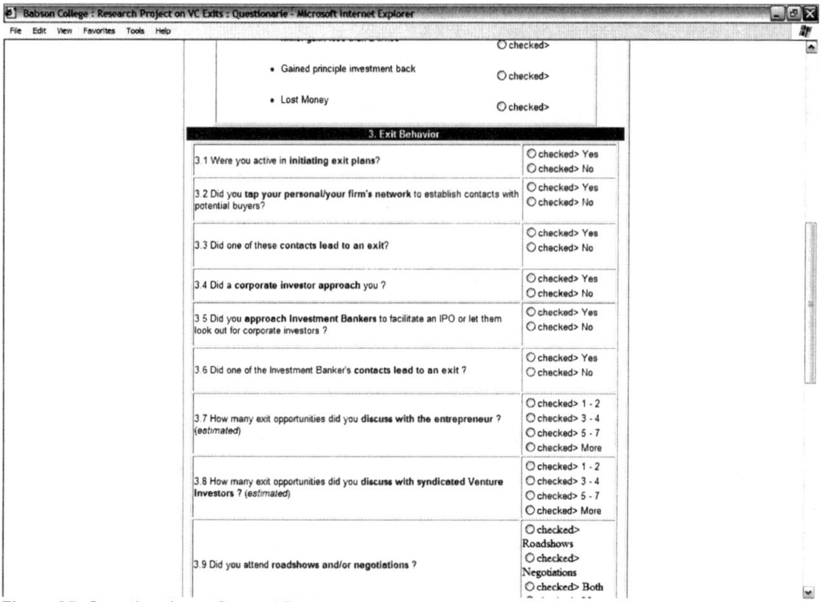

Figure 35: Questionniare - Second Page

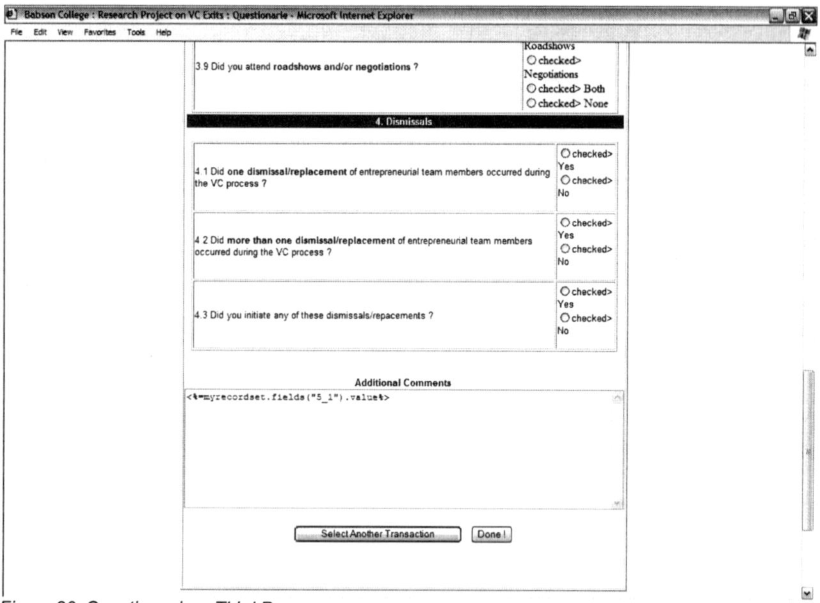

Figure 36: Questionnaire - Third Page

A.2.5 Check-Out

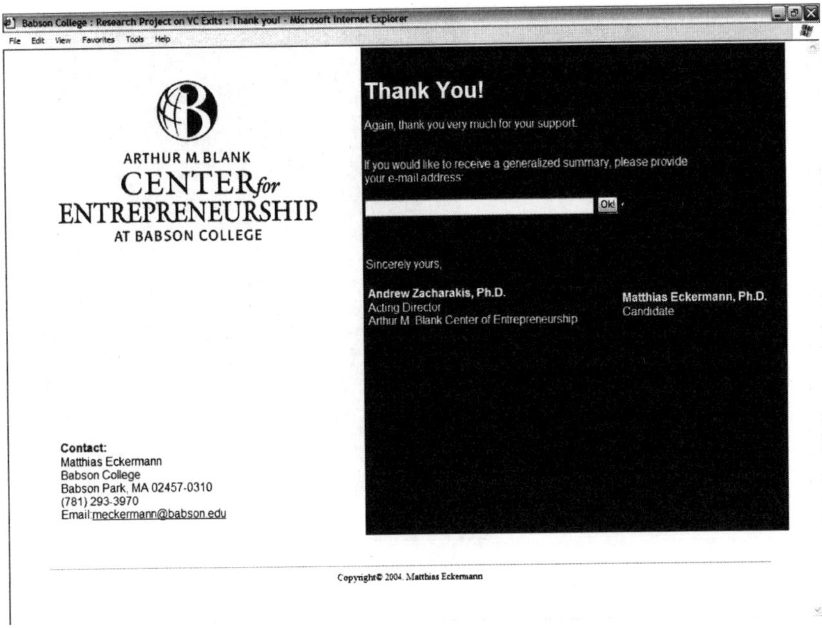

Figure 37: Check-Out

A.2.6 Final Page

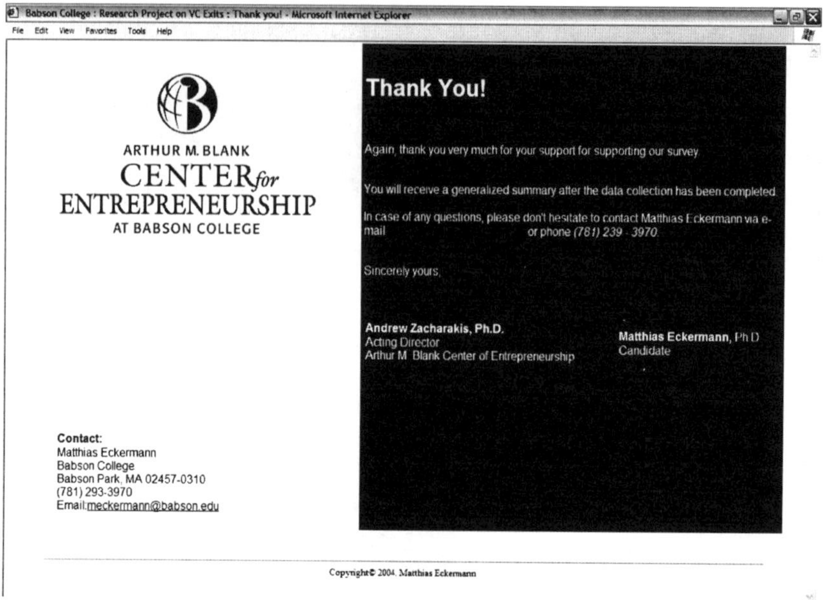

Figure 38: Final Page

A.3 Contact Letter and Mails

A.3.1 Initial Letter

Dipl.-Wirtsch.-Ing. Matthias Eckermann, Ph.D. Candidate
Arthur M. Blank Center for Entrepreneurship
Babson College
Babson Park, MA 02457-0310

(781) 239 - 3970
(781) 239 – 4178 Fax

<< Title>> << First Name>> <<Last Name>>
<<Company Name>>
<<Address Line 1>>
<<Address Line 2>>

<<Insert Date>>

Dear <<Title>> <<Last Name>>:

We would like to ask you kindly to support **Babson College's online survey on exit success factors.**

My name is Matthias Eckermann. I am writing my Ph.D. thesis on exit strategies of VC investors under the guidance of Professor Zacharakis, the Director of the Arthur M. Blank Center for Entrepreneurship at Babson. The purpose our study is to identify success strategies for exiting ventures. For instance, we compare exit strategies across industries and development stages. To identify successful exit approaches, we require data from those people who have been directly involved. We would like to ask you few questions on those exit transactions you are familiar with (e.g., << Identified Transactions>>). **Completing the survey will take not more than 10 minutes.**

For your convenience, we have set up an online questionnaire. **Please visit www.babson.edu/vcexits and use the log-in '<<Log In>>'.** The site will list a number of deals on which we have collected data. Please answer the questions for those deals you are familiar with.

Your answers will be confidential, reported only in an aggregated form and coupled with widely available secondary data on similar deals.

Thank you very much for devoting your time to our project. If you have any questions or would like a summary of the results, please drop me an email (*meckermann@babson.edu*).

Best regards,

Matthias Eckermann

A.3.2 First Reminder Mail

RE: Babson online survey on VC exits

Dear <<Title>> <<Last Name>>,

I am writing to follow up on my earlier invitation for you to take part in the **Babson College's online survey on VC exits**.

My Ph.D. thesis looks into the factors that influence VC's decisions to exit their investments in young ventures. It also explores the actions VCs take to make these exits happen. Therefore, I have developed a questionnaire that hopes to capture your thoughts on these issues.

Given the importance of this study for my graduation, I would appreciate it very much if you help me with this study by providing information on some transactions you decided to terminate (e.g., << Identified Transactions>>). The questions I ask are simple and do not require a lot of details. **The survey takes no more than 10 minutes to complete.** To share your views, thoughts and experiences, **please visit www.babson.edu/vcexits and use the log-in '<<Log In>>'.**

In case of any questions, please do not hesitate to call me at 781 – 239 – 3970 or write me an email (*meckermann@babson.edu*).

Again thank you very much for your help and support of this project.

Best regards,

Matthias Eckermann

A.3.3 Second Reminder Mail

RE: Babson online survey on VC exits

Dear <<Title>> <<Last Name>>,

I am writing to follow up ***one last time*** on my earlier letter and mail in which I invited you to participate in the **Babson College's online study on VC exits**.

This academic study focuses on exit transactions and tries to provide solutions to questions such as:

- How can VCs facilitate exits?

- How are the entrepreneurial team and co-investors integrated in the exit preparations?

The information you provide in the questionnaire will be kept strictly confidential. If you would like, summary results can be sent to you, as soon as the survey is completed.

This study is an essential part of my dissertation. Please take a few minutes of your busy time to fill out this independent academic web-based survey on exits with information about transactions you are familiar with (e.g., << Identified Transactions>>).

Please visit www.babson.edu/vcexits and use the log-in '<<Log In>>'.

Please feel free to contact me if you have any questions regarding the survey.

Best regards,

Matthias Eckermann
Ph.D. Candidate
Babson College
Babson Park, MA 02457-0310
Phone: 781 – 239 – 3970